CW01502481

ACKNOWLEDGEMENTS

My thanks go first of all to my husband Ricardo, who had the foresight to ensure that all my telexes to the *Morning Star* and the *Scotsman* over 6 years were safely packed away and sent to London in my absence. Without these and my own diaries it would have been impossible to write this memoir. His encouragement and conviction that my book would be an important contribution to people's understanding as to why socialism failed in the USSR has been the main driver behind my decision to attempt it.

My particular thanks go to our historian son Victor, who read the typescript and made several useful comments and helpful suggestions. Our daughters Liza and Martha have assisted in many ways with reminiscences from their Moscow childhood, and with thought-provoking comments and advice.

I am also grateful to our wider family and friends who have been unfailingly supportive over the several years it has taken me to write this book.

My book was completed before Russia's invasion of Ukraine, therefore that event is outside the scope of this memoir.

TWILIGHT
of the
SOVIET
UNION

Kate Clark
Memoirs of a Moscow correspondent

First published in Great Britain in 2023 by

Bannister Publications Ltd
Office 2A Market Hall,
Market Place, Chesterfield, Derbyshire. S40 1ARG.

ISBN 978-1-916823-02-0

Typeset in Sabon by Bannister Publications, Chesterfield, Derbyshire

Cover designed by Geoffrey Arias, London

www.geoffreyarias.com

Fornt cover image shows statue of Worker and Kolkhoz Woman,
by Vera Mukhina, Moscow

Printed and bound in Great Britain by CMP (UK) Limited, Poole, Dorset

BANNISTER
PUBLICATIONS

To my family

FOREWORD

By Dr David Lane

Emeritus Fellow of Emmanuel College, University of Cambridge

Kate Clark represents a generation of British people who in the post Second World War era pinned their hopes for a transition to socialism on developments in the USSR and who, following Gorbachev's perestroika, saw their aspirations destroyed in the subsequent dismantling of the Soviet Union and the transition to capitalism. This book tells the story from someone living and working in Soviet Russia in the period of perestroika. Kate has a long-standing interest in the Soviet Union and first visited Moscow in the 1960s. In those days, there were relatively few ways that people could visit or become acquainted with Soviet life. Kate, however, utilised the channels of the British-Soviet Friendship Society (BSFS) which actively promoted Russian publications and exchanges, especially for youth. The BSFS and organisations such as the Society for Cultural Relations with the USSR (SCR) provided an alternative route to study the socialist states for those who were unsuccessful in the British Council student exchange. As Kate shows in this book, the 1960s – the time of Nikita Khrushchev – was a period of optimism in the Soviet Union and many people in the UK were confident that the Soviet system, despite its deficiencies, would eventually outstrip Western competitive capitalism.

The story told in the book focusses on the period when Kate, as the Moscow correspondent of the *Morning Star* (and later, the *Scotsman*), lived and worked in Moscow with her family between 1985 and 1990. Unlike other British press correspondents who lived in a rather secluded set of apartments allocated to foreigners, Kate lived among, and interacted with, Moscow people. These were momentous days in the history of the Soviet Union. Her book provides a personal documentary of this period. It delivers a fascinating account of the family's experiences in Moscow. Unlike in present times, when the media portray a unidimensional view of Russia, the book illustrates the ideological differences between a journalist from the *Morning Star* and other Western correspondents. The author, however, is not uncritical of Soviet practices and illustrates how the heavy-handed top-down leadership was often out of touch with the reality of people's lives. The book provides intriguing examples of the absurdities of the planning system as it affected daily life – planners locating different though complementary retail shops miles apart. The book is illustrated with pictures and illustrations showing the reality of the Soviet Union.

One of the problems for the interpretation of the Gorbachev reform movement, especially for correspondents sympathetic to the Soviet cause, was explaining the deficiencies and inadequacies, caused by Soviet planning, which were revealed by Gorbachev. Ever more disturbing were the reinterpretations of history which, for example, questioned the heroic role of some Soviet leaders in the Second World War. The book then is also an account of how the author came to terms with the reality of Soviet society and the ways its history was reinterpreted during the period of glasnost'. Reporting on the reversal of historical interpretation by the Soviet leadership and mass media created significant problems for the home editors of papers such as the *Morning Star*. Perestroika was not only problematic in the USSR but also for pro-Soviet comrades in the West.

Kate's book is not just an account of her stay in Moscow and her many visits to places in the USSR, but also contains her experience of life in Russia and comparisons with the UK. She raises many of the concerns of people living in the USSR, rather than, as many correspondents, observing life inside a transparent jar. Bureaucratic management with its insistence on excessive paperwork and the lack of response of the planning authorities to public needs portray a realistic picture of life. These negative aspects however are evenly balanced with a positive appraisal of Soviet achievements. One attribute of the book is that Kate's aspirations of her early visits in the 1960s are compared with the reality and shortfalls of the late 1980s. The examples, drawn from her life experience, combine with her own commentary to deliver a montage of the anomalies, ambiguities, and contradictions in Soviet life; the book, however, does something more – it conveys the sense of pride on the part of Soviet people in the achievements of Soviet power and the positive attitudes of people to Soviet life – something that few Western people appreciate. She also reflects on, and explains, the changes which have taken place and the role of the West in bringing down not only the Soviet system but also the aspirations of many who strove to build socialism.

This is a well-written accessible book which portrays a lively picture of life in the USSR as it was lived and also how it was interpreted by a friendly but critical journalist - a 'bottom up' perspective. It deserves a wide readership.

INTRODUCTION

I arrived in Moscow in February 1985, a couple of weeks before the last of the Party old guard died, and the new broom Mikhail Gorbachov took over as Party leader.

Little did I know that the next six years would shake the world as much as the initial ten days of the 1917 socialist Revolution, described in John Reed's gripping account - *Ten Days that Shook the World.* John Reed witnessed the beginning of the seventy years of socialism in one country, and I witnessed the end of that historic experiment, as the socialist system came to an end and the world's first socialist state - the Union of Soviet Socialist Republics - disintegrated.

Had it all been worth it? Can socialist society work efficiently? Or is capitalism the only way that society can be organised? Is it pure idealism to attempt a society without rich and poor, without an exploiting class and a working class?

These thoughts were in my mind as I began the task of writing this book. As a long-time socialist, I wanted to help readers understand what the USSR was like, not from a hostile viewpoint, which is the usual thing among books about the Soviet Union, but from a broadly sympathetic viewpoint, one which understood the aims of the October 1917 Revolution and appreciated its many gains and achievements over the seven decades that followed.

The trouble with writing about the USSR is that unfortunately readers are likely to have many preconceptions, even prejudices, about that country. The years of the Cold War coloured most people's thinking about that country, and its distance and our unfamiliarity with the language meant that few people travelled there. Russian culture, its literature and arts, much less those of the other, non-Russian parts of the USSR, were little known. Apart from Russian ballet and the country's space achievements, practically everything else about the country was for decades portrayed in a negative light.

I'd like to invite readers to come with me on this journey through the final, tumultuous years of the Soviet Union, to learn with me what people's lives were like in the eighties, to catch a glimpse of their hopes and dreams, to share in their fun and their pride in their country. I'd like readers to learn something of the other, non-Russian republics, of which we know so little.

In the process, we can reflect on why it was that the USSR was so different from Britain, what its aims were and to what extent these were achieved. Was the USSR a great country? Was it well served by its leaders? Was the new, socialist, system ever really feasible in a fairly backward country as Russia in 1917?

How free did people feel? How free was I, or was the KGB tracking my every move? I hope readers will get a feel of what everyday life was like for me as a journalist and for my family, living as we did among Soviet people and sharing their interests, problems and aspirations.

I invite readers to come with me, leaving preconceptions behind, on the journey I and my family made through the USSR from 1985 when we arrived, until 1990 when we left.

CHAPTER I

It wasn't exactly an auspicious start. A temperature of 39 degrees and three children in tow who also had varying degrees of colds, coughs and high temperatures.

But, on Tuesday, February 19th 1985, I was on an aeroplane, we were on our way to Moscow and the nightmare of preparation, packing, saying goodbyes and leaving our London home was at last behind me. That was surely a plus.

It hadn't been easy. Our three children were happily settled in a nice, small London primary school and I was enjoying my work as a journalist in the London offices of the *Morning Star*. Some might have thought it crazy to give all that up to go to a largely unknown future.

But my husband was already working in Moscow, and waiting for us to join him. Bureaucratic delays meant that I had to stay behind in London with the children for seven months before our family reunion became possible. The children were longing to see their Daddy. And I too was longing to be with him, for our family to be complete again and to start this new chapter in our lives.

Ricardo was waiting for us at Sheremetyevo airport and with few formalities we were whisked away in a car headed for the centre of Moscow. It was already dark and the children marvelled at the wide streets and big blocks of flats along our route. Ricardo whispered to me: "Just wait till you see where we're going to live!" I was intrigued and excited, but at that stage, with my mounting temperature, I would have been glad to lay my head anywhere.

The car entered through a high archway and into an inner courtyard. "See?" said Ricardo, "this is it!" Ill as I was, I had failed to notice that the archway was the main entrance to one of the seven "wedding-cake" buildings of the fifties, for which Moscow is famous. This building, straddling the intersection of the Moscow River and the River Yauza, is one of the most impressive of the seven, overlooking the Kremlin from its dizzying heights.

The driver and Ricardo swiftly took our cases inside, past the *dezhurnaya* – a small, elderly woman who would be a somewhat doubtful source of news and gossip over the coming years – and into the old-fashioned lift, its heavy concertina doors clanking impressively as they shut. Up to the ninth floor, and through a high, solid wooden exterior door, then another, equally solid, interior door into our flat – and we were "home".

We were met by a kindly middle-aged woman, Anna Nikitichna. She had a meal ready for us, which she had brought from the Party Hotel (the CPSU[1] had two such hotels for Communist leaders from other countries) to help us out for the first few days. She immediately saw that I was ill – I had a raging temperature - and as we sat down to our first Russian meal, Anna Nikitichna produced a bottle of Stolichnaya vodka and poured out a small glass for me. "100 grams three times a day, with meals!" she pronounced gravely, as if administering pills, "and you'll soon be right as rain!" It was my introduction to the benefits and all-encompassing uses of vodka, which I soon learnt Russians used not only for curing colds and flu, but also minor scratches, grazes and skin infections.

It was 19th February 1985. Konstantin Chernenko was the elderly and infirm General Secretary of the CPSU and there was much speculation in the West as to who would take over after his death, which, judging by his rare appearances on TV, would not be far off. Little did I realise, obediently sipping the vodka under Anna Nikitichna's watchful gaze, that within three weeks a much younger and energetic new leader would emerge – and change the course of history forever.

It was a rude awakening, for me personally, as there was much to do arranging the children's new school and generally settling in, finding out where the shops were, and fitting out the children with warm winter coats and boots, as the temperature that February was around -15 °C. Our first few days were spent enjoying our spacious new flat, with its spectacular views over the Kremlin and the Moscow and Yauza rivers, and the famous power station opposite the Kremlin, which bore Lenin's famous dictum: *Communism is Soviet Power plus the Electrification of the Whole Country!*

The flat we had been given was on the ninth floor of a side wing of the huge block of flats. We found out from our neighbours that it had been built by German prisoners after the Second World War as reparation, being completed in 1952. It had a central building of 32 floors and one lateral wing on either side. The ceilings inside the flat were very high. Four of the windows – the lounge, two children's bedrooms and the spacious kitchen – looked out over the Kremlin and the two afore-mentioned rivers. The Moscow River is wide, like the Thames, and big slow barges, laden with heavy goods, plied the river, day and night. The lounge and 2 bedrooms on that side had small semi-circular balconies, and my favourite place for looking through the papers every morning was the lounge balcony, which was just big enough for a couple of chairs. Ricardo and I had a large bedroom on the other side, overlooking the courtyard, and adjacent to it was my study, just outside the flat's back entrance.

We had a smallish table in the kitchen against the window, so Ricardo and I had a privileged view of the river and the Kremlin when enjoying a lazy breakfast after the morning rush of getting our three children to school. We

---

1 Communist Party of the Soviet Union, thenceforth CPSU.

would often breakfast and read the papers at the same time, commenting on anything new or unusual.

The kitchen had a rubbish chute on one wall, which went all the way down to the ground floor, where the rubbish from all the flats in that wing was collected and disposed of. It was very convenient, in the sense that you didn't have to take out black bin bags or bins as we do in Britain. The only disadvantage was that cockroaches manned the bin chute like an occupying army, and we had to resort to making little balls of poison mixed with egg yolk (our neighbour's recipe) to scatter around.

Ricardo and I wanted our children to go to a Soviet school. I think as a general principle, if you're living for a longish period in a country and its education system is reasonably good, it's better for the children to attend a nearby school where they will meet and make friends with local children. And as Russian speakers, Ricardo and I looked forward to our children learning Russian.

We chose a school a short tramway away from where we lived on *Kotelnicheskaya* embankment, down the pleasant tree-lined *Yauskiy* boulevard. It was one of the schools that specialised in English. At that time there were specialised schools for different foreign languages, maths and sport. Or you could choose your nearest local school with no specialism. My secretary, Olya, recommended the nearby English-specialism school (*spetsshkola*), pointing out that the children would find it an easier introduction to Soviet school life.

We bought the children their uniforms at GUM, the big department store on *Krasnaya Ploshchad'* (Red Square)[2]. All schoolchildren throughout the whole of the USSR had the same uniform, one for girls and one for boys. The boys' uniform was very attractive – a navy blue jacket with epaulettes and shiny metal buttons down the front, white cotton shirt with shoulder flaps and matching navy trousers, half-lined down the trouser legs for extra warmth. The uniform for our six-year old twin girls was a chocolate-brown woollen dress, with long sleeves and a white collar and cuffs, and with a black woollen pinafore to go over the dress. For more special occasions, like ceremonies, concerts or class performances, the girls' pinafores were white cotton with a frill round the edges.

Getting the kids to school on time was no mean feat, especially in winter. School started at 8am, so they needed to leave the house at 7.30 in order to get the tram three stops to the cul-de-sac where the school was. Once dressed in their school uniforms the girls had to put on *shtany* (sort of loose woollen leggings that went on top of their woollen tights), then their fur boots, their fur coats, fur hats and woollen scarves tied tightly round the collars. Victor had a *shapka* which had ear flaps you could release if the

---

2 *krasnaya* nowadays means "red". But formerly it meant "beautiful", so *Krasnaya Ploshchad'* simply means Beautiful Square.

weather was particularly cold, and a blue fur-lined coat, as well as scarves and gloves. They each had to take their satchel with all the books they had needed for their copious homework the night before, and if it was a sports day, they had to take skis, ski boots and sportswear.

Once the children were settled in their new school, life took on a more ordered shape. Since school No. 35 specialised in English, the pupils had more English lessons than in a non-specialised school. The teachers sometimes gave our children books to read while the other children were having English class. Senior boys and girls even had certain other subjects taught in English and could express themselves very well in the language. Occasionally, our children would come home and ask me whether a particular word was really said like that, as their teacher of English had obviously mispronounced a word, or put the stress on the wrong syllable.

One day a few months after our arrival, I suppose it was, our daughter Liza told me how the teacher of the second class, Zoya Ivanovna, had come into their classroom and dragged some children off into the corner "by the scruff of their necks", as she put it, because they had been giggling. I asked Liza if she had also got into trouble – had she also been laughing? She said no, she hadn't. I asked her why not – and she replied, in all seriousness, "Well, I didn't understand the joke!" As I wrote in my diary at the time: there are clearly some advantages in not knowing the language perfectly.

Years later, our children have often related the story of their first day at school, which it seems was pretty traumatic for them. At the time, they did not make a fuss or even tell us that they had suffered. But the twins tell how I took them to the class they had been allotted, handed them over to their new teacher, Lyudmila Petrovna, and left. They felt abandoned and scared. But it seems the teacher and the other children were very nice to them and took them under their wings.

As for Victor, I think it must have been even worse for him, since he was on his own and in a different classroom. At home, he never complained about it to us, he was stoical and just got on with the challenge of learning the language, so that he could join in the fun he saw the other boys were having.

It is incredible how fast children learn a language if they are surrounded by children of their age and in a situation where everyone speaks that language. Only four months later, after a month-long stay at a pioneer camp, all three of them were fluent in Russian and had numerous friends.

At first I had a secretary, Olya, who spoke good English. She was very efficient in showing me the ropes, taking me to the big department store on Red Square - GUM - and recommending what winter coats, hats, gloves and boots the children would need. I admired her decisiveness – she knew exactly where to go, what to buy, even the right sizes.

But as the weeks went on, and Olga realised that my Russian was pretty good, I could easily do interviews without help and read the newspapers on my own, it was decided that I could manage the *Morning Star* office on my own, and soon, any trips outside Moscow would be without Olga's help. But she was always there if I needed to call on her, and she frequently gave me tips and useful advice which were invaluable in steering through the at times turbulent waters of life in the USSR.

Shopping for a family of five, three of them growing children with voracious appetites, is time-consuming wherever you live. We had a big supermarket on Taganka Square, but you could not guarantee buying everything you needed in that one shop, since supplies could be somewhat erratic. Over the first few weeks, we learnt that it was more convenient to buy from the shops on the ground floor of our block of flats – fruit and vegetables, dairy products of all kinds, bread and confectionary – and buy other foodstuffs here and there, at shops we happened to be passing. Both Ricardo and I, like all Soviet working citizens, had the right to a weekly order through our workplaces. There certainly wasn't the range of foods a typical London supermarket would stock, but shopping was not the nightmare that you would imagine if you read Western media reports at the time.

I knew that one of the issues I would need to investigate and report on for the *Morning Star* was that of supplies and quality, and from my earliest articles, I reported on the situation as I saw it, giving the context and without the overtly anti-Soviet stance the hostile Western media adopted. How often, in their reporting, did you find the same clichéd phrases: "serried ranks of grey, dilapidated flats", "run-down housing", or "monotonous blocks"? I wanted to report fairly, taking into account Soviet history, and try to get to the bottom of why supplies were erratic, why there was *defitsit,* and why the quality of goods on sale was often not as good as in the West.

One of the main issues which the socialist societies that have existed up to now have not successfully solved is that of productivity and innovation.

All kinds of industry competition schemes existed at various times in Soviet factories and plants. I visited many during my six years, from small factories employing 200-300 workers to massive plants like Uralmash, with its 45,000 workers and facilities like crèches, nurseries, hospital, holiday clubs, choirs and other hobby clubs, holiday schemes, Pioneer camp places for the workers' children and a series of other benefits. Uralmash, in the Urals city of Sverdlovsk (now reverted to its pre-revolutionary name Yekaterinburg), was more like a self-contained town than a large steel plant.

At every factory I would visit, workers seemed to be working diligently enough, as you might find in a British factory, yet for all the competition between teams (*brigady*) intended to raise productivity, much of Soviet industry lacked competitiveness on a world scale.

In the early years after the Revolution, workers' enthusiasm for Soviet power and their participation in the new organs of state power – the *soviety*, or councils – helped boost productivity. Readers may have heard of Stakhanov and the Stakhanovite movement, which started in the thirties as the first national phase of socialist competition in industry and the countryside. Aleksei Stakhanov had mined 102 tonnes of coal in less than 6 hours (14 times his quota) on 31 August 1935, and his example was followed by many other "stakhanovite" workers in other parts of industry.

There is no doubting the real enthusiasm of these early pioneers of industry in the USSR. Even decades later, when I first lived for a year in Moscow in 1967-68 (the year my husband Ricardo and I first met), that enthusiasm and national pride in being a citizen of the Soviet Union was still tangible. A good friend of mine, who later in the Gorbachov[3] era became Deputy Editor of the CPSU's theoretical journal *Kommunist*, Otto Lacis, and his wife Tamara, who edited a literary magazine, often talked of their work as young university students in the fifties when they went to work on the ambitious BAM (Baikal-Amur Mainline) railway project. BAM was one of those heroic projects for which the Soviet Union became famous.

Thousands of students or recent graduates, like them, volunteered to work in freezing conditions to build the 4,324 km long railway which runs north of the famous trans-Siberian railway and is built on permafrost. In the fifties enthusiasm and belief in the system, in socialism, was still widespread and undeniable. They worked hard, and played hard. They made lifelong friends on the BAM and were proud of the progress it meant for their country, enabling oil to be transported westwards from the new Siberian oilfields that were opening up at the time. It was only later, during the seventies, that for many the flame of that new socialist society, with all that it was meant to bring, started guttering in the hearts of many ordinary people.

One problem connected with productivity, visible in the time we lived in the USSR, was the generalised problem workers, especially female workers, had in obtaining food and goods. Since supplies were erratic, if something desirable appeared in the shops, people would hear about it through the grapevine and would take time off to go and queue. People from the Central Asian republics and other non-Russian parts of the Soviet Union would fly to Moscow on some pretext or other so that they could buy shoes for the children, or fur coats, or TV's, that were not easily available in their own regions. It did not make for smooth production schedules and increased productivity.

I remember once we sent our daughters down to the greengrocers on the ground floor of our building, as we had seen that apples were being sold there for the first time in a week or so. They went down and dutifully queued for about half an hour, but when they got to the head of the queue the shop assistant announced: "*Vsyo! Konchilis'!*" "That's it! "No more left!" so

---

3 I am going to use this spelling throughout this book. The surname is often transliterated from the Russian as "Gorbachev", which unfortunately results in English speakers pronouncing the surname wrongly. The [ë] letter in the name's last syllable is pronounced [yo] in Russian, and is stressed, so although for historical orthographic reasons it may be correct to transliterate [ë] as [e], if you want non-Russian speakers to approximate the Russian pronunciation of the name, it is better to use [o]. The *Morning Star* and the *Times* were the only newspapers to adopt this pronunciation convention during the eighties.

they came back empty-handed. In Moscow during the eighties you could always get some kind of fruit, and meats, fish, eggs, cheese and vegetables – but not necessarily when and where you wanted to find them.

Another even more serious problem concerned innovation, or the lack of it. During the Stakhanov period, workers were encouraged to find and devise better, more efficient ways of doing their jobs. But by the seventies, during the period of *zastoi* (stagnation) many workers had come to feel indifference to their work. It was something you had to do, to keep body and soul together, but it wasn't something you had any pride in or any interest in suggesting new, better ways of working.

There were, of course, innovators who managed to cut through red tape and get their ideas put into production, but usually only after years of fighting their corners. One such was the famous eye surgeon Svyatoslav Fyodorov, for instance, who was the first in the world to devise the conveyor-belt system of corrective myopia surgery.

In 1980 he became the head of the Moscow Research Institute of Eye Microsurgery and eight years later founded the Fyodorov Eye Microsurgery Complex, which was a self-financing concern outside the national health system. I visited this clinic, and saw the patients lying on what looked like a slow-moving circular conveyor belt, each eye surgeon swiftly and deftly carrying out one particular step of the surgery on their eye. Once done, the belt was set in motion once more and the next patient moved into position for the surgeon to do the next operation. It was very impressive, and Fyodorov became famous for his "assembly line" eye surgery throughout the world. His fame later catapulted him into politics, in 1989 being elected to the new Congress of People's Deputies and later, to the Duma, or parliament.

Dr Fyodorov told me how hard it had been to get the authorities to agree to finance his new Eye Microsurgery Complex and introduce the new operation which, if it had been available to people outside the USSR, would have been an extremely profitable enterprise for the state.

"I had to struggle for this," Fyodorov said. "I was opposed by all the professors in the Soviet Union. I broke medical canons by introducing new technology and those who violate canons are revolutionaries, pioneers. If they emerge victorious, they become popular," he added, smiling.

Another example was Gavriil Ilizarov, a doctor from Crimea who was the first to patent and introduce bone-lengthening by means of a frame. He worked as a family doctor in a remote area of Siberia, and perfected his surgical techniques mainly by research from books and from practice. Ilizarov had earlier been on a six-month course in military field surgery and became interested in bone reconstruction because many of his patients were wounded soldiers coming back from the front during WWII.

Up till then only casts and skeletal traction had been commonly used to treat serious fractures, but Ilizarov felt sure there must be a better way. He moved to the big city of Kurgan and there at the regional hospital developed the idea of a frame or external fixator ring with cross wires round the site of the fracture, which, once in place, would gradually lengthen the bone.

The first patient to be treated with the new external fixator was a worker from the factory where the metal parts for the new frame device were made. As in Fyodorov's case, Ilizarov's revolutionary invention was met with scepticism and only achieved wider recognition after he successfully treated a Soviet high jumper, Valery Brumel, in 1968.

In these days of increasing resistance to anti-biotics, scientists in our country are re-discovering the use of anti-bacterial agents called bacteriophages – which had been used in the Soviet Union and Eastern Europe for decades. As a result of pioneering work done by Georgi Eliava and others in the Soviet Republic of Georgia, bacteriophages were used in the treatment of Red Army soldiers coming back from the front in WWII.

There are many other examples where Soviet science was ahead of the game, and many advances were never given publicity in the West due to the prevailing anti-Soviet Cold War atmosphere. This is even true of the space race: if you look at children's books about space, for instance, you are lucky if you can find a mention of Yuri Gagarin or Valentina Tereshkova, whereas there are always pages and pages of pictures and text about NASA and the US landing on the moon.

In a country with such a big population, and with a good education system where maths and science were given great importance, one can only wonder that there were not far more great innovators.

It was a scandal, brought to readers' notice by the press in the new conditions of *glasnost*[4] (transparency or openness), after 1985, that a large number of very clever inventions and innovations were patented and sold abroad rather than developing them for the domestic economy. The fact was that the economy, centrally state-planned as it was, could not absorb and develop new ideas and techniques. It was not just due to *zastoi*; it was that the way that *gosplan* (the state planning committee) worked actually militated against their incorporation, since the success of an individual enterprise was judged, not by new inventions or innovations, but by whether or not it fulfilled its plan, handed down to it from *gosplan*.

"What's the use of a tractor factory every year fulfilling its quota of the five-year plan if nobody actually wants or needs these tractors?" I clearly remember economist Otto Lacis saying. "We're producing tonnes of steel for the same old products, year after year – and no one stops to ask whether they're what we really need!"

I remember our nine-year old son, Victor, on one of the first days after our arrival, looking out of the kitchen window overlooking the Moscow river embankment - *Kotelnicheskaya Naberezhnaya* – along which would

---

4 *glasnost*' is sometimes written with a final apostrophe, to indicate that the final 't' is soft in Russian. Henceforth I will write the word without the apostrophe, for simplicity's sake.

regularly trundle rather old-fashioned-looking lorries, all seemingly of the same model, asking: "Why do their lorries all look old?"

It was a simple question, but one which certainly gave room for thought. Whereas British lorries were all shapes, sizes and colours, here they all seemed to be grey and the same uniform shape, with the bonnet sticking out in front like those used in Britain during the war.

We had arrived on a Tuesday. Two weeks later the children started their *spetsshkola* No. 35. Four days after that, Soviet leader Konstantin Chernenko died. The following day, Mikhail Gorbachov became General Secretary of the CPSU, after veteran Soviet Foreign Minister Andrei Gromyko gave Gorbachov his backing and urged the Central Committee to elect him.

It was a baptism of fire for me. There would be no comfortable first few weeks of settling in, helping the children to get used to their new school where they would be taught in Russian, and finding my feet in the new job as a foreign correspondent.

One of the reasons we had decided to move to the USSR was that we wanted to find out what was really happening there and what it was like to live in a socialist society, as opposed to simply visiting the country for a few weeks. Ricardo, in particular, was especially interested in having the real, live experience of living daily life much as the Russians do. When living in Chile together from 1969 to 1974, we had both been keen supporters of the constitutional Popular Unity government of President Salvador Allende, whose programme aimed to make socialist transformations to Chilean society. We had experienced its brutal overthrow in September 1973, both of us sacked from our university posts, Ricardo imprisoned for months without charge or trial and had seen many friends and colleagues imprisoned or killed. It was clear to the whole world that a country intent on introducing socialist transformations – even if it were a government *elected* on such a programme – would be likely to suffer the same fate as Allende's Chile. So what was *existing* socialist society really like, we wondered. Was it a society of the kind the Chilean left had wanted for Chile? Was it a society where I, a British woman, would feel at home, a society I could admire or envisage as the sort of society I, or the British left in general, would want for Britain?

All these questions were in our minds in 1984 as we mulled over whether to apply for jobs in the Soviet Union. We had lived in Moscow in 1967-68, as postgraduate students, and we had spent a month there in 1982, on a refresher course for teachers of Russian (both of us had been teaching Russian that year at the SCR[5]), so we had some fairly recent knowledge

5 SCR: Society for Cultural Relations with the USSR, founded in 1924. Among founder members were E.M. Forster, Julian Huxley, Maynard Keynes, Bertrand Russell, Sybil Thorndyke, Alexei Tolstoy, Virginia Woolf and Konstantin Yuon. Since 1992, following the break-up of the USSR, the Society changed its name to Society for Cooperation in Russian and Soviet Studies. The SCRSS houses an important library on Soviet science, education, philosophy, art, literature and social and economic life, organises lectures and events and continues to teach Russian.

of the country. Initially I was not very keen on the idea, now that we had three young children, especially because on our last visit in 1982 we had seen shortages and queues at the shops and I envisaged that daily life could be quite hard.

We had noticed then that people looked careworn and even sullen in the streets and shops, which seemed a stark contrast to the mood we had sensed 14 years earlier. And from our conversations with Russian friends we gathered that daily life was indeed quite hard. Whereas in 1967-68 people had seemed optimistic and enthusiastic, now people seemed more discontented. It is always dangerous to generalise, but impressions gained over a longish period and after many conversations *do* have validity, and this was definitely the feeling both Ricardo and I had after our month there in 1982.

Mikhail Gorbachov's appearance as the new leader gave rise to huge optimism among our Russian friends. After so many elderly leaders since Leonid Brezhnev – who was largely blamed for the stagnation in the Soviet economy – Gorbachov came over as young, energetic, attractive and well-educated. On TV he appeared surrounded by people in the streets, close enough to touch him, which was something entirely new and fresh. Of recent past leaders, only one – Yuri Andropov, head of the KGB (USSR State Security Committee) - seemed to have enjoyed much public support, because in his short time as leader (15 months, cut short by his death in 1984) he actually seemed to be the sort of leader who would get things done. Gorbachov was seen as in the same mould as Andropov – a reformer.

One of the first measures announced by Gorbachov in May 1985 was the anti-alcohol campaign. It was clear that something needed to be done to halt the heavy drinking which afflicted the country, affecting industrial and rural production, safety at work, absenteeism, family life and the health of the male population in particular. Once the anti-alcohol edict from the leadership had been announced, vodka, dinner and dessert wines very quickly disappeared from the shops. Then sugar also became very hard to find, as people found a way round by making their own moonshine. We were surprised by the immediacy of the measure's results and the fact that not only spirits were the target of the campaign, but dinner wines too. Ricardo, as a Chilean patriot, accustomed to having a decent wine to accompany our dinners with guests, railed against its sudden and total disappearance from the shops.

Previous Soviet leaders had tried, with varying degrees of success, to stem alcoholism. Gorbachov's campaign, which included severe penalties against public drunkenness and alcohol consumption, was temporarily successful in reducing per capita alcohol consumption and improving quality-of-life measures such as life expectancies and crime rates, but it was deeply unpopular among the population and it ultimately failed.

We read of the destruction of ancient vineyards in Georgia and Moldavia, where most of the wine the Soviet Union produced came from. It is well-known that wartime leader Josef Stalin's favourite wine - *Kindzmarauli* - was from Georgia, his native country[6]. Such drastic measures seemed destined to fail: civilised wine drinking is acceptable and even considered beneficial, accompanied by food, in much of the world. And how could local farmers in the state and collective farms in those republics not be furious at the measures ordered from above, when this would affect not only their production and incomes, but their way of life, as wine-drinking cultures? Ricardo and I both felt sure that the drastic nature of the anti-alcohol campaign would not end well.

In my daily reading of the Soviet press – *Pravda, Izvestia, Sovietskaya Rossiya, Literaturnaya Gazeta* and others – I became increasingly convinced that the campaign was on the wrong track. Articles appeared which were blatantly ridiculous, one suggesting that even one glass of wine or vodka was enough to give you all manner of dire health problems. Such articles would never convince anyone, I thought, since everybody knows this is not true. The campaign was extreme, lumping together both spirits and wine, in one dire warning. No subtlety, no gradual approach, no convincing use of statistics. I couldn't help but compare this campaign with the anti-smoking campaign in Britain in the seventies and eighties, which had been so effective in getting a large percentage of the population to give up smoking.

Thirty years later, in an interview published in *Komsomolskaya Pravda*, former Soviet President Mikhail Gorbachov admitted that his anti-alcohol campaign in the 1980s had been too swift and sweeping, and combating heavy drinking — which remains a major problem in today's Russia — should have been handled more patiently.

"The sobering up of society cannot be done in one fell swoop," Gorbachov was quoted by *Komsomolskaya Pravda* as saying. "It takes years. And the fight must go on incessantly, constantly."

"We should not have shut down trade, provoking moonshine production," he said. "Everything should have been done gradually. Not by an axe to the head."

The campaign continued for two years. Mortality rates and accidents declined, the birth rate increased and the health of newborns improved. But the state lost 20 billion roubles, according to *Komsomolskaya Pravda*, due to the drastic reduction in the lucrative vodka trade.

Later I would travel to the capital of Georgia, Tbilisi, and nearby rural areas and hear for myself the complaints of local Georgians, even those in the political establishment there, about that misguided anti-alcohol campaign.

It was an exciting time to be a correspondent in Moscow during those years. Whereas I would probably have had an easy life if I had been there during the Brezhnev years, now it was hectic in the extreme. There were frequent press conferences, and books and films that had long been shelved

---

6 Georgia: at that time one of the fifteen constituent republics of the USSR.

by the state's censorship body began to appear.

I always felt lucky, though, in one sense, compared with other British correspondents for the UK's national press, radio and TV: I spoke good Russian, we lived in a Soviet block of flats with Russians (and other Soviet nationalities, such as Kalmyks) as our neighbours and our children went to a Soviet school, all of which meant that I chatted frequently to a variety of ordinary Soviet people, from repairmen and street-sweepers to car mechanics, teachers, other parents and office-workers, just in the course of daily life.

You might think that other correspondents had the same advantage, since they too were living in Moscow. But their problem was that they lived in certain blocks of flats reserved for foreigners, with a militiaman in a kiosk at the entrance to check who was coming or going. Their children went to the Anglo-American School, which was a private school for the children of ex-pat diplomats, business people and correspondents. In 1985 practically none of the British media correspondents even spoke Russian, something I found incredible. I couldn't imagine that the BBC would have a Paris correspondent who didn't speak French, for instance. It would be inconceivable. Yet somehow it was considered fine to have correspondents in Moscow who did not speak any Russian.

I remember a conversation I had on this with the British Ambassador at the time, Sir Bryan Cartledge, at a reception held at the British Embassy. I raised the problem – as I saw it – of British media correspondents not speaking the language, and his reply was on the lines of: "Well, Russian isn't a major world language, is it?" Many of us would think that a language spoken by nearly 300 million people might be classed as an important language, but our ambassador at the time did not. Sir Bryan's comment seemed to exemplify the Cold War mentality I had grown up with ever since the fifties.

It is also true that at that time, in the eighties, Russian departments of British universities were either being merged with other language departments or closed entirely, so there were fewer and fewer Russian-speaking graduates available for mass media editors to recruit.

A visitor to Moscow from Britain is bound to be struck by the enormous width of the roads, with big housing blocks bordering the main thoroughfares leading out from the centre, such as *Leninskiy Prospekt*, *Kutuzovskiy Prospekt* or *Komsomolskoye Shosse*, many with evocative revolutionary names.

To get from one side of *Leninskiy Prospekt* to the other you have to walk the width of a motorway just to get to the central verge, then another such width to get to the opposite side. I used to think to myself jokingly – either all this essential walking makes the population very fit, or it's the reason average life expectancy is not among the highest in Europe!

It seemed to me that everything was on a monumental scale – like the block of flats we had come to live in, or the building of Moscow State University on Lenin Hills, which was another "wedding-cake"-style building similar to ours. Of course our big cities, in Britain, also have multi-storeyed blocks of flats, some situated quite close together, but we have many other smaller, lower buildings, and of course, houses with gardens, in different architectural styles.

Perhaps, I used to think when walking the long distances between one shop and another, it's because the country itself is so vast – it must do something to the mentality which feeds into the architects responsible for building such vast structures. Or perhaps, I would muse, it's because women - who actually do most of the shopping - have never been consulted. Otherwise why have a bread shop in one block, a butcher's in the next block and a grocer's in the following one? Who wants to walk such distances just to get three items of shopping?

In my diary entry of 20th January 1987, I wrote: "....then I walked to the *khozyaistvenny magazin* (shop selling household goods) and got 2 bags of washing powder and various powders and liquids for kitchen and bathroom. It's all there – but, why oh why do you have to go to a special shop to get such everyday needs?"

The heroic British miners' strike of 1984-85 was drawing to its sad conclusion at the time of our arrival in Moscow. The end of the strike in March 1985 was undoubtedly a defeat for the miners, who had held out so bravely for so long to defend their jobs and their communities. The mining industry was still a viable one; there was plenty of coal in the ground and the nationalised industry had a good safety record. It seemed to many that Prime Minister Margaret Thatcher had some sort of vendetta against the miners and the NUM leadership and was determined to break the strength of the miners' union. I had grown up in the Derbyshire coalfield, my family knew well the local Derbyshire and Yorkshire miners' leaders, Bert Wynn, Peter Heathfield, Mick Kane and Jock Kane. Living in London at the time of the strike, I had been active in raising funds for the miners, going on marches, attending protest meetings and sending money, clothes and toys to the soup kitchens of the mining communities hard hit by the strike. The Women against Pit Closures movement was especially inspiring, and I remember hearing Betty Heathfield's rousing speech in London and the standing ovation we all gave her. I had known Betty and her sister, Del, since I was a child, and remember our meetings as Young Communists at the Grassmoor Coalboard house she shared with her husband Peter, along with their cheerful little dog called Timoshenko[7].

As a child I would sometimes accompany my mother, Win Clark, as she sold copies of the *Daily Worker* (later the *Morning Star*) to miners coming off the night shift at local pits around Clay Cross and Grassmoor. Always friendly, always respectful, sometimes teasing and good-humoured, the

---

7 Marshal Semyon Timoshenko - Soviet military leader who fought in the Civil War (1918-20) and was one of the outstanding commanders of the Great Patriotic War (1941-45).

miners' reaction to my mother and the paper was invariably positive.

I had read in the *Morning Star* of the support Soviet miners had given our striking miners, as had several miners' organisations from different countries. International solidarity is typical of the working class and its organisations, the trades unions. Liverpool dockers, for instance, had refused to unload ships coming from Chile during the Pinochet dictatorship, and Scottish workers had blacked work on Rolls Royce engines sent for refit by the Chilean dictatorship. Those engines never did get repaired and were left to rust outside the factory, due to the Scottish workers' refusal to repair them, in solidarity with Chilean workers who at the time were being arrested, tortured, murdered and disappeared by the military junta. This story is beautifully and movingly told in Felipe Bustos's 2018 film *Nae Pasaran!* British workers through their trades unions have a very proud history of solidarity with workers in other countries who are being persecuted.

So one of the first trips I wanted to make after my arrival as the *Morning Star*'s Moscow correspondent was to a mining region which I knew had sent money to help the strike. I wanted to have the chance to thank the miners in person for their solidarity with the NUM and our British mining communities, who were now having to swallow the bitter pill of defeat. They had to try to rebuild their shattered lives in areas where the local pit had been practically the only livelihood available, and now faced a bleak future after the Thatcher Government's mass closure of pits.

I had met NUM leader Arthur Scargill a couple of times in March when he came to Moscow invited by the Soviet miners' trade union. I found him surprisingly buoyant despite the defeat, which spelled the end of the coal industry in Britain. Pits all over the country were closed within weeks and months on the orders of the Margaret Thatcher Government. The vast majority of those pits had coal reserves for many years ahead, but that was not considered important by her Government, who preferred to import oil from Saudi Arabia, brought halfway across the world in ocean-going tankers, than continue to exploit our own coal reserves and give work to thousands of men.

So it was then, that in July 1985, 4 months after arriving in Moscow, I found myself on my way to meet with Soviet coalminers who had shown solidarity with our miners and communities. I had chosen Karaganda, in the republic of Kazakhstan[8], one of the non-Russian republics of Central Asia. It was a three and a half hour flight by Aeroflot, the USSR's state airline. This was the second of many Aeroflot flights I would take over the next six years to many parts of the Soviet Union, and I found them to be without exception, comfortable, punctual, with decent food and good service.

Karaganda is three hours ahead of Moscow, and it was my first introduction to the several time zones the USSR had. As the world's biggest

---

8 Kazakhstan was one of the fifteen constituent republics of the USSR.

country covering an expanse of over 22,402,200 square kilometres, the USSR encompassed 10 different time zones and covered one-sixth of the Earth's land surface. Its western portion, more than half of all Europe, made up just 25 percent of the Soviet Union, but the overwhelming majority (about 72 percent) of the people lived in those regions and it was where most industrial and agricultural activities were concentrated.

The Karaganda coalfield, smaller than the more well-known Donbass (Ukraine) and Kuzbass (Siberia) coalfields, was first developed in the 1930's to supply coking coal to the Magnitogorsk steelworks and to support the industrial development of the Kazakh republic, which, like the other Central Asian republics, was considerably less developed than Russia at the time of the Revolution in October 1917.[9] Coal was the region's main resource. During WWII, known as the Great Patriotic War in the USSR, Karaganda's coal was able to compensate in large measure for the loss of coal from the Donbass, as that region in Ukraine[10] was under occupation by the Nazi invaders.

I didn't know what to expect, but I was sure that meeting other miners from a Soviet coalfield would be a wonderful experience, and I was looking forward to the chance to say thank you on behalf of the British miners.

I was surprised to see that Karaganda was a big town, with a population of 700,000. In fact it is Kazakhstan's second biggest city, after the capital, Alma-Ata (now Almaty). Today Kazakhstan is well-known for hosting the Baikanur cosmodrome, from which cosmonauts and astronauts are launched into space to the International Space Station. Valentina Tereshkova, the first woman to fly in space, was launched from Baikanur on June 16th 1963. On my visit to Karaganda I learnt that a 19th century scientist, Sergei Nikitin, was sent into exile to Baikanur for preaching the idea of space flights, which of course seemed pure fantasy back then.

I went to meet the miners of a pit named after Kornei Osipovich Gorbachov, the man who had first opened up the coalfield. It was the third biggest pit in that coalfield. I was able to meet the pit's trade union and Party leaders and thank them for their solidarity, but what I really wanted was to be able to meet with ordinary miners themselves, and I didn't get that chance. Perhaps I should have insisted more on my own programme, but having told the Ministry of Foreign Affairs Press Office back in Moscow that that was the purpose of my visit, I assumed they would arrange that for me.

It was my first trip outside the Russian Federation and I was still a novice as a foreign correspondent. I gradually learned that one had to be quite insistent about what I and my newspaper wanted, not only what the local authorities wanted to show me and impress upon me.

I did learn that 8,500 roubles had been collected from one meeting alone to send to the British mineworkers. And that 200,000 roubles had been

9 USSR in Maps, J.C. Dewdney, Hodder and Stoughton, London 1982.

10 Ukraine was one of the fifteen constituent republics of the USSR.

raised from the 26 mines in the mining conglomerate. I asked in what way the moneys were collected, and was told that individual miners signed their names alongside how much they wanted to give, and that amount was then deducted from their wages. Most men gave 10 to 12 roubles – more or less a day's wages.

I learned quite a lot about the mine and its workforce and social conditions, which seemed impressive. 3,500 worked at the pit, 600 of whom were women. There were 30 different nationalities – mainly Russians, Kazakhs, Ukrainians and Germans. I learned it was the best-performing pit in the coalfield and the most dangerous one, being very deep. It was fully mechanised, using only Soviet technology.

Kindergartens, sports complex, football stadium, its own holiday resort outside the city, its own sanatorium where miners and their families could recuperate after illness; a 6-hour day, 300-rouble monthly pension at 50 if you'd worked at least 10 years underground, 2 days off per week, opportunities for miners to study at specialised mining colleges, bonuses, free coal, free medical care, 27 working days annual holiday or 42 days where more dangerous work, free transport to and from work – the statistics were impressive.

Some of the seams were 1.5 m high, some 2 m, never more than 3.5 metres high, and in some places they could be as low as 0.9 m. I shuddered at the thought of how claustrophobic working in that sort of seam would be in the heat of the deep underground. Later, on a visit to the Donbass, I would have the experience of crawling along such low seams myself, in unbelievable heat. I take my hat off to miners everywhere, who do such a gruelling and dangerous job.

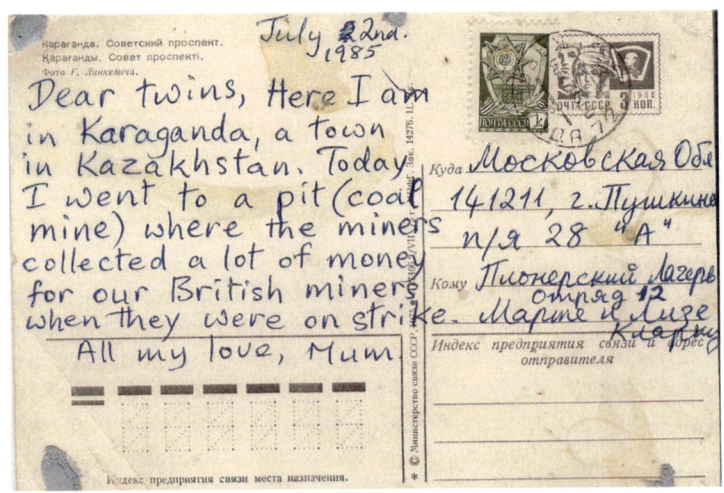

My postcard from Karaganda to our seven-year old twin daughters

"There's 25 to 30 years more coal in our pit," the Chair of the miners' union committee, Kazakh national Tulegin Albiyev told me. "We only close mines when they are fully worked out."

"This mine is not really profitable," he went on, "but taken as a whole the coalfield does make a profit, so we share it out among all the pits."

Wherever you went in the Soviet Union there were the inevitable reminders of the Great Patriotic War, when large parts of the country's territory was occupied by the Nazis.

It never ceased to amaze me, living in Britain in the sixties, seventies and eighties, that the impression had somehow managed to be created in the minds of many British people that the Soviet Union was a country ready to attack us in the West. Yet, from the Mongol invasion in the 13th century to Napoleon's in 1812, to the Nazi invasion of 1941, it is precisely the other way round. By the fifties, when I was growing up, the USSR began to be seen as the ogre stalking Europe. Somehow, from us being great allies during WWII, in the space of only a few years of Cold War propaganda we had imperceptibly become "adversaries".

And as I write now, in 2021, Russia is again seen as a country menacing its western neighbours and the whole of Europe. Our media has, it seems, successfully painted this picture, despite the lack of evidence. Yet, which side has advanced on the other since the dissolution of the USSR? Shortly before the Soviet Union disintegrated, on 9th February 1990, at a meeting between Mikhail Gorbachov and US Secretary of State James Baker, the latter assured Gorbachov that NATO would not expand "even one inch eastward".

Gorbachov only accepted German reunification - over which the Soviet Union had the legal right of veto under treaty - because he received such assurances - given by James Baker, President George H.W. Bush, West German foreign minister Hans-Dietrich Genscher, West German Chancellor Helmut Kohl, the CIA Director Robert Gates, French President Francois Mitterrand, British Prime Minister Margaret Thatcher, British foreign minister Douglas Hurd, British Prime Minister John Major, and NATO secretary-general Manfred Wörner.[11]

According to George Washington University National Security Archives researchers, Svetlana Savranskaya and Tom Blanton, referring to newly declassified documents, Mikhail Gorbachov was given a host of assurances to this effect - that the NATO alliance would not expand past what was then the East German border in 1990. "The documents show that multiple national leaders were considering and rejecting Central and Eastern European membership in NATO as of early 1990 and through 1991", they wrote. But NATO went on to extend an invitation to Hungary, Poland and what was then Czechoslovakia to join the alliance in 1997 at the Madrid Summit - in

---

11 *Not One Inch: America, Russia, and the Making of Post-Cold War Stalemate*, M.E. Sarotte, Yale University Press, 2021, p. 49.

contravention of assurances to the Soviet Union before its 1991 collapse.

Both Russian Presidents Boris Yeltsin and Vladimir Putin complained bitterly about the expansion of NATO towards their borders despite what they had believed were assurances to the contrary. "What happened to the assurances our western partners made after the dissolution of the Warsaw Pact? Where are those declarations today?" Putin said at the Munich Conference on Security Policy in 2007. "No one even remembers them. But I will allow myself to remind this audience what was said. I would like to quote the speech of NATO General Secretary Mr. Wörner in Brussels on 17 May 1990. He said at the time: '...the fact that we are ready not to place a NATO army outside of German territory gives the Soviet Union a firm security guarantee.' Where are these guarantees?"[12]

But to return to my Kazakhstan trip: in Karaganda, far away from the European parts of the USSR, much of which was occupied by the invading Nazi army, there is a monument to Nurkan Abdirov, a Hero of the Soviet Union. Abdirov had been a miner but became a pilot during the war. He deliberately crashed his burning plane on to a Nazi tank column near Rostov rather than save his life by parachuting out.

I also saw a monument to the women who worked in Karaganda's mines from 1941-45, while their menfolk were away at the front. I learnt that both a tank and an aeroplane were named "Women of Karaganda" in their honour.

Before this trip I had no idea that there was a German community in Karaganda. I had seen that the writing on these monuments was in Kazakh and in Russian, but I was really surprised to find that German was also one of the languages spoken by a German community in the city. They were the descendants of Volga Germans, invited to Russia in the 18th century to farm that region.[13] But during WWII many thousands of these Volga German descendants were forcibly moved from the Volga region to Kazakhstan and parts of Siberia for fear of them collaborating with the German Nazis who had occupied the western parts of the Soviet Union.

If this measure, usually painted as an example of the 'Stalinist repressions', does indeed seem harsh, we have to remember that during WWII, people of German, Austrian and Italian nationality living in Britain were forcibly removed to the Isle of Man for the course of the war. They were housed in internment camps to hold enemy aliens – civilians who were believed to be a potential threat or have sympathy with the enemy's war objectives. It was

---

12 from an article in *The National Interest*, by Dave Majumdar, Defense Editor, Dec. 12th 2017.

13 The first German colonists—some 30,000 people—came to settle in Russia in 1763 at the invitation of Catherine the Great, herself of German descent. The majority of the early German colonists were refugees fleeing war, conscription and poverty. The purpose of the invitation was to populate the lower Volga frontier, which had been acquired by the Russian Empire almost two centuries earlier but remained sparsely settled by Russians.
From *The Tragic Saga of the Volga Germans*, Asya Pereltsvaig, 2014.

not only the Soviet Union that regarded Germans living on its territory as suspicious, or likely to side with the enemy.

By 1985 there were 109 nationalities living in Karaganda: 13% were German, 11% Kazakhs, and the rest were Russians, Ukrainians, Byelorussians, Koreans and others. In an industrial city like Karaganda, which was only founded in 1931, it was not surprising that the proportion of indigenous people – the Kazakhs – was lower than that of Russians, since traditionally the Kazakh population were farmers and peasants, and industrial development in the republic was a twentieth century phenomenon.[14]

Some schools taught in Kazakh, others in Russian and some in German, in the communities where the German population was concentrated. I saw that there were newspapers in German and I visited a publishing house in the city which published books in German. I spoke to a German miner – a tall, fair-haired man in his thirties – who told me that although some of the Germans kept their language and traditions alive, and the state helped them in doing this, there were also a lot of inter-ethnic marriages resulting in quite a mixed population in the city.

One pit team-leader ("brigade-leader", in Russian) – Sotsial Isayevich Imanov – invited me back to his home for evening tea. He lived with his wife, Maria Imanova, who was a school cook, and their 8-year old daughter, Almagul, in a typical block of flats, which he told me had been built by the mining conglomerate where he worked. The living room was a good size, with a red oriental carpet adorning the long wall. We drank weak tea out of a *piala* which is like a cup without handles and ate *baursaki* – a sort of Kazakh doughnut – and *chak-chak* which are like chips doused in honey.

We talked in Russian and laughed at little Almagul's questions. Sotsial told me their 3-room flat cost them 18 roubles a month in rent, and their electricity and heating costs were another 2 roubles. So although a monthly wage of 400-450 roubles (a miner's average wage there) might not sound much, with low rent and amenities, wages like these enabled a pretty good lifestyle.

My brief stay in Karaganda over, I flew back to Moscow, eager to see Ricardo and hear about the children, who, like many Soviet children, had gone off to Pioneer Camp, as the long summer vacation had begun in early June.

When I got back to our flat, I was horrified to see Ricardo in bed, alone and in terrible pain. He had started with a slight pain in his knee a few days before, but I had no idea it would have got so much worse. He was in agony. He had been to his Polyclinic (one for foreigners) and they had given him some heat treatment, which had apparently made things worse. I immediately called my secretary, Olga, who arranged for him to be transferred to the

---

14 Kazakhstan was only made a separate constituent republic of the USSR in 1936. Before that it had been the Kirghiz Autonomous Socialist Soviet Republic, established in 1920.

same Polyclinic as me – one which catered for CPSU functionaries and their families. A doctor came within half an hour or so, and proceeded to examine Ricardo's swollen knee joint. Then she got out a canister, which I learnt on asking was liquid nitrogen, and squirted a massive jet of this from a distance of over a metre on to his knee. You had to see the funny side - seeing her aim so accurately from some distance.

It certainly did the trick, having an immediate beneficial effect in bringing down the temperature the inflammation was causing.

But he needed an operation on his knee to remove an abscess, so he was taken by ambulance to No.1 hospital on the outskirts of the city, set among woods of silver birch and pines. One week after I had returned from Karaganda, Ricardo had his operation and spent the next 3 weeks recuperating there.

I took the children to see him in hospital, which was a fascinating experience. He shared a room with an elderly man, who told Ricardo interesting wartime stories he had lived through and shared opinions as to Soviet life. Though ill and frail, this man was a pleasant and friendly companion for Ricardo during his recuperation.

The hospital was modern and clean and the nursing efficient. Ricardo had to have 6 injections a day after the operation, and there was one particular nurse whose injections always hurt, whereas other nurses did the job more or less painlessly. One day he asked her: "How come your injections are always so painful?" She replied: "How do you expect to get better unless it hurts!"

Readers might just laugh at this and think no more of it, but actually, in that one question is encapsulated a Soviet philosophy which I found again and again. 'No pain, no gain', I suppose, would be the English equivalent, but these days that attitude is no longer prevalent in British society – quite the opposite, I think, as more and more we tend to feel that pain should never be tolerated.

But the Russians are hard – *zakalyonniye* – and proud of it. It was the same when the children were vaccinated against TB, whooping cough and measles at their Moscow school: the nurse told Victor: "It has to hurt, otherwise it won't do you any good!"

Thinking about it over the years, I do think that the USSR's wartime experience has something to do with it. When you think of the Nazis' barbarism to the population they overran in Ukraine, Belarus and the western part of European Russia – torture, hangings, detentions in death camps, forced labour, forced exile to work in Germany for Nazi families, and other crimes too numerous to mention, you had to have been tough to withstand all that. Not to mention the courage and sacrifice of all the partisans and those who risked their lives to help and sustain them.

Their climate, too – winter temperatures of anything between -10°C to -20° C surely makes people tougher than those who live in sunny climes.

We had seen our children off to Pioneer Camp on 5th June, taken by a fleet of coaches with their brown suitcases and in Pioneer uniform, which for girls was a blue skirt, white blouse and red Pioneer scarf, and for boys, white shirts with gold buttons and a red and yellow pioneer badge on the upper sleeve. They would spend 5 weeks at the camp, which enabled Ricardo and me to continue working without having to worry about them.

Druzhba (Friendship) Pioneer Camp was in a forest about 40 kilometres outside Moscow. The children lived in wooden chalets with trees all around them and clearings for activities here and there among the trees. Russians are very fond of woods, and firmly believe that breathing forest air is good for you.

I was slightly worried about whether the children would like the Camp, as they had only been in Moscow three and a half months, so their Russian was still not very good and they hadn't really had time to make friendships. We went to see them the first weekend and were briefly allowed to see their sleeping quarters, the sports field and running track, and managed to get ourselves bitten by the many mosquitos which thrived in the humid forest air.

The kids were having a good time and were full of all the activities they were doing, tripping over themselves excitedly to tell us about their new friends at the camp. I was so relieved that they weren't pining for home and were obviously having a good time. The only objection from the twins, who were just 7, was the regulatory afternoon rest for an hour after lunch. "Why do we have to rest, as if we were babies?" they complained. But they adapted, resting on their camp beds, lying on their right sides, as they were instructed, not on their left sides.

The thought did cross my mind that perhaps the enforced hour's rest was a way for the *vozhaty* (pioneer leaders) to get a well-earned break for a while from their hundreds of charges....

Our children were covered in mosquito bites; probably the fact that they had never been bitten by mosquitoes before made them especially delectable for the horrid insects. But they weren't particularly bothered by them and seem to have developed an immunity to mosquito bites.

Parents weren't really supposed to go and see the children; there was no provision for that, and neither could you take them out for a few hours. It seemed unnecessarily strict to me, and I did not like at all having to talk to our children through the bars of the tall iron gates, as we handed in biscuits and fruit for them. But we did not think we should ask for any special treatment, so we didn't.

When the kids came back after the camp was over, their Russian had much improved. Five weeks of being surrounded by the language had done the trick, and from then on their fluency increased by leaps and bounds. They also learned to enjoy raw garlic cloves sliced on to thick wedges of *borodinskiy khlyeb* – the Russian black bread which is so tasty with savoury food and snacks.

Whilst they were away at camp, I was getting on with my work, reading the Soviet papers, going to press conferences and ringing up people I knew to try and get under the official news to find out what the new leader, Mikhail Gorbachov, meant to them and to the country as a whole.

In early July, 1985, there was a visit by British MP's on the Foreign Affairs Select Committee, led by Sir Anthony Kershaw, and a press briefing at the British Embassy, which occupies an elegant old mansion on the banks of the Moscow River opposite the Kremlin.

At the Embassy briefing, Sir Anthony took out a gold tooth-pick on a chain and proceeded to pick his teeth with it, then carefully screwed the top back on and put it back in his top pocket, deftly readjusting the white handkerchief therein. My sardonic comment in that day's diary was: "Quite charming!" Closing the press conference, the Chair said: "Kate Clark and gentlemen, that brings us to the end of our press conference."

In answer to a question of mine, Kershaw said that our knowledge (in Britain) of the Soviet point of view was rather lacking, in his view, and added: "Not that your efforts, so to speak, are not dedicated towards it (i.e. giving the Soviet view), but we can't, in the House, concentrate on everything, and people have their specialities and do tend to read reports by their own people."

This kind of barbed remark was typical of what I would get from British establishment people, whether embassy staff or visiting parliamentarians. I decided right at the start that I would develop a thick skin, and not give them an easy ride by staying away, as some former correspondents had done. As far as I was concerned, I had as much right as any other British journalist to be invited to Embassy press conferences and events, and I wasn't going to let their hostility to me change my mind on that.

I was to learn later what "giving someone the cold shoulder" actually meant. When Margaret Thatcher went to Moscow in March 1987, all the British journalists were told to meet outside the Kremlin walls one morning to find out which of us would get accreditation to go inside the Kremlin where she would meet Gorbachov. I was standing talking to one or two of the other correspondents – from the *Times,* the *Telegraph,* the *Financial Times* and the *Guardian*, plus a couple of special correspondents from London - when the British Embassy's Press Attaché, a Scottish laird with a posh English accent, who liked to call himself Donald McLaren of McLaren, walked up to address the group, and all of a sudden I found myself completely outside of the circle, literally facing the "cold shoulders" of my fellow journalists as they edged me out. As I am barely 5' tall, and slim, it's not hard to imagine how they did that.

In this sort of situation, I always find that a foul-mouthed insult sworn inwardly helps.

In general my relations with the other journalists were good. Soon after my arrival as the *Morning Star*'s correspondent, I met the *Times* correspondent, Richard Owen. He made some witty remark about the *Morning Star* - I can't remember what - and I reminded him that our two papers used to be very friendly, so much so that we shared the same correspondent for a time - Claud Cockburn[15]. I told him: "Maybe your paper would like to do the same now - I could do your job!" Richard took it in good heart and laughed. The other British journalists saw that I was a very active correspondent, I asked questions in Russian at press conferences and I was fairly knowledgeable about what was going on, since I read the press, watched TV and talked to people. Most of them didn't, since they didn't speak the language and their editors only wanted stories about "dissidents" anyway. Cloistered in their foreigner-only blocks of flats in Sad Sam[16], as they called it, they did not mix with ordinary people as I and my family did.

A 1986 BBC TV film, *Caviar and Cornflakes*, made by Richard Denton, in which I was interviewed, gives an inkling of British diplomats' and journalists' lives in Moscow at that time. (See Appendix V for reviews of this film).

I wouldn't say I was exactly *friendly* with any of my fellow British correspondents, but I think 'with grudging respect' might sum up how they looked on me. Remember that these were the years of the Cold War, when anti-Communism was very strong in Britain. The election of Mikhail Gorbachov to the Soviet Party leadership was to change that somewhat in the next few years.

The British Embassy was terribly, terribly "establishment" at that time. From Sir Bryan Cartledge and McLaren of McLaren down, they all had accents you could cut with a knife. I was once invited to dinner with a British diplomat and a couple of journalists and at one moment they were all swapping stories of their days at Eton – it turned out they'd all been at the same public school. (Eton's fees in 2017 were nearly £40,000 p.a.)

I suppose, as the odd one out among 'establishment' journalists, it was to be expected that I would be the butt of snide comments and worse – such as a piece in the *Guardian* by their correspondent, Martin Walker, who claimed I wasn't really a journalist at all[17] – but I could hold my own. On a visit to Moscow by Tory MP Sir Malcolm Rifkind, his Private Secretary facetiously remarked to me that "it would be rather fun to hang up a banner on the British Embassy façade, opposite the Kremlin, with the words: "SDI rules OK!" I replied: "Oh, I thought you were going to suggest a banner with the number of Britain's unemployed on it!"

SDI (US President Ronald Reagan's pet Strategic Defense Initiative) was no joking matter. It was the height of the Cold War. Both sides had vast arsenals of nuclear weapons targeted at each other - each more deadly than

---

15 Claud Cockburn worked for the *Times* and the *Daily Worker*, for the latter under the pen-name Frank Pitcairn. He reported on the Spanish Civil War for the *Daily Worker* and worked as its Foreign Editor for a time.

16 Sad Sam was made up of three adjoining blocks, each with nine storeys, on the Sadovo-Samotochnaya stretch of the Sadovoye Koltso, the Garden Ringroad encircling the Kremlin and the ancient heart of Moscow.

17 See Appendix III for Walker's letter and my reply.

the atom bombs the USA had dropped on the Japanese cities of Hiroshima and Nagasaki at the end of the Second World War, which had killed an estimated 200,000 people. The world was crying out for detente and de-escalation, but what we had instead was an actor-President of the USA, totally out of his depth in arms reduction talks, but wedded to his naive belief in a space-based 'shield' which would destroy incoming missiles.

"They seek to create an anti-missile shield over the US, to simultaneously deploy strategic first-strike offensive weapons and new strategic space-based forces intended to hit targets on earth, in the sea, in the atmosphere and in outer space," Soviet Defence Minister, Marshal Sokolov told journalists, condemning SDI as a blatant attempt to achieve military superiority over the Soviet Union.

"The anti-missile shield would frustrate any retaliatory strike from the USSR and would "finish off" any Soviet missiles which survived a first American nuclear strike," he explained.

Mikhail Gorbachov, after becoming CPSU General Secretary on 11th March 1985, soon set about announcing a series of initiatives to ratchet down the tension and bring about lasting peace, which earned him considerable popularity in the West from people tired of the increasing tensions of the Cold War.

On 8 April 1985, he announced the suspension of the deployment of SS-20 missiles in Europe as a move towards resolving intermediate-range nuclear weapons issues. Then, in August, on the 40th anniversary of the atomic bombing by the USA of Hiroshima and Nagasaki, the Soviet Union announced a 5-month unilateral moratorium on testing nuclear weapons. The USA did not agree to stop their nuclear testing, however, even though the Soviet Union renewed their testing moratorium several times, until February 1987. In September 1985 Gorbachov proposed that both the Soviets and the Americans cut their nuclear arsenals in half. In November the USSR proposed a summit in Geneva between Gorbachov and Ronald Reagan, which, although not achieving any concrete agreements, did set the scene for further summits at which important agreements were reached.

"The Soviet Union will not be the first to make the step into outer space with weapons," Gorbachov assured the American Union of Concerned Scientists in July that year. The militarisation of outer space would inevitably increase the threat of nuclear war and give impetus to an uncontrolled arms race, he said. Later at the Geneva summit he declared that the Soviet Union was for a complete ban on the development, testing and deployment of space attack systems.

Meeting the visiting British parliamentary Foreign Affairs Select Committee in July 1985, Soviet spokesman Boris Ponomaryov said that the stationing of US first-strike missiles aimed at the USSR "cannot but have an effect on Soviet-British relations". There was "no Soviet threat", he told the MPs, explaining: "In our country you will not find classes or social groups that

24

have an interest in war or profits from war work."

January 1986 would see Gorbachov make his boldest international move so far, when he announced his proposal for the elimination of intermediate-range nuclear weapons in Europe and his strategy for eliminating entire nuclear arsenals by the year 2000.

It's hard to underestimate the excitement that accompanied Gorbachov's coming to power. After so many very elderly leaders, especially the last one, Chernenko, who on TV appeared stiff as if he were being propped up, this new, much younger leader, who looked full of vigour, was bound to gain their support.

It was refreshing to see him in the streets, on a visit to Leningrad in May 1985, answering questions off the cuff, surrounded by ordinary people. It was clear that people were enthusiastic about the new leader and there was a wealth of goodwill towards him at that time.

For the first time people heard their leader denouncing the shortcomings in the economy: "Try to get your flat repaired," he told a meeting in the Smolny Institute – headquarters of the Bolsheviks in the October 1917 Revolution – "and you will definitely have to find a moonlighter to do it for you – and he will have to steal the materials from a building site!"

And later that summer he told workers on one of his many visits to factories and towns: "You can understand the consumer who wonders why we know how to make spaceships and atomic-powered ships, but often produce defective modern household gadgets, shoes and clothes!"

He immediately set about making changes. The veteran Foreign Minister, Andrei Gromyko, who in the Politburo had supported Gorbachov's election to General Secretary, was replaced by the much younger Georgian, Eduard Shevardnadze. At first the talk was of acceleration of the economy. The aim of the reforms was to make the existing centrally planned economy work better, not to do away with it in favour of the market – what would later be termed 'market socialism'.

After 'acceleration' Gorbachov started to talk of 'perestroika' of the entire economy – the need to overhaul or restructure the whole economy. And from 1986, in social and political life, he introduced the concept of glasnost (openness, transparency) arguing that Soviet society had been closed up for too long. This heralded an incredible period when previously banned books were published and previously censored films and plays shown. New-found freedom existed for journalists in the media to explore for themselves the boundaries of what was permissible with little or no supervision from editors or political overseers. It's interesting that glasnost now figures in the vocabulary of many languages.

My work as correspondent was very busy, though in subsequent years the pace would become even greater. But alongside the heavy workload, we managed to enjoy life and spent as much time as we could with the children. They had a number of good friends and had managed to find their feet at school, so we were not unduly worried about them. Being Chilean, Ricardo found compatriots also living in exile in Moscow, so we sometimes socialised with them.

Schooldays were always a rush in the mornings, especially in winter, when we had to make sure the children were wearing the necessary layers of clothes, taking their heavy satchels with homework and sometimes having to carry their skis, too. Looking back, I think to myself: "How on earth did we manage?" But we did. The children were really good at getting ready on their own, with just a bit of help from us. And they cheerfully set off each day, taking the old clattering lift down to the ground floor, walking across the little park we could see from our windows and along *Ulitsa Obukha* (Obukha Street) to the nearest tram stop on *Yauskiy Boulevard*. There they would clamber with all their encumbrances up the tram steps, put their 5 kopecks in the pay-box, get off after a few stops and walk the 100 metres or so to their school on *Bolshoi Vuzovskiy* cul-de-sac.

Yausky Boulevard

There were no conductors on Soviet trams or buses. You simply put your 5 kopecks in the box with a slot in the top – or, in the case of some children, you rode *"zaitsa"* (hare), i.e. without paying! The fare – standard on the metro too, for whatever distance you rode – was so cheap that very few people avoided paying.

Our children - Victor, who was now ten, and the twins, Liza and Martha, who were seven, adapted very well to their new lives. Perhaps our happy household gave them the security needed to help them through those early months before they had made friends and learned the language well.

Victor had a nice group of schoolfriends. His best friend was Artyom, who was part Dagestani[18], and Victor would often go to his flat near *Ploshchad' Nogina* after school. Artyom and their other schoolfriends would also come to our flat, where there was more room to play. Much of the time the children played outside in the *dvor* (inner courtyard) of the block of flats, where there were pleasant grassy areas and trees and little mounds they could sledge down in winter. They also used to sledge on pieces of cardboard down the slopes of a green area near our flats on their way home from school.

In spring and summer the girls would play skipping, jumping over a long piece of elastic with their friends who lived in the same *dvor*, or playing the Soviet equivalent of hopscotch.

Liza and Martha soon made friends with Masha, who was a bit younger than them, and lived in a different wing of our building, and Baira, who lived a few floors down from us. She was part Kalmyk and her grandparents had been early Bolsheviks from that nationality in the north Caucasus[19]. She lived with her father, Lev, who used to come and visit sometimes, bottle of vodka in hand. Then we knew we were in for a long session of chat, and stories about Kalmykia and his family and their camel-herding past. In Kalmykia, Lev told us, you had to leave your door open for any traveller to stay with you, that was the custom: tradition had it that you could not refuse anyone hospitality.

He had had a hard life, I think. Both his parents had done time in the gulag[20] and he lived with his elderly mother and his Russian wife – Baira's mother – who for at least part of the time we lived there was in prison for some sort of fraud, we heard. So his home life was not exactly rosy. But Baira was a cheerful, enterprising girl, and the four girls played very happily together throughout the five years we lived in Moscow.

Daily life wasn't that easy in Moscow, compared with our lives in London. There were supermarkets, and we sometimes went to one on Taganskaya Ploshchad' which was our nearest, but the variety of goods on sale was inconsistent. At times there would be no meat or fish at all for sale, although if you called back in an hour or so, there might be. We did not have a market nearby, but if we had invited guests to dinner, we would use the Central Market, where a great variety of meat, fruit, vegetables and herbs were on sale from the *kolkhozy* (collective farms) and farmworkers' private plots.

---

18 Dagestan was an Autonomous Republic within the Russian Federation.

19 Kalmykia was an Autonomous Republic within the Russian Federation.

20 Gulag: *gosudarstvennoye upravlyeniye lagerei* – state administration for labour camps.

So Ricardo and I tended to do what most Soviet people did – have a weekly order through their place of work. Ricardo had that right, as an employee of *Agentstvo Pechati Novosti*, where he was a translator and style-editor on a monthly magazine in Spanish, *Socialismo Teoría y Práctica*. I had a weekly order, too, at GUM, the big department store on Red Square, and between these two weekly orders, which were delivered to our flat, we managed very well for basic foods such as meat, cheese, tongue (our kids never will forget that the tongue sent in our order was, literally, a cow's tongue – and as a result, they wouldn't touch it, although it was actually very tasty) tinned fish of all kinds (there was a big variety of fish species we have never heard of in Britain, both tinned and fresh, swimming in tanks in the big *Okean* shops situated here and there throughout the city) soups, rice, pasta, cakes, biscuits, butter and eggs. Honey, jams and *vareniye* – a sort of runny jam containing small pieces of fruit, which Russians serve in a small dish with a spoon, alongside tea (served without milk, with optional slice of lemon) and *halva* from Central Asia were also available on the order list.

Fresh fruit, bread and dairy products we would buy ourselves, either from the shops in our block of flats, or in shops on our way back from work. Ricardo was a dab hand at finding good-quality ready-made meals (*polufabrikaty*), which came in square tin-foil trays, with a big chunk of beef in gravy, for instance, and cooked rice or *grechikha* (buckwheat) to accompany it. We would make a cabbage or carrot salad to go with it, and hey presto! our evening meal was ready.

Dairy products were always in good supply everywhere: *kefir*, a sort of liquid yoghurt, *toplyonnoye moloko* (baked milk), *varyonnoye moloko* (boiled milk), *prostokvasha* (sour low-fat buttermilk), *ryazhenka* (fermented baked milk), bottles of milk with different amounts of cream, *smetana* (soured cream), *slivki* - fresh cream of different thicknesses.... *Smetana* is an essential part of everyday Russian cuisine, used for topping salads of all kinds – tomato, cucumber, spring onion, grated carrot....

As I write, my taste buds remember the really tasty small, fat cucumbers that you could buy – so much tastier than the long, slim cucumbers we are used to here. From the market we would buy a variety of fresh herbs and whole marinated garlics, purplish in colour, which you eat just as they are. They are softer than raw garlic, and delicious. We all loved them.

Many blocks of flats had shops on their ground floors. Along with a baker's and confectionary, fruit and vegetable shop, butcher's and dairy products shop on street level, we had the renowned *Iluzion* cinema, which showed foreign films as well as Soviet ones.

In Britain during the Cold War much was made of the so-called "privileges" of the *nomenklatura* "class" – as if there were no privileges accorded to the elite in Britain through simply being wealthy and having attended fee-paying schools which ensure their alumni progress to key jobs in the economy, the media, the Church and the military. In my experience in Moscow, I could see that even a top journalist on *Pravda* or *Izvestiya*, or a factory director, would be likely to have a three-bedroom flat, instead of a two-bed one which was more common. They might have access to a better Polyclinic through their work and status than their local one, or to slightly better-quality weekly food orders. But nothing on the scale of our rich people, or of the Russian oligarchs who took over the heights of the Soviet economy after 1991.

As a *mnogodyetnaya mama* (i.e. mother with three or more children) I had the privilege of being able to buy children's clothes from a special section in big department stores like GUM. It was a help, since I didn't have time to go round scouring the shops for winter boots, fur coats, hats and other clothes, which had to be replaced as the children grew, of course. But such special sections did not have a big variety or offer all sizes, so I wouldn't exactly call it a privilege.

Why was it that such essential goods as children's clothes and footwear were not available everywhere all the time? I have already alluded earlier in the book to the problem emanating from the centralised planning system, but the question remains: were such shortages an *inevitable* result of centralised planning, or due to a malfunction or lack of checks and balances in that system?

The output plans were agreed at national level, by *Gosplan*, the State Planning Committee, so each factory and plant knew exactly what they had to produce each year according to the annual plan. But what was the mechanism for deciding how those plans responded to the needs and desires of the population? Why did factories keep churning out old-fashioned shoes, furniture, unstylish clothes and poor-quality buttons, for instance - thus meeting their plan targets, but failing to satisfy the population's wishes?

I mention buttons, because one incident illustrates this vividly. One day, I took my English raincoat for dry-cleaning to a little shop on *Ploshchad' Nogina*. It was such a culture shock that I wrote about it in a piece for the *Morning Star*:

"Before me in the queue were two girls handing in thirteen big net curtains from their workplace, and a middle-aged man with a raincoat for cleaning.

"The attendant had to write out two sets of forms for each item with the client's address, telephone number, etc, then measure the curtains and calculate the price.

"Then she had to write a number with pen and ink on to thirteen little slips of material, which the girls had to then sew on by hand one by one, while everyone waited.

"After waiting about half an hour, the man with the raincoat began to protest. The recent Party Congress (in February 1986, K.C.) had shown the way, he said - now it was up to everybody at every workplace to think how their work can be better organised. "And there must be a better way than this!" he said, to murmurs of agreement from everybody else in the queue.

"The overworked shop assistant answered rudely that things were all

29

right as they were. "Let everything stay just the same," she muttered, "and everybody mind their own business."

"And she had the last laugh - because the man ended up having to sew the raincoat belt on to the bottom of the coat - yes, all the way round - before she would accept it for cleaning. "That's the rules," she said, pointing to the wall.

"Finally it was my turn. The assistant took it, looked at it, then said to me: "Take off all the buttons, give them in here, then tack the belt on to the bottom of the mac." And she produced a needle and thread with which to do it. Amazed, I asked why I had to do this. She replied that with the chemicals they used, buttons on coats from abroad melted. And the belt had to be attached because otherwise it might get lost.

"Seething at the stupidity of this, I nevertheless complied, since I knew that it would be the same in any other dry-cleaners. All the time I was thinking of the time lost by Soviet women – because it was mainly women - in ridiculous tasks like this. No wonder women were nowhere to be seen in the top echelons of Party and Government, I thought to myself – they haven't got time!"

Before we left for the USSR, I was aware of economic studies which described the decline in growth and inefficiencies of the Soviet economy. These were serious studies produced not by anti-Soviet economists, but by people who supported the socialist system and who knew its benefits and shortcomings very well. I, with our three small children at that time, had not been keeping abreast of such literature, but my brother who, like me, had been a Communist since his teens, had warned me of the gravity of the Soviet Union's economic situation.

"By 1970 the period of stagnation under Brezhnev had resulted in an obvious collapse of the existing system," a St Petersburg academic, Leonid Seleznev, wrote.[21] "It was evident that sources of growth were exhausted. Gross National Product (GNP) continued to fall. Industry was skewed on the one hand towards the production of armaments, on the other hand away from making consumer goods. Agriculture was at a stalemate. Living standards had stopped rising by the early 1980's."

"While Marxists agree that "public ownership" must replace private ownership, there has always been debate about how public ownership should be controlled and how the economy should be ordered and organised – how in practice the general interests can be furthered by a system of planning. Recognising the evils of capitalism is one matter, but agreeing on how to improve on its system of production and exchange is another," writes Professor David Lane.[22] This centralised planning structure which existed in

---

21 SCRSS Digest No.1, spring 2016.

22 *Soviet Society under Perestroika*, London Routledge, 1992, David Lane, p.28 & 29.

PLANNING AGENCIES	Gosplan (along with the state bank; commissions for supplies, prices, science and technology; and so on)
	PLANS
	↓
PRODUCTION	Government ministries for all industries (coal, electronics, fish, food, gas, petroleum, autos, and so on)
	↓
Production Units	Government-controlled factories seek fulfillment of output defined in plans.
- -	- -
FREE MARKET	Collective farm surplus and private plot produce

Figure 2.2 Control of the Soviet Economy from Stalin to Brezhnev

the USSR of the eighties is illustrated above.

But in 1985, the talk was so far only about *uskoreniye* (acceleration) of the economy, and then, later that year, of the need for a "restructuring" of the economy – *perestroika*. *Glasnost* (transparency or openness) was to come to the fore in 1986, when former editors of influential newspapers and magazines were replaced by men (yes, they were all men) considered reformers in the mould of Gorbachov.

In June 1985 I had the chance to visit the Crimean peninsula, for centuries a holiday and recuperation favourite for Russian leaders and famous writers like Mikhail Lermontov, author of *A Hero of our Time*, Anton Chekhov (his famous short story *The Lady with the Little Dog* was set in Yalta) Lev Tolstoy, author of *War and Peace*, whose family lived for nearly a year in an old mansion in Gaspra, Fyodor Dostoyevsky and many other prominent Russians of pre-revolutionary times.

For his poems about freedom, Russia's most famous 19th century poet, Alexander Pushkin, was exiled from St. Petersburg to the Crimea. And in the 20th century, Marina Tsvetaeva, Maxim Gorky and Alexei Tolstoy found inspiration in Crimea's warm air and beautiful scenery.

31

"During the civil war, Crimea was the last foothold of resistance for the White Army. Refugee ships departed from its ports carrying scientists, artists, and writers. 1920, the year of the Bolsheviks' final victory, was an important milestone for Russian literature. The play *Flight* by Mikhail Bulgakov reflects the last days of that old Russia. Crimea was a sort of Noah's Ark in distress. Here White Army soldiers, priests, and aristocrats from St. Petersburg were trying to understand what happened to Russia and how to find their place in the world," Aleksandra Guryanova wrote in *Rossiyskaya Gazeta*[23].

"Crimea has always attracted creative people who disagree with the actions of the authorities in Moscow," Guryanova continues. "One of them was the young poet and translator, Joseph Brodsky. In his narrative poem *Homage to Yalta*, Brodsky talks about the fragility and randomness of earthly life, which is ruled by invisible, ruthless fate."

We know about the Crimean War, 1853-1856, in which the Russian Empire lost to an alliance of the Ottoman Empire, France, Britain and Sardinia. Lord Alfred Tennyson's poem *Charge of the Light Brigade* celebrated Britain's success at the Battle of Balaclava on 24 October, with, one historian writes, relatively light casualties – "only" 118 killed out of 620. The human cost of the Crimean War was immense: 25,000 British, 100,000 French and an estimated 41,000 Russians died, mainly fighting the Ottoman forces in the Caucasus region. Many of the casualties died from disease and neglect. Florence Nightingale and Mary Seacole became national heroines for their work in improving hospital conditions for the wounded.

Another key battle in the Crimean War was that of Sevastopol, an important port on the Black Sea. Founded in 1783 as the base for the Black Sea Russian Navy, it was besieged by the British in the Crimean War. Since the 1917 Revolution it has been the home port of the Soviet Navy's Black Sea Fleet and as such, of great strategic importance to Russia.

As I write now, in 2021, probably what most British people know about Crimea is that Russia invaded the peninsula in 2014. A referendum was held which showed that the vast majority of Crimeans wanted to be part of Russia - not surprising, as Crimea had been part of the Russian empire since 1783 and its population is primarily Russian and Ukrainian.

It was only in 1954, under Soviet leader Nikita Khrushchov, himself a Ukrainian, that the peninsula was transferred to the jurisdiction of what was then the Soviet republic of Ukraine, rather than that of the Soviet Russian Federation. It was an administrative transfer, effected within the boundaries of the same country – the USSR, a federation of 15 constituent republics, of which Russia was one and Ukraine another. This fact puts a different complexion on the so-called "invasion" by Russia of Crimea.

This sunny Black Sea peninsula is famous for hosting the Yalta Conference, held in February, 1945, where the heads of government of the allies –

---

23 In *Rossiyskaya Gazeta*, 5th May 2014.

Roosevelt, Churchill and Stalin, of the United States, Great Britain and the Soviet Union respectively, met to agree on how Europe would be reorganised after the Nazis' defeat in the Second World War.

I visited the Livadia Palace, in pre-revolutionary times one of the tsar's palaces, now a museum, where I was told of Lenin's decree, following the 1917 October Revolution, that all such palaces would henceforth belong to the workers and peasants. In the large white hall I could see a big photograph of Winston Churchill.

Soviet partisans had saved the palace from destruction by the Nazis, who had stolen wall decorations, chandeliers and objets d'art. "Nothing of the 800 or so precious objects they took was ever returned to us," our guide told us.

Another room held documents from the three postwar conferences – Potsdam, Teheran and Yalta. Among the many topics discussed at Livadia was the need to de-nazify Germany, the Soviet Union being in favour, our guide stressed, of "a strong, democratic and unified Germany."

Once more on this visit, as in so many others in different parts of the Soviet Union, the dreadful effects of the war were highlighted. It was like a painful scar which never completely healed. It is estimated that some 388,000 Britons died in WWII, but the USSR lost some 27 million citizens, including military and civilian. It is hard to take in the enormity of such loss, the effects caused to the economy of a generation of missing men and the demographic effects on the country.

My trip to the Crimea was a bit of a rude awakening as to what I could expect on subsequent ones: visits to *sovkhozy* and *kolzhozy*[24], oodles of statistics bombarding you (in Russian, of course) and the difference between the British "million" (one thousand thousands) and the US "million" and "billion", the Russian term *milliard* (one thousand millions) and between "tonnes" and "tons" ready to trip you up at every turn.

I'll give you an example. Information given me on my visit to Crimean state farm Shirokoye (wide): 5,000 hectares (I'm thinking, er, what's a hectare?) with 2,700 head of cattle, 4,500 pigs, X number of rabbits for the many sanatoria there – good for the diet; they grow wheat, barley, oats, peas, maize, herbs, alfalfa, etc. 70 tractors, 100 other farm vehicles, 40 combine-harvesters, 620 farmworkers, 4,600 litres milk p.a., automatic milking 2x a day. 280mm average rainfall, harvest average 43.6 centners (help? what's a centner?) per hectare on non-irrigated land; 9000 tons (English tons, or metric tonnes?) grain p.a., 800 tons meat sold to the state every year, 1000 tons fruit, 3000 tons onions..... etc, etc. You get the idea..... It was a bit of a nightmare, which is why most journalists never included such statistics in reports they filed.

Crimea is a wine-growing region, and when I was there in June 1985 the

---

24 *Sovkhoz*: state farm; *kolzhoz*: collective farm.

farmers were having to reassess their production in the light of the drastic anti-alcohol measures taken by the new leader, Mikhail Gorbachov.

"We'll go over to 10% of non-alcoholic wines," Professor Pavel Golodriga, of the Magarach Institute told me. "We'll produce more table wines in future rather than the stronger dessert wines we make at present. And we'll produce more juice and raisins, instead of importing them from Turkey."

In his striped shirt and navy cords, Golodriga spoke with enthusiasm of the scientific work they were doing at the Institute to produce new drought- and frost-resistant vines, and vines producing faster-ripening grapes.

A wine culture has existed in the Crimea since the 4th century BC; presses and amphoras from this period have been found on the southern coast of the peninsula, which became part of the Russian empire in 1783 under Catherine the Great (1729–1796). The Magarach viticulture research institute was founded in 1828. Famous for its wines, champagne and sparkling wines, Magarach had to destroy many of its vineyards during Gorbachov's anti-alcohol campaign. In a feature I wrote:

"Pesticides would not be needed in the world's vineyards if wine-growers concentrated on new multi-resistant vines," Golodriga told me. And people would be much healthier as a result. Multi-resistant vines are new varieties able to withstand disease, frost and drought. All these pesticides being used throughout the world are causing untold damage to future generations – we don't really know yet just how much damage. Pesticides can cause mutations in the genes which in turn can lead to disease in human beings. But without international cooperation it will be impossible to stop their use," Professor Golodriga went on.

Driving for hundreds of miles around the Crimea, you get the impression of a rich agricultural region. Neat vineyards, stretching up hillsides at crazy angles, ripening fields of wheat, barley, oats and corn. It's an area famous for tourism – both Soviet and foreign – but the good weather for tourists means a low average rainfall (280-300mm) which causes problems for agriculture. This was being overcome, I was told, by a vast irrigation network, started 20 years ago, which takes water from the River Dnieper and channels it into the North Crimean canal system.

Driving along I could see machines like giant dragonflies with elongated wings, going up and down the fields spraying the crops with water, pumped through thick long pipes from the canal. Man-made irrigation is costly to set up but very worthwhile - one irrigated acre produces as much as 4 non-irrigated acres. By 1990, when the third irrigation stage was due to be completed, nearly 50% of the arable land would be irrigated.

At *Shirokoye* state farm, where they always fulfil their share of the five-year plans, Dmitri Volkov told me with pride, they have 70 tractors, 100 different farm vehicles and forty combine-harvesters. The farm comprises two villages with a population of over 2,500.

They have their own schools, both primary and secondary, nurseries, their own theatre, clubs, medical centre, shops, public sauna, and are at present building their own museum.

A farmworker's average wage is 201 roubles per month, but some get more than 300, depending on age, qualifications and the job they do. Out of their wages they pay 3-5 roubles per month on rent for a flat or a house in one of the villages. I saw modern three and four-storey blocks of flats, and many cottages with their own gardens, orchards and vegetable patches.

Many farmworkers and their families prefer to live in cottages, so many people buy their own, paying some 3,750 roubles over 15 years. This is for a 4-roomed cottage, plus kitchen, bathroom, verandah, garden shed and all mod cons – gas, hot water, electricity and central heating.

The collective farms I visited had big modern cultural centres, with theatres seating several hundred people. I even noticed a revolving stage in one of them. One had its own art gallery, with a children's art exhibition at one end. You could not fail to be impressed by the nursery-school at *Friendship among Peoples* collective farm, in *Krasnogvardeisky* district. For 330 children, the nursery has its own workrooms, playrooms, film-room and dormitory for the sacred afternoon nap. They have their own little greenhouses, with child-size spades, forks and rakes in them, and all sorts of plants growing there. Any child needing a nursery place is assured of one, and parents pay 2 roubles per month per child, for 6 days a week if they wish, from 7am to 7pm (or less if the parents wish).

At this collective farm 19% of the arable land is irrigated. They have achieved a 14% increase in production over the last 4 years, due to new incentive schemes, greater mechanisation and irrigation. Under the incentive scheme, the collective farmworkers' pay is tied to results – and the system has proved successful, we were told. The farmworkers' average take-home pay is 215 roubles – about the same as the average industrial wage.

Friendship among Peoples comprises 8 villages and has a population of 10,000, with a labour force of 3,700. Last year they sold 36 million roubles worth of produce – mainly fruit, vegetables, milk and meat. Last year's net profit, the farm's head agronomist, Yevgeni Yeroshenko told us, was 12 million roubles, which represents 42% profitability.

And the *kolkhoz* has a rosy bank balance of 130 million roubles. "We've got so much money we don't know what to do with it!" Yevgeni joked. In fact they use that money for putting up new buildings, improved facilities for the farmworkers and their families. And we were told at another collective farm that *Friendship among Peoples* had given one of the less successful collective farms in the area a 3 million rouble, interest-free credit.

In his recent speech at a CPSU Central Committee conference on scientific and technological progress, General Secretary Mikhail Gorbachov said that Soviet society was faced with the "urgent tasks of improving food supply, increasing the output of commodities and services for the people. During that first year - 1985 - living in the Soviet Union, I was surprised at the amount of criticism you could see in newspapers and hear on TV, even before the era of *glasnost* had kicked in.

One feature I wrote began like this: "Surely no country on earth criticises itself in public as much as the Soviet Union. Can you imagine Margaret Thatcher seriously analysing the problem of Britain's nearly four million unemployed, in a speech of an hour and a half, relayed at peak time on British TV news?"

Unemployment was not a feature of Soviet society, but I realised from my first trip outside Moscow that there was much to criticise – one being the gap between words and deeds.

"We have to face up to the truth even if it hurts," Gorbachov told a Party leaders' conference in the western Siberian coalfields of Tyumen and Tomsk in September 1985. Berating the living conditions of oilworkers and their families in such harsh climes, he cited complacency "and even a certain dishonesty" on the part of some officials.

"It is difficult to proceed correctly if the information we have is not objective," he told them. "Lenin's teachings were always to stick to the truth, whatever that may be. Any doctoring of the truth can only do harm to our great endeavour."

It was this "divergence between words and deeds" which could make people lose faith in their representatives. In words, you heard wonderful statistics, but often what you found in practice was very different. You could read much about eliminating the discrepancies between town and countryside - yet you could find, as I once did, that a rural restaurant's toilet was in a field some metres away. Or, on being shown round the recreational facilities of one enterprise and seeing an empty swimming pool, I was told that it was just awaiting repair – when it was obvious to me that it had not been used for months, if not years.

Gorbachov highlighted one problem on that Siberian visit of enterprises modernising already outdated equipment, rather than bringing in fundamentally new systems.

My brother Joe had already made me aware of this, from his own experience as general manager of a small engineering works in Clay Cross, Derbyshire - W.R. Clark & Co. (Engineers) - which our father Wilfred had set up in 1948. Wilf had had to set up on his own as he had been unfairly dismissed - for being an outspoken and active Communist during the Second World War - from the big Sheepbridge Stokes engineering works, where he had risen to be General Manager. At that time my father was one of the Party's outdoor speakers in Chesterfield's Market Square and was an active Communist. As manager at

Sheepbridge Stokes, he may have been something of an embarrassment to the directors, but he used to tell the family how during WWII the workers would write "Good old Joe", referring to Josef Stalin, on the sides of the crates with arms and parts destined for the USSR.

In a 1990's discussion within the British Communist Party on the problems of the Soviet economy which were partly responsible for the collapse of the USSR in 1991, Joe wrote the following, from his personal experience:

> "We had bought a Soviet lathe in 1964. In 1977, although we'd passed that technological stage, we needed a simple lathe of robust proportions, so we bought another – essentially to the same design. When I met the fitter in 1990, he told me that they were still making thousands of these lathes. Twenty five years with little development. They sold for peanuts in the UK – but no-one bought them. Why? Because new Japanese lathes at 10 times the price had such high productivity and accuracy that we couldn't afford to use Soviet lathes even if they had been given away."

> "Meanwhile in the capitalist world the electronics revolution was ruthlessly pushed into all sectors causing radical new designs across industry."

On that same Siberian trip, Gorbachov slammed the wastage there was in the economy, calling it "extravagant".

As I noted in a feature at the time for the *Morning Star*, "even on the domestic level, I suppose it is extravagant to wash the dishes in constantly running hot water, as people do here. Foreigners have been known to complain of the lack of plugs – but running water is considered cleaner than water in a bowl."

Five years later, I wrote a feature, under the pen-name Tess Armand, for the *Scotsman*, highlighting another aspect of Soviet extravagance. We used to go swimming in the big circular pool next to the Kremlin – which was an experience in itself. To obtain a pass to swim there you had to take stool samples and a doctor's note, then wait for your pass to be granted. From the changing rooms, you had to swim down a sort of tunnel, emerging straight into the water from the tunnel.

This open-air pool – the world's largest at the time - was built in 1958 on the foundation of the abandoned Palace of the Soviets, which had been begun in 1938, but had had to be abandoned so that steel from the building's foundations could be used for war materials during World War II.

Kropotkinskaya swimming pool near the Kremlin

During the Yeltsin years, in 1995, the pool was destroyed in order to rebuild – at huge cost - the Cathedral of Christ the Saviour, whose original building had been demolished in 1931 in order to build the Palace of the Soviets in that location. The 1990's re-build was an initiative of the resurgent Russian Orthodox Church, which organised donations from over 1 million people to help finance the construction, completed in the year 2000.

Our first year in Moscow, 1985, was still at the height of the Cold War. Nuclear missiles East and West were stationed, pointing at each other. The Campaign for Nuclear Disarmament in Britain constantly campaigned for Britain to get rid of its nuclear weapons, arguing that they made us a first-strike target. I had been a member of CND for years and my first meeting with a survivor of the atomic bomb dropped by the Americans on Hiroshima, Japan, at the end of WWII, convinced me even more of the sense of CND's stand.

I met 57-year old Yuji Yegusha at the World Youth Festival held in Moscow in August 1985. In 1945 he had been in the city of Hiroshima to start a music teacher-training course, but, like all students, had been mobilised by the army during the holidays.

So on August 6th, 1945, he was in the army canteen, he told me, having an early morning cup of tea.

"All of a sudden at 8.15am, a wave of heat like from an open furnace swept through the room scorching my face. A few seconds later a gale force wind raged through the building, the floor shook, window panes shattered sending glass shards in all directions."

The United States had dropped the first-ever atom bomb on the city of Hiroshima.

The army barracks were 6 kilometres from the epicentre. "The heat from the blast was unbearable," Yuji told me, "several hundred people who happened to be near the epicentre that morning simply vanished, vapourised by the intense heat."

"We were told we had to go to the opposite end of town to give help to our teaching staff. I shall never forget that nightmare journey across the city," Yuji Yegusha said, his dark eyes gazing fixedly from behind his gold-rimmed glasses, as if reliving the experience yet again.

"We saw many, many injured people on our way. Their hair was all burnt off, their skin was charred. Some people's hands had been completely burnt off and they stood there dazed with pieces of skin hanging down from their arms.

"Some who had been facing the explosion had had their eyes burnt out. When we got to the river we saw hundreds of people who had fled to the water in a desperate attempt to escape the terrible heat. They were terribly injured, with raw flesh and blood pouring from open wounds. They died in the water."

This is just an extract from the feature I wrote after meeting Mr. Yegusha. His account, so horrific, so graphic, has stayed with me to this day. I was surprised to hear him say that current Japanese school textbooks omit the fact that it was the USA that dropped the world's first-ever atomic bomb on Hiroshima – killing 100,000. By 1950 a further 50,000 had died of radiation sickness.

The United States, of course, has always maintained that it was the dropping of their atom bomb on Hiroshima on August 6th 1945 that put an end to the Second World War. Yet the truth is very different, and makes the appalling deaths of so many innocent Japanese citizens completely senseless.

Japan was already in surrender talks, before August 6th. This was known by Truman, the US President. And US generals knew that once the Soviet Union entered the war in the Pacific, Japan would be defeated. The first atom bomb was dropped on 6th, the Soviets invaded Manchuria at midnight on 8th August, before the second US bomb on Nagasaki, which killed a further 80,000. The war in the east would have been over without the US dropping a second bomb.

The American military leaders knew the bomb was unnecessary. The US had eight five-star admirals and generals in 1945. Seven of the eight are on record as saying that the atomic bombings were either militarily unnecessary, morally reprehensible, or both.

Truman's personal chief of staff, Admiral William D. Leahy, who chaired the meetings of the Joint Chiefs of Staff, later commented:

"The Japanese were already defeated and ready to surrender. The use of this barbarous weapon at Hiroshima and Nagasaki was of no material assistance in our war against Japan. ... In being the first to use it we had adopted an ethical standard common to the barbarians of the Dark Ages."

Professor Peter Kuznick, a professor of history at Washington's American University, where he founded the Nuclear Studies Institute, thinks the bomb was "not only dropped on the Japanese, it was dropped on the Soviets. The Cold War had already begun."

As CND and other peace organisations and many ordinary citizens know, nuclear weapons are abhorrent. At the very least, nuclear states should declare that they will never be the first to use them.

In the Cold War atmosphere of mistrust and hostility, expulsions of diplomats and journalists were par for the course. On September 12th 1985 the British Government expelled 25 Soviet diplomats from London, and a few days later, the Soviet Union reacted tit-for-tat.

The *Morning Star* dedicated much space to peace initiatives and to the evils of the arms industry. The fact is that too much profit is made from the sale of arms. After Britain's ill-fated intervention in Libya in 2011 I learned, for instance, that each Tornado aircraft cost £35,000 per hour to fly; each missile cost £800,000; and each Cruise missile £750,000-800,000 (data given by Francis Tusa, ed. *Defence Analysis*, quoted on the BBC's *Today* programme, 22.03.2011).

The Cold War mentality permeated all aspects of reporting about the Soviet Union. The British mainstream press never wrote about Moscow life without describing the "drab" apartment blocks, the "dreariness" of Moscow's streets, the shortages and queues outside shops. You would imagine, reading those pieces, that Muscovites' lives must be utterly depressing.

Yet we knew, living among Russians, and having friends who invited us to their flats, that Soviet people were no less happy or unhappy than people in Britain: they took life as it came and got on with their lives, as most of us do.

One thing that never failed to surprise us was the veritable feasts our friends would prepare when inviting us. One of our friends, Irina, a teacher, lived in a *kommunalka*[25] and she, her husband and their 11-year old daughter had to share one fairly small room. On our visit, the table took up a big part of the room, and some of us had to sit on cushions on their sofa to sit at table. There was a whole variety of little dishes with hors d'oeuvres, very attractively displayed on a beautifully embroidered white linen tablecloth – pickled cucumbers, fresh cucumber with *smetana*, salted herring, mushrooms in sour cream, grated radish, spring onions in *smetana*, *bliny*, *stolichnyi salat* and little *pirozhki* with different fillings, as well as *wurst* of different kinds.... We loved *svyokla s chesnokom* (grated beetroot and walnut in mayonnaise).

Soviet cuisine, despite the fact that you couldn't always buy exactly what you wanted all of the time, was excellent. And the nice thing was that you

---

25 *Kommunalka*: communal flat, in which families would each have one or sometimes two rooms and share a kitchen and bathroom. They were meant to be a temporary solution to the housing shortage after the war.

knew that the cucumbers and mushrooms had been grown and harvested by your hosts, and then pickled or marinated in big jars which they stored on their balconies over the winter.

Russians love mushroom-hunting: they make a day of it, going out into the woods round Moscow and gathering the different kinds, seemingly always knowing which ones to choose safely. It was an eye-opener to us, as neither we nor the children had ever picked mushrooms in England.

The only problem with these invitations was that you invariably ended up eating far too much, because after trying a little of each of the many hors d'oeuvres, there would come the hot main course, by which time you didn't have much room left for it. And then the sweet – and the Russians have a wide variety of desserts, from the delicious Soviet ice-creams that you could buy from kiosks (*eskimo* was the children's favourite) and eat in the street, to *ptichye moloko s shokoladom* (chocolate sponge cake), *vafelnyi tort* (a layered waffle cake) and *kompot* (juice from boiling fruit or berries).

Our neighbours, Galina Gyorgiyevna together with her daughter Lucy, husband Viktor and son Kirill, were wonderful hosts and put on the most sumptuous meals, using quite basic ingredients. They would suggest a break from the table after the hors d'oeuvres, when we would play a game or chat, then be called back to the table a couple of hours later to be given the hot main course and dessert. It was a good solution, but anyway meant eating far more than is good for you in one day!

Galina was a tall, striking-looking woman of about 65. She was the widow of a military historian, author of the multi-volume History of the Soviet Armed Forces. He had been considerably older than Galina, who was his second wife. She was very close to his daughter by his first marriage, and they frequently went on holiday together. Galina, judging by the photograph on their piano of her as a young woman, had been a real beauty, but quite apart from her looks, she had a lovely personality – kind, affectionate, cheerful, intelligent and a mine of information of all kinds, from history and experiences during the war to helpful tips about everyday living.

When the cranky old lift outside our door was being replaced in 1987 (which took months to complete), Galina insisted we use the lift outside her back door, instead of us having to walk up the nine floors to our flat. This, however, meant walking through her flat to get to ours. Whenever we had bags of shopping we were very grateful for Galina's kindness, though we tried not to abuse her hospitality too much.

Though it was clear right from the start that Mikhail Gorbachov was a new broom, the emphasis during our first year in Moscow – 1985 – was on "acceleration" of the economy at home and in foreign affairs, the unilateral nuclear testing moratorium and November summit.

Analysing Gorbachov's aims in introducing the subsequent policy of *"perestroika"* (restructuring) of the economy and society, Cambridge academic Professor David Lane paints the following picture of the situation which obtained before *perestroika*:

"Under Brezhnev, a "social contract" between leaders, government, and people developed. The political leadership provided a framework of stability and peace. The government apparatus was secure under the traditional forms of central planning. The working class enjoyed full employment, an undemanding work environment, and a steady but slow amelioration of pay and conditions. There was a liberalization of conditions for the intelligentsia: within restricted circles discussion was not curbed. (Many of the policies adopted by Gorbachov were worked out by reform-minded intellectuals under Brezhnev). When reforms were suggested, they were experimented with but when problems or resistance arose, reforms were quietly dropped. These are the roots of what is now called the "period of stagnation."[26]

The relative decline in living standards, problems with supply of foodstuffs and everyday items, the slow improvement in housing (several of our children's friends still lived in *kommunalki*, on the waiting list for flats of their own), led to many Soviet economists, sociologists and political scientists arguing for reform. One sociologist, Tatiana Zaslavskaya, in her "Novosibirsk document", which had circulated quite widely in 1983, wrote that the contradictions in Soviet society – whilst not class contradictions such as found under capitalism – had to be addressed. She argued that the structure of Soviet society did in fact generate group and class interests and that the antagonisms between groups were at the heart of the Soviet economy's lack of growth and dynamism.

Gorbachov's wife, Raisa, was also a sociologist and had written her doctoral dissertation on *The Development of New Features in the Life of the Peasantry in Collective Farms*, published in 1967. She was thus well aware of the many problems of Soviet rural life.

Economist Otto Lacis was another reformer who came to prominence under Gorbachov. Abel Aganbegyan, Ivan Frolov, Leonid Abalkin, Stanislav Shatalin - there were many highly-educated people in the CPSU, the Ministries and the media who agreed with Gorbachov's views on the urgent needs for reform. The truth is that a great number of people within the system had, through their work and their observations of society, come to the same conclusion – that urgent reform was necessary if Soviet society were not to go backward.

I remember an early conversation we had over dinner at the flat of Otto Lacis and his wife Tamara. The Soviet economy had worked well, he told us, in conditions of war, when everything was geared to winning the war and citizens were highly motivated by the need to repel the invading Nazi army

---

26 *Soviet Society under Perestroika*, David Lane, Routledge London, 1992, p.12.

and support the troops. But in peacetime, that sort of "war communism" was no longer adequate for the needs of the economy, he said.

One example of this was close to home: being a family of five, with three children, we really needed a washing machine. My secretary, Olya, took me to a wholesalers where they sold Soviet-made washing machines and, as there seemed to be no other choice, we ended up with a primitive little machine which was not automatic at all; the only thing it did was to swish the clothes round, most of them getting fast round the central steel pin of the machine. It did not rinse or spin the clothes and as far as I was concerned, it was a complete waste of space.

How was it possible, I thought, that in the eighties, Soviet households did not have access to essential items like a fully automatic washing machine? It seemed incredible, and once again, I was forced to confront the reality that the socialist society we had come to the USSR to experience was very far from the ideal we had had in our minds two decades earlier.

Because it wasn't just a question of the lack of good-quality, labour-saving machines. It was what lay *behind* that reality – which was a lack of consideration for the women of that society, who bore the brunt of domestic labour such as washing, cleaning, shopping. You could not get away from the sobering fact that the society which was capable of sending a woman into space was not, apparently, capable of producing labour-saving devices to enable women to play a fuller part in the political, social and economic life of that society.

I would rail against articles I read in the Soviet press or in CPSU documents about making life easier for women to play "their dual roles" – work outside the home, and their domestic work as wives and mothers. It was, it seemed, totally accepted that women should have these two roles, and the only question raised was "how to ease the burden for women", so that they could continue to do the two jobs. There was never any mention or examination of whether domestic work should be shared by both parents in the home. It seemed such a far cry from the days of the early women revolutionaries, such as Inessa Armand, Nadezhda Krupskaya, or Aleksandra Kollontai, who fought for women's equality and for the provision of communal dining-rooms, for instance, as one way of lightening the burden on women and going some way to achieving equality between the sexes.

The role of Bolshevik women in the years leading up to and during the Revolution was hugely significant. On International Women's Day 1917, tens of thousands of middle class and working women converged on Nevsky Prospect with banners demanding better rations for the soldiers in the First World War in which Russia was still embroiled. Other banners demanded "Bread!" And "Down with the tsar!" During the days that followed, more and more contingents of factory women converged on the centre of St Petersburg. These mass women's demonstrations, fearless in the face of the tsarist police, played a key part in the success of the October Revolution.

After the victory of the Revolution the Bolsheviks immediately removed discriminatory legislation. Children outside wedlock were granted equal rights, divorce was made available on request and both spouses given equal rights to property and earnings.

Women achieved full equal rights to education, which was a turning point in the progress of women towards equality, especially in the backward Central Asian republics of the Soviet Union, which by the early twenties had become part of the USSR.

A Women's Section (*Zhenotdel*) of the Russian Social Democratic Labour Party had been set up in 1919, its aims being to inform and educate poor working and peasant women, check enforcement of the new legislation and set up political education and literacy classes for women throughout Russia.

It is salutary, looking back now at the Russian Revolution and its legacy throughout the world, among which is the fight for true women's equality, to continue to analyse why women's equality has not been achieved either here in Britain or in Russia. Here we have laws on equal pay – but employers continue to get round them by describing the same or similar jobs done by women as different and thus paying them less than men doing similar work.

In the Soviet Union by the thirties there was not one single woman on the Central Committee of the CPSU; when I worked in Moscow in the eighties there was only one woman in the top leadership.

The *Zhenotdel* was dissolved in 1930. In a Soviet encyclopaedia published in 1987, you can find the following words: "The women's movement reached the Caucasus and central Asia only after the Civil War. As a result of the cultural revolution and in the course of the building of socialism, the women's question in the USSR *has been completely solved*." (my emphasis, K.C.)

This experience – of how the "stagnation" of Soviet society affected women and the women's question – contributed to my formulating my own ideas as to the importance of campaigns within any society. I became increasingly convinced as to the need for citizens to be able to band together to form campaigns around issues they believed strongly in and which were not necessarily included in the programmes of parties in power.

Would we in Britain have had the Sex Discrimination Act 1975 or the Equality Act of 2010, had it not been for the decades-long campaigns of women's groups such as the early suffragettes who campaigned for women to have the vote, or the Women's Liberation movement of the sixties and seventies and other feminist organisations throughout the twentieth century?

Would the environment and global warming be taken seriously today (though not seriously enough by governments) had it not been for organisations like Friends of the Earth, Greenpeace and the Green Party?

Would the various treaties reducing stockpiles of nuclear missiles and banning nuclear testing in the atmosphere have been signed had it not been for the constant consciousness-raising and publicity generated by the Campaign for Nuclear Disarmament in Britain?

I came to the conclusion, after six years living in the Soviet Union that the lack of any social organisations or campaigns outside the CPSU had definitely contributed to the stagnation in society, which was to the detriment of society's democratic development.

On the personal and family level, life was good. The children were happy at school, it seemed, and they had fun after school and at weekends, playing in our flat or outside nearby with their friends. In winter they would take their sledges down to the inner courtyard of the huge block of flats where we lived, and sledge down the mounds and hillocks there, dodging between the trees. It was a very safe area, away from traffic, and we did not worry about them unduly. They had a very free childhood, apart from the pressures of schoolwork, and to this day, they all have happy memories of their years in Moscow.

The absence of advertising billboards and advertising on TV was refreshing. I also liked the fact that if you wanted to buy, say, detergent, you weren't befuddled by the vast array of different brands and prices as we are used to here in Britain. You might have two or three brands, at most, for the same sort of item – and personally that's enough for me. I don't want to have to spend minutes scanning the shelves just to find one essential item like washing powder.

I liked the fact that when you bought butter, it was cut, according to the weight you asked for, from an enormous chunk, and wrapped, without packaging, in brown paper. Sugar, similarly, was scooped into a hand-made cone shape of the same brown paper and the top twisted by hand to seal it. As I write this, in 2018, we in Britain are discussing how our country will deal with all the plastic and other waste that we have been shipping off to China for decades, now that China has decided not to accept any more of our waste. I look back on our life in the Soviet Union and realise that the USSR was acting in a much more environmentally friendly way by minimal packaging, the ubiquitous use of string bags to carry loose apples and oranges, instead of the pre-packed plastic trays of fruit we use now in the UK and which create so much damaging plastic waste.

I always felt glad that I could speak Russian and that we lived among Russians and other, non-Russian nationalities. Shortly after the Geneva summit between Gorbachov and Ronald Reagan, in November 1985, I got talking to a man on a bus. About 45 years old, he told me he was from North Ossetiya, an Autonomous Republic within the Russian Federation, to the north of Georgia, and was in Moscow on trade union business. Unfamiliar with the capital, he asked passengers where Podkolokolny Lane was. Nobody knew, apart from me, so I explained what bus he had to catch next.

We got off the bus at Revolution Square in the city centre and I accompanied him to the bus-stop of the K circular. Once on the bus, I asked him what he thought of the results of the recent Geneva summit. "Well, obviously we would have hoped for more," he said, "in the sense that we haven't yet managed to get agreement on banning space weapons or on arms control."

"But we didn't really expect we would, at this stage," he went on, fumbling in his pocket for change to pay the fare. He fished out a 10-kopeck coin and put it in the pay-box for both of us, since I hadn't got the right money. "It's a good beginning, I think," he went on, "After all, you can't get further progress without a beginning, can you?"

"It's the most important problem of our time," my fellow passenger continued. By this time, he had realised that I was not Russian. "From Britain?" he exclaimed, surprised. Then he immediately asked, in that very direct way Soviet people have, "and why does your Government support SDI?"

As the bus was just approaching Podkolokolny Lane, I couldn't reply. But it was typical of many conversations I so often had, with acquaintances and sometimes with total strangers, and I was always struck by 'ordinary' people's knowledge of current affairs and how strong their anti-war feeling was.

In an interview around the time of the Geneva summit, the Soviet Foreign Ministry's spokesman, Vladimir Lomeiko, told me that his country considered SDI (Strategic Defense Initiative) to be "exceptionally dangerous".

"Not only for the Soviet Union, but for the whole world," he said. "The US plans are for first-strike space weapons which hide behind the innocuous formula of SDI." The USA proposes reducing some weapons in certain cases, he said, but in other cases, creating *new* weapons, which would change the balance of forces.

Whereas what the USSR was proposing was to freeze present stocks of nuclear arms, then reduce levels on the basis of equality. "What we need," Lomeiko told me, "is a serious approach. That means thinking of the other side's security as you would your own."

It's difficult, no doubt, for today's young people, to sense how much of a danger we in Western Europe felt we were in during the seventies and eighties, with ground-launched US cruise missiles stationed at Greenham Common and RAF Molesworth, as well as US Army Pershing II ballistic missiles stationed in West Germany.

The Soviet Union had its SS-20 missiles facing west. When in 1980 it was announced that RAF Greenham Common was to become the first site for cruise missiles, there was an outcry from the Campaign for Nuclear Disarmament, giving rise to the establishment, outside the high perimeter wire net fence, of a women's peace camp which, incredibly, lasted for 19 years, till the year 2000. In the early eighties I had been to several demonstrations at Greenham Common, to support the core group of women who were camped there to protest at the stationing in Berkshire of such dangerous missiles, making us a direct target in the event of a nuclear war.

The Greenham Women's struggle was nothing short of heroic. They were vilified, slandered and insulted by the media and largely ignored by the public.

They lived under canvas in cold and wet weather, constantly being dislodged from their tents by police and bailiffs, facing arrest and rough treatment. I will never forget my first impressions of Greenham Common base – the high strong wire fence for miles around the base, the rolls of barbed wire between the outer and inner fencing, the men in unfamiliar uniforms of the American military police, with their great Alsatian dogs straining at the leash, and their unfamiliar police vehicles, all underlining the fact that this was alien territory, not a British base at all.

But then you were struck by the contrast of the little things the women protesters hung on the mesh of the perimeter fence – diminutive baby clothes, knitted teddy bears and strands of wool, crochet patterns and bright scarves - which, in their own inimitable way, declared for all to see: "We are for life, for creation, not for death and destruction!"

Some peace activists at the time would equate the Soviet Union and the West, in terms of nuclear weapons. And in a sense, one could see their point, since it was undeniable that the Soviet Union had over 200 SS-20 missiles, each carrying three highly accurate and independently targetable warheads, believed to be in the 150 kiloton range, permitting them to strike three objectives simultaneously. (A kiloton is the equivalent of 1,000 tonnes of conventional TNT explosive. The atomic bomb dropped on Hiroshima was in the 12 to 15 kiloton range).

Having interviewed the Japanese Hiroshima survivor I told about earlier, like many people I was filled with dread at the thought of a nuclear attack, especially since there had been a number of near-accidents, when human error could have resulted in a missile launch by mistake.

But everything I knew about the Soviet Union and its peoples convinced me that they were not the aggressors: the USSR was responding to weapons already developed in the USA, and felt itself obliged to develop similar weapons as a deterrent.

There are many reasons to support this view. It was the West which first set up NATO – the North Atlantic Treaty Organisation, in April 1949 – only 4 years after the end of the Second World War. A US State Department website explicitly states:

> "NATO was created in 1949 by the United States, Canada, and several Western European nations *to provide collective security against the Soviet Union.*" (my emphasis, K.C.)

When you think that the Soviet Union had been the greatest ally of the UK, France and the USA during that war, in fact had borne the brunt of the war, losing some 27 million citizens in the fight against German fascism, it seems odd, to say the least, that only four years later the NATO alliance was formed, excluding the USSR, ostensibly to provide security *against* the former ally. It is testament to the power of western media that the Soviet

Union went from staunch ally, respected and admired by most British people, to Cold War adversary.

The US State Department website continues:

> "In the 1950s, one of the first military doctrines of NATO was that of "massive retaliation," or the idea that if any member was attacked, the United States would respond with a large-scale nuclear attack. The threat of this form of response was meant to serve as a deterrent against Soviet aggression on the continent."

Whilst the USA poured money into rebuilding West Germany after the war, by means of the Marshall Plan, the Soviet Union had the mammoth task of single-handedly rebuilding its bombed cities, clearing its mined fields to restore agricultural land and providing housing for the millions displaced by the war – a war which, unlike in Britain, had meant invasion and occupation of much of its territory for four years.

It is often overlooked that the Warsaw Pact[27] – the equivalent organisation of the Soviet Union and its East European allies - was only set up in response to the formation of NATO six years earlier.

Which side developed the atom bomb first? Again, it was the United States, and they used it to devastating effect in 1945 to bomb Hiroshima and Nagasaki. As a result, the Soviet Union felt forced to use its depleted resources to develop its own atom bomb, to deter any similar attack in the future against the USSR.

The Soviet Union will also have been mindful of the duplicitous attitude of our wartime leader, Winston Churchill, who had always been a vociferous and convinced anti-Communist and who, up to the point when Britain declared war on Germany, had hoped that Nazi Germany would first turn its *lebensraum* intentions eastwards, invade the Soviet Union and destroy communism once and for all.

The British Communist Party leader at the time, Harry Pollitt, wrote: "For six and a half years, the Chamberlain government helped Hitler with money, arms, and political support.

"They backed up everything (Hitler) did in Austria, Czechoslovakia and Spain. ..... They smashed up the League of Nations and refused to sign a pact of mutual assistance with the Soviet Union. They did all this to build up Hitler's war machine so that he would go and fight against the Soviet Union."[28]

It is true that Soviet leader Josef Stalin had signed a non-aggression pact with Hitler Germany in August 1939. Soviet agents had informed Stalin of the Nazis' invasion intentions, so the pact was a ruse by the Soviet wartime

---

27 Set up in May 1955.

28 From the *Daily Worker*, 15 February 1940.

leader to buy time so as to prepare for a likely Nazi invasion. It never meant, as many Western historians have claimed, that the Soviet Union and Hitler Germany were "allies". To claim this is a travesty of the truth, whatever one might think of Stalin.

In a socialist society, where the means of production, distribution and exchange are in the hands of the people, i.e. are socially, not privately, owned, there is no incentive to make money from manufacturing arms. Whereas in the west, for instance, the German firm Krupp made massive profits from manufacturing arms for Hitler. After World War II, Alfried Krupp was convicted of war crimes at Nürnberg, specifically for employment of slave labour, but the company had also been guilty of plundering property and plants in all the occupied countries. There are many statistics proving how arms companies vastly enriched themselves as a result of war work - and today's arms firms continue to do the same.

Under socialism there are no shareholders profiting from arms sales. In fact the production of arms like nuclear weapons, which cannot be sold or used, constitute nothing but a drain on the socialist economy.

Ricardo and I had wanted to see what a socialist society was really like. We wanted to experience life there at firsthand and I looked forward to looking up old friends from my days as a postgraduate student 18 years earlier. Instead I found myself swept up by the whirlpool of hectic activity that characterised the years of Gorbachov's leadership.

Gorbachov set about removing old-timers from the politburo – people like Grigori Romanov[29] who he knew would not be likely to support radical reform. By the end of his first year in office he had also replaced one-third of the government ministers and 40 out of 157 of the party first secretaries[30].

I had never been a "Kremlin-watcher", as my fellow British journalists were (to a greater or lesser extent), but, as correspondent for a daily paper, I had to report on every change, demotion and promotion, of course. Which left precious little time for reviving old friendships, like Olya, a young woman married to a well-known actor, who once came to our meeting with bruises round her eyes resulting from his having hit her during an argument over his drinking, or like Slava Doskach, a Ukrainian scientist who was doing his Ph.D when Ricardo and I met in 1967, and who was a great character, cheerful, funny and popular. He had four front gold teeth, as a result of them having been knocked out during a football match, he told us. Despite that, he was a good-looking fellow and his gold teeth merely added to his idiosyncrasy. He was friends with another research student from Iraq, who

---

29 Romanov, like many Soviet leaders including Gorbachov himself, came from a peasant background. Socialism gave them the chance to study and achieve leading positions as economic managers and rise to political leadership positions – in Romanov's case, to the Leningrad Party leadership. Romanov was promoted in 1983 by the respected CPSU General Secretary Yuri Andropov, with responsibilities for industry and the military-industrial complex.

30 from Patrick Cockburn *Getting Russia Wrong*, Verso, 1989.

was in love with a fellow Russian student, Olga. Where are they all now, I wonder? I am 78 as I write this, so I have to presume that not all of our friends from those years will be alive.

Soviet children started school after the long summer holidays on the first Monday in September, at 7.45am. The custom was to take flowers for the teacher, so the children, dressed in their best school uniforms, the young girls with their white cotton pinafores over their dark brown long-sleeved dresses, carried bunches of flowers as I accompanied them on their first day back to school.

It was a lovely sight, to see lots of children on the streets, all with bouquets. Flowers were always available in Moscow, sold in little kiosks here and there. The children's first lesson of the day was a Peace Lesson, which I attended that year in a 9th form class, equivalent to a sixth form class here in Britain. The teacher spoke, in English, of the need for peace and what the Soviet Union was doing to promote peace; some children spoke of their hopes for the future and one or two read poems they had written.

That September, as in future years, the veteran British Communist Andrew Rothstein was on holiday at one of the CPSU's sanatoria outside Moscow in Barvikha, a beautiful countryside resort surrounded by a zone of pine forest nature reserve on the south bank of the Moscow River. Leading government and Communist Party officials could holiday at the sanatorium, and this right was extended to a few foreign Communists or friends of the Soviet Union. The famous Bulgarian leader Georgi Dimitrov[31] died there, for instance, in 1949. In 1961 the renowned black American singer and actor, Paul Robeson, was treated there for several months.

At the turn of the 20th century, before the Revolution, an architectural folly in the style of a German castle had been built there as a private residence for the rich Meyendorff family, who, like many of Russia's wealthy, left Russia after the October 1917 Revolution. The castle was later used by Vladimir Lenin and other Bolshevik leaders.

Famous Soviet people who vacationed in Barvikha were the playwright Mikhail Bulgakov, the renowned space scientist Sergey Korolyov and the first person to fly in space, Yuri Gagarin. There is also a cemetery there with a smaller copy of the impressive Mamayev Kurgan monument in Volgograd (Stalingrad during the Great Patriotic War) by the Soviet sculptor, Yevgeny

---

31 Dimitrov, forced to live in exile during the 20's and 30's, was a renowned anti-fascist, arrested in Nazi Germany for alleged complicity in setting the Reichstag on fire. He famously decided to defend himself against his Nazi accuser Hermann Göring. Explaining why he chose to speak in his own defence, Dimitrov argued:

"....I am defending myself, an accused communist. I am defending my political honour, my honour as a revolutionary. I am defending my communist ideology, my ideals. I am defending the content and significance of my whole life. For these reasons every word which I say in this court is a part of me, each phrase is the expression of my deep indignation against the unjust accusation against us Communists of this anti-Communist crime, the burning of the Reichstag."

Dimitrov became Bulgaria's first Communist leader after the Second World War.

Vuchetich.[32] Nowadays Barvikha Castle is an official country residence of the President of Russia.

Russian Prime Minister Dmitri Medvedev with Venezuelan President
Hugo Chávez in the grounds of Barvikha Castle, September 2009

Andrew Rothstein was a revered figure in the USSR at that time. He was born in London in 1898 to Jewish parents, both of whom were political exiles from Tsarist Russia. Andrew won a London County Council scholarship to Balliol College, Oxford to study history. However, in 1917 he was drafted into the army as a corporal. His regiment was not permitted to be demobbed at the end of the war. Instead they were ordered to go to Archangel (Arkhangelsk in Russian) in order to engage in hostilities against the new Soviet republic[33] – something Andrew, as a young Communist, would never agree to do.

Encouraged by Corporal Rothstein, the vast majority of the regiment declined and elected Andrew as their spokesman.

Andrew was a foundation member of the Communist Party of Great Britain in 1920 and served as the London correspondent of ROSTA (later TASS), the Soviet news agency. He spoke Russian well and, as a veteran

32 Mamayev Kurgan is a hill overlooking the city of Volgograd (formerly Stalingrad) in Southern Russia. The name in Russian means "tumulus of Mamai". The hill is dominated by an impressive memorial complex commemorating the Battle of Stalingrad (August 1942 to February 1943).

33 The British Government was among 14 foreign powers which intervened militarily in the young Soviet state on the side of the Whites in the 1918-21 Civil War which broke out shortly after the Revolution.

British Communist, was always invited to holiday at Barvikha. So each year Andrew, who by then was in his late eighties, but in good health, would ring me up and come to our flat to see us or I would go to see him either in his hotel in Moscow or in Barvikha at the sanatorium.

I was very fond of Andrew. Despite his history as a leading Communist, historian and author of many books, he was extremely modest and always showed a kindly interest in me and my work and my family. I always found him very helpful in the days when I would get criticism of my work from the *Morning Star*'s then Foreign Editor, Roger Trask, since Andrew was at the same time unfailingly supportive, whilst giving the odd suggestion as to something that might be worth thinking about.

This is part of one of his letters to me, from 16th February 1986:

"Just a line to congratulate you on the quality of your messages to the paper, about which quite a number of people have spoken to me lately. Keep it up!

"All the more because a colleague has shown a lamentable failure to understand (at best) that concentrating on criticism in the Soviet Union is a means of pushing progress forward – especially as readers know what big strides have been made – whereas retailing only the criticism, while carefully omitting the positive background, has been the 67-year old trick of bourgeois hacks, and help only the enemies of socialism to sow doubt, confusion and contempt."

He would mention articles of mine he had seen in the *Morning Star* that he thought were very good and managed to be encouraging whilst at the same time recognising and sympathising with the difficulties I faced in reporting the dramatic changes which were going on after the advent of Gorbachov and which many of our readers found it difficult to comprehend the need for.

This was, indeed, something of a dilemma for our paper: for years we had been stressing the positive side of socialism in the USSR, as the main example of a real socialist society, and now, all of a sudden, we were reporting on the many failings Gorbachov and the new leadership were highlighting.

In that sense it was a complex and difficult time to be a correspondent for a Communist paper, and I had quite a few problems over these years with my editors back home. From my friendship with other British correspondents, however, I know I was by no means alone in this – most of them had rivalries with Special Correspondents sent over to "intrude on their patches" and feelings of being misunderstood from time to time by their editors, so I knew it was just par for the course.

However, whilst the job was far from easy, it was an exciting and exhilarating time to be in the USSR and witness the beginning of the historic changes which were to come.

Abroad, the changes were causing quite a stir throughout the world.

Everybody was suddenly interested in coming to Moscow, and we hosted several visits from friends and comrades coming to see for themselves.

One of them was a writer, Emma Smith[34], who had been invited to Moscow by the Soviet Writers' Union, and was staying at the Ukraina Hotel – one of the seven "wedding-cake" style skyscrapers in the capital. I had met Emma a few years earlier in 1980, when she had been a student of mine in a Russian class at the SCRSS. As a published British writer, Emma had been invited to spend a couple of months in the Soviet Union, to give her the opportunity to gather material for a book, which was why she was learning Russian. She stayed in three rural villages, one in Byelorussia and two in Siberia, writing an account of her impressions of rural life in these far-distant places in *Village Children: A Soviet Experience* published in 1982.

So now Emma was visiting again, this time in October 1985, six months after our arrival, eager as ever to find out how our children had adapted to Soviet school and how we were finding life in Moscow. Like many British people, she was excited by the new wave of hope that Mikhail Gorbachov's arrival on the scene seemed to herald, for world peace and a possible end to the relentless anti-sovietism which had characterised the post-war years in Britain, whereby practically everything in the Soviet Union was reported on negatively.

Emma came to the children's school, sat in on a couple of lessons and our children proudly showed her round their new classrooms. She was able to hear for herself that they had very quickly learnt Russian and could chatter away quite happily in Russian with their friends. Everyone connected with learning foreign languages knows that total immersion in the language is the best way, if at all possible, and they, having been 'thrown in at the deep end' that first day at School No.35 back in March 1985, certainly proved the truth of that.

Emma, having tried to learn Russian from me a few years earlier, was suitably impressed by their fluency, and by how quickly the children had been accepted by their classmates and had obviously made friends in those few months since our arrival. Their teachers invited Emma into their classrooms and showed her round the entire school during the break.

The school, housed as it was in an old building, with no real playground or much room for extra-curricular activities, probably would not have impressed Emma greatly. I'm sure she would have seen much superior school buildings in London, where she lived. Yet I know she would not have found a friendlier, more curious or hospitable welcome anywhere than on that day in a Moscow cul-de-sac, surrounded by excited, laughing girls and boys.

As we were leaving the school building, strains of a hymn being sung next

---

34 Emma Smith's novels include the prize-winning *Maiden Trip*, about her canal working experience during WWII, *The Far Cry, Out of Hand, Emily's Voyage, No Way of Telling, The Opportunity of a Lifetime, The Great Western Beach, As Green as Grass,* the latter two being memoirs of her early life.

door at the Baptists' chapel could be heard in Bolshoi Vuzovsky Cul-de-Sac. I had learnt earlier from the children that the Baptists had their services and rehearsals in the building next to the school.

We enjoyed having Emma to dinner in our flat and taking her round the sights of Moscow. Her quick mind and her writerly observation skills made her a good companion – one you could bounce ideas off and get interesting and insightful responses from. We became good friends over subsequent years; I was privileged to read her typescript of a novel whose central character was a Chilean refugee in England (that novel, unlike her other novels, never did get published, unfortunately). In the seventies, after the Chilean military coup, she herself, true to her ideals, had taken in a Chilean refugee – Rita Contreras – into her London home for some months, until Rita could be offered housing.

Emma was very encouraging to me when, years later, I was writing my second book, *Chile in my Heart*. When this was published in 2013, she was full of praise for it, which, to me, was gratification enough for the years it had taken me to write it, reliving as I did so the harrowing time Ricardo and I had lived through in Chile during the 1973 military coup and dictatorship that followed it.

One of the initiatives of Gorbachov's first year in office was to issue a new draft of the CPSU programme, to replace the 1961 programme, and which would be approved at the next CPSU Congress in February 1986. In the sixties, Soviet leader Nikita Khrushchov had declared that the Soviet Union would already be well on its way to communism and would surpass the West's capitalism. The new draft recognised that that prediction had been premature and that the period called socialism, before communism, might well turn out to be longer than originally thought.

Observing Soviet society as it was in 1985 was sometimes puzzling: you could find side-by-side examples of cutting-edge technological breakthroughs and incredibly backward infrastructure. I remember, for instance, once when I was doing research in the Lenin Library, which is the USSR's equivalent of the British Library, being horrified to see that the Library's ladies' toilets were of the kind without toilet seats and automatic flushes, but simply a tiled hole in the floor with room for one foot either side. I had seen that sort in a Normandy village years before – but could not imagine such a thing in the Soviet capital, moreover, in a seat of learning.

It was hard to understand, except in terms of such things being low on the list of priorities. But, why so? Decent toilets are part of the dignity of human beings, and modern appliances surely cannot have been so expensive to install.

Yet overall, one could not fail to be impressed by so much that was positive in the Soviet Union, and the indubitable advances they had made in transforming their country from a backward, peasant economy to an advanced industrial society capable of putting a man and a woman in space and erecting modern housing in a short space of time for the millions left homeless by the Second World War.

Russia had only relatively recently – 1861 - abolished the extremely backward and inefficient system of serfdom. Having read books like Gogol's *Dead Souls*, Goncharov's *Oblomov* and Dostoyevsky's *Idiot*, I knew that rural life was much more primitive and backward than in Britain at that time for the serfs, who made up about a third of the population in the vast expanses of Russia. Serfdom tied Russian peasants to their landlords and was only abolished at Tsar Alexander II's imperial command after Russia's serf soldiers had been found to be inadequate during the Crimean War, when Russia was defeated. In Russia the traditional relationship between landowner and serf was based on land and it was because he lived on his land that the serf and his family were bound to the landowner.

"The Russian system dated back to 1649 and the introduction of a legal code which had granted total authority to the landowner to control the life and work of the peasant serfs who lived on his land. This included the power to deny the serf the right to move elsewhere, thus endlessly perpetuating the system.

"Serfdom was manifestly not working. It had failed to provide the calibre of soldier Russia needed. So it was that in 1856, the second year of his reign, Alexander II (1855-81) announced to the nobles of Russia that 'the existing condition of owning souls cannot remained unchanged. It is better to begin to destroy serfdom from above than to wait until that time when it begins to destroy itself from below'." [35]

One of the lessons I have learned in life is that much of what one observes in another country is, in part at least, the result of the specific history that nation has experienced. So vestiges of authoritarianism still prevalent in the 1980's – the ubiquitous *nyelzya* (it's forbidden, you can't), for instance, were probably a result of the authoritarianism of the serfdom era and later, of the Stalin era.

Nyelzya was a word quite commonly heard. I think I first became aware of it years before, in 1967, when I was waiting for a friend whom I had arranged to meet at the Pushkin monument on Gorky Street. The monument was surrounded by a little area of lawn, enclosed by a low pavement kerb stone. While waiting, I stood with my heels on this low kerb. An elderly woman came up to me saying "*Nyelzya!*" and remonstrating with her hand that I should not be standing on that kerb. I was not touching the grassed area, I was not damaging anything, but "it was not allowed".

Another time, in the Hermitage museum in Leningrad, one of our daughters perched on the seat below a big window in one of the galleries. Immediately "*Nyelzya!*" could be heard as an attendant shooed her away. It was the

35 *The Emancipation of the Russian Serfs, 1861: A Charter of Freedom or an Act of Betrayal?* Michael Lynch, *History Review* Issue 47 Dec. 2003.

peremptory tone of voice that grated with us; the attendant could simply have approached my 10-year old and asked her not to sit there. Since there were no notices saying sitting was not allowed, I did not see why she should have been shouted at.

But, I always thought to myself, this nation has gone through such dreadful hardship and suffering that it has made them hard and tough and, yes, when in positions of authority and wearing a uniform, somewhat authoritarian.

As I said earlier, Gorbachov's main emphasis in his first year was on *uskoryeniye* (acceleration) of the economy. The central precept of the planned economy was not at that stage being questioned. In fact, in the new Party programme put out for discussion in the months before the 27th CPSU Congress, centralised economic planning was considered to be one of the great advantages of socialism.

Some economic experiments in certain large enterprises had already initiated new schemes with the aim of increasing productivity, and in December 1985, I had the chance to visit one of the foremost examples of this at two big Leningrad plants, *Elektrosila* and *Krasnogvardyeiyets*.

In these experiments, wages were linked to performance. If a workplace met its production targets, the work collective got more pay; if it failed to meet targets, no extra pay.

"One of the greatest boons of socialism – guaranteed employment for all citizens – conversely constitutes one of its problems," I wrote in one of my articles. "A worker who is a poor time-keeper, or who is always having time off for no good reason has the same constitutional right to a job under socialism as his/her fellow-worker who is more socially responsible."

"He can't be sacked as he can in capitalist society. He can have certain privileges withdrawn, he might get put lower down on the housing waiting list[36], for instance, or be asked to take his holidays in November – but that's about as far as it goes."

In a feature to celebrate 68 years since the Great October Revolution, I wrote:

"The Soviet people have a great deal to celebrate. 68 years of socialism have brought them from backwardness, poverty and illiteracy to a highly advanced and powerful nation, which is spearheading the fight for peace in the world today."

"Socialism has meant jobs for all, security and confidence in the future. It has welded a society where over a hundred nationalities live peaceably and amicably together.

"It has brought women equal status, respect and confidence in themselves.

"It has brought health and happiness to Soviet children.

"It has brought a high level of education and culture to working people.

---

36 Many Soviet factories and plants provided their own housing for their workforces.

56

"It's the most equal society in the world, with no rich and no poor.

"It's a society where old people are respected and still have a role to play in society.

"It's a society without violence on the streets, without sexist abuse, child kidnappings, pornography or video nasties."

This was how I viewed Soviet society in 1985. Yet only a year later, I was to become increasingly horrified and perturbed by the unfolding information released under the next phase of Gorbachov's reforms – *glasnost* (transparency or openness), in which most of the old shibboleths were rejected or undermined in a veritable onslaught by the mass media.

My visit to Leningrad, in December 1985, was memorable for many reasons. Firstly, because it reminded me so vividly of the time in 1968 when Ricardo and I had been there together, on a trip with other postgraduate students from the Russian Studies course we were on. Then it was deep winter, there was snow and ice on the ground, and one evening, Ricardo and I took a local bus – just any bus – to its terminal, had a walk round there, and then caught the same bus back to the centre where our hotel was.

We were in love. The dazzling white snow glistened in the moonlight, and we could hear the crunch, crunch of snow beneath our boots as we walked. Hand-in-hand, we walked and talked, who knows about what... It was then that an elderly woman in a woollen headscarf wrapped tight around her head and neck came up to us, shaking her finger, saying: "*Nyelzya, tovarishchi!*" (You shouldn't, comrades), an admonishment because we were holding hands in public!

We, of course, despite being astonished, immediately released hands and walked on. We had too much respect for the old lady's generation that had lived through the dreadful Leningrad siege, which lasted from 8th September 1941 to 27th January 1944, to do anything else.

After the Nazis invaded the Soviet Union in the summer of 1941, the German army surrounded the city. Although supply lines from the Soviet interior were later established for minimal food supplies and to evacuate its citizens, using a hazardous "road" - the Russians called it *doroga zhizni* (road of life) - across the frozen Lake Ladoga, it took until January 1943 before a successful land corridor was created, and it was only the following year that the Red Army finally managed to rout the besieging Nazi army. Altogether, the siege lasted 872 days and resulted in the deaths of 1.5 million of Leningrad's civilian population.

Twenty or so years later, I was sitting in the balcony at the Moscow Conservatoire, listening to a concert – it was Tchaikovsky's Concerto No. 1 for Piano and Orchestra, according to my diary entry for 1st July 1986, played by Barry Douglas of Northern Ireland, who that year won the Gold Medal at the Tchaikovsky International Piano Competition in Moscow.

During the interval, I got chatting to the middle-aged woman sitting next to me. She asked me to read something from the concert programme, and I noticed she wore dark glasses. It emerged that she had poor eyesight - as a result, she told me, of having lived through the Leningrad siege as a child during WWII. She was six when the siege began and doctors had told her that her poor eyesight was most probably due to the prolonged malnutrition of those siege years. Now she only had 25% vision, due to the muscle atrophy she had suffered as a child. "Most people who survived the Leningrad siege have some health problem or other," she added.

Whilst in Leningrad, both in 1967 and now in 1985, I had visited the famous Piskaryovskoye Memorial, which each time left an indelible impression on me. The cemetery holds the graves of around 420,000 civilian victims of the siege, the majority of whom died of cold and starvation, and of 70,000 soldiers who died defending the city.

Nazi Germany declared war on the USSR on 22 June 1941, and by September German forces had laid siege to Leningrad. As the harsh winter of 1941-1942 set in, Leningrad's citizens began to suffer the full effects of the lack of food and fuel supplies. They died in their thousands daily. On 15 February 1942, for example, 8,452 bodies were delivered to the cemetery; on 19 February 5,569 bodies; and on 20 February 10,043. By the following winter, the Red Army had managed to open a small land corridor to the city, and the mortality rate never reached the same heights again, but as the siege was only lifted on 27 January 1944, the total civilian and military death count reached over 1.5 million. The total buried in the mass graves of the Piskaryovskoye Cemetery number around half a million people, most of whose names remain unknown.

At the cemetery there is a small museum dedicated to the Siege of Leningrad. I remembered having seen on my first visit the tiny rations of black bread the population had to survive on, decreasing in size as the siege went on. And the tragically bleak handwritten notes on display of a little girl called Tanya Savicheva, a Leningrad schoolgirl who witnessed and recorded in single phrases the deaths of her sister, her grandmother, her brother, her two uncles and her mother during the siege, with the final three entries reading: "The Savichevs have died/ They all died/ Tanya is left alone." Tanya herself died of alimentary dystrophy - basically, starvation - two years after her evacuation.[37]

Behind the monument, a wall of granite slabs is adorned with bas-reliefs and lines of verse by Leningrad poet Olga Bergholz, whose radio broadcasts during the siege made her a symbol of the city's resilience. The last lines read "Nobody is forgotten, nothing is forgotten."

Leningrad (in 1991 the city reverted to its pre-revolutionary name of St Petersburg) is an impressive city. Founded by Peter the Great in 1703, it was

---

37 For personal accounts by siege survivors of their lives during the 900 days of that cruel siege, readers may be interested in Caroline Walton's book *The Besieged: a Story of Survival*, Biteback Publishing, London, 2011.

seen by him as a "window on the west" - a progressive city which would be a centre for science, technology and innovation. He decided to build this major city on what was barren marshland, to better integrate Russia into Western Europe and secure a Baltic port for Russia. Today's St Petersburg is a beautiful city, interwoven by a network of canals, with original 18th century buildings and ornate wrought-ironwork, cathedrals and monuments, and the wide River Neva visible from its graceful central streets.

The city was renamed Petrograd in 1914, at the beginning of World War I, because that sounded less German than St Petersburg, then the city was renamed Leningrad in honour of the leader of the Russian Revolution after Lenin's death in 1924. The city had a population of 4.8 million people and is Russia's second-largest city, an important industrial centre, with heavy industry, research and development and military-industrial production.

"We've built two more Leningrads in the last 32 years!" leading Leningrad Communist Vladislav Korzhov told me, "we've built 78 million square metres of housing, but we still have a housing problem."

"In 1960, 24% of citizens had a place of their own, now (in 1985) it's 70%," he went on. The effects of the years of Nazi bombing were still being felt by Leningrad's citizens in the shortage of housing.

As in hundreds of Soviet cities throughout the western regions occupied by the Nazi armies, the damage to homes and hospitals in Leningrad was enormous. The Nazi air attack of 19 September 1941 was particularly brutal, 276 German bombers hitting the city, killing 1,000 civilians. Many of those killed were recuperating from battle wounds in hospitals that were hit by German bombs. Six air raids occurred that day. Five hospitals were damaged in the bombing, as well as the city's largest shopping bazaar. Artillery bombardment of Leningrad began in August 1941, increasing in intensity during 1942. It was stepped up further during 1943, when several times as many shells and bombs were used as in the year before. Torpedoes were often used for night bombings by the Luftwaffe. Altogether, according to one estimate, German shelling and bombing killed 5,723 and wounded 20,507 civilians in Leningrad during the siege.

On 17 May 1985, the new General Secretary Mikhail Gorbachov gave a speech at Leningrad's Communist Party headquarters which was televised nationwide. In that speech he admitted that in the past the country's performance had been sub-standard and openly mentioned for the first time publicly the problems besetting the Soviet economy. He pledged to introduce policies to correct past mistakes, saying, "We have to travel a long road now but in a short space of time."

It was obvious that the current Leningrad Party leader, Grigory Romanov, would not be likely to head the new reforms set in motion by Gorbachov, whose Leningrad speech, scolding the Party leadership as it did for all the shortcomings, acted to undermine Romanov in his stronghold. Romanov was forcibly retired from the Politburo by the Central Committee on July 1

1985, with barely a word of thanks, "for reasons of health."

When I visited the city 7 months later, I was told that only the First Secretary had been changed, but that the rest of the Party cadres had remained in situ. Party officials that I spoke to were at pains to stress that their region's "Intensification-90" programme of economic improvements was in line with Gorbachov's rhetoric, and that it was being successfully implemented.

I spent a few hours at Leningrad's big Krasnogvardyeiyets plant, which made medical instruments – heart and lung machines, ventilators, electrocardiograph (ECG) machines, fibre-optic bundle endoscopes, machinery for blood transfusion and skin grafting among others. Whilst the works looked modern enough inside, the building itself was old. The works General Manager admitted: "Our endoscopes are not as good as Japanese ones. Our operation still entails too much manual work." But 20 million roubles had been allotted, he said, for new technological processes which would improve the instruments' quality.

My eye was caught by a series of photographs on the entrance hall wall: they were of workers who had been fined – 30 roubles - for drunkenness at work. "In the past such workers often got off too lightly," works Party Secretary, Nikolai Chirkin, told me. "But now (under the anti-alcohol campaign, K.C.) we exert both moral and financial punishment."

The *Elektrosila* plant was a much bigger works, comprising 3 factories and a research institute. The plant had taken part in two economic experiments, whereby top engineers had been able to earn higher salaries, equalling the high salaries of production workers on the shop floor. This, I was told, had resulted in a 37% increase in productivity during the two years of the experiment. Computer-programmed lathes had been introduced over the previous year.

Everywhere we went in Leningrad it was the same story: the management, Party committee and trade unions were keen to tell us of their achievements – and they were not inconsiderable. They always seemed proud of their works, proud to be taking part in experiments to raise wages and productivity, proud to have realistic plans for the future. When you talked to the workers, the ones we had the opportunity to talk to were equally proud of their "brigade", their factory, their output.

Yet it was clear from Gorbachov's May 1985 speech in the city that all was not well, by far – and the coming months and years would reveal more of the shortcomings that were not so evident in December 1985 when I visited.

We had the opportunity to visit the Smolny Institute, which I had first visited in 1967 with Ricardo. Smolny was the building where the Great October Russian Revolution was planned and organised, and where Lenin lived for 124 days, organising, leading, discussing strategies and tactics with his fellow Bolsheviks at meetings held day and night in that febrile revolutionary atmosphere.

Painting by V. A. Serov showing Lenin speaking at the
Second All-Russia Congress of Soviets, which proclaimed the
transition of all power in the country into the hands of the
Soviets of Workers', Soldiers' and Peasants' Deputies

A beautiful 19th century ochre-painted building, Smolny, now with a statue of Lenin in front, had been a finishing school for young ladies before the Revolution.

The first decrees of Soviet power were passed there on October 26th (November 8th in the new calendar) 1917: the Decree on Peace, which proposed an armistice and talks on universal peace, without annexations or contributions; the Decree on Land, under which landowners were deprived of their land estates without compensation. All land was declared state property, i.e. the property of the whole people.

This Smolny Congress also set up the first Soviet government – the Council of People's Commissars, electing Lenin as its Chairman.

When I was a young student of Russian at the University of Manchester I had thrilled to read about the Revolution and admired Lenin, both as someone with a colossal brain, a theorist of revolution, and as an activist and leader, someone obviously immensely capable of winning over the hearts and minds of people during the first two decades of the twentieth century, when a host of other parties and left groups existed in the Soviets (councils) of People's Deputies all across that vast country.

I knew from reading about the Revolution that since the late nineteenth century there had been Marxist groups in Russia, like for instance the League of Struggle for the Emancipation of the Working Class, and the forerunner to the CPSU – the Russian Social Democratic Labour Party, which was formed from a number of revolutionary organisations in 1898.

To me, as a student in Manchester, the city where Friedrich Engels, friend of Karl Marx and fellow revolutionary, had lived and worked, the Russian Revolution was inspiring. In Marxist classes organised by our Communist Party Manchester University students' branch, we studied Engels's *The Condition of the Working Class in England*, based on his Manchester research, which had been published in 1845 and, of course, *The Communist Manifesto*, which Engels co-wrote together with Marx, published in 1848.

We had regular Marxist classes, mainly taught by a Manchester University academic, Dr Ted Rowsell, studying works by Marx, Engels, Lenin and even Stalin. I remember reading Stalin's *Dialectical and Historical Materialism*, for instance – a very manageable and readable introduction to the topic – and articles by Stalin on the National Question and on Linguistics.

I admired the courage and selfless activism of Lenin and his co-revolutionaries, and the bold assault on the Winter Palace in St. Petersburg, the ousting of the pro-capitalist Kerensky government and the taking of power – for the first time in history - by the working class and peasantry. It was, it seemed to me at that time, what the Paris Communards had fought for, and the English Chartists too, so to me the Bolsheviks epitomised what I wanted for my country – a system where the ordinary people would be in charge, where capitalist exploitation would be done away with.

And here I was, in December 1985, inside Lenin's flat in Smolny, the actual building where Lenin had directed proceedings during the October Revolution, looking at his desk where he wrote over 110 articles, lectures and letters, our guide told us, during the four months or so that he lived there during and after the Revolution. He had returned from exile in Switzerland, by train, arriving at the Finland Station in St. Petersburg on 16 April 1917, with the aim of organising the revolution. I couldn't help feeling some of the exhilaration of those revolutionary events nearly seventy years earlier.

As with Lenin's flat in the Kremlin in Moscow, you could not fail to be impressed by the total lack of any ostentation: the flats in both cities where Lenin and his wife, Nadezhda Krupskaya, had lived were very simply furnished, utilitarian even, with nothing but books as a luxury.

To me, St Petersburg will always be Leningrad; in general, I would say that I'm not very much in favour of name-changing of towns or streets. Usually people continue to use the old names anyway, and you get incongruous situations like the fact that present-day Volgograd is the city of the heroic Battle of Stalingrad. And you might end up with absurdities like a little lane near where we lived in Moscow – *Kommunisticheskiy Pereulok (*Communist cul-de-sac).

This topic leads me to muse on the specifics of the Russian character, as I have observed them over the decades: along with their undoubted heroism and stoicism, the emotional tendency to go from one extreme to the other. After the denunciation of wartime leader Josef Stalin's crimes by Soviet leader Nikita Khrushchov at the 20th Congress of the CPSU in 1956, everything connected with Stalin was thrown out, statues taken down, towns and streets renamed and his body removed from the Red Square mausoleum. And after the collapse of the Soviet Union in 1991, again – wholesale removal throughout the country of statues of Lenin and other revolutionaries like Sverdlov and Dzerzhinsky.

It is interesting that Lenin himself had never wanted to be embalmed, and had actively opposed attempts to deify him after the Revolution. But apparently in November 1923, when Lenin was terminally ill, Stalin suggested that the dead body should be "preserved using embalming" to give the opportunity for everyone to say goodbye.

Part of the Bolshevik leadership met the idea with indignation. Leon Trotsky, who was considered to be the second most important person in the party after Lenin, compared the preservation of the body with the creation of "holy relics," worshipped by Christians: an unheard-of sacrilege for ideological communists. Lenin's widow, Nadezhda Krupskaya, was also opposed to the embalming of her husband's body.

The Mausoleum became a symbol of loyalty to the ideals of Leninism. A visit to this place in Moscow became like a pilgrimage, both for Soviet citizens and for delegations from friendly countries. And close to 2.5 million people apparently still visit the tomb each year.

It's still a subject of debate in today's Russia. Some Russians, especially those critical of the Soviet past, demand that his body be buried. This idea is supported by a number of human rights advocates and members of the clergy.

But Russia's Communists want to keep Lenin in the mausoleum, arguing that Lenin is already buried (the sarcophagus with the body is at a depth of three metres below ground), while the Mausoleum is a unique historic monument.

So far the government – I'm writing this in 2018 – has kept a neutral position. The current President, Vladimir Putin, commenting on the possibility of burial, said that the issue should be approached carefully, so as "not to divide society." According to the most recent opinion poll, a majority of Russians (60 percent) generally support the idea of burial. And the topic continues to be aired from time to time, as it has ever since the era of *perestroika* and *glasnost* thirty years ago.

1985 was busy for Moscow correspondents – but that was nothing compared with subsequent years, as I was soon to discover. I sometimes envied other correspondents who worked for weekly or even fortnightly papers. I had to file daily not only in-depth features about serious topics like the economic experiments going on in different places, or a new peace initiative, or particularly harsh criticism from the new leadership of this or that problem, but also the everyday reports of press conferences at the Soviet Foreign Ministry's press centre on Zubovskiy Boulevard, alongside the Moskva-Ryeka (River Moscow). I used to go there most days and was a very active correspondent, frequently asking questions of whatever leaders, officials, ministers, leading artistic figures or foreign dignitaries happened to be holding press conferences there.

So it was especially galling for me when I found out that the *Guardian*'s correspondent in Moscow, Martin Walker, with whom I had established quite friendly relations, published a shameful article in the *Guardian*, "Rotten to the Moscow Corps" on 23rd September 1985, insinuating that I, as the *Morning Star* correspondent, was not a real correspondent at all. It should be viewed in the context of the British Government's expulsions of Soviet diplomats of 12th September, so it clearly fitted into the heightened anti-sovietism of those weeks of tit-for-tat expulsions. But on a personal level, I found it contemptible that Martin would have lent himself to such an unworthy act.[38]

Galling it certainly was that anyone could state that I wasn't a real correspondent, since I frequently felt that I was neglecting my young family to do the best I could as a correspondent for a daily newspaper published on 6 days of the week.

Several times during my years as Moscow correspondent I had angry exchanges with the *Morning Star*'s Foreign Editor, who, it seemed to me, often had difficulties expressing clearly what he did want from me, whilst sometimes demanding a piece urgently at the last minute.

One such exchange, with me resisting having to re-write an entire piece, which I didn't see as necessary – and remember, it was transmitted by old-fashioned and laborious telex at that time – ended thus:

> Foreign Editor: "OK, sorry if we have had wires crossed. Best regards, Roger.
> Me: "It's OK. It's just a pain, since it's Sunday and I haven't spent any time with the kids yet today. Sniff, sniff. Kate. (Verbatim, from my 1985 diary).

Life was tough – trying to give the family enough love and attention, whilst striving to do as good a job as I was able as the paper's Moscow correspondent. Knowing that the "bourgeois correspondents" had drivers, secretaries, plus maids or nannies to help with the children even when their wives did not work, whereas we didn't have any of these (my paper couldn't

---

38 See Appendix III.

possibly stretch to such luxuries) I sometimes used to joke: "What I need is a wife!"

But we managed, the children seemed to thrive, and Ricardo was a great help, often buying food on his way to and from work, and helping with the children if I was still filing a story at 9 o'clock at night.

Fortunately the *Morning Star* at that time, in its well-located premises on Farringdon Road, went to bed at 6pm, which was 9pm in Moscow, so I knew I couldn't file after that hour. But very often, if there had been an important CPSU Plenum or Conference or Congress I used to have to file until the very last moment to try and make sure that our paper got the best information possible. I have a very clear memory of one such evening, when I was busy reading some such lengthy TASS report on some such Party meeting, trying to decide on the salient points for my piece, which might well be the front page splash the next day, my daughter Liza appeared sorrowfully at the door to my office, which was adjacent to our flat, and said "Mummy, I've got a tummy ache!" I didn't even get up to see to her, but just said, "Well, go and tell Daddy, he'll have to see what to do! Sorry, love, I must just finish this before the deadline - 9pm, you know!" And she dutifully disappeared back into the flat. I distinctly remember feeling really mean.

I frequently felt I was neglecting the children, but what could I do? It was such a busy time. In my diary entry for November 15th 1985, I wrote: "Kids came home after 4pm. Made dinner. Took me till 9.15pm to finish typing and sending Lomeiko piece over. Had no time to help Victor with homework and the kids got themselves to bed. Poor little abandoned things they are."

Because *perestroika* and Gorbachov had become so popular throughout the world, we had many visitors, from people we knew and some we didn't know, but who wanted to meet the *Morning Star*'s correspondent and soak up a bit of the atmosphere. One memorable visit was by a Jamaican MP called Manley, accompanied by a colleague of his, Desmond, from the People's National Party. Ricardo had met them in Sochi that November 1985, when he was recuperating in a sanatorium there. Desmond read bedtime stories to the kids and told them about his country, Jamaica, and the benign climate of the Caribbean. With Manley we talked of his hopes as an MP for the PNP which was campaigning for a democratic socialist future for Jamaica under the progressive leadership of Michael Manley. He had been Prime Minister until 1980, and went on to win again in 1989. It was already 10.30pm when Manley and Desmond arrived at our flat, but we had a great impromptu party with lots of laughter. They left at 03.30am, and my diary entry records that the following morning "I slept in, starting work at 1pm." It had been one of those meetings of minds and views that remain in your memory forever. They called again on their way to the airport leaving for home, saying how much they had enjoyed getting to know Ricardo during their stay at the sanatorium and then meeting our family in Moscow. We hoped that we would meet again somehow some day.

One of the main problems I faced as a correspondent of a socialist newspaper broadly supportive of the Soviet Union was the discrepancy I could not help but observe between official statements and reality on the ground.

Take anti-social behaviour and crime, for instance: during one 1985 session of the Supreme Soviet, for instance, the Procurator-General told deputies: "The violence and vandalism common in the West are unknown in Soviet socialist society."

"Socialism creates favourable conditions for overcoming crime and consolidating legality in all spheres of public life," Aleksandr Rekunkov went on. "The number of such serious crimes as murder, grievous bodily harm and assault has gone down steadily, as has the number of crimes committed by young people."

Yet Soviet leader Mikhail Gorbachov, in his memoirs, says: "By 1973 crime had become a serious problem in Stavropol. A series of crime waves swept through urban and rural areas. After several cruel murders and rapes, the situation had to be taken in hand. People were frightened and began to question whether there was any effective authority in the *krai* (territory)."

And he described in some detail the drastic measures taken, including sacking and appointing new police chiefs. It was, Gorbachov relates, "an all-out operation to uphold legality, first and foremost in law enforcement."

So clearly there *was* crime, and we learned later the scale of economic crimes, such as embezzlement and corruption by people in leadership positions in certain republics and regions.

It is true that one felt very safe in general, walking the streets of Moscow, either in the daytime or at night. But our son Victor was once confronted by an unpleasant band of young teenagers in a wooded area near the hospital where his Dad was convalescing, who told him to get out of their turf or they'd beat him up. And our daughters were once confronted by a man flashing his private parts at them.

I once interviewed an old Bolshevik, Maria Leontyevna Kuznetsova, born in 1900, and 87 when I met her. She was upset because she'd been persecuted by hooligans, she said. Members of the ZHEK (residents' housing Committee) and residents of her block had organised a *tovaricheskiy sud* (comrade court) against her. The hooligans had kicked her door in, so now she had several locks on her door. She told me that they had shouted *chekistka* (nark – from the forerunner of the KGB, the *Cheka*) at her.

She didn't think much of Gorbachov, and didn't believe all that was coming out in the media about wartime leader Stalin. "He was our one real leader, he was a Leninist," she told me, "what they're saying now is all lies!" I found the interview disturbing – whatever had happened to upset the old lady I had no means of knowing, but it showed that serious problems did exist in society.

It was difficult to know what was true and what was "propaganda". I tried, in my reporting, to keep a fair balance, to report what the authorities were saying, whilst in my features showing the very real problems I knew still needed to be tackled and overcome.

It was not all work, of course. I had the opportunity, in June 1985, to presence the 5th International Ballet Competition. I love ballet, and learnt so much from seeing the initial stages of the competition, when not all the competitors were top-knotch, and so one could compare the different competitors as they each danced the same routines. It was fascinating and most enjoyable. To my delight, Argentinian dancer Julio Bocca won joint first prize that year, together with Soviet dancers Nina Ananiashvili, Vadim Pisarev and Aleksandr Vetrov.

Before we moved to Moscow our six-year old daughters Liza and Martha had been taking weekly dance classes at the Ballet Rambert in London's Notting Hill. We had obtained a special reduction in price (we were very hard up at that time) due to the intervention of Joan Jara, the widow of murdered Chilean folk-singer Victor Jara, who as a professional dancer herself, had close relations with the Ballet Rambert. Joan had gone to Chile as a young dancer and made her life there. We never met when I lived in Chile; she lived in Santiago and I lived in Chillán in the south and we moved in different circles. After the 1973 military coup in Chile against the Popular Unity Government of President Salvador Allende, Joan's husband Victor, who was an immensely popular singer and well-known supporter of the constitutional government, was detained by the military, tortured and killed in the National Stadium and his body dumped by the roadside in a Santiago suburb[39].

Joan received a tip-off from someone that Victor's body had been seen in a morgue. She had to suffer seeing his broken and tortured body there. Shortly afterwards with her two young daughters she left Chile for Britain, where she tried to make a life for herself and them whilst dedicating herself to telling the world about the horrors of the Chilean Pinochet dictatorship and contributing to whatever solidarity work she could.

We had met in London in 1974, shortly after our return from Chile after the 1973 coup and Ricardo's imprisonment there, and became friends during those years which were full of sadness for Joan. She later went back to Chile in the eighties with her daughters Manuela and Amanda, setting up the Victor Jara Foundation and a dance school, Espiral, now run by Manuela, which is still going strong.

But to come back to our twin daughters and their dance classes: they had only been going to the Ballet Rambert's classes for a couple of terms when we left for Moscow. So we wanted them to have the opportunity to continue dance classes in Moscow, since they had been enjoying them.

So I asked around, and it was arranged that we should take them to a dance class at the famous ZIL car plant in Moscow. I knew that big factories

---

39 I describe this in more detail in my book *Chile in my Heart*, Bannister Publications, 2013. Joan's book *Victor: An Unfinished Song* was published in 1983 by Bloomsbury.

in the Soviet Union invariably had all sorts of clubs and groups, choirs and dance groups, drama clubs, photography circles and a host of other activity groups. So it did not seem surprising.

We collected the twins' ballet shoes and leotards and met my secretary, Olya, to go to this ballet group. It turned out, however, to my surprise, that it was a sort of audition, which was not at all what we had had in mind. After all, they were only just seven. After they had performed the steps the very stern-looking middle-aged man in charge of the group had ordered them to do as best they could, he came over and told me: "No, no good, it is clear they have had no training at all, *nikakaya formatsiya u nikh, nikakaya!"*

Not so much disappointed as annoyed, I could see that he was not the sort of person you could reason with or ask questions of, so we left and that, I'm afraid, was the end of our daughters' foray into dance at Zil!

Thinking this over, I concluded that it simply reflected the very strict notions they had as to what constituted a dance group. I think the Ballet Rambert training our twins had had, which fostered bodily expression through dance, rather than choreographed steps and postures, was outside the narrow framework of what he considered "dance".

The following month the twins started ballet classes at a nearby Pioneer Palace – Kirovskaya - which were more informal and fun, so everything worked out all right. Victor joined a Chess Club there too and they enjoyed their weekly sessions. The twins took part in a little play which we went to see - although their part was to hold up a big cardboard painted car and move it along as if it were being driven, so we couldn't actually see them behind it!

The main Pioneer Palace on the Lenin Hills in Moscow was an imposing building, with every conceivable club, from chess to joinery, sewing to dance, painting to space technology. I visited a couple of times and was impressed by the scale of activities and the lively atmosphere. On one visit I was with an old friend, Genia Browning, who at the time was working at Moscow Radio, and from an upper balcony we watched dozens of children below, in the main foyer, in Pioneer uniform, marching, as if in military formation, to martial music, which Genia, as a long-time peace activist, found disturbing.[40] Having been a Girl Guide myself, I did not find it so very different from the kind of formations and uniforms that were common in British scout and guide troupes.

That winter 1985 our children were given the opportunity to go to a winter Pioneer Camp. As the accommodation was in chalets, which were heated, camps such as these were a boon for working parents, although in my experience, not nearly as many children went to the winter camps as to the summer ones. It was here that they learned to cross-country ski, which is one of the most magical experiences, skiing through the snowy paths in the wintry woods that encircle Moscow, the snow glistening in the bright sun peeping through snow-bedecked trees.

---

40 Genia's book *Back in the USSR 1967-1970 A Russian Memoir* was published in 2022.

Summer pioneer camps lasted 5 weeks, and some 40,000 of them were to be found throughout the Soviet Union, on the edge of towns, in the countryside, by rivers and at the coast. Parents paid a *putyovka*, which was very affordable and usually obtained by parents through their place of work. It was one of the many benefits of the system, and in our experience, the children had a great time at the different camps they went to over the years we lived there - their walks in the woods, the friendships and camaraderie they found as well as the many activities organised for them. They also recall fondly the delicious anticipation of the food parcels parents would take and hand in at the gate - with biscuits, doughnuts and fruit.

It was at Pioneer camp, too, that they learned the ubiquitous qualities of iodine and *zelyonka*, a bright green antiseptic lotion, which would be painted liberally on any scratch or graze the child had suffered.

Delicacies our children tried for the first time were *vobla* and *cheremsha* - smoked fish and wild garlic, which they would press into a slice of Russian black bread somebody had saved from breakfast and share round.

Victory Day – May 9th in the USSR – was another occasion when I could blend work with pleasure. On that day, Second World War veterans would gather in Gorky Park alongside the Moscow River and meet old comrades and wartime acquaintances, swap stories and meet some of the children – Pioneers – who would also go there that day to meet them.

On one such Victory Day, I met some British visitors, some wearing their war medals, who had come to Moscow from Leningrad to take part in the 40th anniversary celebrations of the victory over fascism. "As soon as people knew we were British, they came up to us and shook our hands and kissed us," said Lindsay Baster, from London's East End.

"We've had such a good reception everywhere," said Mrs Irene Fitzpatrick, who worked in a munitions factory in Yorkshire during the war. Having visited the Piskaryovskoye cemetery where the 400,000 civilian victims of the Leningrad siege are buried, war veteran Stanley Fitzpatrick, who took part in the D-Day landings, told me they had found the experience very moving.

MP Denis Healey, Shadow Foreign Secretary at the time (1985), was also in Moscow for the Victory celebrations, representing the Labour Party. I met up with him at a posh Kremlin reception, held in one of its splendid halls, lit by magnificent chandeliers, with long tables covered in brilliant white starched linen tablecloths and silver cutlery, laden with smoked salmon, glistening black and red caviar, cold meats of all kinds, jellied white fish of unknown-to-us species, fruit, cakes and delicious sweet tarts. And of course, vodka and Soviet champagne, served by attendants frequently coming up to fill empty glasses. On catching sight of me, Denis, who had already had a few drinks, I suspect, put his arm round me, gave me a squeeze and said

"Hello Gorgeous!"[41] I still remember his bushy eyebrows hovering very close to my face.

Healey, who had met Gorbachov earlier in the day, told me he was convinced the new Soviet leadership was working hard to bring about arms reduction and nuclear disarmament.

The Victory Day parade itself that 40th anniversary year was a grand affair. Top Party and Government leaders were standing as usual on the tribune of the Mausoleum in front of the high dark red Kremlin wall, where many of the famous figures of the early revolutionary period are buried, the beautiful towers and golden domes of the Kremlin visible beyond. The troops filing past were of all nationalities – blond European Russians and Ukrainians, dark-eyed Kazakhs with their high cheek-bones, Uzbeks, Tadzhiks, Kirghiz[42] and from a host of other, smaller nationalities that make up the different constituent republics, autonomous republics and regions of that enormous country. I learnt that there had been people of 41 nationalities, for instance, in the partisan detachments operating in Nazi-occupied Ukraine.

In one report to the *Morning Star,* I wrote: "It was a moving moment when the veterans in the uniforms of the different forces to which they belonged marched past to the cheers and applause of the onlookers."

"And there were tears as the partisans came past, in ordinary suits and dresses, some with grey caps, some in blue berets, some of the women in headscarves, their war medals glistening in the bright May sunlight. A huge cheer went up as they came into view, many people no doubt remembering the heroism of the partisans and resistance-fighters in the territories occupied by the Nazi invaders."

The partisans played an important part in bringing about a radical change in the course of the war. Their daring raids on occupying Nazi forces, their sabotage of the railways communication system not only caused huge problems for the Nazis, but raised the morale of the people in occupied zones. There people were forced to work like slaves in Nazi-held factories and farms, with starvation rations, and many people were forcibly transported to Germany to work.[43]

"Then came the tanks, cannons, lorries, guns and rockets. The Soviet people around me buzzed with excitement as the faithful old tanks of the

---

41 The reaction of my boss, the Foreign Editor, Roger Trask, when I told him about this, was: "Oh well, all in the trials of a reporter!" I must say that in all my time as a correspondent, I did not experience any kind of "sexual harassment" from any Soviet men encountered in the course of my work, except for one minor incident in Georgia. My Soviet colleagues and interviewees were invariably extremely respectful.

42 People from Kazakhstan, Uzbekistan, Tajikistan and Kirghizia – four of the 15 constituent republics of the USSR in Central Asia.

43 See appendix IV– the true story of Tamara, who was one of these people transported to work in Germany, as told by herself to Ricardo when they shared a train carriage from Moscow to London in 1985. She was on her way to meet a sister she had not seen for about 45 years, due to their separation during the war.

war years dinned past, leaving the air blue with smoke behind them."

"*Nashi, nashi!*" shouted one small boy near where I was standing, to one side of the Mausoleum – "They're ours, ours!"

When Hitler's Wehrmacht attacked the Soviet Union in June 1941, it was in breach of the Soviet-German Non-Aggression pact contracted by the Soviet leader in August 1939 with the aim of holding off the Germans as long as possible to give the Soviet Union breathing space to prepare for the war which intelligence reports indicated was coming.

At that time the forces of the two sides were extremely unequal. The Nazis attacked with 153 divisions and powerful infantry and tank units. Romania, Hungary and Finland sent another 37 divisions against the Soviet Union.

Fascist Germany had long been preparing for war; the Soviet Union, on the other hand, was not nearly so well prepared, their troops at the start of the war being outnumbered by nearly two to one.

The enemy's rapid advance into Soviet territory deprived the country of many of its armaments factories; only a few managed to be evacuated eastwards in time.

By early December 1941, Hitler's army had reached a distance only 30 kilometres from the capital, Moscow. Yet, despite overwhelming German superiority in men, tanks and aviation, the Soviet counter-offensive launched on 6th December 1941 managed to halt the Nazis' advance and start forcing their retreat.

All material and labour reserves had been quickly put on a war footing, the entire economy of the country mobilised and directed towards providing for the needs of the front. Soviet experts have always considered that the centralised nature of the Soviet socialist economy was an advantage in this, in that it enabled the economy to react relatively quickly. Soviet factories during the Great Patriotic War (1941-45) produced 96% of required overall industrial output, and received 4% under the lend-lease agreement, whereby the USA and Great Britain provided aid to their Soviet ally in the shape of planes and tanks.

What the USSR really needed in those early years of the war was for a second front to be opened, but the western allies did all they could to delay this, despite an agreement in principle at the Teheran Conference in late 1943. The Second Front was finally opened with the allied landings in Normandy on June 6th 1944.

By the end of that year the Soviet Union had driven the Germans out of the country and went on westwards to liberate the occupied countries and the Nazi death camps like Majdanek in July 1944 and, later, Auschwitz, where they found hundreds of emaciated and exhausted prisoners. Soviet soldiers marched all the way to Berlin, where the Soviet hammer and sickle flag was famously raised on top of the Reichstag.

"We've always been told that the Soviet Union is a threat to peace," I remember a miner's wife from Barnsley, Cath Bostwick, saying to me, "yet people's main concern here is peace."

Not surprising after all that they suffered during the Great Patriotic War. Cath was one of a group of 50 Yorkshire miners' wives and 100 of their children who had been invited to holiday in the Black Sea resort of Sochi by the Soviet Coalminers' Union in 1985, after the long British Miners' Strike of 1984-85. I met them as they spent a sightseeing weekend in Moscow before their return home.

"Onwards to Berlin!"[44]

"They've suffered so much themselves in the last war," said Maureen Stubbings. "The genuine warmth of everybody we've met here is amazing."

There were always visits from organisations and important individuals in the peace movement, and I was fortunate to meet some of them. A delegation of Greenham Common women came in June 1985 and in September I met with Joan Ruddock who came as part of a CND delegation. A Labour

_____

44 Original poster by courtesy of SCRSS archives.

Councillor from Chesterfield, Jill Jones, came as part of a Derbyshire peace delegation and met with the Soviet Peace Committee. From Pax Christi came Mary Brennan, a nun. Everyone who was anyone from the various sections of the British peace movement wanted to come to Moscow to drink in the new atmosphere created by the peace momentum of the Geneva and the following year, Reykjavik, summits.

One of the most memorable and important peace ambassadors was Professor Dorothy Hodgkin. A Nobel Prizewinner for Chemistry in 1964, Dr Hodgkin had been active for many years in the Pugwash[45] peace organisation, and when I met her in Moscow she was already in her seventies. Dorothy Hodgkin's husband, Thomas Hodgkin, a socialist, historian and specialist in African affairs, was the cousin of a great friend of ours, Mary Cowan, from whom we learned a great deal about this eminent couple, whose lives were dedicated in great part to peace and socialism.

Both Dorothy Hodgkin and Joseph Rotblat, whom I met later on, were eminent scientists, absolutely dedicated to ridding the world of the permanent danger of nuclear weapons and risk of an all-out nuclear war on the planet, which would be a disaster for all humanity.

The war was something very close to the hearts of the Soviet people I met, and not just those of middle-aged and elderly people.

I remember one farmworker called Anya Monakhova who had worked on a state farm during the war telling me how all the farm's tractor-drivers were away at the front as tank-drivers. It had been very hard for those left on the farm – women, teenagers and old men – who had had to knuckle down to provide potatoes and grain both for the country and for the front.

"The women left behind had small children, with all the problems that can entail," she told me, "but they never shirked, even though it was very hard. They amazed me! They were all young lasses, living away from their families, but not one of them left the farm," she said. "They stayed throughout the war and pulled together."

"They dug trenches in bitterly cold weather, poorly dressed and with no proper boots. But we always managed to feed everybody and provide hot water." Out of the 400 or so people who worked on that state farm, she said, 150 were either killed or died of their wounds during the war.

Another woman I once met told me her story, which was by no means untypical: Galina Korbe, who was 69 when I talked to her, a small, lively woman with bright eyes and short grey hair, still worked full-time as a production engineer at the Moscow tyre factory. When the Soviet Union was

---

45 The Pugwash Conference on Science and World Affairs is an international organization, set up in Pugwash, Nova Scotia in 1957, which was awarded the 1995 Nobel Peace Prize together with its founder Sir Joseph Rotblat. The purpose of the Pugwash Conferences is to provide scholarly insights into the prevention and resolution of armed conflict, including nuclear and conventional disarmament, control of the arms trade, the peaceful settlement of disputes and to contribute to solutions for environmental threats to human security.

attacked by Nazi Germany in 1941, Galina was 25 and working at Kauchuk rubber works in Moscow.

She had graduated from a chemical institute 3 years earlier and already had three small children, who were looked after at the factory crèche and nursery before the war. After the Nazis invaded in June 1941, Galina's parents took her three children to their home about 30 miles from Moscow.

"This enabled me to work the long shifts that we had to work at that time due to the war," Galina said. "I was lucky in that my Mum was able to help me out in this way, as we all knew it was important for me to continue working, as it was for all those engaged in production."

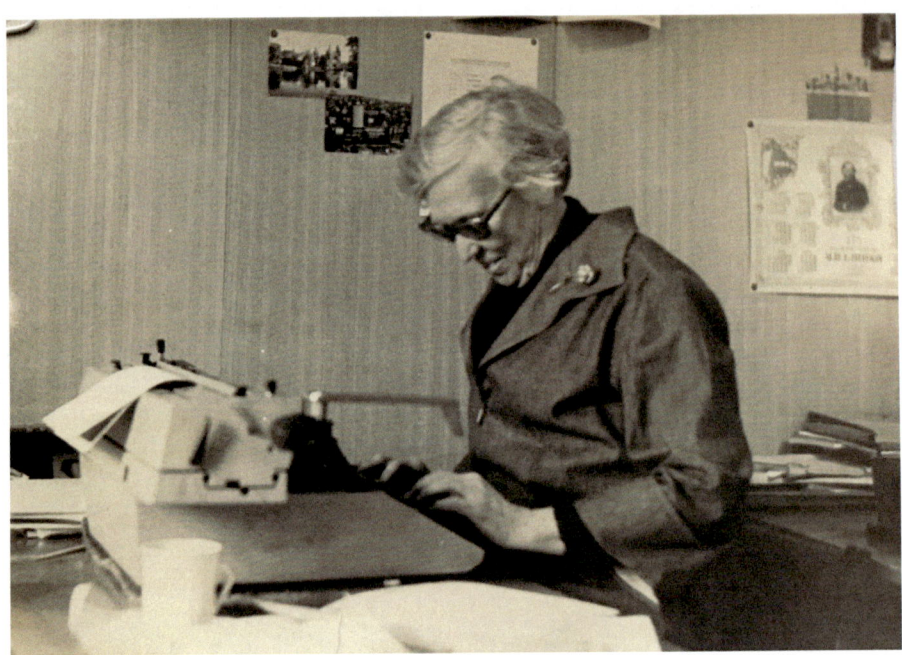

Galina Korbe after the war

Between the summer and October of that year, Kauchuk works was bombed by the Nazis practically every night. "Fortunately the bombs never actually landed on the production shops, only on the stores, so we were able to continue."

But in October that year the factory had to be evacuated east to the Urals. "I was in charge of one train, with 28 wagons carrying the factory's machines and equipment, and another 6 with people – there were about 70 of us," she recalled. Her mother and Galina's three small children travelled with them, to safety in Sverdlovsk.

"It took us 29 days to get there. The train was bombed several times, but we were lucky – equipment was damaged but nobody got hurt."

On more than one occasion, the bombs hit the track, so the train had to stop and the track repaired before they could continue.

"We finally got to Sverdlovsk on December 19th 1941, and the temperature, I remember, was minus 38 degrees Celsius. We immediately got the machinery and equipment out of the train and started production of rubber tank parts on site."

"At first we didn't even have a roof over our heads! We just worked in the open air, in those temperatures," Galina remembered, smiling at my incredulous expression.

Whilst in Sverdlovsk, Galina's sister tragically died of typhus, leaving a six-month old baby girl. "I was told the baby could go to an orphanage, since I had three small children of my own to look after, which wasn't easy in those harsh war years."

"But it was my own sister's child. How could I? So the baby came to live with me, and became my fourth child."

It was immensely hard, with four young children, and working all hours, she went on, but the local people were wonderful. "They helped us so much, and I shall always be grateful for the relationships I formed during those years."

"It's hard to imagine the hunger at that time," Galina told me. It was very difficult to get milk, and everything was in short supply. "Since I had such a young family, the factory gave me a little goat – it was barely bigger than a cat – so that I could at least get a little goat's milk for the children," she said, laughing out loud as she remembered how she – a city girl born and bred – first tried to milk the goat, which kicked the jug over with its hind legs.

It produced one glass of milk morning and evening, and lived together with Galina, her four children and her mother in one room, for two years.

"Yes, times were hard all right," Galina mused. "We had no furniture, only a few boxes. And yet I remember those years as among the happiest of my life."

"We worked a 12-hour day," she said. "After work, we'd go on social duty, helping to feed soldiers who had been wounded in the face, and who had to be spoonfed very carefully."

She returned to Moscow a few days before victory on May 5th 1945. Luckily her husband survived the war and life slowly returned to normal. But the enormous destruction caused by the war, the many bombed-out buildings, meant that Galina and her family had to live in one room in a communal flat until 1954 when they finally received a flat of their own.

Important political changes were being made. Brezhnev-era leaders were losing their jobs. At the very end of 1985, the long-standing and elderly Moscow Party leader, Viktor Grishin, was replaced by Boris Yeltsin, an energetic and bombastic leader from Sverdlovsk in western Siberia.

After the November 1985 summit in Geneva between US President Ronald

Reagan and CPSU General Secretary Mikhail Gorbachov there was a new atmosphere of optimism – that here at last was a world leader who seemed determined to put nuclear disarmament and peace at the top of his agenda, who began to talk of "new thinking" and who put out a detailed plan for the world to be rid of nuclear weapons by the year 2000.

And on the home front - talk of accelerating the economy and the first signs of a leader who seemed closer to the people. Filmed surrounded by enthusiastic and friendly crowds in the streets, Gorbachov seemed to emanate optimism about the future of the Soviet Union and the socialist system. All the omens seemed good.

CHAPTER II

By the start of 1986, it was clear that things were going to change, but not that much had actually changed so far. The talk was around "acceleration" of the economy, rather than "market socialism", which came much later. Yet only four years later, the once considered impregnable fortress of the Soviet Union had crumbled from within. It is still hard to understand how this happened, especially for those who did not witness it. This is the main reason why I decided to write this book, in an attempt to enable readers who are not unsympathetic to the ideas of socialism to gain a better understanding of the processes which were at work at the time.

One author, Chris Miller, comparing China's reforms with those of Gorbachov, writes that Deng Xiaoping, the Chinese leader credited with introducing market economy reforms in China during the nineties, "had seen enough of Russia's tumultuous politics to know where he stood: China was right to sacrifice political liberalisation for stability's sake, because the alternative was chaos and collapse."[46]

And certainly, as the years 1987-91 went on, "chaos and collapse" increasingly seemed adequate words to describe what was happening.

By 1986, Soviet economists in the various institutes and think tanks that existed in the USSR were well aware of the economic problems besetting their country. They knew that the countries of Eastern Europe, which were part of the Comecon economic bloc - mainly sustained by the Soviet Union through generous fuel subsidies - were largely in debt to Western banks since their imports of consumer goods from the West were not offset by corresponding exports to Western countries.

The economic assistance to many third world countries considered within the USSR's orbit was also a heavy burden on the Soviet economy, as was the military intervention in Afghanistan of December 1979, which lasted ten years.

There was a consensus among Soviet economists that something needed to be done, but little agreement on *how* to reform the system without introducing a full-blown market economy - which would be equivalent to introducing capitalism.

After all, as recently as the 1960s, many thought the Soviet Union's rapid growth seemed to prove that socialism had by no means outgrown its

---

46 *The Struggle to Save the Soviet Economy*, Chris Miller, University of North Carolina Press, 2016, p. 6.

economic capabilities. And anyway, its "rival" - the United States – also had many economic problems of its own.

You can often find, in books on the relative benefits of socialist and capitalist economies, statements to the effect that "America and Western Europe had higher standards of living than the USSR". One could, of course, ask: whose standards of living are we talking about? The homeless person eking out an existence on the streets? The young drug addicts and delinquents virtually excluded from society? People on zero-hours contracts, who find it hard to make ends meet? Single working mothers finding it hard to meet the costs of childcare? Usually the comparison is between middle and upper class people's living standards in the West, and their middle-class counterparts in the Soviet Union – and in terms of housing and consumer goods, yes, the latter could be said to enjoy a lower standard of living in the eighties than similar professionals in the West. But for the working class and the unemployed in Western societies, the same was never true. Those sectors were much more on a par with workers in the USSR, and, of course, it must be remembered that in the USSR there were no unemployed people. Not to mention the psychological benefits of long-term security, knowing that you'll always have a job, a pension, guaranteed housing of some sort. It is also true that poverty has not been entirely eliminated in the West, even in Scandinavian countries, which are generally considered success stories.

Writing in 2018, the General Secretary of the UK's Communication Workers' Union (CWU), Dave Ward, said: "The world of work is a terrifying, insecure, poverty-stricken world – in-work poverty is higher than ever."[47] Job security in developed capitalist countries is becoming a thing of the past in the era of globalisation and fast-changing industries. Yet job security, enabling working people to buy their own home and bring up their children without fear of job loss or repossession, is greatly valued by most people.

"Many Soviet scholars and policymakers, even those who recognized their country's deep flaws, nonetheless believed in socialism as an ideal, and feared that emulating Western capitalism would introduce inequality and poverty to the Soviet Union."[48]

Living among Soviet people I could see that they did have a deep sense of security. Even friends of ours like Irina, a teacher of Russian as a second language, who, when we first met her, did not have a flat to themselves, but lived in a *kommunalka,* seemed to be happy in the knowledge that sooner or later they *would* get a flat of their own – which they did, during the years that we lived there. She and her family moved to a brand-new flat just outside the outer ring road that encircles Moscow, part of a new housing scheme of tower blocks.

Job security was taken for granted, although it was possible to apply for

47 *Morning Star* feature, 10 April 2018.

48 Chris Miller, ibid, p.19-20.

a different job and move elsewhere to work. Having experienced quite a lot of job insecurity ourselves (firstly, after the 1973 military coup in Chile, and then later in Britain) I envied people the job security I sensed everywhere I went in the USSR.

Looking at job security from another angle, however, I could see that such security did not always produce the desired effects: you couldn't help but notice that there was a good deal of slovenly work going on (road-workers filling in holes in the road without proper preparation, for instance) and that people would think nothing of slipping out from the workplace during working hours to do shopping or go to appointments - with no fear of retribution or demotion. When the old-fashioned lift in our block of flats was being replaced, it took weeks for the work to be completed, meaning that we and other residents had to climb 9 or more flights of stairs every time we came back home.[49] Absenteeism and shoddy workmanship were what had resulted from the Brezhnev-era "stagnation" – *zastoi* – which one heard sharply criticised whenever the economy was being discussed.

"Standing in the queue at the cash desk of a Moscow foodstore," I wrote a year or so after our arrival, "is not the best place to reflect on the advantages of socialism. You have to get to the head of that queue, remember what it is you want to buy, the cost of each item and from which section of the shop. Then, armed with your receipts, you have to go back to the different sections, where there may also be queues, to get the items you've paid for."

Supermarkets were much more convenient, but they were still relatively new at that time. The other thing that any Westerner would notice in Soviet shops, even in the capital, was the ubiquitous use of the abacus at the cash desk, rather than tills. It was totally manual, of course, but the cashiers were incredibly adept at calculating.

By the time of the 27th Soviet Communist Party Congress in February 1986, I had been the *Morning Star*'s Moscow correspondent for just a year. It was Mikhail Gorbachov's first Congress as Party General Secretary – and his opportunity to get much-needed changes agreed by Congress. *Perestroika* (restructuring) and *glasnost* (openness) became keynote words.

1986 had begun with Gorbachov's historic call for a nuclear-free world, with a timetable for all nuclear weapons to be decommissioned by the year 2000. This was the first time any world leader had put forward a vision of a world without nuclear weapons, a world without the constant threat of nuclear war. Though the new leader's dramatic proposal was not given the prominence in the Western media that it deserved, I personally found it inspiring and visionary.

I had been at the 12th World Youth Festival a year before, in July 1985,

---

49 In Richard Denton's BBC film *Caviar and Cornflakes* (1986) about the British diplomatic and journalist community in Moscow, I can be seen traipsing up the 9 flights of stairs with our children.

when the new Soviet leader spelt out his vision of a world without wars. Greeted with great enthusiasm by the young crowd, he told them that the goal of Soviet policy was "a world of good-neighbourliness and cooperation in good faith."

"Socialism's ideal is a world of friendship among nations," Gorbachov said. "Forty years ago the world shook from the first atomic blast. The echo of that blast appeals to every decent person's conscience and reason."

"We are for people's strength and energy being channelled, not into creating new means of destruction, but into the elimination of hunger, poverty and disease, and to work for prosperity and peaceful development."

How the young Nicaraguans and Salvadoreans, dressed in military fatigues, a few on crutches, who attended that World Youth Festival, must have echoed his words, wishing for an end to conflict in their countries. And the delegates there from apartheid South Africa and Chile under the Pinochet dictatorship, who knew and felt the Soviet Union's support for their bitter struggles against oppression and injustice. One example of this solidarity was Moscow Radio's *Escucha Chile* (Listen, Chile), a daily programme beamed into Chile which helped sustain the resistance during the 17 years of dictatorship.

1986 was the start of a very busy year for the country – and for me as correspondent.

"Acceleration" and "restructuring" of the economy – what did it mean? To find out I visited several important industrial plants, in Sumy, Ukraine, and Volokolamsk, in the Moscow region, to examine how they were introducing self-financing (*khozraschyot*). That year too I visited the northern city of Arkhangelsk, where I experienced the famous White Nights, and the republics of Georgia and Armenia; the Chernobyl nuclear power station disaster was on 26th April - and only 2 weeks later I was in the first group of journalists allowed near the exclusion zone. In June that year I was the only British newspaper journalist to cover the trial of Ukrainian nazi collaborator Fedorenko, extradited from the USA; in September I flew to the formerly secret Soviet nuclear testing site of Semipalatinsk; and in October the Reagan-Gorbachov summit took place in Reykjavik. In December the ban on nuclear physicist and human rights campaigner Andrei Sakharov was lifted, allowing him to return to Moscow from internal exile in Gorky, a town previously off-limits to foreigners. It was a busy year.

Even a correspondent as sympathetic to the ideas of socialism as myself could not help but see the problems in the Soviet economy. The choice of goods in the shops was poor, food supplies erratic and many of the consumer goods on offer were poor quality and old-fashioned.

One TV report in January showed a factory that made work gloves apparently to fit hands with five equal-length fingers and no thumb! Under the centralised planned economy, factories like that one could keep churning out the same poor-quality goods, year after year, achieving their plan targets, but by no means satisfying the needs of the population.

I travelled to Sumy, a city in north-eastern Ukraine, to find out more about the self-financing experiments, meeting local Party leaders, works managements and brigade-leaders of the plants taking part.

Sumy's history goes back to the tenth century Kiev Rus', immortalised in the Old-Russian legend *Song of Igor's Campaign*, which recounts the exploits of Prince Igor's troops against Polovtsian raids. Readers may be familiar with the Polovtsian Dances from Borodin's opera *Prince Igor*.

But in the twentieth century, Sumy people endured the Nazi invasion during WWII and thousands were captured, tortured and shot. The entire region was famous for its great partisan movement whose daring exploits under the very noses of the German fascists were the stuff of legend in the Soviet Union.

Even in 1986, the region's CPSU First Secretary Ivan Grintsovy told me that the region's population had still not managed to get back to pre-war levels, such was the extent of the destruction, which still told on industrial output.

Like most people, I enthusiastically welcomed Gorbachov's "new thinking" as a refreshing and much-needed change. Here are some lines from a feature I wrote in February 1986 after visiting the profit-making Frunze plant in Sumy – "the first in the country to operate under a completely self-financing system".

"The Frunze plant, with its 25,000 workers, made automated gas-transfer plants, centrifuges, compressors and pumps for nuclear power stations. The plant had become profit-making, workshop No. 2 foreman Yevgeny Adyekin told me, "by making the workers materially interested in the results of their work – linking wages to output and quality of output..."

"When President Reagan imposed his embargo on equipment supplies from Western firms for the Siberian gas pipeline, the Frunze plant suddenly found itself obliged to make the whole gamut of equipment for the pipeline." There had been a spontaneous protest meeting when the workers heard of the US embargo, Adyekin went on: "In our own way we told Reagan to get stuffed – we'll make the whole lot ourselves!" By early 1986 the whole of the gas pipeline from Urengoi in the far north to the Urals was provided with equipment made at Sumy's Frunze plant.

"After a year under the experiment, the plant was a success: "Our factory was profitable even before the experiment. But in the past we used to receive from the state what it saw fit to give us, and we had to spend it on what they decided we should spend it on. Our collective lived, as it were, on state subsidies. What it meant was that the ministry used advanced plants like ours to 'patch up the holes' and help sustain the backward ones," Frunze works Deputy General Director Vladimir Moskalenko explained."

Now the CPSU's policy was that all enterprises should be self-financing, and those that were unprofitable would simply go to the wall. It would be a real shake-up to the system.

It sounded drastic – but in line with Gorbachov's words at the February

1986 27th Party Congress, when he did not mince words in talking of the deficiencies to be overcome:

"The problems in the country's development built up more rapidly than they were being solved. The inertia and rigidity of the forms and methods of administration, the decline of dynamism in our work and an escalation of bureaucracy – all this was doing no small damage. Signs of stagnation had begun to surface in the life of society. The situation called for change, but a peculiar psychology – how to improve things without changing anything – gained the upper hand in the central bodies and, for that matter, at local level as well...."

On a visit to Stankoagregat, a big engineering works in Moscow, in January 1986, I was told that even where workers' jobs had been made redundant by automation, as in the case of crane-operators at their works, they would never be made unemployed. Aleksandr Korenblit, head of the works economic planning department, told me twenty crane-operators had been transferred to other jobs in the same works at the same or higher pay. "Nobody will be left without a job here," Stankoagregat's Director, Vladimir Isanin assured me. How did that fit with the Party's new policy of all enterprises having to be profitable, I wondered.

I looked forward to seeing, as the months went on, how the Congress resolutions on *khozrazchyot* (self-financing) would be put into practice.

In mid-February 1986 I flew on a lightning visit to Yerevan, the capital of Armenia, one of the 15 constituent republics making up the USSR. It had a warm climate, and I was glad to escape the harsh Moscow winter for a couple of days.

Yerevan is a pleasant city, with the stunning backdrop of Mount Ararat, and some beautiful central buildings. With its balmy temperatures and friendly people it is a lovely place to escape to for a winter break.

It was in this city that I first learned of the tragic 1915 Armenian genocide. I visited the city's impressive monument to the 1.5 million Armenians massacred in that savage event. By the early 1920s, when the massacres and deportations by the Ottoman Turks finally ended, between 600,000 and 1.5 million Armenians were dead, with many more forcibly removed from the country. Today, most historians call this event a genocide: a premeditated and systematic campaign to exterminate an entire people. However, the Turkish government still does not acknowledge this.

Obviously for a small republic like Armenia – 3.5 million in the eighties - such a huge loss of citizens produced something approaching a national trauma, and the resulting diaspora brought problems of its own.

In 1920, 90% of its population was illiterate; now Soviet Armenia made computers, lathes, radio-electronics and precision machine-tools.

When I studied Russian at the University of Manchester one of my fellow students was a great niece of the famous Soviet Armenian composer, Aram Khachaturian, and she bore the same family name. Whilst in Yerevan, I was treated to a performance of the ballet "*Gayaneh*" with music by the famous composer, at the Academic Theatre of Opera and Ballet. Khachaturian's original *Gayaneh* was the story of a young Armenian woman whose patriotic convictions conflict with her personal feelings on discovering her husband's treason. In later years the plot was modified several times, emphasising romance over nationalistic zeal.

Yerevan, with Mount Ararat in the distance

This was my first trip as a journalist to one of the non-Russian republics. Many years earlier, in 1963, I had been to neighbouring Azerbaijan, to its capital Baku, and fallen in love with the middle-eastern sounding music you could hear everywhere, wafting through the summer air of the beautiful park set alongside the Caspian Sea. Yerevan, too, made a similarly pleasant impression on me on this very short visit. Driving to the Masis shoe factory I could see rather rickety little houses seemingly perched unsteadily on the steep, stony hillsides of the ancient city. Housing, as in many parts of the USSR, was clearly still a problem: Yerevan had grown, I was informed, from less than 30,000 in 1920 to 1.1 million in 1986, so despite the visible construction of tower blocks, many people still lived in inadequate housing. The Masis factory produced attractive leather footwear – shoes, boots and trainers (only leather being used for children's shoes, I was told).

I was there – in February 1986 – to get an idea of the work going on in preparation for the forthcoming 27th CPSU Congress. The republic of Armenia, like all the other 14 republics, had had its own Congress at the end of January, when 900 delegates represented the republic's 186,000 Communist Party members, and from that Congress, 50 Communists were elected to the national, All-Union 27th Congress, to be held in Moscow in February 1986.

In the spirit of the day – criticism and openness concerning problems – I learnt that 7-8% of factories had still not reached planned targets. Poor management, slack work discipline, and complacency on the part of the Party factory branch were some of the reasons mentioned.

Western journalists in the eighties often used to talk of the "russification" of the non-Russian republics. Personally, I always felt this a very unfair accusation, given that in Great Britain, for instance, the Welsh language had, until relatively recently, been actively discouraged in schools. As late as the 20th century, the so-called "Welsh Not"[50] was still used as a means of forcing Welsh children to speak English at school. English was deemed to be the only appropriate medium for learning. I remember a Welsh family friend, Kath Westacott, once telling me that in her childhood (in the 40's) schoolchildren were told off if they were heard speaking Welsh in the playground.

In 1986, I found that Yerevan's street names were all in both Armenian and Russian, and you could hear Armenian spoken in the streets. I reproduce here the *Gayaneh* ballet programme I still have among my memorabilia from that trip, where you can see that Armenian is in first place, with the Russian translation at the back of the theatre programme:

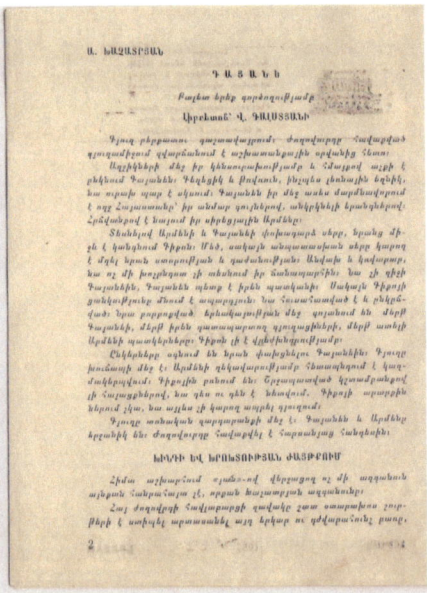

This was typical of what I would find everywhere I went in the Soviet Union: whilst Russian was the *lingua franca* for the whole of the country,

---

50 A stick or plaque was given to any child heard speaking Welsh during school, to be handed on to whoever next was heard speaking the language. At the end of lessons, the child left holding the Welsh Not was punished.

the republics and some regions had their own languages alongside Russian.

Only a year after the October Revolution, in 1918, it had been decreed that all nationalities in the Soviet Union had the right to education in their own language. At first, the new orthography used the Cyrillic, Latin, or Arabic alphabet, depending on geography and culture, but after 1937, all languages that had received new alphabets after 1917 began using the Cyrillic alphabet. That way, all citizens, from whatever republic or region, would be able to communicate with every other citizen of the USSR. Clearly, in a country where people could go and work in a far-off region, alongside people of many different nationalities, there had to be a common language and orthography. Similarly, at higher education level, there could be Uzbek, Armenian or Kirghiz students, for example, all being taught in the language that was common to them all - Russian.

Lithuania's Deputy Minister of Culture once told me, in July 1985, that all school, college and university subjects were taught in Lithuanian. The tiny republic of only 3.5 million people had 5 publishing houses, Mr Kibildis said, putting out literature in Lithuanian. What is more, works by the republic's novelists and poets were translated into Russian and other languages of the Soviet Union and sold in millions throughout the USSR.

I found much that was praiseworthy in Soviet nationalities policy during the years I lived in the USSR, and the more I travelled, the more convinced I became of the big lie of what Western correspondents called "russification". Leaving aside the fact that most correspondents based in Moscow in the eighties did not even speak good Russian and were thus hardly in a position to chat to the local population on any topic, in my travels around the USSR I found the very opposite of "russification". Kazakh and German newspapers published in Kazakhstan, street name signs in Moldavian *and* Russian in Kishinau, Uzbek *and* Russian-language schools in Tashkent, books published in all the national languages in huge volumes *and* translated into Russian for distribution in other republics..... I could give many more examples of excellent practice from Soviet nationalities policy.

If "russification" were true, how was it that, after the USSR's collapse, these now independent republics had their parliamentary proceedings, TV, radio, newspapers and magazines in their own languages? Did all the parliamentarians suddenly have to undergo crash courses in their national languages that had supposedly been so suppressed under "russification"? It is obvious that their languages had not been stamped out – far from it, they had been encouraged and promoted by Soviet nationalities policy.

It is true that there were mistakes and crimes involving certain small nationalities, a fact that has been amply recognised since the Gorbachov era. But overall, the Soviet Union, with its numerous nationalities and languages, many at very different stages of historical and economic development, did manage to live in peace for 70 years and encourage feelings of friendship among its peoples. "For the Friendship of Peoples" doesn't seem such a bad motto, especially if you compare it with the racist and xenophobic headlines that scream at us from our newspaper stands and which are contributing to the most fractured and hate-filled society we have ever seen in Britain.

The *Morning Star* was firmly on the side of peace and nuclear disarmament, so gave a lot of space to any peace initiatives. "The new Soviet disarmament plan, announced by Mikhail Gorbachov last Wednesday," I wrote on 20.1.86, "is a bold step to rid the world of nuclear weapons over the next 15 years."

"It provides for the stage-by-stage reduction of nuclear weapons – both delivery vehicles and munitions – right down to their total destruction under appropriate international control, on condition of a ban on space strike weapons." These were the days of US President Ronald Reagan's Strategic Defense Initiative – widely dubbed his Star Wars project.

Meanwhile the Soviet press was arguing for enterprises to become self-financing and for the work collectives to put "socialist self-government" into practice by increasing workers' participation in the running of their enterprises.

The Party newspaper *Pravda* called the mass media "democracy in action": "Where could you find a state outside the socialist system where, on the pages of the press, on TV and radio life's burning issues are discussed so openly, frankly and arousing such interest?" *Pravda* asked. It was true that the press in the USSR, even before *glasnost,* always carried critical articles and letters from readers.

At the 27th CPSU Congress, the emphasis was on all enterprises becoming self-financing, i.e. profitable, and on raising the quality of the goods produced. Wages should depend on an enterprise's productivity and efficiency. Tying profits to performance would help put an end to the manufacture of low-grade goods which nobody wants, the Party's General Secretary, Mikhail Gorbachov, told the Congress.

In a hard-hitting speech Gorbachov told the 5000 delegates: "We can no longer accept a situation where the personnel of enterprises producing worthless goods lead an untroubled life, drawing their full pay and receiving bonuses and other benefits!" Managers' mentalities had to change, in line with the new demands, he went on, to prevent the economy from being drawn into capital-intensive but low-productive projects.

As always, fraternal delegates attended this five-yearly event. Cuban President Fidel Castro spoke, calling the Congress "truly historic", as delegates got to their feet, applauding the revolutionary Cuban leader. Vietnamese Communist Party delegate, its frail-looking General Secretary, Le Duan, was also given an especially warm welcome.

It was during this Congress that we heard the shocking news of Swedish Prime Minister Olaf Palme's assassination in the Swedish capital - a crime which continues to puzzle to this day. Was it a political assassination, because Palme had actively worked for peace and disarmament and for international cooperation? Like all the delegates, I stood in a minute's tribute to Olaf

Palme, and listened to Politburo member Viktor Chebrikov, who was chairing the session, say that the Soviet leadership was "outraged and shaken by the murder of such an outstanding political figure."

Six years earlier, John Lennon, whose songs *Give Peace a Chance* and *Imagine* had had huge resonance throughout the world, had likewise been assassinated in New York. Many people doubt that this was the act of a lone crazy gunman, but instead, a political assassination of someone who was capable, due to his huge popularity among the youth of the entire world, of influencing global opinion towards peace and disarmament. When we think of the massive profits of arms producers, it is not outside the realms of possibility that Palme and Lennon could both have fallen victim to the dark forces of the so-called "deep state" which want to perpetuate the system that produces those huge profits for arms manufacturers.

As 1986 went on, in the spirit of the new *glasnost,* some previously-banned films and books started to appear. The following year would see release of Abuladze's anti-Stalinist film *Repentance (Pokayaniye)*, Rybakov's novel *Children of the Arbat* which features the 1934 murder of Leningrad Party leader Sergei Kirov, and many other previously-shelved works.

I read as much as I could of the newly-released literature. It is true that literary journals such as *Novy Mir,* even before the Gorbachov era, had always pushed the boundaries, printing excerpts from such banned works.

But as more and more damning criticism, stories from the gulags and even gory crime reporting became daily fare from 1986 onwards, I began to feel uneasy at the extremist tone of a lot of it. It was as if all balance had disappeared. Everything belonging to the past was suddenly negative, from the repressions of the thirties to the lack of preparedness for WWII, from the reforms of the Khrushchov era to the stagnation of the Brezhnev years – everything was painted in solely negative colours. It worried me, firstly because I knew that not everything *was* negative, and secondly because I felt it would have an unsettling and destabilising effect on the mass of the population.

The new Moscow leader, Boris Yeltsin, was increasingly getting the reputation of a firebrand, frequently criticising the sluggishness of the reforms. But instead of being an ally of Gorbachov's in his attempts to introduce the agreed reforms, he became a thorn in Gorbachov's side, firing off criticisms as and when he saw fit, as if he were not part of the leadership that had agreed them. And as the reforms failed to show any tangible results – at least in the economic sphere – so many Muscovites began to warm to this firebrand figure, who was unafraid to call a spade a spade, and who gave the impression that he was a man who could get things done. Whereas Gorbachov's star began to fade, Yeltsin's began to rise.

As a journalist you had to be ready to drop everything and file a news story immediately - and my family can attest to this. Often I could not be around to prepare meals or sit at table for dinner with the family, due to having to file. When the USA bombed Libya in April 1986, killing many civilians, including one of Libyan leader Muammar Gaddafi's own family, I had to report on the angry reaction of the Soviet Government and media, who called it "gangsterism".

Soviet news agency TASS condemned the British Government's "kowtowing" to the USA by allowing US aircraft to take off from British soil to bomb Tripoli. The Foreign Ministry's spokesman, Vladimir Lomeiko, called the bombing a violation of international law. According to Japan's ambassador in Tripoli, who witnessed the bombing, embassy buildings of Romania, France, West Germany, Greece and Switzerland had all suffered damage by the ostensibly super-accurate laser-guided missiles, supposedly targeted on military facilities. TASS said the death toll was probably several hundred, as a hundred houses had been destroyed in the first night's raid alone. The BBC reported "at least 100" had died in the raids.

Though life as a journalist at this time of change was busy, we managed, as a family, to enjoy at least part of our weekends. There was no Sunday edition of the *Morning Star*, so I did not have to file anything on a Saturday, although if I was working on a feature or trying to keep up with reading the Soviet press, I often spent part of the day working. Anyway, the children had school on Saturdays till about 1pm, so it wasn't often that we had the whole day off.

One of our favourite excursions was a trip down the river on a *raketa* – hydrofoils that ran up and down the Moscow River, stopping at various embarkation points along its route. There was a convenient stop just near our block of flats, so we could easily catch the *raketa* and disembark somewhere new up- or downstream. We would find ourselves in a hitherto unknown quarter of the huge city, have a walk round, find a cafe or ice-cream kiosk and then walk back to take the hydrofoil back home. With very low fares, they used to run about every 20 minutes, so you could go back whenever you felt like it. We would often get talking to people, on park benches, on boulevards or in the ice-cream queue. Russian people are very friendly and open, and it is easy to get into conversation with them. Many of them learned English at school, and whilst I can't say that the average Russian knew English well, many did have a smattering of English and were keen to try it out on us once they heard that we were from Britain.

Raketa (hydrofoil) on the Moscow river

Mostly though, people used to think I was Russian, or if they detected a slight foreign accent, they thought I was probably Latvian. And quite often Ricardo would be stopped to ask the way to somewhere, people simply assuming he would be from one of the non-Russian republics like Georgia or Azerbaijan, judging by his dark skin and hair. Moscow's population was pretty mixed: there were lots of non-Russians who lived and worked there, just as in the republics there were Russians who had gone there to work and stayed. I didn't detect any racism in Moscow, though it now seems clear that there must have been prejudices that had long lain dormant. The first overt signs of ugly nationalism were to surface later.

One of Victor's closest friends was half-Dagestani, one of the children's schoolteachers was Armenian, one of the twins' best friends was of Kalmyk origin, we had Soviet Jewish friends, Ukrainian friends, an old university friend from Bashkiria.... We always felt the warmth of the Soviet people we met, and, of course, of our friends and acquaintances both where we lived and on trips to the different parts of the vast Soviet Union. I was lucky enough to get to see quite a lot of the USSR - but still only a fraction of what there was to see - in the six years we lived there. Ricardo, too, travelled to various cities to see Chilean compatriots who had been studying in the USSR at the time of the 1973 military coup in Chile and had therefore been unable to return home.

Two months after the 27th CPSU Congress, where the reform programme was outlined and agreed upon – and I was keen to see how much of that ambitious programme would actually get implemented, if any – a terrible event occurred which shook not only the entire Soviet Union, but the world. On Saturday 26th April there was a meltdown of a reactor at a nuclear power station at Chernobyl in Ukraine, near the border with Belarus, situated in the north western part of the Soviet Union.

Initially the accident was not reported in the Soviet media. But on 29th April the 9 o'clock news programme *Vremya (*Time*)* gave a brief factual report. Swedish authorities had alerted the world, having detected radiation at their Forsmark nuclear power plant early on 28th April, as the winds had blown radiation from Chernobyl westwards. Only then did I begin to take in the enormity of this tragic accident.

The Chernobyl Nuclear Power Plant, comprising four reactors, was about 81 miles (130 km) north of Kiev, the capital of Ukraine, and about 12 miles (20 km) south of the border with Belarus. The nearest town to the power plant was the newly built town of Pripyat, which housed almost 50,000 people in 1986, according to the World Nuclear Association. A smaller town called Chernobyl, was home to about 12,000 residents. The rest of the region was primarily farms and woodland.

The deserted town of Pripyat is seen against the background of the damaged reactor at the Chernobyl nuclear power plant in Pripyat, Ukraine, April 23, 2013

Obviously all correspondents were desperately trying to find out as much as they could about what had happened and what the dangers were. I rang all my Russian contacts and friends, but no one knew anything more than the official announcement had revealed. Among these, I rang a Ukrainian journalist I knew from *Radyanska Ukraina*, the main newspaper in the Ukrainian language, but if he knew more, he wasn't telling.

Five days after the accident, May Day in Moscow was a muted affair. The authorities in Kiev went ahead with their demonstration through the streets as if nothing had happened, and were later rightly condemned for putting showy appearances ahead of people's safety.

At the May Day demonstration in Moscow I met up with Patrick Cockburn of the *Financial Times* and Christopher Walker of the *Times* who were of course keen to see if I knew anything more than they did. Sometimes

I *did* know more than the other British correspondents – but not on this occasion. At that time the *Morning Star* was on sale at kiosks all over the Soviet Union, so the Soviet authorities would know that anything I managed to glean from contacts would be accessible to millions of Soviet people. Perhaps understandably, they were keen to keep information to a minimum, partly so as not to cause panic, but also because the authorities were only recently emerging from the period when there was what one might call a news blackout on accidents that could be seized upon by the Western media to denigrate the country.

In a speech on 13th May 1986, Soviet leader Gorbachov slammed Western news media for the lies they were telling about the accident - reports of "thousands of casualties", "mass graves" and that the entirety of Ukraine had been poisoned. Calling this media onslaught "a highly immoral campaign", Gorbachov said the Western media were accusing the USSR of lack of information, yet they said "not a word about how to stop the arms race or how to rid the world of the nuclear threat."

"Not a word in reply to the Soviet initiatives, to our specific proposals on termination of nuclear tests, on ridding humankind of nuclear and chemical weapons," he went on. As to the supposed "lack of information" on the Chernobyl accident, Gorbachov said: "Everybody remembers it took the US authorities ten days to inform their own Congress, and months to inform the world community about the tragedy that took place at Three Mile Island atomic power station in 1979."

Soviet TV showed how military helicopters were flying hundreds of missions dropping sandbags on to the damaged reactor. The pilots knew that their lives were in considerable danger. And we saw conscripts and volunteers in long, heavy radiation-proof aprons over protective clothing and headgear working on the reactor site itself, clearing debris and making it possible for robots to work ridding the site of contaminated material.

Though the initial death toll was very small, we knew that the doses of radiation the decontamination personnel were exposed to would probably either be lethal or at least, very damaging to their health in the long run.

In the case of Chernobyl, 31 people died as a direct result of the accident: two from blast effects and 29 firemen died as a result of acute radiation exposure in the days which followed.

Even now, so many years later, there is no consensus on the number of people who were impacted by long-term radiation exposure, but in its 2005/06 assessment 'Chernobyl's Legacy: Health, Environmental and Socio-Economic Impacts' the World Health Organisation (WHO) estimated that the total number of long-term deaths will be around 4,000. Other estimates have put the figure considerably higher.

Our daughters' friend Masha's father, an atomic scientist, worked on decontamination at Chernobyl for many months. We knew that was why he was away from home for weeks at a time, but nothing more than that.

Like the "liquidators", as they were called in Russian, he selflessly worked to lessen the radiation effects, putting to one side the danger or any long-term effects. Years later, we found out that he had been awarded a prestigious State Prize for his contribution to the development of nuclear power.

Radiation is a strange thing: I remember once on a visit to the Soviet nuclear testing ground at Semipalatinsk, in northern Kazakhstan, talking to an elderly man who had been a conscript during the time when atmospheric nuclear tests were held regularly there, before they were outlawed by the Partial Test Ban Treaty in August 1963. He told me that he was in good health, yet others who had presenced such explosions alongside him had died of cancer. Sometimes it depended, I was told, whether you were directly facing the blast, or were shielded in some way, as to whether you received a bigger or smaller dose of radiation.

As we watched on TV the massive efforts at clean-up in the days after the Chernobyl explosion, I was struck by the dedication of so many workers – volunteers who risked their lives to do this supremely difficult and dangerous job simply because it had to be done.

I was in the first group of journalists allowed to go to the Chernobyl area after the accident. It was a group of correspondents all from Western Communist publications, "privileged" to be the first to gain access to the region at the centre of world attention. My secretary, Olya, advised me of the dangers of radiation exposure and told me quite honestly that she wouldn't go if she were me. But I felt I had to go. I think my journalistic instincts and feeling of duty and loyalty to the *Morning Star*, which I knew had so many difficulties and disadvantages compared with other wealthier media owned by magnates like Rupert Murdoch, made me keen to go, if with a certain amount of trepidation on account of the radiation risk. I was the only female correspondent on that trip, and we stayed in Kiev from Sunday 11th May to Wednesday 14th May.

On our arrival that Sunday we had meetings with Ukrainian Government ministers, with health specialists and members of the republic's Academy of Sciences. After filing my story by phone, I took a walk round central Kiev together with the correspondent from the Israeli Communist Party's newspaper, Leon Zahavi. Kiev centre was very green and pleasant, the pavements shaded by the many horse chestnut and poplar trees. When I got back to the hotel, I immediately showered to rid myself of any radiation I might have been exposed to. At that time – 2 weeks after the accident – radiation was 0.4 milliroentgens per hour (mR/hr) in Kiev, we were informed. (Compare natural background readings for radiation of anywhere up to about 0.1 mR/hr).

On Monday, 12th May - more meetings at the regional Party headquarters, where we met the Kiev regional (Obkom) First Secretary and other Party officials. They were all keen to stress the ongoing work to decontaminate and keep the local population safe. A thirty-kilometre exclusion zone had

View from our kitchen of Moscow River and Kremlin

Ricardo and the children in front of our building

Skipping in our yard

Class in school no.35

Victor with writer Emma Smith and his teacher Anna Oganyezovna (centre)

Leaving for pioneer camp

The twins at their first New Year party with Dyed Moroz
(Grandpa Frost) and Snyegurochka (Snow-maiden)

Speed skaters at Alma Ata Sports Stadium, Feb 1987

Chernobyl "liquidators" after decontamination shift, May 1986

Testing locals for radiation, Chernobyl, May 1986

Hosing away radiation, Kiev, May 1986

Back to school with flowers, 1 September 1986

With Jamaican PNP friends Manley and Desmond, 1985

Derbyshire Peace
Delegation at
Soviet Peace
Committee, 1986

Councillor Jill Jones gifting the Soviet Peace Committee a scroll
from Derbyshire Peace Federation, 1986

We had a little gym in our hall

Yamal. Nenets baby in cradle suspended from *chum* roof. April 1988

Yamal. Welders working on gas pipeline in freezing temperatures, April 1988

Woman roadworks operator in Moscow

Meeting miners' leader Mikhail Srebny, 1985

Nazi war criminal Fedorenko in the dock, Simferopol, June 1986

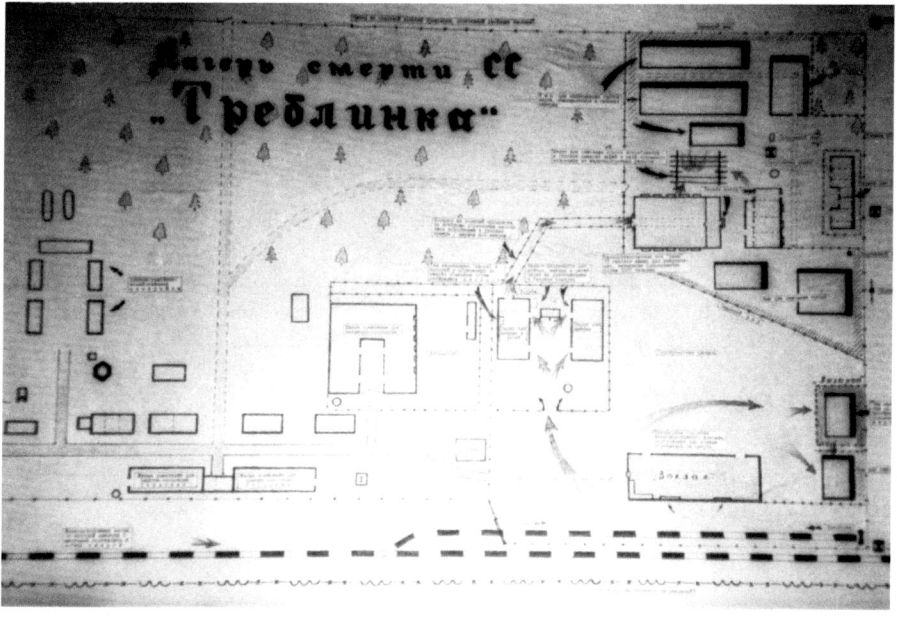

Map of Treblinka Death Camp, where Fedorenko worked as Wachmann

A national dance, Georgia, Oct 1986

Prensa Latina correspondent, Teresa, Tbilisi, Georgia, Oct 1986

Ancient church,
Gagra, Abkhazia

Underground nuclear test tunnel, Degelen Hills,
Semipalatinsk, Kazakhstan, September 1986

With Bob Evans, Reuters Bureau Chief, Semipalatinsk

Statue of nuclear
physicist Igor
Kurchatov, near
Semipalatinsk

Cruise ships, Ryechnoi Vokzal (River port), Moscow

Tretyakov Gallery, Moscow

40th anniversary of
Victory Day, Bolshoi
Theatre, 9 May 1985

Military parade, Victory Day, Red Square

immediately been established around the damaged plant and residents from that zone had been evacuated, which was no mean feat. But we all knew that it was an exercise in damage limitation and one had to take what was said with a big pinch of salt.

We were taken to Nyemeshayevsky Medical Centre to see radiation monitoring and the ongoing blood-testing of the population. We saw a farm to which cattle from the zone had been evacuated and met some of the evacuees from the Chernobyl region, who, though worried, seemed very accepting of their situation. We met emergency workers at "Lesnaya Polyana" pioneer camp, which had been commandeered as a residence for the hundreds of emergency staff working 2-day shifts at the nuclear power station.

One young worker, Aleksandr, tall and well-built, told me his family had all been evacuated from the exclusion zone to Kiev, some 80 miles to the south. Like so many Russians and Ukrainians, he was cheerful, matter-of-fact, open and optimistic about the clear-up they were engaged in. You could sense his pride, too, in being involved in what was, after all, a heroic job, given the dangers everyone knew they faced.

This is from one of my reports filed by phone from Kiev during our 4-day stay in the area:

"Another Chernobyl victim has died of burns in a Kiev hospital, Ukrainian Health Minister Anatoly Romanenko told the *Morning Star* yesterday. This brings to three the toll of dead from the nuclear power station accident there two weeks ago.

"In a no-holds barred 2-hour talk with Mr Romanenko, Ukraine's Deputy Prime Minister Yevgeny Kachalovsky and others, Communist journalists visiting the region learnt that altogether, 90,000 people and 50,000 cattle had been evacuated from the 30-kilometre zone round the damaged reactor.

"But it's already safe for people within that zone, said Kiev Regional Council leader, Ivan Plyushch. The temperature inside the fourth block reactor was down to 230°C yesterday, proving beyond doubt that the graphite fire is extinguished.

"Victor Trefilov, Ukrainian Academy of Sciences Vice-President, said the republic's Food Programme would not be seriously affected by the Chernobyl accident. Consistent monitoring of vegetables and milk had not shown above-normal radiation levels, he said. Water in rivers and the Kiev reservoir had been normal at all times.

"Mr Kachalovsky insisted that people had been told the facts as soon as proper, objective information was available. "We can't give information like some papers do in the West, first saying there are 2000 dead, then later denying it. We don't give information until we are sure of what we are giving.

"Kiev's streets are alive with people on this early summer day. Majestic horse chestnut trees in their pink blossom and slim poplars line the bustling streets of this greenest of Soviet cities. Yet, driving from the airport a few kilometres outside the city, you meet the first radiation monitoring checkpoint - and you remember Chernobyl nuclear power station is only 130 k away.

I phoned this report on 12th May:

"The bus stops. Radiation control. We're nearing Kiev. The manual monitor runs over the wheels of our bus. We wait inside. If the needle flicks to red, we're in for a long wait. It stays in the black. We're all right. We breathe sighs of relief.

"We're on our way to a Rest Home. But it's a Rest Home with a difference. "Forest Glade" is where Chernobyl emergency shift workers live after their dangerous work at the damaged nuclear power station. We drove up to the entrance, in the midst of a tall pine forest. A recent rainfall made the earth give off a pungent woody smell. We saw some men in track suits, talking in groups. These are the Chernobyl emergency workers. They're the troubleshooters, dealing with the Chernobyl nuclear accident. These are the men the nation is depending on.

"Chernobyl is 90 kilometres away. These men work there amidst danger - the unseen danger of radiation. The graphite fire is out, say the men, but the radiation is still polluting the atmosphere.

"Aleksandr Lukienchenko is 31 years old. He's an electrician at Chernobyl nuclear power station. He wasn't on duty that fateful morning of 26th April. But when he heard of the accident, he reported for duty just the same. He is one of the 150+ volunteers on shift duty at the stricken reactor.

"When I spoke to him after his stint, it was hard to believe that he was one of those up against it, on the front line of the battle against the reactor. In his navy blue sweatshirt and jeans, Aleksandr looks a typical Soviet worker. Medium height, blonde, blue-eyed, a Ukrainian, he is modest, unassuming, matter-of-fact.

"'We're all volunteers here,' he told me. 'All Chernobyl workers were given the possibility of either transferring to work elsewhere, going on holiday, or simply leaving.'

"'But the job has to be done. We've got to see to the other 3 blocks of the station, and keep up maintenance work there,' Lukienchenko said. I asked him how he felt. 'Grief, of course, that's my main feeling after this tragic accident.'

"'But that's why I'm working there, and why all of us volunteers are working there. To put things right, so that we can get on top of the situation.'

"He smiled his broad wide-toothed smile. His lower lip trembled slightly. A doctor in a white gown came up and nudged his elbow: 'It's time to stop,' he said, 'I think you've had enough.' They are kept under careful observation for 2 weeks at Forest Glade after their 2-day stint at the reactor.

"The Chernobyl workers are indeed on the front line. And it is their lives they are putting on the line when they go in for their 2-day shift after a 2-week rest and treatment break.

"What precautions do they take on the job, I asked. Aleksandr told me they wore special clothing and breathing apparatus on entering the nuclear power station to do their essential job. When we were leaving "Forest Glade" we met three workers who had just returned from their shift in a jeep. "What's the situation," I asked. "It's stabilising," they said. "The radioactivity is less and less - but the work still has to go on."

"The lads looked cheerful. I noticed their personal radiation monitoring apparatus, clipped to their heavy twill overalls. "What's it like out there?" someone asked. "It's all right," they chorused. "The other three blocks of the power station are all fine, everything's under control."

Aleksandr is from Pripyat' - the power station workers' town only three kilometres from the accident. It was evacuated the day after the accident, as soon as radiation levels started to climb. He wants to go back, we were told, as soon as it's feasible. "It's a young town," he told me. "We all went to school together, we all work together, and now we're all scattered."

"His wife had been evacuated to Kiev. Next week she and their older 7-year old child were off to a sanatorium in the Crimea. The younger, 4-year old boy was staying with his grandmother in Kiev. Aleksandr echoed what other evacuees said earlier: "It's nice to go visiting, but there's no place like home."

"Decontamination of the 30-km danger zone around the stricken nuclear power station will take time. And nobody here is saying yet when the evacuees will be able to return home."

This, of course, was wildly optimistic, as we now know. Pripyat' is a ghost town that will never be fit for inhabitation.

This is my last report from Chernobyl, sent with considerable difficulty, as phone lines were in great demand and attending to journalists was not a priority for the officials we met:

"Anatoly Amelkin looked tired and strained. The hardest 10 days of his life began at 03.40 am on April 26th. When Chernobyl's Communist Party Secretary answered the phone from his sleep, it was like awakening into a nightmare. *Accident at the power station - 4th block - fires burning in reactor hall and engine room - not yet known what effects will be…..*

"In ten minutes, Amelkin was dressed and at the Party's District headquarters, together with other Party secretaries from surrounding districts. First measures: to organise information to work collectives in the area, to keep discipline and avoid panic. Next, a meeting of Party activists, to hear a full report on the accident.

"Meanwhile the Government Commission, formed on the 26th April, the day of the accident, had issued their first instructions based on their initial analysis of the situation at the damaged reactor. As radioactivity continued escaping from the destroyed shell of the fourth generating unit, it became obvious that there was nothing for it but to evacuate the nearest population.

"Amelkin and his comrades did not sleep the following night. The population of Pripyat', where most of the power station's workers lived, had to be got out as soon as possible.

"By 2pm on the 27th, the whole operation was beginning: 2,172 buses drove into Pripyat' and up to every block of flats. Starting with women and children, the evacuation lasted 2 hours 45 minutes. Finally, the police went round every block and every flat checking that no one had been left behind. Dogs and cats went with their owners. 50,000 head of cattle were also evacuated in 1,786 lorries.

"First, the Government Commission led by Deputy Council of Ministers Chairman, Boris Shcherbina, set up a 10-km danger zone around the burning reactor. Then a 30 km zone was established and evacuation started from Chernobyl itself - 18 km from the reactor - and the villages and farms around.

"While frantic helicopter sorties were going on to plug the invisible, but steadily seeping, radiation from the fourth block, people in villages roundabout were having to be persuaded, if not bludgeoned, into leaving their homes. This was one of the many problems Amelkin and other leading Communists faced in the first few days after the atomic reactor explosion. As a helicopter bound for Chernobyl whirred above our heads, Amelkin told me how older village people had been especially hard to convince. You can't see radiation and all around, trees are in blossom and gardens bursting with the fruits of the earth.

"The strain told on his good-natured face as he related the human difficulties they had surmounted. I spoke to several evacuees, and workers from Chernobyl power station itself. There had been no panic, they said. Everything went off smoothly and in a disciplined way.

"And that is the abiding impression I have after talking to people in Kiev and Borodansky district in the Kiev region - calm, responsibility, stoicism. Borodansky district, 68 km from Chernobyl, is one of the four districts which has received the Chernobyl and Pripyat' evacuees.

"I saw old folk at a specially organised Medical Point in the local village's Cultural Centre (*Dom kul'tury*). Young and old were there, being monitored for radioactivity on their clothing and footwear, having blood tests and consultations with a team of doctors. So far, radioactivity was normal, only two people had been hospitalised, both of whom had now been discharged, I was told.

"The lab assistants and all the equipment had come from Leningrad. A small fleet of ambulances standing outside had been sent from Odessa. "The whole country is rallying round us in our time of need," Anatoly Amelkin said. And for a moment the strain lifted from his tanned face.

The apparent optimism that I encountered on this brief visit - the first by any Western journalists - was clearly, with hindsight, misplaced. On my return to Moscow, I heard that seven of the 35 critically injured in the accident, most of whom were firemen, had already died.

Optimism, plus pride and bravery was typical of the attitudes we found among "liquidators", other emergency workers and evacuees. As one of the liquidators in Svetlana Alexievich's book[51] writes: "We remember that they couldn't have made it without us. Our system, it's a military system, essentially, and it works great in emergencies. You're finally free there, and necessary. Freedom! And in those times the Russian shows how great he is. How unique. We'll never be Dutch or German. And we'll never have proper asphalt and manicured lawns. But there'll always be plenty of heroes."

The Soviet public reacted to the tragedy with customary generosity: according to Finance Minister Boris Gostev, speaking in September 1986, so far 500 million roubles had been donated to the Chernobyl Disaster Fund, plus 1.5 million from abroad.

One of the most curious events during those few days in April 1986 spent near Chernobyl was when our small group of journalists was taken to lunch – not as on other days, to some hotel or restaurant, but in the middle of a forest. When we first arrived the food on the tables was covered by white cloths. We milled around chatting until we were invited to have lunch, and only then saw that the long trestle tables with their crisp white linen tablecloths were laden with cold meats and fish, salads of various kinds and fruit, together with jugs of *kompot*.

One correspondent, no doubt in an attempt to be gallant, came up to me and presented me with a pretty wild flower he had picked from the forest floor. My immediate thought was: *"that must be covered in radiation, better not touch...."* But my polite upbringing got the better of me, and I accepted the flower, equally graciously. I thought then, and still think now, that this was the craziest idea - to have lunch in the open air, only 3 kilometres from the edge of the exclusion zone, and 2 weeks after the accident. What was the point? Surely not to show us the beauty of the Ukrainian woodland. It was the same reason the authorities had for not cancelling the May Day demonstration in Kiev, despite the known risks of contamination – i.e. to show the world that everything was fine, the area was safe. And none of us complained, whatever we might have thought to ourselves.

---

51 *Voices from Chernobyl, The Oral History of a Nuclear Disaster,* by Svetlana Alexievich, Picador, 1997.

In fact, one or two of the correspondents – I remember the Italian correspondent of *L'Unita* in particular – had asked the organisers of our trip if we could accompany emergency workers on board one of the helicopters flying right over the stricken reactor so as to get an exclusive picture from above. And they continued to demand this more and more vociferously.

I had already decided I wasn't prepared to subject myself to that dose of radiation. I thought of my three young children and anyway, to me it seemed a crazy request, especially when you could see that all the emergency workers were working flat out to try and control the situation. So I was glad when we got the answer next day: "*Nyet!*" No possibility of us being allowed to fly over the reactor – all available helicopters were needed for the urgent work of dropping sacks of sand, clay, lead and boron on to the reactor.

The *L'Humanité* correspondent, Gerard Streif, nearly exploded when we were told this, demanding to go back to Moscow immediately, not to waste another day in Kiev. Obviously he and Giulietto Chiesa, of *L'Unitá*, who had both been the most vociferous in demanding we be allowed to fly over the reactor, represented large-circulation newspapers and thus faced the sort of pressures of any Western mainstream media – and the desire for a scoop, the big story, the exposé.... The French and Italian Communist Parties in the eighties were mass parties and both countries' Communist press had enviable circulation figures.

I wrote in my diary: "I didn't mind. I was glad we weren't going to fly over the (nuclear power) station – after all, it's 100 roentgens above there." Before our flight back to Moscow on Tuesday 13th May, I filed a feature by phone, then went with our translator, Sergei, who was a friend of Ricardo's, to see the War Memorial complex up on a hill in Kiev. Sergei suggested I should wear a hat to shield me a little from the radiation, but I didn't have one, so we walked like everyone else in the city, freely and seemingly without a care in the world. Radiation - invisible, undetectable by smell or any other sense - yet we knew it was all around.

When I look back at my diaries from that time, some of my comments make me laugh. Like the entry on that same day, when I wrote how cross I was that the Soviet functionary who was in charge of our group left our hotel for the airport without waiting for me as I was 3 minutes later than the appointed time. Several of my fellow journalists came up to me at the airport to say that they had tried to make him wait, but he had insisted they had to leave, even though they arrived at the airport with 40 minutes to spare. "He's an idiot, that bloke," I wrote. "A little man given a bit of power – like a Sergeant-Major giving out orders!"

And I went on: "Just my luck I had to sit next to him on the plane, where he spent nearly the whole journey worrying about the effects the radiation will have had on his health. Pathetic. Can't imagine *him* in a war situation!" I didn't mince my words in those days.

When I got back to our Moscow flat later that night, I insisted on going straight to the bathroom to take all my clothes off, stick them in the washing machine and shower thoroughly, before emerging to hug and kiss Ricardo and the children. They were thrilled when they saw me that very evening interviewed on TV in the prime-time *Vremya* programme, giving my impressions in Russian. I can't remember what I said, but several correspondents rang me afterwards to congratulate me.

My *Morning Star* colleague, Colin Williams, told me next day that I had also appeared on British TV, filmed in Kiev. Fame indeed.

Talking of fame – a British TV producer, Richard Denton, came to Moscow in May 1986, with the idea of filming members of the British diplomatic and journalistic community; he wanted to film me as the only example of someone who lived among Soviet people, spoke Russian and whose children went to a local Soviet school. The result, later that year, was the film *Caviar and Cornflakes*, which showed the British Ambassador at the time – Sir Bryan Cartledge – and the Embassy's terribly posh Press Attaché, McLaren of McLaren, in a far from favourable light. The British correspondents came over in the film as bored and only interested in the "dissidents" story. The film showed me at home and at our children's school, surrounded by the children's lively classmates, and in an interview I slammed the British press for only being interested in the so-called dissidents, when there was so much more to life in Moscow if the correspondents ever ventured to find out.[52]

At a meeting of the Supreme Soviet in November I met up with Bob Evans, who headed up the Reuters team in Moscow. "I've just seen that film you starred in!" he told me. "You're the only one who comes out well in it." And another journalist, Chris Walker of the *Times*, told me that the Embassy was "hopping mad" about the film. He revealed that the other British journalists had been shown a preview of the film – to which I hadn't been invited. So I rang the Embassy asking why not, and was promptly invited to a special viewing on my own. "It's just my personal view," Press Attaché McLaren confided to me, "but I think you came over very well – and made a rather firm point in the film." Somewhat hypocritical, since I had been expressly excluded from the preview.

When Ricardo and I went to the Embassy for Christmas drinks on 15th December, the Ambassador smilingly welcomed me at the top of the steps with the words: "Oh, here comes our TV star!" or some such comment.

Being a Moscow correspondent at that time was far from easy. Many times I would have worked all day, going to the frequent press conferences, filing (laboriously, on old-fashioned telex machine), reading the press, as well as the usual chores of food shopping, washing, cleaning, or taking the kids by bus across town to the Polyclinic – and then I would get an urgent request for a piece, say, on some street protest in faraway Alma-Ata, wanting me to contact people there for a story - at 9pm Moscow time....

---

52 See Appendix V for a *Caviar and Cornflakes* review in The Times.

One extract from my diary, dated 18th November, put it like this: "Came home [after an earlier press conference and a Supreme Soviet session, K.C.], filed stories on both, finished at 8.40pm. Cooked meal concurrently. It's not a job for a woman with three kids, I say to myself for the 100th time."

Or the following entry, on 17th October 1986, "Came back from UB-40 press conference, Tony (*Morning Star* Editor) wanted 15 pars on economic results, quite rightly. So did that, then 7 pars on UB-40 in Moscow, finished 7.30pm. Made dinner at last for my poor kids."

Whereas the mainstream western press correspondents had maids and even chauffeurs, we had no such thing. We did our own cleaning; in any case, both Ricardo and I felt that it is good for children to grow up having to share in the chores.

Despite the many frustrations and problems, the *perestroika* era for journalists was an invigorating and exciting experience, and one coped as best one could.

One of the great things about speaking the language was that you could get talking to people you met by chance and find out what they were thinking. It's one thing to find out what decision-makers are thinking, but it's also important to find out what ordinary people think, what their concerns are.

Once on a bus my neighbour started chatting to me. She had been shopping for a winter coat. She told me: "After the war, we were short of everything, and the main concern for many years has been to produce enough goods, in terms of quantity."

"But now," she went on, "we've got enough of everything. Now what we want is better quality." Like most women in Moscow, she was very well dressed. But I knew from personal experience that to get such good-quality coats or boots, you had to queue somewhere for them. And of course, as I wrote in one of my reports, "while women are in queues, they are not at work."

Another time I got into conversation with an elderly woman at the No. 8 bus-stop. She asked me if I could read the price on a jar of baby food she had bought. I couldn't see the price anywhere, but listened with interest as she proceeded to tell me how you couldn't get any information from shop assistants these days, how rude they were and how they were always telling you off. I commiserated, as I agreed with her – shop assistants in general were often unsmiling and could be downright impolite. "It's the same with the health service," she went on, telling me how she had been to her Polyclinic recently and the doctor there – a Georgian, she added – had "ordered her about" and been very rude to her. I asked her why she thought it was so. She said she didn't know, but ever since Stalin had died it had been like that. There's no order anywhere, she complained. Of course doctors and nurses ought to be better paid, she said, but there has got to be elementary respect between people too.

Lenin had said the most important thing was people's "revolutionary spirit"- but that's been lost, she went on. "Now people just don't care!" she declared. As she was leaving the bus at the Rossiya Hotel, she said: "You're from the *pribaltika* (Baltic republics), no?" I wondered if she would have said all that she did if she had known that I was a 'western' correspondent.

The chrome yellow No 8 bus ran along the embankment of the Moscow River from our block of flats towards the centre. I often used to catch it, before I had a car, as it went near the press centre and anyway, I love riding alongside a river. The Moscow River was a busy working river, with big slow barges laden with coal and other heavy goods, as well as the pleasure hydrofoils. Our children would sometimes go down there to the landing stage on the embankment with their Soviet friends. One of their games was to find leeches in the water and throw them against the walls of the embankment. Ugh! Thank goodness I only found out later what they had been up to.

Although school was a very serious business and they had copious homework every day, our children were very free, compared with children in London today, who tend to be ferried everywhere. Our children used to go out to play in the afternoons after they came home from school (and they used to go to the after-school club till 5pm or so, so it was a long school day for them) with their friends, Artyom, Masha and Baira. They would meet other children from the same block of flats and play in the *dvor* on top of the big underground car park.

They were probably a bit too free. One day I was working in my office next to our flat and when I emerged for a break I saw that our twins' little friend Masha, who had lovely shoulder-length blonde hair, now had a rather lop-sided short haircut, courtesy of our daughters, who had agreed to Masha's request to have a haircut! I didn't know whether to laugh or cry. I remember they all seemed very pleased with their handiwork. I demanded that they accompany Masha back home to somehow explain themselves to her Mum.

Masha came round one day and said: "*poidyomtye v bulochnuyu, u menya 10 kopeek yest'*!" ("Let's go down to the bread shop, I've got 10 kopecks!") This became a saying among the three of them, and they would collapse into laughter on saying it - it was such a small amount, and Soviet children weren't in the habit of getting pocket money.

Not long after my return from the scary Chernobyl trip, I met some of the world's scientists in Moscow for a nuclear disarmament conference, including Professor Joseph Rotblat, of the Pugwash[53] movement. There were scientists there from 47 countries, and the conference was one of many, including another slightly earlier, of delegates from women's organisations from 57 countries, addressed by the world's first woman cosmonaut, Valentina Tereshkova.

Professor Rotblat told the conference about the consequences of the USA's atomic bombs dropped on the Japanese cities of Hiroshima and Nagasaki in

---

53 See Footnote 45.

1945: "Thousands of civilians are still dying, even after so many years." The Chernobyl accident, he said, had involved a considerable number of medical personnel, but "in a nuclear war, it would be *millions* in need of medical aid."

"Doctors would be unable to cope," he stressed, adding that in the UK, for instance, there were relatively few centres where radiation and burns victims could be treated.

In June 1986, I was invited to attend the trial, in Simferopol, Crimea, of a former Nazi war criminal. Covering the trial was harrowing, listening to the terrible things that happened in the death camps and in the Nazi-occupied Soviet villages and towns, but it gave me a better understanding of what the population of Soviet territory under German Nazi occupation during the 2nd World War went through. Fyodor Fedorenko was a Ukrainian collaborator who had served the Nazis at the Treblinka death camp in Nazi-occupied Poland. He had escaped to the US after the war and obtained US citizenship, but in 1984 was extradited to the USSR.

During the trial I learnt the following statistics: 250,000 Soviet soldiers killed in the Crimea during the Great Patriotic War; 90,000 Crimean citizens killed during the three years of Nazi occupation; 85,000 Crimeans deported to Germany for hard labour; 127 towns and villages destroyed in the peninsula during the war; 11,700 partisans operated in the Crimea, blowing up Nazi troop trains, destroying bridges and carrying out daring raids.

Treblinka, as I wrote in my despatch from Simferopol, was not a concentration camp: no inmates were kept there, there were no survivors. It was a death factory.

"As the victims - Jewish people transported from different parts of Europe - were let out of the stifling carriages at Treblinka, they saw what looked like an ordinary station.

"Ticket office, station manager's office, timetables, posters on the walls saying "Palestine is waiting for you…"

"But it was all a fake. On the pretext of "delousing" the victims' hair and clothing, Fedorenko and the other *wachleute* (watchmen) pushed, shoved and beat the unwilling people into so-called "cloakrooms".

"Men into one, women and children who could walk into another. Infirm or disabled people and tiny children were driven to a shed with a red cross on the door - the "infirmary".

"Here Fedorenko showed his German masters what he was worth: he was personally responsible, behind the closed door of the "infirmary", for shooting the elderly, disabled and babies. "It was an everyday occurrence. It was our work," said Fedorenko, referring to the "infirmary" shootings.

"Witnesses told the trial how, using sticks and clubs, the SS forced the terrified people along the open-air path and into the gas chambers. In 7 gas chambers, 2000 people could be exterminated at one go in Treblinka.

"800,000 people were exterminated in Treblinka, where Fedorenko served. One trainload a day arrived - 52 carriages with no windows, packed to capacity. Many did not even survive the journey. The stench of cremation of so many thousands of bodies reached miles away."

It was painful and emotionally draining to hear these testimonies. Were there no depths to human cruelty and inhumanity?

It came as a surprise to me that so many of the witnesses who testified against Fedorenko had themselves served long prison sentences in the Soviet Union after the war for varying degrees of collaboration with the enemy. It was disturbing listening to Ukrainians who had served as SS Wachmann at Nazi concentration camps, when you knew that other patriotic Ukrainians had given their lives as partisans... One former Wachmann, looking at Fedorenko in the dock, burst out, bitterly: "You ran off to the United States after what you'd done. Not like me: I stayed here and served my term! I stayed to rebuild!"

One witness had worked as a kitchen maid at Treblinka, but the most interesting witnesses were former Soviet inmates at Stutthof[54] and Pelets concentration camps where Fedorenko had also worked. I had a chat with one of the former inmates – one of only four Soviet prisoner-of-war survivors of Pelets – who had gone on in later life to work as a lecturer at the Patrice Lumumba Peoples' Friendship University[55] in Moscow.

Whilst attending the Fedorenko trial, I also had the chance to meet fellow journalists from *Radyanska Ukraina* – the main newspaper in the Ukrainian language. I was later asked to write a couple of articles for this newspaper. One I wrote was the story of Tamara (see Appendix IV), which was also a story borne of that dreadful World War.

The evidence against Fedorenko was irrefutable: he was found guilty of taking part in mass executions and sentenced to death for treason.

It had been a hard few days, listening to grim testimonies, filing my stories and telephoning them over to the *Morning Star*, always mindful of the high cost of the calls. But in those days there were no well-equipped press facilities in provincial places, so if a story was needed on that day, you had to phone it. I decided I could do with a day to relax a little after the trial, so I took

---

54 In September 1939, the Nazis created the concentration camp of Stutthof, near the Baltic port of Gdansk. Originally, it was a civil prison camp for political enemies of the Nazi regime. In November 1941, Stutthof was labelled an "SS special camp", and from January 1942 on, it was officially declared a concentration camp, comprising dozens of concrete buildings, a crematorium and gas chamber. In 1940, the total area of the main camp was 12 hectares, while by 1944 it was ten times as large. The prisoners were guarded by 3000 SS members and Ukrainian auxiliaries. In total, around 110,000 people were deported to the Stutthof camp, out of whom at least 65,000 died there (Holocaust.cz website). Another camp was near the small village of Pelets.

55 A year after its foundation in 1960, the University was named after the progressive Congolese independence leader, Patrice Lumumba. He was the first legally elected prime minister of the Democratic Republic of the Congo, but was assassinated on 17 January, 1961 in a US-sponsored plot using Congolese accomplices and a Belgian execution squad to carry out the deed. The stated purpose for establishing the university was to give young people from Asia, Africa and Latin America, especially those from poorer families, an opportunity to receive higher education and go back as specialists to help their countries' development.

a car the 50 miles to Yalta on the Black Sea just for a few hours. I visited a Donbass miners' holiday home near the beach, where I met miners who had recently finished a decontamination stint at Chernobyl. I had a lovely swim in the warm sea, then it was time, after lunch, to drive back to Simferopol and catch my plane back to Moscow.

I hadn't needed to rush back since our children, having finished the school year at the end of May, were now at a Pioneer Camp outside Moscow. I was a little worried as to how they were faring, so the first thing I did on my return from Simferopol was to go and see them. Visits from parents were not encouraged for some reason I could never fathom, so at the perimeter fence, we asked a child who was within earshot if he could find our son Victor for us. Victor soon ran up and we chatted through the fence. "Have you made any new friends here?" I asked. "Yes," he said grinning, "all the football team are my friends!" He told me he was trying to do what I had apparently advised him to do – to try and be on good terms with everybody.

Reading such entries in my diary (from 15th June, 1986) makes me realise now more than I think I did then that Victor, probably more than the twins, who by then were eight and had each other for company, found the experience of going away to Pioneer Camp, with hundreds of children he didn't know, quite daunting. He would probably have preferred to stay at home, but with both Ricardo and myself working, and no school to fill his time, I know he would very soon have got bored.

Whilst it is true that children are very adaptable, I think all our children, especially our son, who was 11 in 1986, went through some hard moments during those Moscow years, and then again when having to adapt to school once back in Britain.

I always went to the twice-yearly Supreme Soviet sessions, which resembled meetings in a hall more than a parliamentary chamber. All the proceedings were done from the platform, where CPSU General Secretary Gorbachov, President Andrei Gromyko and Prime Minister Ryzhkov and other top leaders would sit and conduct the business, including taking the votes - on the five-year plan, for instance, and on other motions.

There wasn't anything like debate, in the sense that most of us know it, but there were quite critical speeches by deputies from far and wide, including all the constituent republics of the USSR, which gave you a flavour of the problems different regions had. The June 1986 Supreme Soviet approved what seemed like a pretty ambitious five-year Plan: national income up by 22.1%, output to increase by 25%, productivity by 25% over the five years; agricultural output to increase by 14.4 % each year and productivity on farms by 21.4%; average pay to go up by 14.7%, 595 million square metres of housing to be built, as part of the plan to give every Soviet family a flat of their own by the year 2000. Consumer goods were to increase by 27% over the five years of the Plan.

Sessions were held in the Palace of Congresses in the Kremlin grounds, or other nearby halls. The snack bars were a good place to find delicious titbits, like smoked salmon and caviar on tasty Russian *borodinskiy khleb,* the black bread which was our family favourite. They were a welcome relief from the sessions which were rather routine and unexciting. Some of the speeches could be critical, like a Latvian farmworker who talked of the potato losses due to poor transport, refrigeration and storage facilities, or a young woman deputy from the Kalmyk Autonomous Republic who asked: "What's the use of sports gyms and clubs when you can't buy sports kit or trainers in the shops?" It seems to me that the *concept* of Soviets, and the Supreme Soviet itself, was democratic, in theory, in the sense that the deputies were voted in by the public, but in practice, they were not bodies which debated or discussed draft laws before being enacted.

Much more pleasurable was to attend sessions of the International Tchaikovsky Piano competition, which in 1986 was the 8th one held. Some 280 pianists, violinists and cellists from over 40 countries came to Moscow to take part in the prestigious competition. Barry Douglas from Northern Ireland had got through to the second round, so I made sure I had tickets to hear him play. I wasn't surprised when he went on to win the Gold Medal that year.

Towards the end of June 1986 I went to Arkhangelsk in the far north of Russia. I knew of Archangel in connection with the "Lend-Lease" programme during World War II, but not much more than that. The city is on the banks of the Northern Dvina and the White Sea coast. The Arkhangelsk region is bigger than France and includes the Arctic archipelagos of Franz Josef Land and Novaya Zemlya.

The city itself is 25 miles long, as I discovered when we drove from one end to the other. I visited a museum which had a mock-up of the city as it had looked in the 1920's, and the guide, an elderly man who had designed and made the exhibit, pointed out to me the huge number of Orthodox churches along the city's whole length. "Most of them were pulled down after the Revolution - those were the years when it was 'away with God, away with religion!'" he said, his eyes twinkling. He was a likeable man of 73, still full of life and enthusiasm.

Founded in 1584, the port's population at the time I was there was about 400 thousand people. There are a number of Russian Orthodox monasteries, including the World Heritage Site of the Solovetsky Islands in the White Sea. The great 18th century Russian scientist, historian and scholar of the Russian language, Mikhail Lomonosov (1711-1765), founder of Moscow State University in 1755, was born near Arkhangelsk.

During the Civil War, when revolutionary Russia was invaded by interventionist armies from 14 countries, including Britain, in an attempt to help the Whites defeat the new Bolshevik Government, Arkhangelsk was invaded by British troops, and there is a captured British tank from the period on display in the city.

Vinogradov statue

Pavlin Vinogradov (1890-1918) was one of the organizers of the opposition against the British and other "entente" interventionist forces in the North and was fatally wounded in battle against the Whites. Now the central avenue in Arkhangelsk bears his name.

In World War II, Arkhangelsk was a major port of entry for Allied aid. It was there, as well as Murmansk, that the Arctic Convoys landed with supplies for the Soviet Union under the lend-lease scheme. Until the Second Front was opened in June 1944 with the allied invasion of Normandy, the USSR had battled on its own against the Nazi invading forces. Soviet leader Stalin rightly complained in 1941 that his country was "waging a war of liberation single-handed", as the allies delayed and delayed opening a Second Front. Neither Arkhangelsk nor Murmansk were captured by the Germans in the war.

I was shown round an ice-breaker named Mudyug, and learned about the difficult transit for shipping through the Arctic seas. Inside, the Mudyug was very comfortable, with attractive individual cabins, lounges, library, cinema, hobby room, gym and sauna. I visited one of the repair workshops of the Krasnaya Kuznitsa (Red Smithy) shipyard, then the yard's museum, then the Dom Kultury – the shipyard's cultural centre.

At the Krasnaya Kuznitsa yard I interviewed a shipyard repair worker. I told him that most of Britain's famous shipyards had closed down. Scratching his head underneath his cap, he replied: "Well, that's a disease of capitalism, isn't it? We haven't got that problem here - our ship industry is growing."

"There's no shortage of work, we're overloaded with work, all the time," he went on. "We have a planned system of shipbuilding and repair here." His shipyard, quite a small one, built and repaired ships for the Soviet Northern fleet. "Trouble is, the yard is old and the machinery outdated."

"Shipbuilding has always used a lot of manual labour. Now we're trying to cut down on this and mechanise as many jobs as possible." This would be done, I was told, by introducing the self-financing model as a result of the decisions of the recent 27th CPSU Congress. Ice-breakers were becoming more necessary nowadays as prospecting and extraction of Russia's natural mineral resources were moving further east and north, in the Arctic regions.

During my Arkhangelsk visit, I saw one very modern port facility for totally mechanised container handling, but I knew that this was the exception rather than the rule. Were the workers worried about their manual jobs getting replaced by machines, I asked. Arkhangelsk's Northern Sea Union chairman, Vladimir Prokofyev, assured me that no-one there would be left without a job. "Fewer seamen will be needed on the newer highly mechanised ships, it's true," he admitted. "But jobs can only be cut if the Trade Union Committee agrees - and there's one on every ship!"

The TU Committee will regulate the process," he assured me. "Jobs will be found onshore, in ship-repair, in ports or in the service industries. And we have comprehensive re-training schemes."

It all seemed very positive and optimistic. But I had the impression that they were only just starting to get to grips with the problems that would undoubtedly arise if the Party's ambitious plans for the economy were really to be put into practice.

It was the magical White Nights season and I enjoyed a memorable boat trip down the River Dvina. The sun never disappears behind the horizon; beyond the Polar Circle days are much longer than nights, the latter resembling dawns. It was so beautiful – and relaxing – standing on deck leaning against the ship's railing, in that eerie blue-tinted light of the warm arctic summer night, the little settlements and villages slowly coming into view and disappearing as we glided past. I had a long conversation with a Soviet colleague, Yuri, usually a rather introverted and shy man, who on that late evening leisurely trip shared with me some of his feelings about life, his work in Africa and the different places we each had experience of.

The next day it was the usual frenetic schedule – a visit to a merchant navy school, then lunch at the Seamen's InterClub, then to a shopping mall to buy souvenirs. I always tried to find something for the children to take back as a little present. And, as on other trips, I ended up with numerous gifts of books about the shipyards, training schools and museums I'd been to, plus a history of the city.

After our 2-hour evening flight back to Moscow, I had to take a taxi back home – and was immediately faced with reality: the new lift in our block of flats still wasn't finished, so I had to walk up the nine flights, with all my heavy books and brochures.

While I was in Arkhangelsk, the 8th Congress of Soviet Writers was taking place, culminating in a third of the old leadership being voted out in the new atmosphere of *glasnost* and change.

Writers in the Soviet Union had a privileged existence, at least, if they were admitted to that august body of published writers. Books and the hefty literary journals, such as *Novy Mir, Znamya* or *Oktyabr* had big circulations and were usually the first in publishing excerpts from contentious or previously-banned works, to "test the waters", before widespread publication. Editors had sometimes found themselves in trouble for their decisions, but that very fact shows how much freedom they actually had in taking decisions on what to publish. There was a censorship body, called *Glavlit,* which had the final say; under the Soviet Constitution pornography, race or ethnic hatred, and glorification of war were outlawed. But, as the popular satirical magazine *Ogonyok*'s Editor, Vitali Korotich, told the Writers' Congress: "Censorship has sometimes been used to block the publication of works the censors simply did not like."

Whilst not having the remit (officially, at least) of checking the literary content of works, nor their political bias, a Foreign Ministry official told me, *Glavlit* also had to check that no military, economic or political state secrets were published.

The popular poet, Yevgeny Yevtushenko, elected to the Writers' Union leadership at this Congress, predicted that *Dr Zhivago* by Boris Pasternak, would see the light of day in the Soviet Union. Pasternak had been a person who had "never found his place in his era", Yevtushenko argued, but had "never been a counterrevolutionary." Yevtushenko was right: it was published two years later, in 1988.

People often ask me: "Did you like living in Moscow?" They often seemed to have a rather negative view of what living there would be like, as if somehow you couldn't have a normal life there. Perhaps it was due to the negative reporting in the West, where Moscow often seemed to be described as "drab" or "grey".... Actually, the centre of Moscow is beautiful, and Ricardo and I used to enjoy walking around the little back streets, finding tiny churches tucked away in some unexpected corner. The Kremlin is really beautiful, its high dark red brick walls surrounding a large area within the fortress walls, where there were yellow and white-painted government buildings, a splendid Palace of Congresses, built in 1960, where concerts and ballets were sometimes performed, well-kept gardens, opulent churches and historical relics like the *tsar-pushka* - a big cannon, displayed on Ivanovskaya Square, between the Ivan the Great Bell Tower and the Twelve Apostles' Church. The cannon was never fired, and today sits on its pedestal, surrounded by tourists.

Our daughters have fond recollections of the beautiful night scene from our flat, with the River Moskva part iced-over and the lights twinkling in the distance among the Kremlin towers and churches.

There are many other parts of the city which are attractive and have historical significance, but it is also true that the outlying suburbs with their many tower blocks were not very attractive. There was little attempt at beautifying the surrounding area, with tree-planting or gardens. Inside, the flats were well-designed and quite spacious, certainly compared with the so-called "*khrushchovki*".

This was an ambitious Soviet housing project that provided urgently-needed housing for millions during the post-war years. A year after Stalin's death, in 1954, Soviet leader Nikita Khrushchov[56] announced a nationwide effort to build housing cheaply and quickly. The distinctive five-storey *khrushchovki*, made either of reinforced concrete and prefab panels, or sometimes of sturdier materials like brick, could be seen all over the Soviet Union. Millions of Russians continue to live in them today. They helped to solve the housing crisis, improving living standards for many, and are thus perhaps Khrushchov's most positive legacy.

Over the years, trees have grown tall around the buildings, making them some of the greenest places in the city. Nursery schools and clinics were usually built nearby, and many blocks were built around pleasant courtyards with trees, benches where old people would sit and chat and children's play areas. We had friends who lived in *khrushchovki* and although they did not have lifts, and kitchens and bathrooms were small, the other rooms were of a decent size.

In 1986, some twenty percent of the capital's population still lived in shared flats, or *kommunalki,* despite an impressive rate of housebuilding over the decades since the end of the war. But as new Moscow leader, Boris Yeltsin, told Moscow's Communist Party leadership in March that year, building was still much too slow.

Our friends Otto and Tamara lived in a better-quality block of flats, built and owned by a cooperative, in the suburb of Cheryomushki. All residents contributed a given amount, the state provided materials and the cooperative organised the work to get the block of flats built. Their flat was very nice, with rooms of a good size.

Our friend Irina and family lived in a *kommunalka* in an old, pre-revolutionary building not far from the centre. Obviously it cannot have been easy to live in those conditions – sharing a kitchen and bathroom with other neighbours. Perhaps that was one of the factors in Irina and Boris getting divorced. Or perhaps Irina had already fallen in love with Kamal, a Syrian postgraduate student, who became her new partner. We were very pleased when we got a call from her one day telling us that she had been

---

56 I use this spelling for the same reason as explained in Footnote 3 concerning the transliteration of Gorbachov's name.

allotted a brand-new 2-bedroom flat in a new suburb just outside the outer ring road. We went to see them with their little boy, Igor, and were glad to see that Nastya, who was 13 by then, at last had her own room.

Moscow summers are short but sunny and warm. We would take a bus or suburban train or *raketa* (hydrofoil) to places outside the city and enjoy the afternoon sunbathing, swimming in lakes and ponds and walking in the woods. Kuzminki Park for instance is beautiful and natural, with ponds and beaches and no traffic for miles – yet it is quite close to the city. Like many other such parks, Kuzminki had been an 18th century stately home, and there were interesting estate buildings, a church and stables to see. I love outdoor swimming, and one of the things I most enjoyed in my Moscow summers was swimming in small lakes and ponds we would come across as we drove out into the countryside. If we saw other people bathing, we would park up and join them. Outdoor swimming gives you a sense of freedom nothing else gives you, and I loved the fact that there were so many freshwater ponds which were readily accessible round Moscow.

There were lots of frustrations about living in Moscow at that time. I wonder if it is any different in today's Russia, now that the Soviet Union and the Soviet system no longer exist? I suspect many things continue to be frustrating, because bureaucracy, high-handedness and surliness, in shops, for instance, may well be throwbacks from history. I have talked elsewhere about the ubiquitous use of "*nyelzya*" (not allowed) probably being a result of centuries of autocracy under the tsars and the creeping authoritarianism which characterised later decades.

In Britain, the Industrial Revolution gave rise to a working class, living close together in towns and cities, from which organisations sprang up such as trades unions, mutual societies and political movements like the Chartists and later, political parties such as the Labour Party, the Independent Labour Party (ILP) and the Communist Party. In Russia most of that long period was under autocratic rule. Russian artisans and craftspeople did set up local cooperatives - *arteli* - which were run by the members themselves and flourished after the abolition of serfdom in 1861. The political parties that were formed, like the Russian Social Democratic Labour Party, though well-organised, were still relatively small and concentrated in the big cities at the time of the Revolution in 1917.

There was not a long history in Russia of people organising themselves in the way that there is in Britain. This is not the place to go into further detail on this, but I am sure that our long democratic tradition of trades unions, working men's clubs, the women's suffrage movement and all the thousands and thousands of professional and popular organisations, from Parent-teacher bodies to golf club committees, from the Women's Institutes and Coop Guilds to Greenpeace, Friends of the Earth and CND, to mention but a few, will stand us in good stead if we ever elect a truly progressive government in our country with the aim of democratic socialism.

One day I got back home about 4pm, and saw that my Foreign Editor was asking about a story the wires had reported on - a *Moscow News* story about former Soviet leader Vyacheslav Molotov. I hadn't seen the story, so phoned *Moscow News* and asked them to give me the gist of their piece. They wouldn't tell me, so I went to a nearby kiosk, but they'd sold out, so I decided to go to their offices, only to find out that their piece was no more detailed than the short piece I had already seen on the TASS wire. "Another complete waste of time," I wrote ruefully in my diary for that day, 3rd July. Why couldn't the person I spoke to at *Moscow News* give me a resumé of their piece, I thought to myself. And like that day, I experienced many other frustrations at the bureaucracy and high-handed attitudes that prevailed.

It wasn't made any easier by the fact that, unlike my fellow Western correspondents, I didn't have a car. I soon realised that if I was going to be an effective correspondent I had to be able to use time efficiently, which meant not having to wait for buses and walking long distances from one place to another. A few months later it was arranged for me to have the long-term loan of a car – a comfortable and very reliable Lada 1700 - which made a huge difference to our lives.

When I look back at my diaries for those years, I often have to laugh. There were things that happened there that I don't think would happen anywhere else. For instance, all flats had central heating emanating from thermal power stations (like the one across the Moscow River from us, which had the Lenin dictum: "*Communism is Soviet power plus the electrification of the whole country!*" emblazoned over the length of its façade. The heating was great on our ninth floor – but you couldn't regulate it by turning the radiators down, so the only way to cool the flat was to open the little windows – *fortochki* – that all Soviet flats have, and let the cold winter air in. I spent all the winters in summer clothes at home because our flat was so warm.

But every summer, in mid July, hot water was cut off for three weeks, for the annual overhaul and repairs. This was a bit of a shock to the system, literally - cold showers only! Heating being centrally controlled, not from the individual block of flats itself, meant that at a certain date in October, your central heating was switched on – but *only* then, even if it had turned cold two weeks earlier! Similarly, central heating was switched off everywhere some time in late spring whatever the temperature outside.

But the heating was very efficient, and incredibly cheap, so in time we accepted the oddities of the system and were grateful for the constant central heating which made the harsh Moscow winters more bearable.

That summer 1986, after the children had spent 5 weeks in Pioneer Camp, there were still several weeks of summer holiday left before they started back at school on 1st September. We decided to spend a month in Britain, to see our relatives whom we hadn't seen for a year. My mother, Win, had had a stroke two years earlier, and it was very hard, when I made my weekly phone call home, to hold a conversation with her, as her speech was badly affected.

111

I was happy, though, to hear my Dad say that when their papers came in the morning, the first thing she would do was to look through the *Morning Star* to see if there was any article by me or if my byline was on any news item.

My mother was a wonderful person, a lovely mother, mother-in-law, grandmother and friend. She had been an active Communist all her adult life, after a few years in the Independent Labour Party; she was also Chair of Chesterfield Cooperative Women's Guild and a founder member and activist of CND. But she always had time for my brother Joe and me, and we had many happy times together, going on walks and picnics as well as accompanying her on Party outings, fund-raising bazaars and jumble sales. I can always remember her playing ball – a game called sevenses – with me in the garden, whilst at the same time testing me on Latin verbs, a list of which she had in one hand, while we threw and caught the ball. It was her way of trying to make revision a bit more bearable for me.

So it was good to see her and my Dad again, though I could see that despite my sister-in-law Shirley's best efforts to help Mum with writing and speech therapy, there had been little improvement and the outlook was poor. My father shouldered the burden of looking after her, doing the shopping and cooking meals, and they seemed to be managing well with help from my brother and family who lived nearby.

I often felt guilty that I had left her and gone to work in Moscow. But I also knew, deep down, that my mother, who was the most unselfish person I've ever known, would not have wanted it any other way. She backed our decision to go and work in Moscow, not only because it was a political commitment that she supported, but also because she knew that Ricardo and I had to think first and foremost of our children and their future, which meant that we needed to work and have an income.

Back in Moscow, our children returned to school on 1st September, holding the traditional bouquets of flowers for their teacher. They looked smart in their freshly pressed uniforms, and were excited and happy to be seeing their schoolfriends again.

But that same day Liza came home complaining of a tummy ache she had had on and off all day. We put her to bed but by evening her temperature had risen to 39.5, and even with wet towels applied and lots to drink, it was still 39. When it rose to 39.7 I rang the Polyclinic and a doctor came in less than half an hour. He diagnosed a stomach infection, or gastroenteritis, and gave her an injection to bring the temperature down. She was very poorly during the night and slept most of the next day, when the doctor came again.

Liza had been ill the year before with gastritis, and had spent several weeks in hospital, but seemed to have recovered completely. Yet now the same thing was happening again. Perhaps again it was something in the school breakfasts that disagreed with her, as she had been fine all summer when she wasn't at school. There were complaints from parents about the quality of the food served at school, but I had not taken them very seriously since she

112

had been well for most of the year after her hospital treatment.

Being hospitalised the year before, when we had only been in the country three months, was somewhat traumatic for Liza, who was only just 7, and still didn't speak the language very well. To make matters worse, due to an infection, her hospital wing had been put in quarantine, which meant that we were not allowed into the building, and could only speak to her through the window.

Yet she had appeared at the window, smiling happily at us and holding up her new toys, not seeming distressed in any way. Later she told us that all the doctors and nurses had made a real fuss of her and she had enjoyed playing with the other children on the ward. Liza herself remembers making the other children laugh by making a squelching noise with her eyes, somehow! She recalls having an exploratory endoscopy, with a camera on the end of a tube and feeling very proud of herself that she hadn't cried. "It wasn't painful, just a bit uncomfortable," Liza says, remembering how amazed she had been at being able to see her insides on the screen. Still, I'm sure it must have been hard for her, especially to be without her twin, Martha, as they had always been inseparable.

Our experiences with polyclinics and hospitals were good, and, as in the NHS, free of charge. The polyclinic system had some advantages over our GP surgery system, in that they could provide X-rays and lab analysis, as well as specialist doctors, so you only went to hospital if you needed to be admitted. On the other hand, in Britain, GP's are much more likely to be local, so a visit to see a doctor is quicker than having to cross town to go to a polyclinic. Both systems have their advantages.

On this occasion, the doctor recommended Liza stay off school for a couple of weeks, so Ricardo and I had to take turns staying with her at home. It's always difficult for working parents when their children are off sick from school.

Living in Moscow we always heard news of the Soviet cosmonauts working on the Soviet MIR space station. TV news frequently showed cosmonauts working there and gave information about their research, the salads that they were managing to grow and how they were managing to keep fit and prevent muscle wastage in conditions of zero gravity. There were joint flights with astronauts from other countries, and when a Houses of Parliament delegation came to Moscow in June 1986, they received an offer for a British astronaut to train and join a future mission.

In fact, it would not be till 1991 that a British astronaut, Helen Sharman, flew to MIR after several months' training at Star City, the cosmonauts' training centre outside Moscow.

You could see the Soviet cosmonauts Leonid Kizim and Vladimir Solovyov live from the MIR space complex, on a giant TV screen on Arbat Street in central Moscow and on special occasions people could put questions to the cosmonauts. From talking to Soviet people, you realised that they knew quite a lot about what the cosmonauts were engaged in: surveys of natural resources, glaciers, mountain ranges, farmlands, also weather forecasting and examination of the earth's ozone layer.

1986 was the year when *glasnost* really became a reality, and became a household word even outside the Soviet Union. We could, of course, have used 'transparency', which also has the connotation, in English, of something desirable in political life. But such was the volume of criticism and revelations about wrongdoings, shortcomings, crimes and privileges that all foreign journalists started using the Russian terms *perestroika* and *glasnost* to describe what was going on under the new leader Mikhail Gorbachov.

Several senior Party officials in Kazakhstan were arrested for bribe-taking. In July 1986 Soviet Communist Party daily *Pravda* asked: "How is it possible for people of this kind to get into positions of responsibility, and who is to blame for this?"

In Ukraine, one in five factories were not meeting targets; in some, machine-building designs were outdated before they were even manufactured. In Kirghizia, the Minister for Light Industry was slammed for allowing defective products to get into the shops and for not updating machinery in good time. Lithuania had problems with alcoholism, unearned income and wastefulness in the economy. There was no end to it - and very little positive or praiseworthy.

We were fortunate in being able to go to concerts of all kinds, as well as plays, ballets, operas and films. You could often see, in the stalls at the Bolshoi Theatre, for instance, a big group from some factory or works, out on a theatre trip organised for them by their place of work, at very reasonable prices. Anybody could afford the tickets: the problem was getting hold of them, as they were always in great demand by Moscow's culture-loving citizens. But in that I was privileged, as a correspondent, and could usually get tickets for whatever I wanted to see. It was very common outside theatres and concert-halls that people would come up to you with the question: "*U vas yest' sluchaino lishniy bilyet?*" (Have you got a spare ticket by any chance?)

One evening we went to a concert at the Rossiya Hotel, on the Moscow River embankment, within walking distance of our block, with the famous poet, Yevgeny Yevtushenko and the Paul Winter jazz group from the USA. Winter had begun travelling to Russia a few years earlier and became a pioneer of ecological music after visiting Siberia's Lake Baikal. At this concert, the music incorporated whale sounds and the haunting calls of wolves in an original and beautiful way. Yevtushenko was a commanding presence: tall, slim, energetic, with his wide Siberian cheekbones, he would stride about the stage as he declaimed his poetry. He was very popular in the Soviet Union, and well-known in the West too, of course. He was somewhat critical of authority, with a rebellious streak that endeared people to him. But he never really fell foul of the authorities, somehow managing to tread the line between sharp criticism of what he saw as the system's failings alongside an acceptance of the basic tenets of the socialist system that his homeland had forged.

That evening he recited his famous *Babi Yar* - a poem about the Nazis' massacre of many thousands of Jews near Kiev in Ukraine. When, as a young man, the poet had visited the site of the massacre, he had found no commemoration stone, no monument, not even a plaque. This disturbed Yevtushenko and inspired his poem. Babi Yar is a large ravine and the site of a mass grave into which the Nazi SS squads threw their victims, killed between 1941 and 1943. After the initial massacre of Jews, the Nazis used Babi Yar as an execution site for Soviet prisoners of war and for Roma as well as Jews. Soviet accounts after the war speak of 100,000 dead. The true number may never be known. Babi Yar became the symbol of the first stage of killing during the Holocaust and of the massacres by the *Einsatzgruppen* - the Nazi mobile killing units.

In 1961, in protest against plans to build a sports stadium on the site, Yevtushenko wrote *Babi Yar*, which begins:

No monuments stand over Babi Yar,
  A sudden drop sheer as a gross grave slab.
I am here terrified.
.....
    The wild grass rustles over Babi Yar.
  Trees stare down stern,
    judicial,
      cold as day.
All things scream silent here.
    Hat in my arm,
I feel myself now
    slowly growing grey.
  And I myself
    am one all-out soundless scream
For the thousand buried thousands in this char.
I'm every old man
          shot in this ravine,
I'm every baby
    burned in Babi Yar.

No fiber in me
  will forget this ever.
.....

(Translated by A.Z. Foreman)

A year later the poem was set to music by Dmitri Shostakovich as part of his choral 13th Symphony, first performed in Moscow in December 1962.

According to Britannica.com website, both Yevtushenko and Shostakovich were reprimanded by the Soviet authorities, who were reluctant to accept the special Jewish significance of a site where so many other, non-Jewish, Soviet citizens had been killed.

In 1966 a small obelisk was put up at Babi Yar, then in 1974 a 15-metre memorial statue was erected.

That memorable evening at the Rossiya Hotel concert-hall Yevtushenko also recited *Hymn to Baikal*, *Ode at the Elbe* and *Sleep my Love*. In general, poetry was popular with Soviet people, and it is no exaggeration to say that the public in that packed hall was enthralled by Yevtushenko's readings. Later, we would have another chance to hear the poet in an even bigger setting, and to meet him in person.

The *Morning Star* had always covered Chile and the struggle of the Chilean people against the Pinochet dictatorship after September 1973. Our paper played a big role in reporting on the Chile Solidarity Campaign, very active in Britain from September 1973 until 1991. At the time we left for Moscow in 1985, I was on the Executive Committee of the Campaign. As several top Chilean Communist Party (CCP) leaders lived in exile in Moscow, I was able to interview them. In September 1986, thirteen years after the coup, a group called the Manuel Rodriguez Patriotic Front[57] which had been set up under the auspices of the CCP, made a bold, but unsuccessful, assassination attempt on the life of General Pinochet. Even more savage arrests, torture and disappearances in Chile followed. I interviewed one of the Party's leaders, Orlando Millas, immediately after the assassination attempt. Millas, who had been a Popular Unity Government Minister in President Allende's Government, told me:

"It was Pinochet who assassinated our constitutional President Salvador Allende; he who ordered the murder of our Armed Forces Chief-of-Staff, General Carlos Prats and his wife[58], it was he who ordered the assassination of Allende's Defence Minister Orlando Letelier[59], and who has had tens of thousands of Chilean citizens killed."

Pinochet was responsible for the recent murder of three young teachers in Santiago, he said, and under his dictatorship victims had been set alight, savagely tortured and thrown from helicopters into the sea. The assassination attempt, Millas told me, was carried out by the MRPF, which was an autonomous organisation responsible for its own actions. "But we admire their patriotic courage." It was distressing for us to learn of the savage reprisals that followed this failed assassination attempt on Pinochet.

---

57 Manuel Rodriguez Patriotic Front, named after the 19th century Chilean guerrilla leader, one of the founders of independent Chile.

58 Killed by a car bomb on September 30th 1974, in the Argentinian capital Buenos Aires.

59 Assassinated by a car bomb in Washington on 21st September 1976, together with a work colleague, Ronni Moffit.

The Soviet Union had declared a moratorium on underground nuclear testing in August 1985. But the US continued testing. In September 1986 a small group of Western journalists, including myself, had the unique chance to visit the Semipalatinsk nuclear testing ground in Kazakhstan.

On the flight to Semipalatinsk, I got chatting to Eileen O'Connor, a TV correspondent for ABC (American Broadcasting Company). I had often seen her lugging heavy TV equipment around and was secretly glad that, at barely 5 feet tall, I didn't have to do that for my journalism. Chatting during the long flight, I discovered that Eileen had been a classmate of the son of a Chilean friend of ours, Isabel Morel, widow of Orlando Letelier, who had been Chile's Ambassador to Washington during the Popular Unity Government of President Salvador Allende. Letelier had held important ministerial positions and in the military coup d'état of September 11, 1973, he was arrested, tortured and held at different concentration camps until finally, due to international diplomatic pressure, he was released on condition that he immediately leave Chile. So in 1975 Letelier moved to Washington D.C. and was a vocal critic of the so-called "Chicago Boys", the group of free-market South American economists trained at the University of Chicago by Milton Friedman, whose neo-liberal policies were being put into practice in Chile under the dictatorship. A year later Letelier was assassinated in Washington by agents of General Pinochet's secret police, the DINA.

So Eileen knew about the military coup in Chile and its aftermath from Orlando's son at university in the US, where Letelier's widow, Isabel, and sons continued to live. During that trip, I also got to know Reuters bureau chief, Bob Evans, who was a pleasant companion.

A helicopter took us to a secret military location some 90 miles from a closed military town which didn't have a name or even figure on maps, on the banks of the river Irtysh.

We were taken to a tunnel which had been prepared for a future underground nuclear test if the moratorium were lifted. We were led inside that eerie dark passage by General Arkady Ilyenko, commander of the test zone, who told us he hoped no further tests would ever be necessary. "We don't need another war," General Ilyenko told us, "because there'll be no victors in the next war!" Geiger counters at the site showed near-normal radiation, we were glad to see. But the strange shattered rocks covering the surface of the surrounding hillsides told their own story - of the massive shocks those Degelen Hills had experienced during all the years of underground nuclear testing. Each tunnel deep into the hillside, prepared for an underground test, could only be used once, due to the massive destruction caused by such explosions, and were therefore a very expensive business, Ilyenko said. "We'd like to seal the explosion shafts off for good and leave the area to nature," Ilyenko said.

As I looked around at the shattered rocks on the hillside, I saw a wild goat – *arkhar* - standing proud on the summit, profiled against the clear blue sky.

These hills were *their* terrain, I reflected, not for nuclear testing.

It was a sobering experience. Now, as I look back, I think the features I wrote then captured not only the drama of the time and place, but my own personal feelings as to the senselessness and futility of nuclear weapons and the enormous danger they pose to the entire human race.

We left the site by helicopter making for the town of Karkaraly, whose population was largely Kazakh. On the way we could see some quite poor buildings and I noticed someone far below pumping water from a roadside well. Once again, I thought of the waste of money that the nuclear arms race entailed, when it could have been used to pipe running water to every home in rural locations like these.

The closed military town we stayed in, which only figured as a number (Semipalatinsk 21) on military maps and which was opened to us foreigners for the first time, was about an hour's flight from Semipalatinsk by light aircraft, flying, I was told, at 400 km per hour. It was quite an attractive place, with the river Irtysh flowing through it, and a pleasant central square with a statue of Igor Kurchatov, the head of the Soviet nuclear programme.

Now officially named after Kurchatov, the town was founded alongside the establishment of the Semipalatinsk Test Site, for which it served as the administrative, logistical and scientific centre for some 40 years. At its peak, it had up to 40,000 inhabitants. But after the closure of the test site, and the departure of the Soviet military, numbers have dwindled to about a quarter of that.

During my trip, I met two American seismologists in Karkaralinsk, in the north of Kazakhstan. From the University of Nevada, they were setting up American seismic equipment there, near the nuclear test site, under a bilateral agreement with the Natural Resources Defense Council, a US non-governmental organisation. Soviet scientists were due to fly to Nevada on September 14th, but by 28th September when I talked to their American counterparts, David Chavez and David Carrel, they had still not been issued with US visas.

A Soviet Foreign Ministry spokesman, Boris Pyadyshev, told journalists that US conditions imposed on the Soviet seismologists due to visit Nevada meant that they could only go to Nevada as "guests of the US Government" and they would be made to witness a US underground test. Since the Soviet side had refrained from testing for 14 months by then, he said: "We have no intention of going to Nevada to sanction US nuclear tests!"

It was an unforgettable trip and I was deeply conscious of this being a privilege accorded to very few journalists at the time – to glimpse the nuclear testing facilities of one of the world's two superpowers and get a feel from talking to the military people who were our hosts that they were deadly serious about the moratorium from their side, as a move that could go some way towards the new Soviet leader Gorbachov's declared aim, in January 1986, of a nuclear-free world.

The following month, in October 1986, Gorbachov and Ronald Reagan held their second summit in the Icelandic capital, Reykjavik. I wasn't there, but from the reports I read and watched, I formed the opinion that Gorbachov could run rings round Reagan, whose grasp of the minutiae of the two countries' nuclear arsenals and of previous agreements reached seemed somewhat tenuous - whereas Gorbachov was smart, well briefed and had a clear vision of what he wanted to achieve. At their two-day summit, the two presidents did, in fact, almost reach agreement on extensive cuts to offensive arms at that summit. Pundits hailed it as a "breakthrough" in nuclear arms control.

It was agreed in principle to remove INF (Intermediate Nuclear Forces) systems from Europe and eliminate all nuclear weapons in 10 years (by 1996), instead of by the year 2000 as in Gorbachov's original outline. Continuing trust issues, particularly over reciprocity and Reagan's Strategic Defense Initiative (SDI), meant that the summit is often regarded as a failure for not producing a concrete agreement immediately, or for leading to a staged elimination of nuclear weapons. It did, however, culminate in the signing of the Intermediate-Range Nuclear Forces (INF) Treaty in 1987.

That October, 1986, UB-40 came to Moscow and I went to see the group at the packed Lenin Stadium, where they had the audience dancing in their seats. The group, very popular in the USSR, told fans they were donating part of their concert fees to the Chernobyl disaster fund. UB-40's impressions of the Soviet Union? "I haven't found it as austere and as grey as it's painted through the Western media," said saxophonist Brian Travers. And they were impressed by the wide-ranging peace initiatives of the new leadership.

"Austere" and "grey" - these were the standard epithets Western correspondents used in their pieces about the Soviet Union at that time. Most used them again and again, to describe the housing estates, tower blocks and streets of any city they were in. I used to wonder if any of them had ever visited some of the older council estates in Manchester, Liverpool, Glasgow or Newcastle .... Was it just lazy journalism, or was it what their editors expected of them?

It was always a welcome break from trips, endless press conferences and keeping up with the press and media when comrades and friends came to Moscow. Ken Gill, who was TUC Vice-Chair at the time and General Secretary of the manufacturing union TASS (later MSF) came to an international conference on the Working Class and the Contemporary World, so we met up a few times. In his speech Ken said that the tragic Chernobyl accident had concentrated people's minds on the nuclear danger. "If one industrial accident can cause such international panic," he said, "how can anyone, under any circumstances, maintain that nuclear arms are anything but a threat to the existence of the human race?"

The Conference dealt with the role of trades unions and their defence of working-class people under capitalism. Ken Gill always said things his way: here he said: "When the motor car replaced the horse, it was great for human beings, but not so good for the horse!" People say that microprocessors will replace people in the workplace, he went on, but "unlike horses, we've got the vote, we've got trades unions and we've got political working-class organisations to defend ourselves."

He told the Conference about the militarisation of the British economy, in which the best-qualified scientists and engineers were creamed off by arms companies and the Ministry of Defence. There was little worthwhile spin-off from military technology to the development of socially useful civilian products. Ken, refuting such claims to that effect by the military, cited the eminent scientist, Sir Monty Finnisten, who was quoted as saying: "That's a hell of an expensive way to invent the non-stick frying-pan!"

"Economic activity is not an end in itself, but a means to creating a better life for all," Ken said. "This is a fundamental principle both for trades unions and the political movement."

I came to appreciate Ken Gill's wisdom and humour, his understanding for the difficult job I was doing and his unflinching support over the years, as a member of the *Morning Star*'s Management Committee.

Labour Party members, including councillor Jill Jones, from my home town, Chesterfield, came that October and we had a memorable meeting with the Soviet Peace Committee's Deputy Chair, Vladimir Oryol, when they presented him with a beautiful "Scroll of Peace" outlining the noble aims of the Derbyshire County Council Federation of Peace Groups, in which my brother and sister-in-law were very active.

This Labour group also handed the Soviet Communist Party a letter for General Secretary Gorbachov, from Tony Benn, MP for Chesterfield, which appeared in the *Morning Star* of October 21st 1986.

At the end of October 1986 I went to Tbilisi, the capital of Georgia. Ricardo and I had dined several times in Moscow's famous Georgian restaurant, the Aragvi, rightly loved for its atmosphere, cuisine and good Georgian wine. *Lobio, satsivi, shashlik,* chicken livers, caviar, dumpling *khinkali* and the chopped salad *pkhali* were just some of the dishes you could enjoy there.

At that time all the restaurants were state-run, and several bore the names of the capitals of the Soviet republics, and of other East European capitals, such as the Prague and Sofia restaurants.

A Soviet booklet in Russian that I brought back with me, titled "Georgian SSR" (Soviet Socialist Republic) says that Georgia has an ancient history and culture dating back to paleolithic times and that at different times it had been subject to attempts at suppression by various invaders, including Rome, Byzantium, the Mongols, Turks and Persians. In 1801 Georgia became part of the Russian empire under Catherine the Great's son, Tsar Paul I.

The old centre of Tbilisi is beautiful, orange-trees and quinces lining narrow roads along the Kura river. Whilst there, I learnt that Georgia provided the Soviet Union with 97% of its tea and 99% of citrus fruits.

I had the opportunity to go round a milk factory in Tbilisi, which, I was told, produced 140,000 tonnes of milk and 4,000 of cheese. We heard statistics of salaries and wage rates, holiday schemes, 70% paid for by the factory's management and 30% by the trade union. They had a 7-hour day, working a day shift only. We learnt of the serious housing problem, though 10,000 flats were being built annually on average, but still not every family had a flat of their own. We learnt that there were 3 metro stations in Tbilisi and five more envisaged in the current 5-year plan. The city had 45,000 nursery places, but 90,000 nursery-age children. City Council Chair - something like our Mayors - Tamaz Paichadze - told me that most children stayed at home with mothers or grandparents till they were at least 18 months old, according to Georgian tradition.

Paichadze told us that Tbilisi had about 100,000 cars, but the Council's emphasis was on developing public transport. I discovered that local schools taught not only Georgian, but Russian, Armenian and Azerbaijani, to cater for the main nationalities living there. We went on excursions to see fruit orchards, saw a road sign "Stalin Avenue" (Stalin was of Georgian nationality) and noticed women playing chess in open-air chess groups (Georgia is famous for its female chess champions). I learnt that the Georgian language has existed since at least the 5th century BC.

Georgia is well known for her innovative film directors and drama theatres, and in the arts in general, Georgia played a role far beyond what could have been expected of a country of a mere 5 million population. The Georgian language "has its own alphabet, which is different from all other alphabets", according to my Georgia guidebook. And I could see as I walked around Tbilisi's pleasant streets, in the warm autumnal air, that street and shop names were all in the totally unfamiliar Georgian script, as well as in Russian. At the Museum of a famous theatre director, Kote Mardzhanishvili, born in 1872, most of the information was in the Georgian script, totally unintelligible to me. I remember a picture on the wall of peasants mashing grapes with their bare feet during wine-making – and being told that the wine made that way tasted even better.

At another museum we visited, dedicated to the poet Ilya Chavchavadze, all the information was in Georgian, with translation into Russian alongside. Chavchavadze was a romantic poet in the 1840's who was credited with reforming the Georgian alphabet and was the first Georgian prince to grant freedom to his serfs in 1861 when serfdom was abolished.

We were lucky to be invited into the flat of a famous Georgian artist, Lado Gudiachvili, who had died six years previously. He had been a friend of Mayakovsky and Pasternak, his daughter told us. I had never heard of Gudiachvili. It is at times like these when one realises one's ignorance - and the limitations of what can be expected of a foreign correspondent, who usually lacks deep knowledge of another country's culture - especially, that of a country so varied and diverse, with so many languages, ethnicities and customs, as the USSR.

I was interested to find out how Gorbachov's anti-alcohol campaign was going down in Georgia, so famous for its good wines. "We mainly drink dry dinner wines," Shota Kutidze, director of one factory we looked round - the Tbilisi *Zhirkombinat* (literally, fat combine). "Even if they've outlawed it, we still find it!" he told us, grinning. "We drink wine in a healthy way." (The inference being "unlike Russian vodka which is not drunk in a healthy way…")

As so often when I would go round factories and works, you couldn't fail to be impressed by a lot of facilities they enjoyed - like sports halls, swimming pool, billiard hall, massage room for 20 workers at a time, holiday sanatorium and holiday homes (called "rest homes" in the Soviet Union), nurseries and housing provided by the trade unions at very low rents. It all sounded pretty impressive - plus, of course, job security which was sacrosanct at that time. I knew, however, that things were far from rosy, since housing was insufficient, food supplies erratic and clothing, footwear and home goods of inadequate quality.

Yet still, when you remembered what the country was like under tsarism, before the Revolution, the poverty and inequality that existed everywhere then, I concluded that big advances *had* been made, and that at least this was a more equal society than capitalist societies.

We visited Kindzmaraulski wine-making concern where, down a passageway built into the hillside, you could see huge vats of wine. "It's a wine mountain!" head of production, Eduard Lekviashvili told us. We took the lift up to the second floor – and emerged halfway up the mountain. From the viewing balcony, you could see kilometres of vineyards stretching as far as the eye could see.

In Soviet times Georgia was home to hundreds of sanatoria and holiday homes, both in the Caucasus mountains and on the beautiful coast, at resorts like Sukhumi and Pitsunda. It was famous both for its cuisine and its excellent wines. I was to experience both at a dinner held for our group, which comprised

A sweet paper wrapper in Georgian and Russian – *Red Riding Hood*

correspondents from the socialist countries and myself. We were driven along a zig-zag route up a mountainside to an attractive hostelry with wooden panels and folkloric features adorning the façade. We hardly had chance to look around and sample the fresh mountain air before we were whisked inside a large room with a long table, lavishly set with immaculate cutlery, plates and crystal wine glasses. I was seated next to Teresa, Cuba's *Prensa Latina* correspondent and opposite a journalist from the Communist Party of Yugoslavia newspaper, *Borba* (Struggle), whose name I forget. Georgian tradition has it that at such dinners, there is a master of ceremonies called a *tamada* in Georgian.

A *tamada*'s job is to make toasts throughout the dinner. The ideal *tamada*, one Georgian website says, should be "well educated, intelligent, sharp-witted, polite, honorable, sociable, have a good sense of humour, have musical ability, be a lover of poetry, be romantic, deeply nostalgic, eloquent, and last but not least, a good drinker."

On this occasion, our *tamada* and our Yugoslav colleague had a friendly rivalry as to who could withstand the most glasses of wine, both of them from wine-making countries and cultures. It seemed a bit silly, but harmless enough.

The toasts came and went, each guest making speeches as they thought fit. Traditionally it is only men who made toasts, and, of course, most of our party were men. So Teresa and I decided: to hell with convention, we would break the mould and make speeches ourselves, as the only women there. We both made toasts in the spirit of internationalism which, despite breaking with tradition, went down very well.

We had begun the lunch around 1pm, and it ended some time in the early evening. And as the toasts became ever more flowery and long drawn-out, I looked across at our Yugoslav friend and saw that his face had gone a greenish colour. Next thing we knew, he had slumped in his chair and collapsed to the floor. The Georgian *tamada* had won.

The rest of my Georgian trip passed in a bit of a haze – whether it was the amount of alcohol we had all consumed, as our glasses kept getting filled up whether we wanted or not, I don't know. But I do remember being chatted up by one middle-aged Georgian Party official at the hotel where we were staying, who ended up making me a proposition he felt he had to apologise for the next morning.

In general I did not experience sexism during my six years as correspondent and felt well-respected. There was, however, the time in December 1985 when I visited the Elektrozavod Kuibishev works in the outer suburbs of Moscow in the company of a young man called Nikolai from the Foreign Ministry staff, who had been asked to accompany me on the visit, which was to look at how they were introducing 'self-financing'.

As soon as he met me and began chatting, Nikolai remarked admiringly: "And you even write about *politics*, don't you?" as if this were an amazing discovery. *What an idiot*, I thought to myself. What can one reply to a remark like that?

Even our neighbour, Viktor, who was a Soviet diplomat on a visit home from Africa, expressed some surprising views once when we were invited to dinner. I noted in my diary at the time: "Viktor came out with his anti-women-in-high-positions theories – that most women high up in management and the Party are blue stockings who as a result lose their femininity." It was depressing to me, especially since his mother-in-law, Galina, was a well-educated and admirable woman who I'm sure did not espouse such views. After so many decades of women's equality under the law, I thought, how could it be that such sexist and male chauvinist attitudes persisted?

Even occasionally in the press you could find disparaging comments

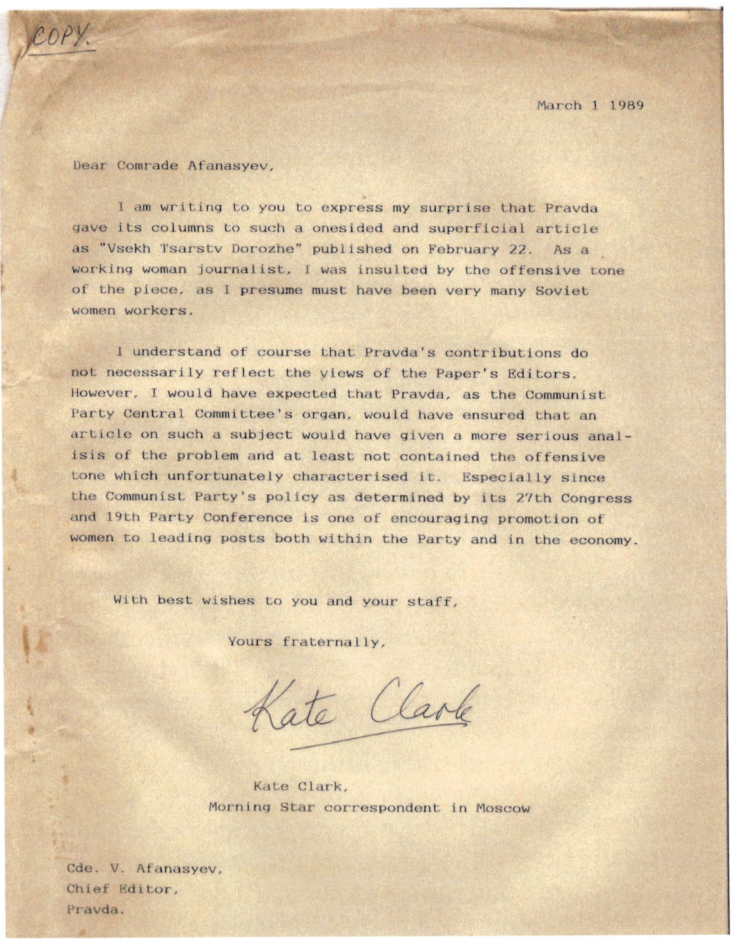

I never received a reply to this letter, which probably speaks volumes

about women at work, especially women in managerial positions, which surprised and dismayed me. Here is a letter I wrote to the editor of the Soviet Communist Party's daily newspaper, *Pravda*, after one such article in the edition of February 22nd, 1989.

It was quite common to find articles about how to lighten women's lives, but never anything about sharing the domestic burden. In practice, however, many men *did* help in the home.

You could see women on the streets doing all sorts of heavy jobs. They were road-sweepers, crane-drivers and builders – yet at home they would be the ones doing all the work.

Once again, on the women's question, I became convinced that the role of campaign groups in society was essential. How else would anything change, since the vast majority of decision-makers in the high echelons of Party and Government were men?

Whilst we lived there, only one woman – Aleksandra Biryukova – was promoted to the Politburo, the CPSU's top body, and even then, not as a full member, but only as a "candidate" member. To me it seemed like tokenism. It was a far cry from the days of the Bolsheviks, when women revolutionaries were on an equal footing with their male colleagues.

I opened this chapter highlighting the new atmosphere of openness, or *glasnost*. On my numerous trips outside Moscow, in press conferences and at factory meetings with managers and workers and Party functionaries, a lot was said about the new *glasnost* and how important it was. But how genuine was this? Did people who were quite high up in their professions and in the Party really want to change? Or was much of what I heard mere lip-service?

At the end of 1986, something unheard of happened: Gorbachov phoned the eminent physicist Andrei Sakharov in the city of Gorky - a city closed to foreigners - and invited him to return to Moscow after six years of exile there. Sakharov was the scientist who created the Soviet Union's atom bomb, in response to the USA's first use of that bomb to destroy the Japanese cities of Hiroshima and Nagasaki at the end of WWII. Faced with the knowledge that the USA not only knew how to make atomic weapons, but was prepared to use them, the USSR decided it needed its own deterrent and called on Sakharov, one of the country's foremost scientists, to work on this. In later life, however, Sakharov had fallen foul of the Soviet authorities for his views on human rights abuses in the USSR. His increasingly vociferous condemnations of these abuses led to him and his wife, Yelena Bonner, being exiled to Gorky (now Novgorod).

Sakharov's return from exile was a momentous piece of news which caused shock waves throughout the Soviet Union and the outside world.

It showed that Gorbachov meant business. The very fact that Gorbachov's phone call to Sakharov was reported and that the previously unmentionable became mentionable seemed to indicate that *glasnost* really was taking root. On the other hand I heard Yegor Ligachov – a Party leader from Siberia who initially supported Gorbachov[60] - in early November 1986 at a Palace of Congresses concert celebrating the anniversary of the October Russian Revolution reveal in his speech the struggle going on by some of the "old guard" in the Party against renewal and reform.

About the same time we learnt that our friend, the journalist and eminent economist, Otto Lacis, had moved from the daily newspaper *Izvestiya* to the CPSU's theoretical journal *Kommunist*. We invited him to dinner, with his wife Tamara and daughter Sasha, and we had a good discussion about the urgent need for economic and social reform. "War communism and diktat from above were all right for wartime," Otto said. "But now we need a very different approach to get the economy moving, to make it actually work for the people."

A new Individual Labour Law was passed at the Supreme Soviet in November 1986. The law gave individuals and families the right to work as private entrepreneurs. People could set up on their own to manufacture consumer goods like clothing and furniture and perform services like repairing cars and decorating people's flats.

The law did not permit individuals to employ others, so obviously this would limit the size of such individual enterprises. In practice, many people were already working on their own, providing many services alongside their day jobs, so it seemed a sensible measure to legalise this rather than continue to criminalise it.

Some of the Party leadership, during the discussion on the Individual Labour Law, were worried that working for pay outside of state enterprises was exploitative, and could pave the way for a return to capitalism. Gorbachov, however, argued, at the Politburo meeting of March 27th 1986: "We can't simply declare individual activity always parasitical. How many decisions have we taken and laws passed on parasitism, on pilferers, on illegal migrant workers! And not one of these decisions is carried out, not one problem solved..... If we close everything off, then we create unbelievable difficulties ...... Is Gosplan thinking about this? Where will people get materials? This is real life."[61]

This certainly was a problem: in a society where absolutely everything was state-owned, down to your local corner shop, the only way individuals who wanted to set up on their own could obtain the materials they needed was by siphoning them off from their official place of work, or similarly, from friends' and relatives' places of work.

One day in November, 1986, I went to a market selling beautifully displayed fruit and vegetables. I noticed the nearby lorry did not have a

---

60 As Gorbachov's policies of *perestroika* and *glasnost* began to take effect, Ligachov distanced himself from Gorbachov, and by 1988 he was recognized as the leader of the more conservative faction in the CPSU.

61 Quoted in *The Struggle to Save the Soviet Economy* by Chris Miller, 2016, p. 90.

Moscow number plate, so I went up to one of the stall-holders and asked him where they had come from. "Voronezh, that's central Russia," came the answer, adding that he and his mates worked on a State Farm there. It seemed strange to me that these stalls were set up outside the official Collective-farm markets in Moscow, at lower prices than those inside. For example, I bought a kilo of apples for one rouble, whereas similar apples inside the Market were priced at 5 and 6 roubles per kilo. At State grocery shops, the price was as low as 70 kopecks per kilo - but you couldn't always find them.

As I noted in one of my pieces about this market, "It is the first time I have seen here a bustling market atmosphere, smiling faces, busy hands weighing out the fruit. For the first time I have seen sellers who actually wanted to sell - because the more they sold, the more money they'd get." It was a contrast with the often surly and bored faces of many of the shop assistants we came across in our six years living in the USSR.

These stalls outside the official Markets were a direct result of the resolution at February's CPSU Congress which for the first time gave both Collective Farms and State Farms the right to sell off surplus produce through a cooperative network. Once they had fulfilled their contractual quotas to the State they were free to sell their output for their own profit. This was one of the ways the Party was trying to boost production and stimulate higher productivity among farmworkers.

Mikhail Gorbachov, who spent many years working for the CPSU in the Stavropol agricultural region, relates in his Memoirs[62] that as long ago as 1977, he argued with high-ups that the Party's agricultural policy was topsy-turvy: "How do we grant credits?" I said. "If a farm is inefficient and operating at a loss, then it'll get more: whereas if it's a well-run farm, it will receive neither credits nor building materials, only to be told "You have to look after yourself." .... Instead of letting rural workers and the *kolkhoz* or *sovkhoz* either earn money or go bankrupt, we introduce guaranteed wages that make everyone equal. The rural population is losing its incentive to work."

It was clear to everybody that there was something wrong with food production, but no unanimity on what needed to be done. As I pointed out in my piece about the new fruit and vegetable stalls: "The process is likely to be a long one. Many problems have still not been solved - transportation, spare parts, storage and refrigeration facilities, improved incentive schemes to raise farm productivity."

Glasnost was certainly going full steam ahead. Everywhere we were hearing of corruption being uncovered, long-serving Party leaders getting removed. In November 1986 I reported on three Turkmenistan Party leaders being sacked and expelled from the Party - something unheard of in the past. Entire Party leaderships had already been replaced in Uzbekistan and

---

62 *Memoirs*, Mikhail Gorbachov, Transworld Publishers, 1996.

Kirghizia, and in Moscow, of course. The sacked Turkmen leaders were charged with fiddling the books, something that had apparently been going on for years.

Gorbachov had quoted Lenin in this respect:

".... we should remember Lenin's warning: 'Illusions and self-deceptions are terrible, the fear of truth is pernicious.' The Party and the people need the whole truth, in things big and small. Only the truth instils in people an acute sense of civic duty. Lies and half-truths produce a warped mentality, deform the personality and prevent one from drawing realistic conclusions and evaluations, without which an active Party policy is inconceivable."[63]

Pravda reported that in the Tashauz region of Turkmenia, the three sacked leaders had ruled like khans, living in comfortable villas while local people complained of inadequate housing, lack of running water and shortages of food and medicines. Speaking at the 27th Party Congress, Gorbachov said that, at some stage, certain republics, territories, regions and cities had become "out of bounds to criticism", enjoying a kind of immunity.

In one single despatch of 5th November 1986, in addition to sackings in Turkmenia, I reported on sackings in Moldavia and in the Ukrainian region of Kirovograd. Ministers were being retired for "figure fiddling" - padding reports to make the situation in their industries seem better than it was. As was to be expected, there was growing resistance to these sackings, and, over the coming years, a re-grouping by such disaffected Party and ministerial leaders, who, whilst professing support for the *perestroika* reforms, were actually doing whatever they could to keep the status quo.

I suppose every correspondent must have something they don't feel proud of. I once arranged a visit to the tokamak at the Kurchatov Institute and was shown round by an Academician, Kadomtsev, who spoke very good English – but to my shame, I never wrote about it. Nuclear fusion and the information I was given there were just way above my head, though I had done some reading on the topic beforehand. I felt bad, because people had gone to the trouble of arranging the visit, the scientists there had given up their time, and I'd done nothing with it.

There was also the time when I interviewed Yoko Ono at the International Forum for a Nuclear-free World, and the batteries in my tape-recorder ran out just as I started. I was obliged to rely on my few notes. I do remember her saying "All weapons are archaic, like bows and arrows. Human love, human wisdom and human unity will be the power, and we will have world peace, because in the end the survival instinct will win."

After the new Individual Labour Law was passed in November 1986, I interviewed Ivan Gladky, a deputy and head of the State Committee on Labour and Wages, to find out more. Was this the beginning of a return to capitalism, I asked him, or was it at least, an admission of defeat? "Perhaps

---

63 from Mikhail Gorbachov's report to CPSU Central Committee Plenum, June 16 1986.

in some ways you could say that," Gladky admitted. But few people would deny that something needed to be done to improve goods and services for the public, he added. Family cafes would be allowed but only if run by a family, not employing outside labour. Services such as wallpapering and decorating, plumbing, electrical work, car and TV repairs and many more had long been provided by moonlighters operating illegally, Gladky pointed out, as well as by state services, which were greatly oversubscribed and therefore unable to meet demand.

If the new law took off, Gladky told me, "we expect perhaps 2 to 3 million people throughout the country to engage in this kind of individual labour by the end of 1987." A drop in the ocean, of course, but a significant new development nonetheless.

The new Moscow leader, Boris Yeltsin, continued to shake things up in the capital. At the Moscow Metro Trade Union Conference in November, Boris Yeltsin was very critical of the Union leadership. As I wrote in my diary, I suspected that if a month ago I had interviewed any Metro officials, everything would have been shown to me as perfectly OK – "yet here Yeltsin uncovers a multitude of sins, including injustices, alcoholism, corruption, smugness and many others..." Yeltsin accused the trade union leadership of doing little to defend Metro workers, pointing out that only six of the thousands of women doing heavy work on the Metro had been relieved of such work in the last five years.

To users, however, the Moscow metro could not fail to impress, both for the frequency and cleanliness of its trains, and for the elegance and beauty of its stations, surely making the Moscow Underground the best and most elegant in the world.

I didn't have much time to indulge my love of art and sculpture, or the arts in general. Daily press conferences, trying to keep up with the avalanche of new initiatives emanating from the new Soviet leader, as well as spending as much time as I could with the children who still needed occasional help (and my company!) were my routine. But occasionally I could combine an art show with reporting on it, with a clear conscience.

I went to the Moscow Artists House on old Kuznetsky Most Street to see a new exhibition by young Moscow artists, and the first thing I saw was the long queue snaking round the side of the hall. It was -10 deg. C that day - not particularly cold if you're moving around, but a bit too cold to stand in a queue, most of us would agree. Inside there were none of the heroic, larger-than-life figures typical of the socialist-realist style of the past. The styles in this exhibition were very varied, some pictures containing obvious social criticism, depicting for instance the destruction of old buildings, the ugliness of some of the newer buildings taking their place and the ravages of industrial society.

People crowded round one exhibit - a picture of three embryonic monkeys

"See no evil, hear no evil, speak no evil", captioned "The Secret of Happiness". What did it mean? Young people were excitedly attempting to interpret it. Other paintings showed the reality of queuing and the overcrowded Metro. It was an exciting, youthful exhibition generating much comment and laughter from the public who had queued to get in.

Our first full year in Moscow had been a baptism of fire for all of us, but perhaps especially for me, as my work level rose in line with the ever-increasing *perestroika* initiatives and the first signs of a growing opposition to the reforms. It was the year of the terrible Chernobyl accident, one despatch of mine in December 1986 giving a glimpse of the huge decontamination work and re-housing effort entailed in housing all the thousands of evacuees.

> "The unique giant structure entombing the ruined fourth reactor and preventing more contamination of the environment used 300,000 cubic metres of concrete, 6,000 tonnes of metal structures; 116,000 people had been evacuated and provided with alternative housing and work. 12,000 new blocks of flats had been built for the evacuees in safe areas; 500 populated areas and some 60,000 blocks of flats had had to be decontaminated. All this in just 8 months."

The Government statement I was quoting from also said that 237 people had been hospitalised after the accident, and that many of the 209 survivors were now back at work. One had to wonder how well they would be in a year or ten years' time....

As 1986 was drawing to a close, I felt optimistic about the future of socialism in the USSR. Surely a country that felt strong enough to air all the wrongs, the corruption and inefficiencies, stood a good chance of being able to overcome them and achieve a better society? At the traditional November 7th Red Square parade for the 69th anniversary of the Revolution, I felt the new mood of confidence and optimism as I watched the floats roll past the Mausoleum, where Gorbachov and other Politburo members were standing waving. It was a cold day with light dry snowflakes falling over the ancient cobblestones of the Square, as thousands of workers filed past, holding brightly coloured balloons and red carnations, holding slogans like "We beat our target for deliveries to agriculture this year!" (workers of the giant ZIL auto plant) or "165 workers have already achieved this year's target!" (Moscow shipbuilding works)

Then there were the peace floats, like one picturing a figure in a cowboy hat bearing the words "US administration", with a missile sticking out of each ear, saying "I can't hear anything!" as the words "The USSR has extended its nuclear test moratorium" were pictured coming out of a megaphone.

Soviet peace initiatives were always worth reporting. The *Morning Star* had a proud tradition of backing CND and all peace organisations and was fully behind the Soviet nuclear test moratorium and the Gorbachov plan for a Nuclear-free World published earlier that year. During the moratorium so far (since it was announced on August 6th 1985), the USA had carried out 23 nuclear tests, Deputy Foreign Minister Yuli Vorontsov denounced, in furtherance of the USA's Strategic Defense Initiative, which was strongly opposed by the USSR. "It's clear to us that the US simply doesn't want an end to testing, it aims for military superiority over the Soviet Union through its Star Wars plans," Vorontsov declared.

At the end of 1986, a new initiative to improve quality control was introduced - *gospriyomka*. It was being introduced initially at 1500 plants and factories. The press reported one case where on the first day of its introduction, half of one factory's TV tubes were pronounced as unfit for purpose and sent back as rejects by the new inspectorate.

One Supreme Soviet deputy from Sverdlosk in the Urals, Oleg Lyubov, explained how the system had operated up till then. "There have always been two quality controls - one by the factory's own Inspection Dept and the other by the customer. The problem is, in the first case, the people checking the goods are employed by the same factory that produces them!"

As for the customer being able to exercise any control - it could happen in theory, but since goods might be produced, say, in Belarus in the west and the customer might live in the far east, it was impractical for goods to be returned over such huge distances.

I also knew that, with the highly centralised system of state planning, you would not be likely to find much, if any, competition, where the customer could find a better-quality product produced elsewhere. I also pointed out in my piece for the *Morning Star* that the *gospriyomka* would not have a say over poor design of products, and this was of paramount importance, it seemed to me. From old-fashioned lorries, as my son Victor had noticed on one of the first days after our arrival, to unfashionable boots and shoes, the lack of contemporary design was evident. Yet in earlier decades, Soviet design was known worldwide for its boldness and innovation.

By the end of 1986, you couldn't open any newspaper or magazine without reading damning articles about some facet or other of Soviet society. One day it was the judiciary in the firing line, another day Kazakhstan's long-time Communist Party leader had been sacked and replaced by a Gorbachov nominee. This gave rise to demonstrations by nationalists, as the sacked leader was of Kazakh ethnicity whereas his replacement was an ethnic Russian.

Trades unions were also coming under fire. Soviet trades unions had a different role, compared with their counterparts in capitalist societies. They were to a large extent responsible for their workers' housing, holiday homes, children's clubs and Pioneer camps. They were more involved with fulfilling production targets, as their argument was that, since all enterprises belonged to the state, and their profits all went into the state's coffers, it was the workers who benefitted from the income generated. Profits did not go to private shareholders as they do in Britain, for instance, but into a common state-run fund from which housing, health provision, education and all social benefits were provided.

That was the theory. But in practice, trades unions, in accepting their role in helping managements to achieve targets, had neglected their primary role which was to defend workers' rights and conditions. In one of his speeches earlier that year, Gorbachov had slammed trades unions for being "toothless" and kow-towing to managements when they should have been standing up for the workers' interests. I spoke to Mikhail Srebny, who had just been re-elected President of the Soviet Miners' Union at its recent conference, and whom I had met a few times earlier when Arthur Scargill visited.

Whilst accepting Gorbachov's criticism, Srebny explained it away by saying trades union officials "might sometimes lack the knowledge of all the laws and regulations" or they "might think that the managing director must know best."

He pointed out that trades union officials at every level could always be voted out at any stage of the run-ups to national conferences of the unions. In practice, though, Trades Union officials often remained in their positions for long periods, their re-election being a formality. But six out of sixty Miners' Union regional leaders were elected for the first time at their recent conference, Srebny told me and roughly half of branch officials had been replaced.

A kindly man in his early sixties, Mikhail Srebny struck me as someone who definitely had the interests of Soviet mineworkers at heart, not someone who was "in it for the money or prestige." And since for decades it had been considered by the Party leadership that trades unions should work *alongside management* to fulfil the plans, this evolving into their *main* function, it was hardly surprising that union leaderships went along with this to the detriment of defending workers' rights and conditions.

The recent miners' conference had shown up problems with the quality of machinery and metals used, Srebny told me. "It's simply a question of growth," he explained. "The machine-building industry can't produce enough fast enough to equip all the 3,200 coalfaces we're currently working."

"People want things to be better all the time, naturally," he went on. "We built 370,000 square metres more housing in the last five-year plan than in the previous one - but it's still not enough!"

The CPSU programme had set the country the target of a separate flat for every single Soviet family by the year 2000. It seemed a tall order, given how many people were living in *kommunalki*.

From next year - 1987 - all pits were to become self-financing, in the attempt to improve efficiency. What would happen to those old pits where the seams were narrow and hard to work, I wondered. How would they compete with larger, more modern pits, which had more modern coal-cutting machinery?

Being a Communist correspondent gave me a special status: most correspondents of Communist newspapers were Central Committee members of their respective Communist Parties. I was not on the Executive Committee of the Communist Party of Great Britain, nor had I ever been, and, moreover, the CPGB was going through an internal crisis - the conflict between the EuroCommunist trend and the, let's say, more pro-Soviet trend. This division culminated in a definite split, when the latter trend, grouped around the *Morning Star*, reconstituted the party, calling itself the Communist Party of Britain. The old rump of the CPGB renamed itself the Democratic Left, and this disappeared altogether after a few years.

I mention this simply to explain why it was that I was invited to some high-level meetings between Communist Parties from all over the world, some of which discussed theoretical questions of interest to Marxists everywhere, such as the viability of the "armed road" to socialism, or whether introducing market elements into a socialist society, which would lead to more inequality, was justifiable, not only in economic, but in social terms too. One such meeting, held towards the end of 1986, discussed this question, and it was very interesting to hear the different perspectives of, say, a South African Communist in the thick of the anti-apartheid struggle, and a Hungarian Communist whose Party was in Government.

What did self-determination mean for a people in struggle? It should mean that they could count on help from friends elsewhere who were in power, *African Communist*'s representative argued, citing Zimbabwean soldiers fighting alongside Frelimo freedom fighters in Mozambique.

Whereas Valeria Banke, Editor of Hungary's *Social Review* journal argued for market elements to be introduced into Hungary's socialist economy: having done this, they "had, however, run into more difficulties than we had thought. The high incomes earned by some," she said, "do cause public anger."

"Socialism has given people security," she declared. "And this is a convincing triumph. But what was wrong in the past was that enterprises had given their workers *too much protection,* she argued. Poorly-operating enterprises producing outdated goods should not be protected at the expense of go-ahead, successful enterprises.

I had the opportunity to talk to Aleksandr Yakovlev, who at that time was a CPSU Central Committee Secretary later to be elevated to the Politburo, and considered a close ally of Gorbachov's in the *perestroika* process. He walked with a limp, having been wounded in WWII. He was an approachable man, and I put to him my concern as to what would happen to workers at the non-profitable enterprises, during the economic reforms just beginning in the USSR.

His reply, in a nutshell, was that they had to shake up the present system because it was stagnating and the ministries and Gosplan had enterprises in a stranglehold, not allowing them to be self-financing even if they wanted to.

"What should the driving force be behind labour productivity in a

133

socialist society?" Yakovlev asked. Thorny questions like these had to be tackled boldly and creatively, he argued, and the Communist movement's theoreticians had to make a full contribution.

Later, when I interviewed Yakovlev for a BBC2 series *Second Russian Revolution*, he greeted me warmly. During that long interview, when my editor, who was sitting behind me, kept leaning forward and whispering instructions in my ear, Yakovlev said to me in Russian: 'Why does she keep interrupting you all the time? Tell her to let you get on with it!"

I think Yakovlev was surprised when he saw, months later, how little of his interview was used in that BBC TV programme.

CHAPTER III

Do Not Call Me, Father - excerpt from Pavel
Antokolsky's poem *Son*, 1943

(Son to father...)

Do not call me, father. Do not seek me.
Do not call me. Do not wish me back.
We're on a route uncharted, fire and blood erase our track.
On we fly on wings of thunder, never more to sheath our swords.
All of us in battle fallen – not to be brought back by words.
Will there be a rendezvous? I know not. I only know we still must fight.
We are sand grains in infinity, never to meet, nevermore to see light.

(Father to son...)

Farewell then my son. Farewell then my conscience.
Farewell my youth, my solace, my one-and-only.

Let this farewell be the end of a story
Of solitude past which now is more lonely.
In which you remained barred forever from light,
From air, with your death pains untold.
Untold and unsoothed, never to be resurrected.
Forever and ever an 18 year old.

Farewell then.
No trains ever come from those regions,
Unscheduled and scheduled.
No aeroplanes fly there.

Farewell then my son,
For no miracles happen, as in this world
Dreams do not come true.

Farewell.
I will dream of you still as a baby,
Treading the earth with little strong toes,
The earth where already so many lie buried.

This song to my son, then, is come to its close.

This poem touched the heart of millions of Soviet people when it was

135

published in the journal *Smena* in February 1943, meriting the Stalin Prize. This extract features in Jeremy Isaacs' comprehensive *World at War* TV series (Episode 11, *Red Star*), narrated by Sir Laurence Olivier, over newsreel footage of Red Army soldiers burying their dead.[64]

The Great Patriotic War was a constant presence in the many meetings, interviews, and conversations we had and in the films, plays, and museums we visited during the years we lived among Soviet people in those *perestroika* years. It was never far from the surface, which is not hard to understand, given the enormity of Soviet losses. Antokolsky's heartfelt poem epitomised for many the grief felt at losing a young son, a brother, husband, father, sister or daughter (many women fought in the ranks of the partisans and in other military roles).

It was hard to keep up with the changes that were sweeping the country in 1987. Practically every day some new initiative was announced, new bills put forward for discussion, new reforms being put to the top Communist Party bodies, like the Central Committee. And all the time novels, films and plays that had been shelved for decades were seeing the light of day – and revealing to ordinary people the extent of the crimes committed in the past. Of course the public already knew of this from the devastating revelations by the leader who succeeded Stalin, Nikita Khrushchov, made at the CPSU's 20th Congress in 1956. But now accounts were being published by victims of the repression, and hitherto unknown tragic episodes in people's lives talked about openly.

The whole question of Stalinism and the harsh repressions of the thirties is an emotive one for many Soviet people and for Communists and socialists the world over. The revelations in 1956 shocked and traumatised communist parties worldwide, as the full scale of atrocities from the thirties to Stalin's death in 1953 came to light.

Is there such a thing as "Stalinism"? Is it a useful term to describe a particular phenomenon or a particular leader? Perhaps it is, in the same way that "Thatcherism" began to be used in Britain to describe the particularly harsh form of conservative rule – the decimation of the coal and steel industries, introduction of the anti-working class Poll Tax and all the neoliberal economic policies that characterised her era.

The arguments as to whether the repressions of the thirties, which resulted in large numbers of Party members and leaders being sent to their deaths as traitors, were justified or could at least be somehow understood in the context of the period after the Civil War, when external forces had joined with anti-revolutionary forces to try and crush the young USSR, will no doubt continue for decades to come.

What seems undeniable to me is that large swathes of capable and

---

64 More information about the poem and its author can be found in an article by author Michael Jones in the SCRSS *Digest*, No. 2, Summer 2020.

committed communists throughout the Soviet Union were lost to the cause of building socialism during those repressions – people like the Leningrad leader Sergei Kirov, for instance. Did such widespread annihilation of supposed opponents and rivals help the cause of socialism? It seems unlikely.

It is true that we must always judge historical events in the context of the events of the time. The immense upheavals intrinsic in the Russian Revolution and post-revolutionary Soviet society cannot be underestimated, and the brutalities on the part of the Whites during the vicious Civil War 1918-21 were no doubt matched by those of the victorious Reds, as in any war. And the harsh and authoritarian rule characteristic of the Romanov tsars preceding the Revolution resulted in strains of authoritarianism prevailing in society long after the demise of tsarism itself.

The exact number of people politically repressed in the USSR remains under discussion to this day. Two approaches exist to measure the total number of victims. The first one suggests that politically repressed people are those charged and imprisoned due to political motives. According to this approach, the number of politically repressed persons in the USSR varies from four to six million people. The USSR's population in 1937 was 162 million.

Another, more extensive approach lists victims of political repression as people denied citizen and social rights due to their ethnicity or religious beliefs, people who suffered after Stalin's policy of collectivisation (consolidation of individual landholdings into collective farms), and people displaced on the basis of their nationality. The numbers according to this approach are several times higher.

In 2001, the then Chairman of the Commission for Rehabilitation of Victims of Political Repression, Aleksandr Yakovlev, stated that "about 32 million people were politically repressed, including 13 million during the Civil War." The Russian human rights group Memorial informs that from 1921 to 1953, some 11-12 million people fell victim to political repressions. Historian Viktor Zemskov estimates the number of victims at 10 million people, including 2.5 million peasants forced to relocate to remote areas of the USSR in the 1930s and 1940s.

Whatever the numbers it is clear that the repressions caused huge suffering, not only to the victims and their families, but to society as a whole, since it was on such a large scale that probably most families had either suffered themselves, or knew someone who had.

Our neighbour, Lev, for instance, had suffered, in the sense that his father had done time in prison, or the *gulag*, as detention camps were known during the repressions. Both his parents, who were of the Kalmyk nationality, were early Bolsheviks in that Caucasus region of Russia, and supported the Party's policies of industrialisation and collectivisation. Yet for some reason, Lev's father fell foul of the region's Party's leadership, was arrested and spent years in prison. Lev never knew why or what his father had been charged with.

We were always surprised that he never seemed bitter or angry when he spoke of these things; he seemed to simply accept that that's how life turned out for his family.

I had a long and interesting conversation with a Soviet biologist, Dr Gabriel Feldman, who had recently edited a book of J.B.S. Haldane's scientific essays. Haldane was an eminent British biochemist and geneticist, Chair of Genetics at University College London from 1933 and populariser of science in many publications on, inter alia, evolutionary theory. He was a lifelong Marxist, who visited Spain three times during the Spanish Civil War to assist the Republican cause, and later served as chairman of the editorial board of the Communist Party newspaper the *Daily Worker*, writing a weekly science column for the paper for some 12 years, from 1937. Later he left the Communist Party, partly because of what he saw as the corruption of Soviet science under the theories of Lysenko[65] which had gained currency in Soviet genetics in the forties and fifties. It's interesting now to look back on Haldane's views of that time, as I quoted in one of my pieces:

".... under communism, there will doubtless be some private property. If we understand how quantity is transformed into quality, we shall realise that private property, like oxygen, can be both a necessity, as in the case of boots, and a public danger, as in the case of armament shares. And we shall steer our way between the extremists of the Left, who think that a Soviet worker is a capitalist, because he lends a few hundred roubles to the State, and those of the Right, who think that because I can own a fountain-pen, the Duke of Westminster should be allowed to own hundreds of acres of London." (from *Quantity and Quality*, 1946)

J.B.S.'s quest for scientific knowledge was so strong that he even used himself as a guinea-pig in various experiments. During WWII, he and another colleague spent 48 hours deep underwater in a miniature submarine to test apparatus:

"After breathing oxygen for five minutes or so at such pressures, one has violent convulsions: and my frequent demand for a soft chair or cushion is due to the fact that I fractured my backbone in such convulsions," Haldane wrote.

Haldane's sharp, witty observations and good humour remained with him even when terminally ill with cancer, when he penned this:

---

65 Trofim Lysenko was a Soviet geneticist who promised greater increases in crop yields than other biologists believed possible. Under Stalin, Lysenko became director of the Institute of Genetics of the Academy of Sciences of the U.S.S.R. but by the sixties his unorthodox theories had become totally discredited.

"I know that cancer often kills,
But so do cars and sleeping pills,
And it can hurt one till one sweats,
So can bad teeth and unpaid debts.
A spot of laughter, I am sure,
Often accelerates one's cure,
So let us patients do our bit
To help the surgeons make us fit!"

Gabriel Feldman's book of Haldane's essays, published by the *Nauka* (Science) publishing house, was testament to his admiration for the British scientist and Marxist. A quiet-spoken man in his sixties, Dr Feldman sat at our small kitchen table overlooking the Kremlin and explained to me the effects, as he saw them, of Stalinism on Soviet society as a whole, not merely on those people who had directly suffered during the repressions. He saw Stalinism as an aberration, an unhealed scar on Soviet society and argued that unless all the crimes of that era were brought to light fully, Stalinism would continue and would not allow society to develop and blossom.

In 1989, a new organisation, Memorial, was set up with the aim of promoting the truth about the USSR's past and to perpetuate the memory of the victims of political repression. Through the efforts of this society, on 30 October 1990, a Memorial to the Victims of the Gulag (a simple stone from Solovki[66]) was inaugurated on Lubyanka Square in Moscow, and a Law on Rehabilitation of Victims of Political Repression was passed in 1991. Today 30th October is a Day of Remembrance for the Victims of Political Repression.

Memorial also helps individuals to find documents and, where possible, the graves of politically persecuted relatives. As of 2005, Memorial had a database of over 1,300,000 names of such people.

In July 2017 an opinion poll carried out by the All-Russia Public Opinion Research Centre showed that most Russians (90%) know about the repressions, with half of the respondents condemning the punitive actions and another 43% saying that it would have been impossible to maintain order in the country without them. 49% of respondents and 57% among those whose family members were subject to repressions disagreed with that and strongly condemned the repressions.

More than two-thirds of Russians (68%) said the Soviet Union's court rulings on the repressed persons were unfair. Some 24% of those polled said their relatives were among those subjected to the punitive measures, including the infamous labour camps. Some 16% of Russians said they believe the punishment during the Stalin era (1922-1952) was fair.

So Russian society today remains divided over Stalin's repressions and this

---

66 Solovki was the name of a detention centre on the Solovetsky Islands in the Arctic White Sea.

may be attributed, the pollster said, to the lack of information on the events of the Stalin era. Most Russians (72%) believe that there is the need to tell the younger generation about the repressions so that they are not repeated in future. But 22% of respondents say this discussion should be reduced to a minimum as it negatively affects the country's image.

I remember on a visit to Tbilisi, Georgia, in 1987, seeing a big picture of Stalin adorning the wall of a factory nursery for the workers' children. Whatever the diktat from Moscow, someone in authority there had clearly decided that Stalin – a Georgian – was still their local hero. Just as everywhere, people will get round rules, especially if they're seen as nonsensical. As far as Gorbachov's anti-alcohol campaign was concerned, the people of wine-drinking cultures like Georgia, Moldavia and the Crimea felt justified in ignoring it.

In 1987 a film by Georgian director Tengiz Abuladze, first made in 1984 but not released at that time, came out and caused quite a stir. The film is an allegory of the Stalinist era: the day after the funeral of Varlam Aravidze, the mayor of a small Georgian town, his corpse turns up in his son's garden and is secretly reburied. But the corpse keeps returning, and the police eventually capture a local woman, who is accused of digging it up. She says that Varlam should never be laid to rest because he was responsible for a Stalin-like reign of terror that led to the disappearance of many of her friends..... At the end of the film, an old woman asks her whether this is the road that leads to the church. The woman replies that the road is Varlam Street and will not lead to the temple. The old woman replies: "What good is a road if it doesn't lead to a temple?"

At the film's preview with Abuladze, the director said the film was based on real episodes in Georgia's history: "Beria[67] wanted to pull down Metekhsky Castle (*zamok*). Five leading cultural figures went to see Beria to try to persuade him not to do it," Abuladze said. "Two days later, three of them were no more."

"The action of the film takes place in all times and everywhere," Abuladze explained. "But it is no secret that we have a dark page in our history."

The novel *Children of the Arbat*, by Anatoly Rybakov, recounts the impact of the 1930's repressions on a circle of friends living in Moscow's intellectual district around Arbat Street. The book deals with the 1934 17th Party Congress, held after the purges of 1933, and the circumstances around the murder of Leningrad Party leader, Sergei Kirov, in 1934.

Told through the story of fictional Sasha Pankratov, a sincere and loyal Komsomol[68] member exiled as a result of party intrigues, the novel is semi-autobiographical: Rybakov himself was exiled in the early 1930s. The

---

67 Lavrentiy Beria: head of the secret police under Stalin, whom he briefly succeeded on Stalin's death in 1953.

68 Komsomol: Committee of Soviet Youth – the youth wing of the CPSU.

book recounts the growing hysteria of the period where simple mistakes or humour were seen as evidence of sabotage or acts of wreckers. In effect the book exposes how, despite the honest intentions of Pankratov and older Bolsheviks like Kirov, Stalinism was destroying all their hopes, and Stalin is portrayed as a scheming and paranoid figure. During 1935, a purge of the Party expelled 250,000 members - most of them suspected as oppositionists by the NKVD.[69]

In April 1987, the 76-year old author told journalists: "My *Children of the Arbat* are the children of the Revolution. The youth today must know the truth about their forebears living 50 years ago."

"They were good, selfless, modest comrades, true to their ideals and to society," he went on. "They weren't out for personal gain."

Rybakov, who fought in WWII, said it wasn't Stalin who had won the war, but "the men, women and children who starved and froze on the home front, who gave their all for the front!"

"I'm convinced," he said, "that unless we overcome what gave rise to the personality cult [around Stalin, K.C.], unless we learn to think independently, it will be difficult for us to make progress."

Just two examples of previously-banned works, both of which revealed the continuing trauma of the repressions 50 years earlier. To what extent these and many other works coming to light in the late eighties were seen as significant by the masses of working people throughout the USSR, I cannot say. But certainly the TV and national media, which most citizens saw, gave them considerable publicity from 1986 onwards.

In February 1987 the Writers' Union officially revoked the 30-year old decision to expel Boris Pasternak from the Union and the following year *Dr Zhivago* was published in the Soviet Union, 28 years after the writer's death.

Through a love story, the novel tells of a Russian bourgeois family's difficult adaptation to revolutionary times and is a truthful portrayal of how sections of the intelligentsia were affected by the sharp class transformations after the 1917 Revolution.

As a University student of Russian Studies, I wrote my final year dissertation on *Dr Zhivago*, and never really understood why it was banned in the Soviet Union. It seemed to me to describe in a sensitive and honest way the kind of contradictions inevitable in such a huge political, social and economic transformation.

"People had to stigmatise a work they had never read!" poet Andrei Vosnesensky wrote in *Literaturnaya Gazyeta*. "We, having breathed the air of *glasnost,* find it hard to believe that most people's comments amounted to 'Well I haven't read Pasternak's novel, but I condemn.....'"

Early in 1987 an important meeting of the CPSU Central Committee heard

---

69 NKVD: People's Commissariat for Internal Affairs, at that time in charge of police work and investigations.

Gorbachov propose unheard-of political reforms, such as multi-candidate elections and the appointment of non-Party people to senior government posts. Lenin's work *On Cooperatives* was invoked to encourage the setting up of profit-making cooperatives – which were in effect like small businesses. That Plenary meeting opposed multi-candidate elections at this point, though that would be voted through a year later at the 19th Party Conference. Gorbachov's reasoning was that while ever you had leaders not having to face any competition, you would get stagnation, nepotism, corruption and a host of other ills that beset the Soviet system.

In February 1987 I had my first chance to go to Alma-Ata (now Almaty) - at that time the capital of Kazakhstan. I had been to Kazakhstan twice before, first to Karaganda, 490 miles from the capital, and then to Semipalatinsk, 525 miles from the capital. But it is a vast country – in fact the world's largest landlocked country - and the ninth largest in the world, with an area of 1,052,100 square miles. Its population in 1987 was 16.5 million. Part of it is in Asia, but the most western parts are in Europe. Kazakhstan is the dominant nation of Central Asia economically, generating 60% of the region's GDP, primarily through its oil and gas industry. It also has vast mineral resources.

Two months earlier there had been serious protests in Kazakhstan arising from the dismissal of the Party's long-standing First Secretary, Dinmukhamed Kunayev, and the appointment of a non-Kazakh, Gennady Kolbin, to head the republic's Party organisation. Not only was Kolbin not an ethnic Kazakh, he had not previously lived or worked in the republic either. Clearly Gorbachov thought a new broom was needed to sweep the Party organisation clean, but one has to question whether he was sufficiently sensitive to ethnic sensibilities in making that appointment.

Demonstrations had begun on 17 December 1986 as 200–300 students, mainly ethnic Kazakhs, gathered in front of the Central Committee building on Brezhnev Square to protest at Kunayev's demotion. The number of protesters increased to 1,000–5,000 as students from universities and institutes joined the crowd.

As a response, the Communist Party of Kazakhstan's Central Committee ordered troops from the Ministry of Internal Affairs, the police and the KGB to cordon the square. The situation escalated around 5pm, as troops were ordered to disperse the protesters. Clashes between the security forces and the demonstrators continued throughout the night in the square and in different parts of Alma-Ata. Two demonstrators were killed, and the protests presaged increasingly unpleasant signs of ethnic tensions which would become a feature of the *perestroika* years in many different parts of the Soviet Union.

"It was nationalism," one Party official told me. "Nobody organised the riots, they were just students and their position was, OK let the new leader be an ethnic Russian – but then he should at least be a Russian born and bred in Kazakhstan!"

"There had been a bit of a cult around Kunayev," he admitted, adding that nepotism was also evident, relatives of the Kazakh leader appointed to positions such as rectors of the republic's higher education establishments. "At first he did some good work, but then he would get praise from every tribune, and it went to his head. He began to think that everything he did was wonderful, and beyond criticism."

It emerged during the conversation with Party officials that one of the problems was that the many non-Kazakh Party leaders and functionaries did not speak the Kazakh language and had not thought that necessary.

The republic at that time had 2,500 Kazakh schools, where teaching was in the national language, and about the same number of Russian schools. There were 11 German-medium schools and 70 Uzbek ones where teaching was in Uzbek.

Now the Central Committee of Kazakhstan's Communist Party had declared that leading cadres should know both Russian and Kazakh. New textbooks for teaching the Kazakh language were being produced, and a special faculty created in *vuzy* (higher education establishments) with the aim of improving the teaching of the Kazakh language.

Given that the USSR had over 130 nationalities and languages, one can understand that as leaders at higher levels might be transferred to work in any republic or region of that vast nation, they might not want or feel able to study the language of the particular republic or region they were appointed to, especially if they might only be in that post for a few years before moving on.

How many Welsh secretaries in our British Government speak Welsh, for instance? I suspect very few, if any.

One can also understand residents of the non-Russian republics preferring to put their children into Russian schools, rather than those teaching in the local language, as they might feel that their child would have broader prospects for work and careers in other parts of the USSR.

Just as Africans whose countries were colonised by the British tend to speak good English and go through higher education in English, not, for example, in Swahili or Yoruba.

Russian was the lingua franca for the whole of the country – all 15 constituent republics and all regions. And in that sense it had a prestige and a practicality that none of the republics' own languages could match.

But it is nonsense to accuse the USSR of 'russification' in the sense of squeezing out or banning local languages: everywhere I went in the Soviet Union over the six years we lived there I found schools teaching in local languages and newspapers, books and street names in the local languages, alongside Russian.

Incidentally, in our country, road signs in Welsh alongside English were only allowed in 1972, but it was several more years before such bilingual signs were introduced widely.

Whilst in Alma-Ata I went to see the impressive Medeo winter sports centre, where director Yesimbekov Selim told me that 14 out of 17 world speedskating records had been achieved. Situated in a wooded mountain valley just outside Alma-Ata, Medeo's outdoor skating rink is notable not only for its beautiful location, but also for its distinction as the highest Olympic-sized skating rink in the world at 1695 metres above sea level. The centre housed a swimming pool, sports hall, sauna, volleyball, basketball and other courts.

Medeo winter sports centre

The speedskating rink was used by the local population at weekends, and for training Mondays to Fridays, I was told. Being shown round these facilities, built in 1973, you sensed the pride of our hosts in this vast sports centre. And it really was something to be proud of, especially when you think how backward Central Asia was before the 1917 Revolution.

I would like to have watched a game of the local ice game, bandy, which is basically hockey — in fact it predates hockey — played with a ball instead of a puck, but time was too short: we had an important meeting with Kazakhstan's journalists.

At the offices of *Sotsialisty Kazakhstan* we were assured that the recent street protests were nothing to worry about. "They weren't as a result of dissatisfaction of the Kazakh population as a whole," I was told, but "due to lack of educational work among higher education students." We were given to understand that they were partly due to Kunayev's appointees at several *vuzy* who had been stirring things up after Kunayev's demotion.

It seemed a rather facile explanation and I was sceptical at the time. One journalist by the name of Leonid Weidmann, who edited a German-language newspaper titled *Freundschaft* (friendship) told us: "We want to foster national pride in each of our nationalities here. But some people went too far, transgressing the line between national pride and *chvanstvo* (self-importance)."

The rector of the republic's main university, Yedil Yergozhin, an energetic man in his forties, whose office looked out on to the mountains, told us that only 14 of their students had been involved in the riots. They had been expelled and had been sent to work in factories and farms, he said. "The road ahead is not closed for them, though; if they do a decent job, they'll be able to come back and study."

We had a meeting with Kazakhstan's Prime Minister, Nursultan Nazarbayev (later the country's President until 2019). For some years he had been an outspoken critic, he told us, of Kunayev's personality cult, nepotism and "regional and clan favouritism". During the disturbances in the square he had mounted the tribune to try to reason with the demonstrating students. Nazarbayev told us that most of the students were from regions which were strongholds of Kunayev, the republic's leader for the last 25 years.

"An entire cult had grown up around Kunayev," Nazarbayev declared, ".... that Kazakhstan gives the country (the USSR) millions, that Kazakhstan gives the country metal, that Kazakhstan gives this and that, that Kazakhstan feeds the whole country – but nobody talks about what Kazakhstan receives from the rest of the country!"

"The education authorities had housed students in single-nationality halls of residence," Nazarbayev told us, "which is contrary to established Soviet practice of mixing nationalities."

But the demonstrators did bring to light real problems, he admitted, such as the city's inadequate housing and erratic food supplies. "These problems are at last being aired and tackled," Nazarbayev told us. "*Perestroika* is only just beginning here."

Nazarbayev had been a Central Committee Secretary with responsibility for industry. When he started to analyse the republic's economy, he had found that there had been virtually no progress over the last 20 years. "When I reported my findings to the First Secretary – Dinmukhamed Kunayev – they were just brushed aside."

"All my reports remained on paper. No action was taken. I was seen as going against Kunayev, and life was made increasingly unpleasant for me!" Nazarbayev told us, with a wry smile.

One of the protesters' grievances, it turned out, was the existence of special shops closed to the general public. There had been special hunting lodges for the privileged few, Komsomol Secretary Margzam Bayandarev told us, but now these and the special shops had been opened up to all. It was clear that things had been going wrong for some time.

In February 1987 ethnic problems were not dominating the agenda as much as they did over the next few years, when they came to play a big part in the collapse of the USSR as a unified country. At that time, it still seemed like a relatively small isolated incident.

Whilst I was in Alma-Ata I got talking to an elderly woman at a market I visited to look for dolls in national costume to take as presents for my children. Her wrinkled face showed her age, and she told me she remembered the time before Kazakhstan became part of the USSR in 1920. "We live much better now than in those times, when there was dreadful poverty," she told me, her wide face breaking into a broad smile.

Many years later I watched a BBC TV series on the *Silk Road* through Central Asia. The presenter revealed the usual anti-Soviet bias against anything belonging to the Soviet era. He showed a Soviet-era bus stop in a far-off area of Tadjikistan, I think it was, dismissing it in a rather sneering way. Was it so bad, I wondered, that in the Soviet Union there were actually buses running to that remote area? Are the inhabitants better off nowadays without buses, then? The presenter may have had a romantic view of peasants living in their old traditional ways in remote valleys, but my guess is that many of them would prefer a bus to give them the chance to see something beyond their, admittedly beautiful, but remote, valley.

So often in the West TV pundits talk of Soviet policy towards the smaller nationalities as if the state had suppressed them. As I watched that TV *Silk Road* series, local wood-carvers, who were at least in their sixties and who must therefore have grown up as children and young people in the Soviet Union, all spoke excellent Uzbek and Tadjik. If their languages had really been suppressed, would they have been able to suddenly learn those languages instead of Russian, and speak them so fluently?

I remember complaining to the BBC for that series' anti-Soviet bias, though I imagine the presenter, an academic, simply believed what some of the people he worked with in Uzbekistan and Tajikistan told him. They, of course, under their present leaders, may have their own reasons to denigrate the Soviet past.

I've never been keen on spas and body massages. But we were told that Alma-Ata's central *Vostochnye Bani* (Oriental baths) were something not to be missed, so of course, I went along. "You'll feel like a new woman after it!" our guide proclaimed.

I was shown into a big room with what looked like marble slabs where a few clients were already having massages. Two of the masseuses looked Kazakh, one looked Russian. The young masseuse assigned to me, an attractive Russian woman who told me she spoke Kazakh as well as Russian, told me to lie face down on the white shiny slab.

She began to work on my naked body, pummelling and kneading, working from my toes upwards. After my back had been pummelled and dug into, the masseuse suddenly got hold of my long hair and yanked my head upwards in a sharp movement. I heard a crack, and I thought to myself "Oh God, she's broken my neck!" "That's the salts," she proclaimed gravely, "all the salts that have accumulated on your bones at your age!" I was 45 then, and in my ignorance, hadn't realised just how many salts get deposited on 45-year old bones to produce a crack as loud as that!

I don't know whether I felt like "a new woman" afterwards, but after all the pummelling and thumb-grinding into my flesh, plus the shock of the certainty she'd broken my neck, I slept like a log that night, and certainly felt wonderfully refreshed the next day.

Back in Moscow, the Congress of the Soviet Trades Unions was held in February 1987. The *Morning Star*'s Industrial correspondent, Mick Costello, was there, as was Ken Gill, General Secretary of TASS. Ken was a leading Communist and an elected member of the TUC General Council.

Since Mick was the *Star*'s well-respected and well-connected Industrial correspondent who had flown out to cover the Congress, I could take a back seat. Mick spoke excellent Russian, so I knew he could do a good job reporting on an event like this. "They're all totally corrupt, you know!" Mick declared, referring to Soviet Trades Unions, "and bureaucratic." It seemed a typically sweeping statement from Mick – but perhaps he was right.

I was simply amazed as the speeches rolled on at how critical they were. Whereas I was sure that if I'd been at the previous Congress delegates would have highlighted achievement after achievement, now all we heard were the failings and the need for *perestroika* in the trades unions as well as everywhere else.

"Some trades union committees dance around managements, instead of sticking up for workers' rights!" Gorbachov told the Congress. "Unjustified bonuses and figure-padding have been allowed. Parasitic sentiments and the mentality of 'wage-levelling' have taken hold. That hit workers who could and wanted to work better, whilst making life easier for the idle."

Wage-levelling meant equal wages for unequal work – those who didn't pull their weight at work got the same wages as those who did work well. Trade unions had become bureaucratic and far-removed from those on the shop-floor, it seemed. To tackle this there would be multi-candidate elections for TU positions, more frequent workplace TU meetings, secret ballots and more accountability.

Once again, I pondered on the tendency of Russians to go from one extreme to another. Were delegates genuinely convinced as to the need for wholesale restructuring of society and the economy? Soviet industry did have many achievements to boast of, so was it correct to leave these out entirely and concentrate wholly on the negative?

I had that niggling feeling that essential balance was being lost, and that so much negativity all of a sudden could not be good for people's psyches.

I had the pleasure of dinner with Ken during that Congress, and would get to know him quite well over the coming years, as I aired with him the problems I faced in my relations with the paper's Editor and Foreign Editor, who gave me little guidance as to what they wanted and often didn't print copy I sent over. I think this was a mixture of reluctance on the part of the *Morning Star* to print the avalanche of criticism of socialist society coming out of the USSR, and the usual problems most foreign correspondents face with editors, resulting from the distance and lack of easy, daily communication.

I always found Ken really helpful and positive, as well as being a friendly and amusing companion. Not only was he a good speaker, and highly respected trades union leader, but an excellent cartoonist, as a later book of his cartoons would show.[70]

Between our busy jobs, Ricardo and I had to find time to look round the shops to buy a piano for our daughters, for whom we were paying to have weekly piano lessons outside school hours. "I cannot do any more for them," their teacher told us sternly, "unless they have a piano to practise on!" Ricardo went to a couple of stores, and I to another, and we finally decided on a decent upright one, made in the GDR; we arranged to buy it on hire purchase, it was duly delivered to our flat – and we still have it with us today, having shipped it over to Britain after we left Moscow in 1991.

At home in our roomy flat we had a big TV in our lounge, whose windows looked out over the Moscow River and the Kremlin. The lounge was rectangular in shape, with a dining table at one end and a three-piece suite at the window end. The kitchen was at the opposite end of the flat, so it meant carrying food on trays to the dining table when all five of us ate together and whenever we had guests. The floors were orangey-brown parquet, and each of the bedrooms and the lounge had good-quality carpets with intricate, colourful designs such as you find throughout Central Asia, regions famed for their carpets.

We used to enjoy watching TV all together as a family on the fairly rare occasions when both Ricardo and I were free. There were some good children's programmes like *Klub Putyeshestvennikov* (Travellers' Club) on Sunday mornings, which featured nature and ways of life in different parts of the world. There were serials, like *Rabynya Izaura* (Slave-girl Izaura) from Brazil. This was the first soap opera aired in the Soviet Union in 1988-1989 and had the nation hooked. Then there was *Robin Hood*, which unfortunately came to a sudden end, as it seemed that Soviet TV had only bought one part of the BBC TV series. We never did find out whether Robin and Maid Marion got it together.....

One thing we really liked about Soviet TV was the refreshing absence of TV adverts. I remember Patrick Cockburn's wife Jan saying the same thing on the BBC TV programme *Caviar and Cornflakes*[71]. Most of us probably don't think much about the ads on our TV interrupting all programmes except BBC ones: we've come to accept advertising as normal. But, if you stop to think about it, it is an infringement of our freedom that commercial firms can interrupt our watching with ads, lasting several minutes at a time, whether we want them or not, without asking our permission.

Before bed-time there were children's cartoons and stories and the same

---

70 *Hung, Drawn and Quartered*: The Caricatures of Ken Gill, Artery Publications, 2009.

71 See Page 99 and Appendix V.

song each night to help put children in the right frame of mind to sleep -
Bayu-bay:

Tired toys are sleeping, so are books.
Blankets and pillows are waiting for kids....

The children's programmes were not dissimilar to those of CBeebies today; they featured lots of cuddly animals, there were goodies and baddies, and they were non-violent and non-political. Our children loved them. Like all children, they loved us reading to them in bed; we had a lot of children's books, and we read to them in English, Spanish and Russian, depending on which story they wanted and on which of us was available to read to them that night.

One night I was tucking our son Victor up in bed, bouncing him lightly up and down in his bed, chanting "One potato, two potatoes, three potatoes, four...." which my Mum used to do to me when she tucked me in at night. But on one of the bounces, as I was leaning down over him, Victor suddenly sat up and our heads banged together really hard. He was hardly hurt at all, but I was. For the next two weeks I sported an impressive black eye, which gradually turned purple and then green. It was a good thing I had a make-up box! I applied purple or green eye-shadow to the good eye to match the other, according to what colour it was that day. I didn't want to look like a battered wife....

New TV programmes came on air, such as *Twelfth Floor* and *Mir i Molodyozh* (Youth and the World) and *600 Seconds*. 70% of young people were now watching these programmes tackling problems of leisure, job satisfaction, moral and social problems of all kinds. Television's Deputy Director Leonid Kravchenko told the Sixth Congress of Journalists in March 1987 that whereas 18 months earlier, only 1% of programmes were live, now (1987) it was 15%. Two thirds of programme editors had been replaced and a quarter of programming was new, he said.

Twelfth Floor was a sort of shouting match between teenagers sitting on the stairs of a typical high-rise block and the "authorities" in the studio, whether they be Young Communist (Komsomol) leaders or Council or Ministry officials, school heads or factory managers. As I wrote on 15 March 1987: "It's hard-hitting stuff. You get the impression the kids are saying all they've had bottled up for years."

600 Seconds was a popular TV news programme, broadcast from Leningrad, in which the host, Aleksandr Nevzorov, would highlight corruption by Soviet officials and crime, drugs and social problems. I was shocked that a programme shown on early evenings would show close up bloodied victims lying dead in the street, which I remember seeing on at least one occasion. Another example of the tendency to go from one extreme (no reporting of crimes or accidents) to the other (close-up shots of bodies). Where was the editorial control, I used to wonder.

In March 1987 British Prime Minister Margaret Thatcher came to

Moscow. The Iron Lady, as the Soviets had dubbed her, came to meet Mikhail Gorbachov, the man she had famously said she "could do business with" when he had visited Britain in 1984. She was interviewed on Soviet TV by two male journalists whose fawning attitude and seeming lack of arguments to counter her staunch defence of nuclear weapons were remarkable.

"....the nuclear deterrent is the only thing which enables smaller countries to stand up to a bigger country. You could never do it with conventional weapons alone - you could not afford them," she argued. During her visit, Thatcher decided to meet with a prominent 'dissident', recently released from jail (on a charge of "anti-Soviet agitation and propaganda") - Josef Begun, whom the Soviet authorities at the time described as a "Jewish activist" or a "leader of the Jewish emigration movement." It was a provocative gesture to her Soviet hosts, I wrote at the time. What, I wondered, would her reaction be if a visiting Soviet leader asked to have breakfast with an IRA inmate of Long Kesh prison?

"Her concern for human rights issues," I wrote at the time, "will doubtless stir the hearts of the four million unemployed in Britain, deprived of the right to work."

Like all on the left in Britain, I disliked Margaret Thatcher. I had arrived in Moscow at the end of the heroic miners' strike, which had held out for over a year, sustained by the NUM, generous public donations, and financial support from trades unions abroad.

To me Thatcher epitomised the harsh, uncompromising determination to destroy British trades unions, starting with the miners, as they were the most powerful and united. Trades unions were painted as sinister organisations controlled by big union bosses, holding the country hostage with their strikes and work-to-rule. Whereas in my book, trades unions were the only organisations that defended their members against the bosses, who always tried to keep down wages so that they could continue to extract maximum profits.

Whereas previous Tory "old school" prime ministers like Harold Macmillan and Ted Heath were no doubt just as harsh in the policies they and their party pursued, they did not exude that harsh, ruthless persona that Margaret Thatcher did.

I found myself, on a visit to Zagorsk, not far from Moscow, practically at her side in the scrum of journalists covering her trip. It was the end of March, so still quite cold.

Zagorsk, named after a Russian revolutionary, Vladimir Zagorsky, is a very beautiful small town with a famous ancient monastery, the Trinity Lavra, one of the greatest of Russian monasteries. The town's pre-revolutionary name was Sergiyev Posad (this name was restored in 1991) and it had grown up around the monastery in the 15th century. The world-famous icon-painter, Andrei Rublyov[72], known to cinema-goers by Andrei Tarkovsky's film of that name, is associated with this monastery.

The building where we lived in Moscow is not far from the Museum of Ancient Russian Art, housed in the medieval Andronikov Monastery on the banks of the Yauza River. The monastery has the oldest surviving church in Moscow where Andrei Rublyov is buried. Ricardo, who is a great admirer of Tarkovsky's films and in particular, his film *Andrei Rublyov*[73], often used to visit this museum, established in 1960, which has a unique collection of the medieval painter's icons.

Like Suzdal' and Vladimir – towns famous for their ancient monasteries and churches – Zagorsk was immaculate and beautifully preserved as you would expect of a national monument. It may be true that the Bolsheviks

---

72 Like for the surname Gorbachov (see Footnote 3) I prefer to use the phonetic spelling of Rublyov's name rather than Rublev, which leads to an incorrect pronunciation of the name in English.

73 Spanish-speaking Tarkovsky aficionados will be interested in Ricardo's book *Tarkovski al Trasluz*, Ceibo, Santiago de Chile, 2014.

destroyed many churches after the Revolution in Russia, as I had been told on my visit to Arkhangelsk a few months earlier, but the many churches which exist today all over Moscow and throughout Russia testify to the vast numbers there must have been before 1917, and, like the religious buildings I saw in Zagorsk, they are well-preserved and restored.

It was one of our undoubted privileges, living on Kotelnicheskaya Embankment, that from our windows we could see the sun glinting on the golden, onion-shaped domes of the Kremlin a short walk away along the Moscow River. The Kremlin has several beautiful churches inside its walls. There is a brightness and colourfulness to them that our British churches do not have, being from a different tradition. I shall never forget a cruise I once made north along the Moscow-Volga canal, when our ship glided smoothly along as typical Russian villages with their golden domes and high white walls seemed to float by to the strains of Shalyapin[74] singing old Russian folk-songs, relayed on the ship's sound system.

In addition to the flood of previously-censored books and films being released, *glasnost* was throwing light on shortcomings like the poor housing conditions of workers in parts of Siberia and the far north, some living in old railway carriages.

In February 1987, a leading sociologist, Tatiana Zaslavskaya, writing in *Pravda*, said: "It's unacceptable that statistics for crime, suicides, alcohol and drug abuse, and the ecological situation in different towns and cities are not published."

"If information about the conditions of people's own lives is hidden from them," she went on, "for example, about the degree of air pollution, industrial accidents, extent of crime and so on, we cannot expect them to become more active either in production or in political life."

The papers and TV were flooded with stories of how bad things were in this or that locality, how corrupt local leaders were here or there and how *perestroika* was just given lip-service by directors, managers and Party leaders in this or that region. Once again, both Ricardo and I felt, on reading this avalanche of bad news stories, that all balance was going out of the window.

I was often in a cleft stick: when I sent over a piece with one of these "bad stories", taken from the press, the *Morning Star* would often not publish it, for whatever reason. Yet at other times, the Editor would demand a piece on, say, the first publication of an anti-stalinist poem[75], for instance, and demand to know why I hadn't filed something on that.

---

74 Fyodor Ivanovich Shalyapin (1873–1938) was a world-famous Russian opera singer with a deep and expressive bass voice.

75 The poem *By right of Memory*, by Aleksandr Tvardovsky (1910–1971) a Soviet poet and former editor of the *Novy Mir* (New World) literary magazine. Written in 1968 but only published in 1987, the poem revealed the guilt he felt at not helping his father who had been accused of being a *kulak*. Kulaks were well-off peasants who opposed agricultural collectivisation during the thirties.

I was a dedicated and hard-working journalist – but I obviously couldn't cover everything that was coming out in every publication. There were times when I felt like giving up, but then the excitement of being in the midst of such interesting changes, plus the sense of duty I felt to the paper, kept me going.

It was a difficult time, and my frustrations were always coloured by feeling that I was not dedicating enough time to our children.

They, however, seemed to be doing fine. At Parents' Meetings at their school, we usually received good reports, except once when I remember our son's teacher warning me that he was "getting into bad company" and advising us to "curb his friendship" with one lad in that group. Since we knew the boy in question, and liked him, we decided to hold off on her advice.

I received praises, too, for my writing: letters from readers sent to the *Morning Star*, and forwarded on to me, showed me that my work was appreciated. On a visit to Moscow by some fifty British trades unionists in June 1987, the train drivers' union ASLEF leader from Sheffield, Bill Ronksley, was loudly applauded when he unexpectedly paid tribute "to the *Morning Star's* Moscow correspondent for all her truthful and informative articles", which, he said, were greatly appreciated.

Winter in Moscow was in some ways a hard time, but in other ways a great time for outdoor pursuits such as cross-country skiing in the parks and woods and skating on the many outdoor rinks. We would sometimes go of an evening to one near the children's school, at *Chistye Prudy* (Clear ponds), on Yauskiy Boulevard. With pop music playing over loudspeakers, and coloured lights strung between the trees, it was a magical scene and I still remember the excitement we felt as we hurriedly put on our hired boots, eager to try out our skating skills once again. *Chistye Prudy* was a smallish rink, so at other times we would skate in Gorky Park, alongside the Moscow River, or at the big Lenin Sports Stadium outdoor rink.

In March 1987, we went to a benefit event for Chile, to raise money for the Chilean underground resistance, held at the Lenin Stadium before an audience of 10,000 people. The main attraction was the world-famous poet, Yevgeny Yevtushenko, who read, or rather, declaimed his poetry to a huge audience. He was always a crowd-puller, a magnetic personality and compelling performer of his work. Here he recited his latest, as yet unpublished, poems:

"There can be no reconstruction
Without reconstructing memory
By constructing monuments to those
Who constructed us." (excerpt from *Monuments still to be Erected*)

This poem is a plea for leading figures of the Revolution and the Civil War who fell victim to the Stalin purges of 1937 to be restored to their rightful place in history.

"Now is your time, monuments, the time of marble,
The dirt is coming off all the slanders forever
And Marshal Tukhachevsky's once smashed-up violin,
Is getting put back together again bit by bit,
And will be turned into marble."[76] (My translation from the Russian, K.C.)

Yevtushenko had visited democratic Chile in the early seventies under President Salvador Allende and had met Chile's Nobel-prize-winning poet, Pablo Neruda - a lifelong Communist - who died soon after the criminal 1973 military coup. "Neruda was a great citizen, not only of Chile, but of the whole world," Yevtushenko declared. In Neruda's company Yevtushenko had discovered that Chile was a land of poetry, where poets were revered.

Yevgeny Yevtushenko

He then read his poem *The Dove of Santiago*, written in tribute to Allende, who died in the presidential palace, La Moneda, on the day of the brutal coup.

Our broadcaster and writer friend, José Miguel Varas, a Chilean Communist leader in exile in Moscow, told the Soviet audience to a storm of applause that at that moment there were 470 political prisoners on hunger strike in Chile's jails.

For Ricardo, as a fellow Chilean, and for me, who had lived with Ricardo in Chile through the three years of Allende's Popular Unity Government, the Yevtushenko benefit evening was very moving. And we were invited backstage to meet and chat with Yevtushenko, who was quite willing to spend time with us, despite no doubt being tired after his solo performance that night. It was clear that his visit to Chile had left an indelible impression on him.

During our years in Moscow, I was fortunate to meet and spend time with a number of important literary and cultural people, among them Elem Klimov, director of the harrowing wartime movie *Come and See*, the famous writer Daniil Granin[77], Natalya Bondarchuk, the actress best known in the West for her role as "Hari" in Andrei Tarkovsky's *Solaris*, and Latvian film director Juris Podnieks, whose film "*Is it Easy to be Young?*" caused quite a stir in 1986, as it showed a cross-section of Latvia's angry and troubled

---

76 Tukhachevsky, Yakir and Blucher, who are also mentioned in the poem, were outstanding commanders during the Civil War, 1918-1924, later shot on Stalin's orders.

77 Granin's novels *Those Who Seek*, 1954, and *Into the Storm*, 1962, among others, depict the struggle between principled, genuine scientists and talentless careerists and bureaucrats.

youth, including disillusioned Afghanistan veterans and colourfully-clad punk rockers.

If *glasnost* was the breath of fresh air that the literary and cultural scene desperately needed, then Gorbachov and the CPSU leadership desperately needed *perestroika* to succeed, if the economy was to satisfy the needs of the masses. Hopes were invested in the new Law on the State Enterprise which enshrined in law that enterprises had to be profitable.

I again went to Leningrad, the Soviet Union's second-biggest city, to report on how *perestroika* was faring in its industries. I visited one of the city's oldest works, the Svyetlana radio electronics amalgamation, employing 35,000 workers. They had introduced shift work so as to make better use of the most advanced and productive machinery they had, and higher rates of pay were paid to evening and night shiftworkers. I was told that earlier incentives such as socialist emulation and prizes had not produced the necessary stimulus for high productivity or high-quality production up till now, which was why more effective incentives were being tried.

"We were restructuring two years before the rest of the country!" boasted Director Oleg Filatov, "so I'm confident that we shall be successful when we go over to wholesale self-financing." But the Svyetlana works had quality problems, he said, and in getting timely delivery of parts from other enterprises.

He explained how 20 years ago Svyetlana had been given the right to deal directly with the Electronics Ministry, instead of having to deal with a go-between body set up by that ministry – "a totally superfluous and bureaucratic link in the chain," he added.

"Up till now, the ministry has had to continually subsidise unprofitable factories – so what incentive did the managements of those factories have to get out of that rut?" Filatov asked. Under the new Law on the State Enterprise, works would be independent entities as they are under capitalism, Svyetlana's Director told me, "the difference being that our profits will go into reinvestment and social programmes, not into private shareholders' bank accounts."

It was fascinating to go round Soviet factories. Many of those I visited over the years were housed in old buildings and sometimes machinery and equipment looked pretty old.

But the photolithographic workshop at Svyetlana works, which made microprocessors, light bulbs and calculators, looked state-of-the-art. A team of about 10 people were working behind sealed-off glass doors in a special microclimate to reduce dust and particles to a minimum. This was one of the enterprise's fifteen *khozraschyot* teams – i.e. teams whose work had to be profitable.

Because they worked in this rarefied air and enforced enclosure, the team received higher wages than the average – 250-260 roubles a month, compared to 200-220 average.

They were given "oxygen cocktails" - a frothy drink intended to oxygenate the lungs - during their breaks. And to avoid psychological stress, the workers rotated jobs within the production-team to reduce monotony. "Each member of the team knows all the operations," I was told.

Once the new Law was operational, the major share of an enterprise's profits would no longer go to the State budget, I learned. A smaller share would go to the State, and the major share would be for the enterprise itself. Where self-financing was already in operation, as at Sumy's Frunze works for instance (see p. 81 for more on this), productivity in 1985 had risen by more than 13% and profits by 32%.

"The bigger the profits, the more the enterprise's own workers get back in terms of wages and social programmes, so they've become much more interested in meeting the higher production targets," said Boris Karyakin, head of one of the assembly workshops, where 15 of the 49 teams had gone over to the self-financing system.

I asked what would happen to workers laid off when teams decided to fulfil their quotas with fewer members. "They are found new jobs either here or at other factories," Svyetlana's Personnel Manager Arkady Tyagushchev replied, "which helps to solve Leningrad's perennial labour shortage."

I knew that experiments such as Sumy's Frunze one and Leningrad's Elektrosila and Krasnogvardyeiyets works which I'd visited the year before were the exception rather than the rule, and that a big percentage of Soviet factories actually operated at a loss. This, plus quality problems, plus the rigid centralised planning system - which meant that factories were able to keep on "fulfilling their norms" whilst failing to produce goods that the population actually wanted to buy - had led to a crisis situation. Why? Because workers on the new cost-accounting system, who were now earning higher wages, did not have the desirable range of goods to buy with their extra money.

I had no doubt that *perestroika* was necessary, and I could see that where enterprises had become self-financing, results were good. It seemed this was the way to make the whole system more efficient and more responsive to what the people wanted, in terms of widespread provision of good consumer goods, housing and leisure facilities.

A friend rang me one morning: "Katya, you couldn't possibly lend me 70 roubles till next week, could you? I've heard there are some Finnish winter boots in our local *univermag*[78], and I really need a new pair!"

I obliged, of course, but it was one of many examples that illustrated the problem: why wasn't *Soviet* industry producing good-quality and fashionable winter boots? Why did people have to seize on what they heard through the grapevine was on sale somewhere?

I found Leningrad a beautiful city. There's something about a city criss-crossed by narrow canals and bridges with statues and wrought-ironwork and

---

78 *univermag* - abbreviation of *universal'ny magazin* - department store.

beautiful 18th century buildings on either side that takes your breath away. I visited the museum in the flat overlooking the Moika river where Russia's national poet, Aleksandr Pushkin, lived and died after the tragic duel which took his life at 37. There I noticed several books by Lord Byron, whose romanticism strongly influenced Pushkin. The Russian poet supported the Decembrists, a group of progressive officers who staged an uprising against the tsarist autocracy and serfdom in 1825, 5 of whom were executed. Pushkin himself was banished and placed under surveillance after that.

> "and long the people yet will honour me
> because my lyre was tuned to loving kindness
> and, in a cruel Age, I sang of Liberty
> and mercy begged of Justice in her blindness..."

On the poet's desk I saw a book by an English traveller, Captain Colville Frankland, with whom Pushkin apparently discussed reform of Russia's political system and how to eradicate serfdom.

Back in Moscow, in April 1987 the Komsomol's 20th Congress was held. We had already read in the popular magazine *Ogonyok* about unsavoury new gangs known as *Lyubers* (the name originated from the small town Lyubertsy, outside Moscow) who were apparently pouring into Moscow on suburban trains and causing mayhem in the capital's discos, squares and parks. They were keen weight-trainers and apparently found fun in picking on other groups of Muscovite youth, like long-haired hippies or heavy-metal fans.

The problem was no doubt exaggerated – you hardly ever saw long-haired youths in Moscow at that time – but *Ogonyok*'s report in February, in which both Lyubers and victims were interviewed, had highlighted the problems of Soviet youth – boredom, poor leisure facilities and alienation from the 'official' youth movement, the Komsomol, among them.

An article in *Pravda,* the CPSU's newspaper, entitled *Where is there for us to go?* highlighted some of the reasons for the emergence of such *informaly* groups like the Lyubers.

A 20-year old technical college student: "I love hard rock .... we wanted to start up a group, but we weren't allowed..." Or Dmitri, also in his twenties: "I've studied music, so my mates and I asked the factory's Komsomol committee to provide us with a room with musical equipment, but we were turned down..."

"The reason teenagers hang around the doorways of their blocks of flats, sitting huddled on the steps, smoking and joking together, is that very often, they simply have nowhere to go," the *Pravda* article said.

It had become something of a joke among Communists from the West that to be a Komsomol leader, you had to be at least 50. We had seen from delegations and events such as the 1985 World Youth Festival that Soviet youth leaders were not what we know as "young". So I was curious to see what the Komsomol's 20th Congress would be like.

"Formalism and bureaucracy in Komsomol work are severely hampering our 40-million strong organisation," new 34-year old leader Viktor Mironenko told the delegates, two-thirds of whom were under 25 - making for a much younger Congress than for many years. Soviet youth may not have faced Western problems like unemployment, but they had many problems of their own. The Komsomol was seen by many as irrelevant to their lives, partly due to Komsomol leaders becoming 'professionals', as Estonia's Komsomol First Secretary, Arno Alman, pointed out at the Congress. "Once the mandate of a youth leader is up, that person should return to his/her old job," Alman argued, unlike present practice, whereby Komsomol functionaries at the end of their terms were usually found executive positions somewhere.

"Stagnation in the Komsomol is because we're suppressing young people's initiative," delegate Valentin Denisov from Ulyanovsk said. What was needed, he urged, was for Komsomol activists to examine young people's requests and proposals, rather than dictate to them what they ought to be doing.

There was no shortage of congresses, CPSU plenary meetings, international meetings and conferences during those heady years. The need for restructuring of the whole edifice of society was constantly being called for, at every level, and much lip-service was being paid at every level. Was it too little, too late? And was there the danger of "throwing out the baby with the bathwater"? I applauded Gorbachov's declared aim of "More democracy, more socialism", but I worried that the pace of change might be too fast for the stability of the country.

Among the *informaly* – groups outside existing officially-recognised organisations - that sprang up were environmentalist groups, like one in Leningrad campaigning to save the old Angleterre Hotel from demolition. It was in one of its rooms that Russian poet Sergei Yesenin, lover of English dancer Isidora Duncan, had committed suicide in 1925. In the end it was agreed that the façade of the building on Isaakiyevsky Square should be kept intact.

May Day in Moscow was a big event, and I was lucky to get a permit to view the parade from the tribunes next to the famous red granite Mausoleum, from which Soviet leaders always viewed the parade. Along with the posters for peace, disarmament and international solidarity with the anti-apartheid struggle and with Nicaragua, in 1987 many of the slogans reflected current economic concerns:

"50 foremen and workshop managers elected by the work collectives – it's self-government!"

Others were satirical: one showed a man - the "reorganiser" - sitting on a tortoise, a poster in his hand saying "Onward!" The slogan read: "He is marking time, he doesn't want to advance!"

Another float had bureaucrats' reports and falsified (padded) figures disappearing into a revolving dustbin.

That year British printworkers' leader Mike Hicks, sporting a bright red tie, was a guest at the parade. Recently released from prison in Britain after serving a 3-month sentence on trumped-up charges during the infamous Wapping dispute, he was given a hero's welcome in Moscow. Mike and his wife Mary Rosser came to dinner that evening at our flat and admired our view overlooking the Kremlin. They were on the *Morning Star*'s Management Committee so we had a much-needed discussion as to how the paper was reporting on all the changes going on.

May Day could be bright and sunny as it was that year – but it could also be grey, cold and rainy, so you always had to go well wrapped up, since you would be there for a good few hours, whilst the serried ranks of people from enterprises and organisations filed past, followed by soldiers, tanks, rockets and other military hardware.

The city was always brightly decorated with red flags, and people were in a good mood since it was a national holiday, which, tagged on to a weekend, meant a few days' break. In the evening we had a privileged view of the splendid fireworks display on Novokuznetsky Bridge, and our kids would shout enthusiastically *Ura! Ura!* from our balcony, along with the hundreds of cheering Russians down on the bridge.

There came a succession of politicians and dignitaries from all over the world, eager to meet the new, energetic Soviet leader Mikhail Gorbachov, amid a groundswell of goodwill towards him in the West. Denis Healey, who was Labour's Shadow Foreign Secretary in 1987, told Soviet TV viewers that unemployment in Britain had trebled since the Tories came to office and hospital waiting lists were longer than ever. Healey pointed out the difficulties of waging an election campaign when practically all the media were unfavourable to Labour; in Britain, he said, "the press belongs to very rich people." I had never heard him say anything like that in Britain, but it's surprising sometimes what people will say when elsewhere.

One day I was invited to *Zvyozdny Gorodok* (Star City) not far from Moscow, where future cosmonauts do their training. I had not expected it to be in the countryside, surrounded by lush forest and long grasses. But it is in an idyllic setting, where training cosmonauts and their families can go for long walks in the woods and cross-country ski in winter.

We saw cosmonauts training in the hydropool, which had an enormous submerged spaceship in it, as water gives the nearest approximation to the weightlessness of space. The pool was very deep and it was quite eerie, looking down into the vast tank below us.

A Syrian, Mohammed Faris, was there training for a joint Soviet-Syrian space mission in July 1987. He had been in training for several months, joking that their work in simulated weightless conditions in the giant hydro-laboratory had lost him two kilos in weight each practice session.

The special pressure suits they wear weigh 220 kilos and they have to be specially lowered into the deep pool by crane. I met a French cosmonaut too – Jean-Luc Chretien – training for work on the MIR space station.

Foreign cosmonauts have to speak Russian so that they can communicate with the Soviet cosmonauts onboard, and from what I could see, they reach a very high level in the language after intensive immersion.

My visit was 5 days after the successful launch of a new, reusable space vehicle called *Energia*. It would be used for large-scale research and for "rendering outer space habitable on a systematic basis," Lt.General Vladimir Shatalov told us. Shatalov had flown several Soyuz missions in the sixties before becoming director of Star City training centre.

Gorbachov had attended Energia's launch, using the opportunity to hold up Soviet space achievements to the rest of the economy. "It provides the example we need," he said, "in tackling new targets that can't be met using old methods, knowledge and professional training."

You certainly could not fail to be impressed by the space technology we saw on display, all of which was Soviet-made. As so often during the years we lived in Moscow, I could not help but reflect on how and why it was possible for the Soviet economy to achieve such stunning advances in space, and yet be unable to produce a decent, affordable washing machine.

1987 - it was not an easy time for the *Morning Star*, with our previously-held shibboleths on the superiority of socialism being trounced daily by Soviet journalists and academics who sometimes gave the impression of vying with each other as to who could come out with the most outrageous thing. Socialism means no unemployment – no, says economist Nikolai Shmelyov, writing in the influential literary journal *Novy Mir* – "limited unemployment is good, to counter the economic harm done by our parasitic confidence in guaranteed employment!"

Gorbachov denied this, but statements like Shmelyov's were coming out all the time. And there was some truth in it: workers *had* become used to getting paid whether they did a good day's work or not. 'Wage-levelling' meant equal wages for unequal input and effort – and it gave conscientious workers little incentive to do a good job.

Another shibboleth was the low, subsidised prices under socialism: "Prices will have to go up," Shmelyov argued, "to more accurately reflect real costs."

"At present," he said, "the Soviet consumer gets from the state more than 50 million roubles in subsidies to cover the loss-making prices of basic foodstuffs and services. Why underpay for meat (heavily subsidised) yet overpay for fabrics or footwear? Why not buy both at real prices?"

Only "cost-accounting socialism" would do, he argued, where all enterprises had to turn a profit or go out of business. The market mechanism had to be recognised and allowed free rein, unfettered by diktat from above – what he called 'management by injunction'.

I had to report such views, but was conscious that our readers would find them very hard to swallow.

In June 1987 I went to Estonia, one of the three Baltic republics which were part of the USSR. Tallinn is a beautiful city, medieval old town in the centre with cobbled streets and steep narrow lanes. You could immediately sense you were somewhere totally different, with no apparent Russian influences like golden domed Russian Orthodox churches, instead tall steeples more like Western Christian churches.

There I learned that new cooperatives were being set up in all the service industries, and that people were keen to try their hands at the new possibilities afforded them by the new Individual Labour Law. At a meeting in the Russian-language daily newspaper *Sovietskaya Estonia* I learned that there were problems with the lack of bilingualism, that some workplaces were mainly Estonian, others mainly Russian, and very often the Russian population did not know the Estonian language. This was compounded by ecological problems such as extraction of phosphorites, which was opposed by many Estonians.

The shops seemed well-stocked and in general Tallinn gave the impression of a prosperous city whose people looked well-dressed. But on talking to residents one could tell that under the surface nationalistic feelings were simmering. I got the impression that at least part of the Estonian population – only one and a half million – resented the influx of Russians who had come to live and work there in the decades since Estonia was incorporated into the USSR in 1940, and who did not speak their language.

One Estonian letter-writer wrote that this resentment was partially caused by historical mistakes – enforced collectivisation, Estonian farmers branded as 'enemies of the people' and banished to faraway Russian regions just because they owned a few cows, for instance. "We have to understand the national question, we must know our past and talk about it openly, not keep silent about it," the letter argued.

Glasnost was just beginning, but you could already sense that not all its effects would be positive, especially when so much negativity about the past was being released all at once.

I was always very busy, as every day brought something new, sometimes sensational, at other times more low-key. And we had no shortage of visitors – both people we knew from back home, and others who just wanted to meet the paper's Moscow correspondent.

One of my best nights out – an evening full of laughter - was with our paper's Women's Editor, Mikki Doyle, and her friend, Tony, the Marchioness of Lothian. They were delegates to a World Congress of Women held that summer in Moscow.

Mikki Doyle was an American Communist who had married Glaswegian Charlie Doyle, who, living and working in the US, became leader of the Gas, Coke and Chemical Workers Union. The McCarthyite purges saw him put in jail, where Mikki married him by proxy, then accompanied him to live in London.

She was the best Women's Editor around, and really put the *Morning Star* on the map among the British press. She was determined, as Ken Gill wrote in his obituary (12.12.95) for *The Independent*, "to get the women's page out of the ghetto".

Mikki was instrumental in founding Women in Media, an organisation which had a lasting effect on contemporary journalism. Her close relationships with "female comrades" as she put it, ranging from the radical *Guardian* journalist Jill Tweedie to devout Catholic the Marchioness of Lothian, was typical of her capacity to "embrace everyone with a good heart".

The Marchioness told me she'd "always felt drawn to Communist ideals". Christ's and Lenin's ideals were very similar, she argued: "if only we could put them into practice the world would be a wonderful place!"

Small in stature, Mikki had a big personality and could dominate discussion by her direct, sometimes vulgar and usually funny interventions. When Tony Lothian started talking that night about the dangers of 'suicide through self-indulgence', Mikki interrupted, joking: "She means alcoholism and smoking – she wants to reform us all!" Mikki, despite having cancer, was still a smoker.

As a colleague, I had always found Mikki kind, supportive and comradely, and we were good friends until her death in 1995. I always remember her telling me before I left for Moscow: "Kate, write it as you see it. We don't want any sunshine stories!" That was what I tried to do during the six years I was the *Star*'s Moscow correspondent.

There wasn't much danger of 'sunshine stories' at this time: quite the opposite, in fact. A previously unpublished letter to Stalin by the writer Mikhail Sholokhov[79], printed in *Moscow News,* described the case of one Red Army volunteer during the Civil War, who later became Chair of the

---

79 Mikhail Sholokhov: author of *Virgin Soil Upturned, Quiet Flows the Don* and other novels; awarded the Nobel Prize for Literature in 1965.

village Council and whose family of seven was deprived of all that they owned – four acres, a horse, two oxen and a cow.

In a telegram to then Soviet Premier Kalinin, this man wrote: "they ravaged us worse than the Whites (counter-revolutionary troops in the Civil War, K.C.) did in 1919." "After this," Sholokhov wrote in his letter, "is there any point in talking of unity with the middle peasants?"

Sholokhov's letter added to the discussions going on as to whether the wholesale collectivisation of the peasantry during the thirties was really beneficial for the country.

One hitherto unpublished novel, *White Robes,* by Vladimir Dudintsev, was published in the Leningrad literary journal *"Neva"* to great acclaim. Written 20 years earlier, it deals with Soviet genetics during the Lysenko period in the forties. It is a profound philosophical work probing the concepts of good and evil and the struggle between them, social conscience, bureaucratism, intellectual honesty and careerism.

It now appealed to the new era of *glasnost,* which was exposing those very same shortcomings of careerism, bureaucracy and deceit which Dudintsev highlighted in his novel.

That summer, 1987, my brother Joe, sister-in-law Shirl and their two children Daniel and Michael came to visit us. Unfortunately I was working and, due to the pace of the changes, I had to file most days, so I did not spend as much time with them as I would have liked. But one weekend we caught the Metro out to Kuzminki park and enjoyed a lovely, lazy afternoon swimming in the lake and sunbathing among hundreds of Muscovites. I was amazed that Mike, who was only 7, swam easily all the way across the lake and back. During the second week of their stay they spent a few days in Leningrad, while Mike stayed with us in Moscow.

In parks and on street corners you could find *kvas* dispensers, which had a rinsing mechanism, so everyone used the same glass. You rinsed the glass, then poured the cloudy, brownish, fermented beer into the glass and paid your 2 or 3 kopecks. It was a good refreshing drink in the heat of Moscow's summers.

Among the *informaly* groups which sprang up that year was *Pamyat'* (remembrance), a nationalistic organisation with racist and anti-semitic overtones. I remember an interview I had with a CPSU leader, Vadim Zagladin, where I expressed concern that such views were being expressed. He argued that, under a forthcoming Press Law, it would be clear whether or not such groups were breaking the law, but if they weren't, then their views would be allowed.

I was dismayed by any such examples of nationalism and intolerance towards other nationalities. It seemed to me that the edifice, constructed so carefully over decades to foster friendship and harmony among so many nationalities and ethnic groups, was starting to crumble. There may have been mistakes made in the past, but in general I remained convinced that there was much that was positive in Soviet nationalities policy.

It was unlike the policy in the USA, where immigrants from all over the world were encouraged to assimilate and form one new nationality – American. Here all the nationalities had their own republics, autonomous republics and regions, kept their own languages and governing structures, whilst forming part of the umbrella nation – the USSR. Personally, I did not want *glasnost* to destroy that edifice, and I began to fear that the authorities were sleepwalking into that danger zone.

The USSR comprised fifteen constituent republics, which represented the fifteen major nationalities of those republics. The national parliament, called the Supreme Soviet, consisted of two chambers - the Soviet of the Union and the Soviet of Nationalities. Each Republic, regardless of size of population, was equally represented in the Soviet of Nationalities, each sending 32 delegates. This might seems surprising, since in the early eighties the biggest Republic - the RSFSR - had 137.5 million inhabitants, whereas Estonia had only 1.5 million.

Some of the republics contained Autonomous Republics; the RSFSR, for instance, had Bashkiria, Yakutia, Komi and 13 others within its borders. These Autonomous Republics were where the inhabitants had their own ethnicities, languages and culture. The Georgian constituent Republic had two Autonomous Republics for the same reasons. These Autonomous Republics enjoyed considerable self-government, whilst still under the higher laws of whichever constituent Republic they belonged to.

Similarly, there was a further tier of governance, which were the Autonomous Regions and areas, or territories (*krai*, in Russian). These were where smaller ethnic groups existed. They had some self-government within their regions and *krai,* but the constituent Republics had the final say in ratifying any laws passed by the lower tiers.[80]

The Communist Party of the Soviet Union was also organised in a similar way: each constituent Republic had its own Communist Party, under the principle of "national in form and socialist in content".

It was a complex system which had been devised in the early twenties, with the best of intentions, the Bolsheviks recognising the sense of identity which a given nationality and the different ethnicities undoubtedly have. It was, as an administrative-political structure, inherently democratic, each tier and sub-tier electing its own *soviets (*parliaments and councils) and it did work reasonably well for seventy years.

In September 1987 I was asked to give talks on *perestroika* by the *Morning Star* Readers' and Supporters' groups in Britain. I spoke to big audiences up and down the country. Everywhere people were really interested to hear about what was going on in the Soviet Union. In Manchester I spoke at the

---

80 for a more detailed description of the Soviet administrative system, read David Lane, *Soviet Society under Perestroika*, pp 188-193.

City Hall at a meeting chaired by left-wing Labour MP, Frank Allaun. I was only halfway through when all of a sudden the fire alarm went off. It was incredibly loud, and there was nothing for it but to discontinue the meeting and leave the building. There was no sign of fire, and it was mid-evening, so it seemed distinctly odd.

Back in the USSR, on a trip to Lithuania in autumn 1987 I was again struck by manifestations of nationalism, encouraged and partly fomented from abroad. Half a million Lithuanians lived abroad, and 3,600,000 in the republic. "Some of our compatriots abroad are keen to sow discord," Minister of Culture Jonas Bielinis told me. "Some of those who collaborated with the Nazis during occupation in WWII have not accepted Soviet power and still hanker after the bourgeois, nationalistic pre-war government." [81]

In August there had been a demonstration in Vilnius by Lithuanian nationalists which was filmed and screened on prime time TV. "We think the film was a good exercise in *glasnost*," said the film's young director, Arturas Baublys, who was Deputy Head of Lithuanian TV news programmes. "There was a core group of about 30, who marched up to the square, and no more than 300 at most at any time," he told me.

Would British television have reported on a demonstration of 30 to 300 people in London, or even a smaller town? Of course not. In Britain you're lucky to even get a mention if you've got a demonstration of a million people. Yet here, knowing that such nationalistic sentiments existed, the Lithuanian TV authorities seemed to be quite happy to exaggerate its importance.

Unlike neighbouring Latvia and even Estonia, Lithuanians made up 82% of the republic's population. The officials we met on our trip – academics, factory managers, journalists and new cooperative entrepreneurs – were all Lithuanian, without exception. We met enthusiasts for the possibilities afforded by the new Individual Labour Law – taxi-drivers who told us how they outdid their state-run colleagues by being willing to take clients to their rural homes whereas state-run taxi-drivers couldn't be bothered, garage mechanics who told us how much more they earned now they were on their own, and others who had branched out into private service industries. Lithuania had always had the private tradition in agriculture, economist Albinas Gulbinskas told me, 30% of farm produce coming from family plots.

How the new private entrepreneurs would fare in terms of overall benefits, such as pensions, paid holidays, access to sanatoria and trade union holiday facilities, statutory sickness benefits and the 8-hour day – on these issues much less information was forthcoming and I came away with the impression that nothing had been worked out so far as regards these.

Everything was changing – and fast.

A new play – *The Brest Peace* – by one of the Soviet Union's most well-

---

81 See Appendix I for more detailed information on US interference in Lithuania and the other Baltic republics during the *perestroika* years.

known playwrights, Mikhail Shatrov, figured heated discussions in 1918 between Lenin, Trotsky, Bukharin and other Bolshevik leaders around the issue of whether or not the young Soviet republic should accept Kaiser Germany's humiliating peace terms at the end of WWI. Trotsky had virtually been airbrushed out of history for decades, so the play trod new ground.

When asked for his opinion on a new encyclopaedia of the Great October Socialist Revolution, which gave information on the roles of Trotsky and Bukharin during and after the Revolution, but omits their subsequent fate, Mikhail Shatrov said it had 'failed to keep up with life.'

"Eighteen months ago I would have been proud of it," he declared, "but now I'm ashamed of it." This was just another indication of how fast *glasnost* was moving.

One day in September 1987 we received a phone call from the son of a Chilean comrade of Ricardo's. Recently graduated from the Royal Conservatoire of Scotland in Glasgow, Galo had arrived to take up guitar studies in Moscow. Well, he *thought* he was going to live in Moscow, but it soon turned out that he had been assigned to the capital of Armenia, Yerevan, to learn Russian for that academic year, before returning to Moscow to undertake postgraduate studies.

So off he went to Yerevan. A few months later, he arrived back in Moscow, complaining that he had come to the USSR to complete his guitar studies, not to spend a whole year learning some unfathomable language he was never going to need in future, i.e. Russian. We tried to convince him that he could not expect to be accepted as a postgraduate student without knowing Russian, but to no avail. "Russian isn't even their language," he complained, referring to the fact that Armenian was the national language in Yerevan. I told him that in Armenia and throughout the Soviet Union, people *did* speak Russian alongside their national and regional languages, especially at higher education level.

I suspect Galo was just lonely, and didn't give himself time to make friends there. So he ended up staying with us for several weeks until he finally went back to Scotland, having convinced himself that there wasn't much of a postgraduate future in Moscow since he hadn't learnt the language.

Whilst he was staying with us, we took Galo to a concert at the Gnessen Concert Hall, on Maly Rzhevsky *pereulok* (cul-de-sac) near Arbat in central Moscow. The Gnessin Institute is a top music school, considered second only to the Moscow Conservatory.

Galo thought the Soviet guitarist that he had hoped to study under – Aleksandr Frauchi – would be there. We did not find Frauchi, but we did meet a Soviet composer for guitar and orchestra, one of whose works was being played that night, and that was Igor Rekhin, a jovial, bearded man in his early fifties, who seemed delighted to meet a young guitarist like Galo, recently graduated from a British music college.

We soon became friends with Igor, who invited us to his flat on Gorky

Street (now reverted to original name of Tverskaya Street), through an impressive archway, and got to know his wife Mila. When Igor heard Galo play he immediately said: "You have obviously had excellent teaching in classical guitar." Then he added: "I am not sure that we can teach you much more than you already know, as guitar studies are not so advanced in the Soviet Union."

I translated all this back to Galo, and that must have been one of the reasons why he decided to return to Scotland and make his career there, which he has done, branching out into ethnic mixes of Latin American and Scottish folk music.

It was wonderful listening to Galo play his guitar in the cosy study of Igor's flat, the walls covered floor to ceiling by bookshelves and untidy piles of books and sheet music on the packed shelves.

On one visit we were invited to stay for a light lunch after Galo had played for a couple of hours, and Igor had shown him some of his compositions for guitar. I still make the lovely carrot salad Igor's wife, Mila, made on that occasion, as it makes a very refreshing light meal.

> 2 grated carrots
> Juice of one orange
> Sugar to taste
> Sultanas or raisins to taste

Rekhin is now a world-renowned composer. Himself a guitarist, he has devoted much of his compositional output to works for solo guitar, as well as works for guitar and orchestra. Among his most well-known compositions are his 24 Preludes and Fugues for guitar solo, but he has also composed two ballets, several works for orchestra, and numerous chamber works.

In terms of the economic transformations Gorbachov was trying to push through, it was clear that entrenched positions and interests were putting the brake on changes that had been agreed at top level. One of the Soviet Union's leading economists, Abel Aganbegyan, told journalists in October 1987 that *perestroika* faced several dangers.

It was being deformed, he argued, by bureaucrats in the ministries and elsewhere who mouthed support for the reforms but continued to work as before.

"In some cases the ministries are making a mockery of the concept of self-financing, by taking away up to 90% of the profits of successful, profitable enterprises."

"Only the *term* 'self-financing' is left! What 'self-financing' can there be if a successful enterprise has no resources left to use as it sees fit?"

Pricing was another complex issue under discussion in 1987. Socialists in the West had always admired the fact that food prices were low and stable in the Soviet Union – but this literally came at a price. As economist

Aganbegyan put it: "It's a tussle between those who favour price increases so as to put an end to '*defitsit*' and those who prefer the current system of low prices, even if these entail shortages and queues." As an example, one entry in my diary (27th June 1987) notes that I spent some 35 roubles on strawberries, tomatoes, salads and meat at a *kolkhoz* market, and that meat there cost 8 roubles per kilo whereas in the state shops it cost 2 roubles per kilo. Obviously the 8 roubles price was nearer to the actual cost of production than the subsidised state price.

Amidst all the problems that were being highlighted daily in the media, it was salutary to think back to the 1917 Revolution that had started it all. On the eve of the Revolution's 70th Anniversary I interviewed a woman who as a teenager had been active in the Bolshevik movement in Saratov.

Maria Kuznyetsova joined the Bolsheviks in 1917, when she was 17. In her simply-furnished two-room Moscow flat, where she lived alone, she reached for an old leather suitcase, opened it, took out a black and white photograph as she was then, and began her story.

"Both my parents were active revolutionaries. My father joined the Russian Social Democratic Labour Party (the forerunner of the Soviet Communist Party, K.C.) in 1905, my mother in 1900.

"My father knew all the members of Lenin's family. He was active in the underground revolutionary organisation in Saratov, where I was brought up.

"My Dad was a building worker and used to take the Party's illegal literature to different towns. He was also in charge of finding safe accommodation for revolutionaries in hiding.

"My Mum had 4 young children and worked as a servant to make ends meet. She hid revolutionary leaflets in the house and helped distribute the Party's paper "*Social Democrat*".

"Times were very hard, so at twelve I was sent to work for a well-to-do family. I hated it there, as I was often punished or made to go without dinner.

"Saratov, on the lower reaches of the Volga river, was a stronghold of Bolshevik activity. It was a big industrial centre and the Bolsheviks did a lot of work among factory and railway workers.

"We used to go out flyposting. Once when I was pasting leaflets on a wall in the dead of night, I heard a police whistle, and I had to quickly dive down an alleyway between two houses!

"*All Power to the Soviets!* and *Down with the War!* struck a ready chord with the workers and peasants. The revolutionary movement was growing in strength under the leadership of the Bolsheviks (so called after the 5th Congress of the RSDLP (Russian Social Democratic Labour Party) in 1907, when the reformists, who were in the minority (*Mensheviks*) split off from the majority (*Bolsheviks*) led by Lenin, K.C.).

"I was active in the February Revolution which overthrew tsar Nicolas II and established a bourgeois government under Kerensky. But under this Government, land remained in the hands of the landowners and the factories with their capitalist owners.

"Dual power existed: the Soviets of Workers' and Soldiers' Deputies on the one hand, and the bourgeois Provisional Government on the other. The Provisional Government was supported by the Mensheviks and the Socialist Revolutionaries, but the Soviets were supported by the masses.

"On September 22nd 1917 a revolutionary staff of Red Guards was set up in Saratov, and our revolutionary soldiers stood guard outside the Soviet building and other buildings we had taken over, like banks and factories.

"On the evening of October 25th (November 7th in modern calendar), red guards were arriving from the nail factory and the ball bearings and other works. There were street clashes between the upper-class people and the masses, most of whom supported the Bolsheviks.

"The Provisional Government people tried to attack our Soviet building with Cossack forces they had approached for help, but our workers were organised and convinced the Cossacks not to take up arms against their fellow workers.

"The Provisional Government representatives in Saratov capitulated, though not before opening machine-gun fire on Bolshevik activists in a battle that lasted all night of October 28th. Two of our Red Guards were killed and ten wounded. We were furious and resentful and would happily have lynched them if it hadn't been for our leaders who called for calm and discipline.

"Of course the displaced capitalist class in Russia was not content to allow the people to take over peacefully. The following year they forced a Civil War, and troops from 14 capitalist countries, including Great Britain, were sent to help the Russian Whites (counter-revolutionaries, K.C.) to regain power.

"I was wounded twice in the head and stomach during that dreadful war. Our Revolution 70 years ago was to make life better for kids like me – a 12-year old girl forced to carry heavy sacks I could barely lift!

"All these years we've been fighting for peace, with the same aim, so that people can live better!"

The aims of that Revolution *had* in many ways been accomplished, I thought, as I headed home after this interview, although I felt somewhat saddened by Maria Kuznetsova's disillusion with today's youth, as she had apparently been shouted at not long before our interview by a gang of youths in her neighbourhood.

It was undeniable, I thought, that the Soviet Union had come a long way from the poverty and political repression of tsarism, and had become a strong industrial economy capable of great feats such as the world's first sputnik and Yuri Gagarin's first space flight. Nobody lived on the streets, everybody had a job, security, free education and healthcare and enough to eat, even if supplies in the shops were somewhat erratic. It was not a paradise, but it was a country with a functioning economy and social life, even if there were problems. And those problems were what the Soviet Communist Party was now trying to tackle.

The 70th Anniversary of the Revolution, held in Red Square on November 7th, 1987, was a grand affair. Soldiers in the uniforms of the historic Red Guards and revolutionary sailors marched across the ancient cobblestones in the biting cold.

Light snow fell as the legendary Civil War Tachanka horse-drawn carts trailing machine-guns rattled across the Square.

Tachanka horse-drawn cart

Then a regiment of soldiers dressed in the uniforms of the Great Patriotic War filed past bearing the victory banner that Soviet soldiers raised aloft the Berlin Reichstag building in May 1945, having finally reached Berlin after liberating not only the USSR, but the occupied countries of eastern Europe too.

The report I filed after the parade said: "It was a day of remembrance and a day of pride. Remembrance for all the losses of these seventy complex years, and pride in the revolutionary achievement which put power into ordinary people's hands for the first time ever."

"Suddenly a distant rumbling announced today's Soviet defence armoury – tanks and armoured carriers, self-propelled artillery and anti-aircraft rocket launchers. Trundling heavily past the thousands of watching Muscovites and international guests, they left behind a pall of pungent, bluish smoke hanging over the Square."

"More democracy, more socialism!" "Citizens, actively participate in managing your country, promote greater openness, criticism and self-criticism!" "Workers of the World, Unite!" were just some of the many slogans people carried on the parade that year.

Among the guests was Labour MP Gerald Kaufman, whom I met at a cocktail party organised by the British Embassy. He was happy to be in Moscow at this "extraordinary time in Soviet history," he told me. "The INF agreement will take us, we hope, to a comprehensive test ban treaty and to a strategic arms reduction treaty – very important for the future of humankind."

He told me he thought the changes in the USSR during its 70 years showed that a "communist revolution", as he put it, was not necessarily inflexible, and he was very happy that Gorbachov was ready to speak publicly about mistakes made. "It occurred to me," he added with a smile, "it would be useful if Mrs Thatcher made a speech about all the mistakes of conservative governments during the last 70 years."

Many, many politicians, artists, writers and celebrities came to Moscow to imbibe the new atmosphere: Annie Lennox, Billy Bragg, Denis Healey, Gabriel García Marquez to name just a few. Anybody who was anybody wanted to come and hopefully meet the new leader, Mikhail Gorbachov.

Earlier that year, in June, a CPSU Central Committee Plenum had heard Gorbachov criticise the head of the State Planning Committee, Gosplan. All enterprises and farms at that time worked on orders from the State: they were told what to produce, how much to produce, in what space of time, and corresponding funds were provided by the State, which in turn received the profits (or covered the losses) of the millions of factories, plants and farms.

Gorbachov gave examples of how a new system of collective contracts was working well in the countryside, where farmworkers had in many cases "become alienated from the land". 54% of rural families, he said, do not keep cows, 33% do not keep any animals at all." This had resulted, he said, in the absurd situation where milk was having to be transported to villages from other regions.

On my visits to rural areas I had observed how many of the village inhabitants lived in 5-storey blocks of flats, rather than individual houses, so I was not surprised at Gorbachov's words. How could you keep a cow or hens if you lived on the third floor of a block of flats?

Gorbachov himself was from a rural background and knew the problems of his region – Stavropol – very well. The collective contract system which was now being introduced, Gorbachov told the Plenum, entailed a small group of farmworkers forming a team which signs a contract with the farm (kolkhoz or sovkhoz), wages dependent on end results. In Pytalovo district in the north west of the Russian Federation, he said, the Party under a new young leadership had decided to introduce the collective contract widely, with 8 subunits of State and Collective farms in the district working under the new system. Weight gain in cattle there had doubled in the last 5 months, he reported, and spring sowing had taken only 6 days as against 15-18 days in the past.

"People are working well in the collective contract because they are sure of getting good wages and independence, the realisation of their human significance, and pride in doing necessary work."

"Does this contradict the principles of socialism?" Gorbachov asked. "Can this method of work corrupt a farmworker? Rather it was the old practice - when negligence at work was paid for from the budget - *that* corrupted the farmworker."

These initiatives at farms, together with the new Law on the State Enterprise, would completely change the function of Gosplan, and render much of its work redundant. Gosplan's role from now on, Gorbachov told the Plenum, would be to plan overall strategy for the economy, but no longer interfere in the affairs of individual enterprises.

"It will be a painful process for many backward enterprises used to being endlessly financed from the State budget no matter how poor their performance. ...but we must introduce competition."

"The situation must end whereby all TV sets or washing machines are made at one works, so that the consumer has no choice to go elsewhere for a better one if dissatisfied with their purchase.... this producer monopoly has led to complacency and poor quality goods, with no redress for the customer."

These were radical steps, and it became increasingly clear over the next few months that they would be resisted fiercely by those who stood to lose – functionaries from Gosplan and the ministries foremost among them.

A *Pravda* article in December 1987 said that in the coal ministry some 700 staff had been cut. "There's nothing else for it," it said, "since from now on it is the enterprises themselves that will decide production and planning matters."

"If the present bureaucratic vertical management is left intact," the article warned, "there'll be nothing left of independence of enterprises at the bottom except the memory! For many administrators "at the top", like puppeteers, are only trained to pull the necessary strings, leading down to the enterprises below. They'll continue to pull them diligently until they are removed from this wasteful work," the *Pravda* article warned.

I was convinced that these economic reforms were necessary – but feared that they were probably too late. And with Moscow leader Boris Yeltsin forming his own 'fifth column', I became increasingly afraid that Gorbachov would not be able to carry the CPSU Central Committee along with him in implementing the reforms. You could sense a backlash from the disgruntled leaders who did not want to stray outside their comfort zone, and Yeltsin's antics were causing a split in the reform-minded leadership.

At a Plenum in October 1987, Yeltsin fired a number of salvoes at his fellow Central Committee members, especially Gorbachov and Ligachov, criticising the "style of work of the Party's leading bodies" and the "progress of *perestroika*", and submitted his resignation. Yeltsin's main attack on Ligachov was over the slow formation of cooperatives, as only some 3,000 had been formed so far, which was, of course, a drop in the ocean.

In November Yeltsin was sacked. The split between reformers could only do damage to the project as a whole and set a dangerous precedent.

It was always nice to meet friends from back home. Our Glaswegian friend, Jane McKay, whom we had got to know during solidarity work with Chile when living in Scotland from 1974 to 1979, came on a STUC delegation that October, and came to dinner to our flat. Jane was on the General Council of the STUC and a good speaker. Tall, striking and capable, Jane was instrumental in forming a broad movement of solidarity among Scotland's trade union movement with imprisoned and disappeared Chilean workers under the Pinochet dictatorship. She organised meetings and rallies, housed Chilean refugees, organised support for them and ran a successful campaign to free imprisoned workers and bring them to Scotland. Jane organised several big rallies where deposed Chilean President Allende's widow, Tencha Bussi – Madam Allende, as she was known – spoke movingly about the 11th September 1973 military coup in Chile which had killed her husband.

Through the Scottish Chile Defence Committee, which was very active at that time, Jane organised support for the Rolls Royce workers of East Kilbride who had decided to black repair work on the Chilean Air Force's engines for its Hawker Hunter aeroplanes which had bombed the Moneda Palace in Santiago on the day of the coup.

Another welcome visit was Tony Benn who was at that time MP for Chesterfield, my home town. He had been invited by the Soviet Academy of Sciences Institute of World Economy and International Relations, and had had meetings with its well-known Director, Yevgeny Primakov. We had a pleasant evening talking about *perestroika* and *glasnost* and the importance of Gorbachov's peace initiatives which were having a big impact on the peace movement in Britain, Tony told us. Like many of us on the Left in Britain, Tony was optimistic about Gorbachov's reforms.

25 years later, Tony Benn kindly wrote the Foreword to my book *Chile in my Heart* (Bannister Publications, 2013), which was published to time with the fortieth anniversary of the Chile coup.

Tony Benn was an admirable man, a Labour politician who was steadfast in his principles and who left a very important legacy, both for those Labour politicians who knew and admired him and for all who are interested in the workings of our political system, as his copious diaries and political letters form an invaluable archive.

The Soviet leadership's peace initiatives had certainly had a big impact on the western world and were a huge boost to the peace and nuclear disarmament movements. It is difficult now in this age of seemingly endless wars and conflicts in many parts of the world to remember how positive and optimistic many of us felt at the tangible thaw in the Cold War and the real, if still distant, prospect of multilateral nuclear disarmament since President Gorbachov's 1986 Declaration for a Nuclear-free World.

Then at the end of that year, 1987, in December, a treaty was signed banning intermediate-range nuclear missiles – the INF treaty, generally credited with being a major step to denuclearising Europe. Scientist and prominent former dissident Andrei Sakharov called it "an event of immense political, military and psychological significance." It was an encouraging end to the year.

CHAPTER IV

If 1987 had been a very busy year for me, as I tried to juggle work and family commitments, then 1988 was an order of magnitude worse. The pace of change was relentless and it was hard to keep up, let alone feel one was doing a good job. When I look through my telexes (I still have them) and my diary notes, I can only say that the volume of copy I sent to the *Morning Star* that year is impressive. I worked on Sundays, because the *Morning Star* comes out Monday to Saturday. I tried to explain to our readers *why* this or that new proposal or measure was being introduced, why *glasnost* was seen as so necessary, *why* hitherto unheard-of eruptions of nationalism could be seen..... I knew our readers must be finding all the changes they were reading about puzzling and unsettling, to put it mildly. So I tried to put things in context, and give background explanatory information to make the reports more comprehensible, wherever I could.

How on earth did I manage that volume of work, I think to myself nowadays.... It was partly due to having a helpful husband, whose job fortunately entailed working mainly from home, so he could spend time with the children after school while I was working. Ricardo often bought ready-made food if he came across it when he was out and about. And it was partly because I was a dedicated journalist who wanted to give as accurate a picture as I could for the benefit of the paper. And I was still in my early forties, in good health and with plenty of energy.

Our children were happy at school, and had a nice group of friends. As they were left to their own devices a lot of the time, they got up to mischief, of course. The twins and their little friend, Masha, had a game jumping off the top of the big, solid wardrobe in their bedroom on to the bed, singing *Orlyata uchatsa lyetat', pryam so shkafa na krovat'*! (Eaglets learn to fly, straight from the wardrobe on to the bed!) In Russian, it rhymes, so it sounds better.... It was all good fun until the single bed they landed on broke and had to be sent for repair.

1988 began with Foreign Minister Eduard Shevardnadze's announcement that Soviet troops would soon leave Afghanistan, followed by Gorbachov's renewed call, in a meeting with the media, for more *glasnost*. This gave editors the green light to throw all caution to the winds and publish ever more incendiary material regarding the country's past. Not only more and more revelations about the crimes of Stalinism, but bribery, nepotism and corruption; self-immolation of women in Central Asia; dire living conditions in Siberia; young people of no fixed abode (*bomzhi*) sleeping rough in the basements of

blocks of flats, problems in the armed forces such as *starikovshchina*[82].......
Where would this deluge of bad news stories lead to, I often wondered.

The year had only just begun when nationalistic demonstrations erupted in a region in the Caucasus - Nagorno-Karabakh. Demonstrations calling for the ethnically mainly Armenian enclave, which was within the territory of Azerbaijan, to be transferred to the Armenian republic turned violent and around thirty Armenians were killed in clashes in the Azerbaijani oil town of Sumgait. I had been to Sumgait, and to Baku, the Azerbaijan capital, in 1963, as part of a youth delegation. I had ridden in the open back of a lorry tearing at speed along the vast network of wooden-planked roads built on pylons above the sea, which was the *Nyeftyanye Kamni* oilfield. I had walked in the park along the coast and had watched open-air theatre there, overlooking the Caspian Sea. I had also more recently been to Yerevan and met Armenia's friendly, hospitable people. I was horrified to think that inter-ethnic clashes between people from these two neighbouring republics could be taking place in this multi-national and multi-ethnic nation of 130 languages and peoples where *Da zdravstvuyet druzhba narodov SSSR!* (Long Live the Friendship of the Peoples of the USSR!) had long been the country's motto.

In January 1988 I reported on a stormy meeting of the Armenian Party leadership, when one District Secretary, Gayk Kotanjan, accused the republic's top leadership of corruption, nepotism and bribery. He had received a torrent of complaints, accusations and proofs of shady dealings from ordinary citizens since taking up his new post. And national Communist Party newspaper *Pravda* told how in Armenia 667 cars had been bought in the names of police officers' relatives, and 596 others did not appear in any paperwork. The paper's correspondent slammed the state of affairs where "people go without water for days on end" and where there were shortages of fruit and vegetables despite the Republic's favourable southern climate.

One thing seemed obvious: not only would it be extremely difficult to redraw borders, but damaging too in many ways, since the populations were quite mixed: about 76% of Nagorno-Karabakh's population were ethnic Armenians, but some 160,800 Azerbaijanis lived in Armenia (out of a population of 3.1 million) and 475,000 Armenians lived in Azerbaijan, out of a total population of 6.3 million.

To what extent the violent clashes were provoked by the economic situation, and to what extent were fomented by the entrenched Party leaderships in both republics angered by the criticisms levelled at them was not yet known. Later it would become clear that there were forces at work which used ethnic tensions to get their own back at the central leadership pursuing the policy of *perestroika*.

The Soviet Artists' Union, at its 7th Congress in January 1988, heard some of the 800 or so delegates slam the authorities for "clinging to outdated and bureaucratic practices which had little to do with creativity." 'Socialist realism'

---

82 *Starikovshchina:* bullying of new conscripts.

had for decades been the mantra of Soviet art. Now it was being questioned. "Fear and refusal to accept what's new and fresh ..... by those who have ruled the destinies of artists and the whole of the country's culture – all this has done immense damage to the spiritual life of society," Moscow artist Igor Obrosov declared.

To outsiders like us, it seemed that quite a lot of Soviet art did *not* fit the 'socialist realist' concept. We would visit art galleries like the one opposite Gorky Park where there were both permanent and special exhibitions, and found that many of the paintings were more experimental in style than, say, the hefty worker or robust farmworker typical of the socialist realist art of the thirties. Ricardo had more time than I to indulge his love of art, and he would always tell me with enthusiasm of particular artists he had discovered.

There was a thirst, among artists, writers and poets, for more artistic freedom. The huge popularity of Vladimir Vysotsky was evidence of this. He was a song-writer, bard and actor who was banned, ignored or at best tolerated during his short lifetime, but whose recorded songs, sung in his unmistakable gravelly voice, "cut like a razor through hypocrisy and philistinism", as I wrote in one of my reports.

Vysotsky sang of the hardships of the soldier's lot, of the tragic fate of prisoners during the repressions of the thirties and of the common man, the worker, the people. "Vysotsky was the first to tell me and other kids the truth about the [Stalin, K.C.] times – that which we couldn't find in our school textbooks," one student said in tribute. As I wrote at the time: "Vysotsky was *glasnost* before *glasnost* times."

The historical revelations that were coming thick and fast were of course very interesting for any Communist or socialist interested in the history of the socialist movement. *Ogonyok* printed a previously unpublished letter dated 28th April 1938 from famous scientist Pyotr Kapitsa, who was at the time Head of the Academy of Sciences, Institute of Physics, to Soviet leader Stalin, in defence of a colleague:

"Comrade Stalin!
This morning our scientific researcher L.D. Landau was arrested. He is only 29, but he, together with Fock, are the most important theoretical physicists we have in the Soviet Union.
With all the failings in his character I find it very hard to believe that Landau would be capable of doing anything dishonest...."

Lev Landau was charged with being a Nazi spy, and was later to say that this letter and others Kapitsa wrote, to Prime Minister Vyacheslav Molotov and to State Security Chief Lavrenti Beria, putting the case for his release, had saved his life, as he was released the following year and went on to have a brilliant career as a physicist.

The *glasnost* revelations were not only of interest from the historical point of view. Those concerning collectivisation of agriculture were relevant to the current food situation. Nikolai Kondratyev and Aleksandr Chayanov, both victims of the repressions, had been attacked as *kulak* ideologues. Now their ideas were being held up as relevant to today's problems in agriculture.

"Chayanov's school, with its in-depth analysis of the prospects for family farms and diverse forms of cooperation, found itself...... opposed to the mainstream [collectivisation, K.C.] view. His misfortune was not in his differences with the official point of view, but in the fact that only one view became entrenched. Only one form of development in any process became possible – that which was approved by Stalin," *Komsomolskaya Pravda* wrote, in January 1988.

We also learnt, in a 28-part TV documentary about Lenin's life, that his widow, Nadezhda Krupskaya, had opposed Lenin's body being put into a mausoleum. "Lenin would never have wanted any kind of deification," she argued at the time. His embalmed body is still on show in the mausoleum and people still queue to see it. The idea of removing it for burial is considered too contentious.

It was Krupskaya who enabled Lenin, during his final illness, to dictate his last thoughts in which he criticised acting leader Stalin:

"Stalin is too rude, and this defect, although quite tolerable in our midst and in dealings among us Communists, becomes intolerable in a General Secretary [of the CPSU, K.C.] That is why I suggest that the comrades think about a way of removing Stalin from that post and appointing another person in his stead who ..... is more tolerant, more loyal, more polite and more considerate to comrades, less capricious....."

The Party's 15th Congress in 1927 agreed that these notes of Lenin's should be published, but they remained unpublished until 1956.

The country's education system was also coming under the spotlight. A 1984 School Reform had "got bogged down", *Pravda* said four years later. The Ministry of Education and the Academy of Pedagogical Sciences came under fire for this "ill-thought out reform".

I became friendly with a journalist, Tatiana, on the popular *Uchitel'skaya Gazeta* (Teachers' Gazette), which came out three times a week and was avidly read by rank and file teachers. Its Editor, Vladimir Matveyev, told me: "What today's world needs is creative thinking. But our schools do not prepare our children for such thinking!"

"The main idea of the (1984) reform was to achieve a new quality of education: it must become oriented towards 'teaching to study', rather than presenting children with a certain amount of regurgitated knowledge that very quickly gets outdated."

"Absurd curricula, stuffed full of totally unnecessary information", "difficult and boring textbooks" and "feeble teaching methods" were just a few of the epithets chosen by one teacher in the Teacher's Gazette.

The paper backed experimental teachers who were trying out new teaching methods, despite facing big problems with the authorities, Matveyev told me. "They've been very courageous, and we back them." These "innovators" favoured what they called 'cooperative pedagogy', in contrast to the existing authoritarianism of Soviet schools.

The Academy of Pedagogical Sciences needed new blood, Matveyev said, and more contact with the real situation in schools, and teachers had to be given the opportunity to work in a creative way.

I had many discussions with Matveyev and Tatiana on what I observed at our children's school. It is true that the textbooks seemed old-fashioned and their presentation quality was poor. The classes were quite big – about 30 children - and they did not have any group work within the class, but simply listened to the teacher at the front of the class, who followed the standard textbooks common throughout the USSR.

For our daughters, who were only 6 when we arrived in Moscow, and who therefore started school at the same time as their Soviet peers, the system seemed satisfactory. At least they felt happy there, and had many friends. They were also fond of their teachers, and they worked diligently both at school and in doing their copious homework.

Their class teacher was Larissa Petrovna and I think it's probably true to say that our daughters both liked and feared her. She would rap a desk with her index finger, quite hard, to get attention. How come, they wondered, it didn't hurt her! One of her favourite sayings was: "*Khot' kol na golovye teshi!*" (you're as stubborn as a mule!)

For our son, who was nearly 10 when he started his Moscow school - and had therefore known what a typical London junior school was like - fitting in and accepting the style of teaching was more difficult. He was told off for sitting with his legs sticking out into the aisle, and for being rough during break-time play. He and other boys got into serious trouble for making a home-made stink bomb which was thrown at a group of girls.

It came to a head when he and his friends were called *khuligany* (hooligans) at a Parents' Meeting at the school. Ricardo stood up after listening to a catalogue of complaints against these boys and ripped into the accusers, saying "Where is the spirit of your great Soviet educator, Makarenko[83]? You accuse, but you don't look at what reasons there are behind such behaviour!"

I had never seen Ricardo so angry – nor so fluent in Russian! We laughed

---

83 Anton Makarenko was an influential educator. In the 1920s he organised the Gorky Colony, a rehabilitation settlement for children made homeless by the Russian Revolution and ensuing Civil War, who were roaming the countryside in criminal gangs. Makarenko's *Pedagogicheskaya poema* (Pedagogical Poem), sometimes translated as *The Road to Life*, recounts his work with these children.

about it many times afterwards, as it does seem that when you *really* need to express yourself, some new powers come to your brain to assist you.... He later wrote an article outlining his views on the Soviet educational system as he saw it, which I include later as Appendix II.

I agreed with Ricardo. The school had a whole top floor, with toys and equipment that never seemed to be used. It had no playground, yet energetic children seated for hours at desks needed somewhere to let off their energy during breaks. There were no facilities at all for that, and the children were not allowed to run or play in the wide corridors alongside the classrooms. I am not surprised that our son did not fit in as well as other, more obedient, children. He made good friends with his class, though, and when he went back to Moscow a few years ago to do research for his Ph.D at London School of Economics (yes, that 'hooligan' got a doctorate later!) he met up with several of his former classmates.

It was the main reason that, when my brother offered for Victor to live with them in order to do his G.C.S.E's in Britain, we agreed. We felt Victor would fit in better in our system and would learn to question and research – which were not features of the Soviet system as it existed then. Victor himself wanted to start the 2-year GCSE course at the beginning, so he left us in September 1989, only coming back for holidays until we returned to live in London a year or so later.

We very much appreciated my brother's offer, and will always be grateful to him and Shirley and their two sons, Daniel and Michael, who accepted Victor in their home for those two years and looked after him like a son and brother.

Strikes were pretty well unheard-of in the Soviet Union. They were not illegal, but because it was a socialist country where the workers were, so to speak, working for themselves, not for private owners of industry and shareholders, disagreements had always been solved by the trade unions and managements together.

This had been the sort of "social contract" referred to by Professor David Lane (Op.cit.).

> "Until 1989 the assumption in the Soviet Union was that a conflict of interest between management and labour was caused by maladministration and could be resolved through management and the trade unions taking the correct action."[84]

But in the era of *glasnost,* workers began to air their grievances as never before. Transport workers in Omsk had gone on strike and ousted the enterprise's director, *Sotsialisticheskaya Industriya* reported in February 1988. Grievances had apparently come to a head when the director had

---

84 *Soviet Society under Perestroika*, David Lane, p.181.

ordered the lorry-drivers to deliver loads of cement without ensuring them loads for the return journey, which meant they would be out of pocket. "He thinks he is a prince here," declared one worker. "He considers us inferior and our ideas not worth listening to!"

The article went on:

> "Isn't it the workforce's inalienable right to assess the management's work? We're fighting for work collectives' independence and initiative, but these won't become real if people are denied the possibility of .... expressing their opinion and demanding equal responsibility."

All that year - 1988 - there was growing nationalism in the three Baltic republics and in the Caucasus. That same newspaper *Sotsialisticheskaya Industriya* accused Western radio stations of deliberately fanning the flames in Estonia. Security forces there had recently caught Estonian nationalists red-handed working for a reactionary émigré organisation, one article said, adding that the father of one of the nationalists behind the demand for a monument "to the victims of Stalinism" had been a Nazi collaborator.

The Baltic republics were always a special case within the USSR, because of the fact that they only became part of the country in 1940 (although they had been part of the Russian tsarist empire since the eighteenth century). Latvia, however, had had its own revolutionary movement at the time of the 1917 Russian Revolution: the *strelki* were Latvian revolutionary riflemen's regiments who were at the forefront both of the Bolshevik uprising in Petrograd and in Latvia itself, part of which, including the capital, Riga, had been occupied by the German Kaiser's army since August 1917, which then went on to occupy the whole of Latvia in February 1918. But in November 1918 Soviets (elected councils of worker and soldier deputies) were established throughout the Republic and an independent Soviet Republic of Latvia was proclaimed. And on December 22nd, 1918, Lenin signed the following decree:

> "The Russian Soviet Government recognizes the independence of the Soviet Republic of Latvia. The Russian Soviet Government recognizes as Latvia's supreme authority the power of the Soviets of Latvia, and pending the Congress of Soviets, the power of the government of the workers, landless peasants and riflemen of Latvia headed by Comrade Stučka."

But Soviet power did not last long. German troops again occupied Latvia and, with the help of anti-revolutionary forces, established a capitalist government there. On the eve of WWII when the USSR signed the controversial Non-Aggression Pact with Nazi Germany (in a bid to gain time to prepare for a likely Nazi invasion) Latvia signed a treaty of mutual assistance which gave the USSR military, naval, and air bases on Latvian territory. When the Nazis invaded Latvia a year later, they set up the infamous Salaspils concentration camp there, where over 100,000 Latvians, Russians and Byelorussians met their deaths.

Latvia's tradition of revolutionary activity dating back to the Russian Revolution itself was a factor in its parliament, the *Saeima*, voting in 1940 for Latvia's incorporation into the USSR. To talk of Latvia being "annexed" by the Soviet Union ignores the proud tradition of the workers' movement in Latvian history.

We had Latvian friends whose grandparents had taken part in the struggle for Soviet power in the early 20th century and I remember seeing a photograph of one of them in a Riga Museum, in an exhibition of revolutionary history. Later I met a Latvian film director who was a descendant of one of the Latvian *strelki*, and very proud of it.

But, as you can imagine with such a complicated history of invasion and occupation, there were people in Latvia who had never accepted Soviet power. And it is true that some 35,000 Latvians who either collaborated with the Nazis, or who were suspected of such sympathies during the war, were deported to eastern parts of the USSR, some to prison camps in Siberia.

I went to Riga, Latvia's capital, in February 1988. As on my earlier visits to Armenia, Georgia, Estonia, Ukraine and Lithuania, I was struck by street names being in the local language. In the kiosks in central Riga you could see lots of newspapers and magazines in Latvian, as well as others in Russian.

After sightseeing a little in Riga's beautiful old town, with its cobbled streets, its 14th century castle by the River Daugava and central buildings looking more like those of Stockholm than of Moscow, I went to interview one of the republic's top Communist leaders, Anatoly Gorbunov.

Despite his Russian-sounding name, Gorbunov was 100% Latvian, he told me. Referring to the first overt signs of nationalism in the Baltics – nationalistic demonstrations in the three Baltic capitals in August 1987 (venues and times of which had been broadcast by Western radio stations in advance) - he said:

> "The August events show that if we don't tackle these problems seriously, certain elements in our society will make political capital out of the situation. The national problem in Latvia has its roots in the extensive development of our economy, which for years has been giving rise to large-scale immigration into the republic. This immigration has resulted in a number of social and inter-nationality problems, both for Latvians and for those who came from other parts of the Soviet Union."

At that time some 54% of Latvia's 2.5 million population were ethnic Latvians, over 30% were Russians and the remainder various other Soviet nationalities. Resentment had been growing, Gorbunov explained, when

Latvians saw that workers - invited to man the new industries - were being given housing ahead of them. There was also a language issue: whereas most Latvians spoke fairly good Russian, most of the newcomers did not speak Latvian.

The Party leadership was now working hard to promote the Latvian language and culture, with TV programmes and courses in the language, but totally rejected the extremist views of some that non Latvian-speaking people should not be allowed to live in Latvia.

Gorbunov argued that the Party should take the initiative out of the hands of nationalistic groups and speak openly about controversial historical events, such as the deportations of citizens considered Nazi-sympathisers during WWII. "The deportations were probably necessary at the time," Gorbunov admitted, "but we can't approve of the way it was done."

> "The nationalists live off the fact that we keep silent about many things. Stalin's positive work can never justify his crimes," he went on. "But if industrialisation had not been carried out in the thirties, it's true that things would be much worse here today. But that time is past, and it went on for too long."

Gorbunov was a big supporter of Gorbachov's reforms and thought that once enterprises went over to *khozraschot* (self-financing) this would solve a lot of the republic's problems. But I had the distinct impression that not all the Latvian Party leadership were wholly behind the reforms.

While I was in Latvia I met some interesting people in the arts, among them the enthusiastic deputy editor of a new polemical youth magazine *Avots* (water-spring), Vladimir Kanivets. Drugs, alcoholism, prostitution .... nothing was shied away from. "What we need is more facts, more research – and less moralising," he told me. The magazine was about to start serialisation of George Orwell's *Animal Farm*. "We want young people to grow up against totalitarianism, and anyway, if people don't like a particular book, they should have the chance to decide that for themselves." *Animal Farm*, required reading in many British secondary schools (and a useful means of attacking the socialist system, some might say) had not previously been available in the USSR.

The most interesting person I met while in Riga was the film director, Juris Podnieks. His documentary *Is it Easy to be Young?* had been widely shown in cinemas and on TV and had shocked and gripped filmgoers the previous year. It was the first time Soviet audiences had seen juvenile delinquency, drug addicts and mystics on film as part of the Soviet youth scene.

I was impressed when I saw the film together with a group of visiting British trades unionists, who were struck by the deeply humanistic treatment of the problems shown, so I was keen to meet its director.

Podnieks, a confident, attractive man in his forties, from an impeccable revolutionary background (his grandfather was in the riflemen's regiment which took part in the 1917 Russian Revolution), told me about one incident he had filmed for his latest venture.

"Some workers in Yaroslavl came out in protest at having to work Saturday overtime at normal rates – what they called 'black Saturdays'. The management hadn't consulted with the workers: they'd simply told them it was necessary."

"I was fascinated by the people themselves – for fifteen years they'd been working these Saturdays without a word.....what made them decide now that enough was enough?"

"People have woken up, they've gained a new consciousness," Podnieks declared. "It's not always easy for the authorities to understand this."

Between easy conversation, cups of tea and anecdotes, Podnieks told me he tried in his films to show conservatism as a brick wall which pro-*perestroika* forces were coming up against.

"Sometimes I try to tear away the masks people put on to find out what's underneath....we have a lot of people wearing masks. After all, you can find very few overt conservatives!"

He slammed the sort of documentaries that showed an idyllic representation of Soviet society, such as those sent to Friendship Societies abroad: "We were afraid to show anything the least bit problematic!" he grinned. "But if the pain shown on film is real, human pain, it will be understood by all peoples – whether Britons, Vietnamese, Uzbeks or Americans."

I sensed that he had a deep concern for his people, not just Latvians, but all the peoples of the Soviet Union. Whether it was social alienation due to living in high-rise blocks, or 'problem' teenagers, ecological problems or the survival of the human race, it was always people that were his main concern.

Unlike some interviews I had with senior people during my six years as a journalist there, with Podnieks I felt a personal rapport, and it became clear during our long chat that we shared a sense of humour. We ended up having tea together, after which Juris invited me to his dacha to spend the evening with a couple of friends. After a meal we all went to his sauna and sat on the hot wooden benches in the sweltering heat chatting about events in Latvia, my work and family and their jokes no doubt helped along by shots of vodka. Every so often, one of them would get up and pour some water on the embers to create more damp steam.

I'm not keen on saunas as I can't bear the extreme heat and humidity, so I had to keep popping out to cool off, loath as I was to miss any jokes. I think Juris was getting a bit the worse for wear for drink, as all of a sudden he suggested we went outside to the lake for a swim - in the dark! The invitation seemed to go a little beyond my journalistic brief, so I declined, saying it wasn't quite my scene, and I really ought to be getting back.....

Ricardo with the *Independent* correspondent Rupert Cornwell, Victory Day, 9 May, Red Square

Morning Star's Mike Hicks with *Pravda* printworkers. War veteran Zinaida Seryogina (centre-left), May 1987

With *Morning Star* women's editor Mikki Doyle and *People's World* Moscow correspondent Carl Bloice

Composer and guitarist, Igor Rekhin

Interviewing President Nazarbayev, Alma Ata, Kazakhstan, Feb 1987

Visiting British Communist Party founder member
Andrew Rothstein, Moscow 1987

With SCRSS Vice-President and film director Stanley Forman in our flat, 1987

Margaret Thatcher meeting Gorbachov, Kremlin, March 1987

At Nikita Khrushchov's grave, Novodevichy Cemetery, Moscow

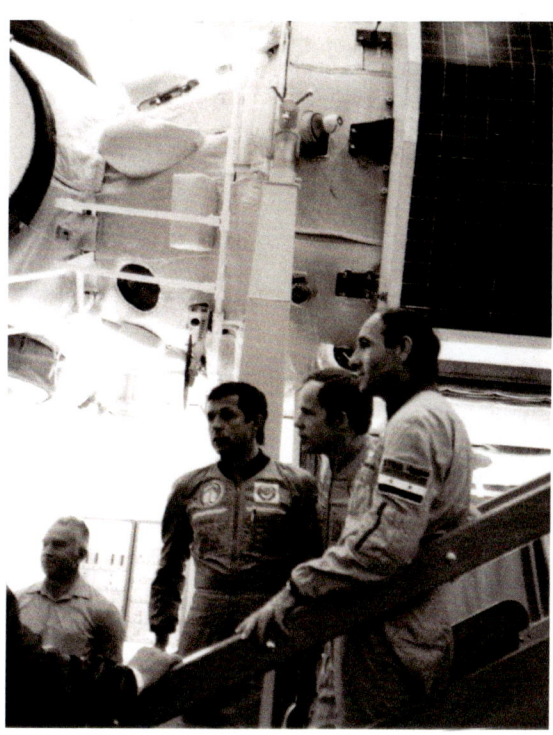

Cosmonauts at Zvezdnoi Gorodok (Star city)

Interviewing Deputy Editor of *Izvestiya*, Otto Lacis

STUC delegation: Ricardo with Jane McKay, Harry McLevy
and John Foster (at back) Oct 1987

With our Kalmyk neighbour Lev, father of Baira, 1987

British Foreign Secretary Geoffrey Howe, next to UK Ambassador Bryan Cartledge, in talks with Gorbachov and Shevardnadze, Kremlin, Feb 1988

Interviewing Latvian film director Juris Podnieks, February 1988

Ricardo with *Guardian* correspondent Jonathan Steele and Israeli
journalist Leon Zahavi, near Red Square, May Day 1989

Soviet troops withdrawing from Afghanistan, May 1988

President Najibullah
press conference, Kabul,
Afghanistan, May 1988

With Lt. Colonel Konstantin Belov at garrison
outside Kabul, Afghanistan, 1988

Weapons captured from the *mujahadin*, Afghanistan, 1988

Enjoying thermal springs, Kamchatka

Koryaksky volcano, Kamchatka, near Petropavlovsk-Kamchatsky

Eternal flame and Tomb of the Unknown Soldier in the Great Patriotic War, 1941-45. It's a custom for newly-weds to visit this monument at the Kremlin wall

Stalin's *dacha*, Kholodnaya Rechka, near Gagra, Abkhazia, Aug 1988

Aftermath of Armenian earthquake, Spitak, Dec 1988

Yevgeny Yevtushenko reciting his poetry at benefit concert for Chile, 1988

A Moscow *kolkhoz* market

A Moscow shop selling *polufabrikaty* (ready-made dishes)

Tiananmen Square, Beijing, China, during Gorbachov visit, May 1989

Side street photographed from rickshaw shared with *Irish Times* correspondent, Conor O'Clery, Beijing, China, 1989

In the mist, Great Wall of China, May 1989

Miners coming up off their shift, Donbass, June 1989

Party pooper possibly, but it didn't seem right, so after a while the friends left and Juris kindly took me back to my hotel.

We met up again on a subsequent visit, but that was the last time. Four years later, I was saddened to hear that Juris Podnieks had drowned one midsummer evening in Zvirgzdu lake near Alsunga, in western Latvia. He was 42.

The month after my Latvia trip, on 13th March 1988, a long letter appeared in *Sovietskaya Rossiya* which attacked the reforms of *perestroika* head-on. Penned by a lecturer at a Leningrad Institute, Nina Andreyeva, the article caused a sensation, being generally considered a call to arms of the conservative forces.

"It is a detailed programme for overt and covert opponents of *perestroika*," a letter by leading arts people in *Pravda* declared in response.

In *Izvestiya,* our friend, economist Otto Lacis, debunked the 'myth' that times had been better under Stalin. He argued that the past *had* to be studied so as to guarantee that such distortions of socialism as under Stalin could never happen again. "*Perestroika* is going through a dangerous time," Otto wrote, "there's not enough understanding as to what the economy requires, yet tangible results are needed now!"

Otto was not one of the hot-headed 'reformers' of the Yeltsin type (of whom there were many, judging by the columns of the newspapers and magazines). He was a serious economist, a Doctor of Economics who had worked on the Communist movement's international journal *Problems of Peace and Socialism* (called *World Marxist Review* in English) in Prague during the sixties and was now Deputy Editor of *Kommunist*, the CPSU's theoretical journal. In our many discussions over all the years that I knew him (I had first met him in 1963) I knew him to be a true Communist, loyal to the principles of Communist theory, but unafraid to raise and find solutions for the very real problems that existing socialism faced. I respected Otto greatly and on a personal level we were all very fond of him, his wife Tamara and their children Alyosha and Sasha.

On my recent visit to Latvia, Otto happened to be there and invited me to his mother's flat in Riga. His sister was there too, and we had a tasty meal together remembering when I had first visited them in the sixties. All Otto's relatives were Latvian, and he was much attached to that country, though I think, like many Communists, he also felt Soviet, in the sense that he felt he belonged to that nation of so many nationalities – the USSR.

He, his daughter Sasha and little grandson Daniel came to visit us in Derbyshire in 2001. Tamara had sadly died the previous year. Driving round the narrow lanes of the Derbyshire countryside where Ricardo and I now live, near Matlock, Daniel asked Otto: "*Dyedushka*, why are the roads so narrow and winding?" I had to laugh, but it was a natural question to ask, since the roads in Russia are very wide and straight, typical of a big country.

I had so many questions I would have liked to ask him on that visit, after the collapse of the USSR, but their visit was short, so many questions were left unanswered. But I remember disagreeing with his evaluation of the Soviet intervention in Afghanistan as mostly negative. Having visited Afghanistan twice during my years in Moscow, I could not help but compare the backwardness, poverty and oppression of women there with the neighbouring Soviet republics of Central Asia I visited, like Uzbekistan, Tajikistan and Turkmenistan, where women were educated and strolled freely in the streets, just as in Russia. I knew that it was the Revolution that had brought the countries of Central Asia into the 20th century practically from feudalism.

There is a wonderful 1965 Soviet film, *The First Teacher,* directed by Andrei Konchalovsky, based on a novel by the Kirghiz writer Chingiz Aitmatov, which shows a young Red Army Communist sent to mountainous Kirghizia in 1923, at the end of the Civil War. His mission is to set up a school in that remote area where elders did not allow children to go to school. He falls in love with one of his students, but the young woman is sold by her father to a wealthy chieftain. The film, a classic of Soviet cinema, gives a wonderful insight into the problems faced by those early revolutionaries in the feudal societies of Central Asia. Reactionary forces in the village burn the school down, but viewers sense that progress will prevail in the end. It is a moving, eloquent film which I first saw in my early twenties, and whose powerful images have stayed with me ever since.

The contrast I saw on my visits in the 1980's between backward Afghanistan, where women are hidden behind all-enveloping blue burkas, with only a rectangular mesh slit for the eyes, and modern Soviet Central Asia was enough proof for me of the huge advantages socialism had brought that region.

On my very first visit to the USSR in 1963 I met a young Afghan student who was studying in Moscow under a governmental agreement with the Soviet Union. I knew little at that time about his country, except that it was a place where wealthier British students than myself went on holiday and brought back the sheepskin coats that became a fashion icon in the West at that time. The student, whose name I can't remember now, told me that his country was ruled by a monarchy, King Mohammad Zahir Shah, and that his country had friendly, neighbourly relations with the USSR. Speaking in good Russian, he told me how happy he was with his engineering course at the newly created Peoples' Friendship University named after Patrice Lumumba[85], set up in 1960 to provide higher education for students from the developing world.

After this one conversation with the first Afghani I had ever met, my 21-year old self was keen to visit that far-off country some day. I had no idea at that time that 25 years later, I would.

Towards the end of March 1988, the Soviet Union's *kolkhozniki* held their 4th Congress, nearly 20 years since their last Congress. The *kolzhozy* were huge agricultural enterprises which had resulted from the wholesale

---

85 See Footnote 55.

collectivisation of the twenties and thirties. They produced half the country's grain and milk and most of its cotton and potatoes. *Kolkhoz* means 'collective farm' in Russian, but of 'collective' there remained little, by the eighties. They were run like any state enterprise, with the same sort of management structures and farmworkers who worked for a wage. These could farm their own plots and sell their produce at *kolkhoz* markets, but since many of them lived in blocks of flats, they often did not have their own plots.

"Lenin's innovative ideas on coops have been seriously watered down," Gorbachov told the Congress, called to discuss the recently published Bill on Cooperatives. There were to be no more state subsidies for collective farms in future, delegates were told. As in industry, so in agriculture – all enterprises had to be self-financing, in other words, profitable.

Lenin, towards the end of his life, wrote about cooperatives, giving them greater importance than earlier. This was after the NEP[86] period, which the young Soviet Government had been forced to introduce as a temporary expedient.

"..... since political power is in the hands of the working-class, since this political power owns all the means of production, the only task, indeed, that remains for us is to organise the population in cooperative societies. ..... But not all comrades realise how vastly, how infinitely important it is now to organise the population of Russia in cooperative societies."

"…..many of our practical workers look down upon cooperative societies, failing to appreciate their exceptional importance, first, from the standpoint of principle (the means of production are owned by the state), and, second, from the standpoint of transition to the new system by means that are the *simplest, easiest and most acceptable to the peasant.*"

"We went too far when we reintroduced NEP, but not because we attached too much importance to the principal of free enterprise and trade — we went too far because we lost sight of the cooperatives, because we now underrate cooperatives, because we are already beginning to forget the vast importance of the cooperatives from the above two points of view."

From *On Cooperatives*, January 1923)

It is interesting to re-read Lenin on this, as it does show that he thought that coops were important as a way of achieving citizens' participation, and that what was "most acceptable to the peasant" was forefront in his mind in working out the best strategies for that difficult period. Would he have been

---

86 NEP: New Economic Policy, introduced in 1922 and lasting till 1928, was a more market-oriented economic policy deemed necessary after the 1918-22 Civil War. The Soviet authorities paused the complete nationalisation of industry (established during the period of War Communism of 1918 to 1921) and introduced a mixed economy which allowed private individuals to own small enterprises, though the state continued to control banks, foreign trade, and large industries.

in favour of wholesale enforced collectivisation such as that carried out under Stalin, who took over as leader after Lenin's death in 1924? It seems doubtful, reading his thoughts on cooperation.

The countryside near Moscow was very attractive. One of our favourite Sunday outings was to get the metro to *Rechnoi Vokzal* (River Station) on the Moscow Volga Canal and take a boat to any of the beautiful beaches and completely unspoilt resorts that graced its banks. One such place was *Bukhta Radosti* (Bay of Joy). We would take a picnic, lay our towels on the grassy banks among the birch trees, have a dip in the river, watch the children play ball and paddle and perhaps have a short snooze. There was sometimes an ice-cream kiosk, where we would buy the delicious Russian ice-creams of various sorts. Further back from the beach, there was sometimes a small cafe, but all these places were very natural, with no formal gardens, just grass, trees and sandy areas for volleyball and other games. The Moscow summer is relatively short, but very warm while it lasts - more or less from June to the end of August.

Sometimes we would go with Chilean friends – exiles like Ricardo, some of whom had been terribly tortured in Chile after the 1973 military coup there. There was always lots of laughter on those occasions, gallows humour never far away as they shared stories of capture, imprisonment and interrogation, now thankfully behind them. The children would play together, usually in Russian, though ours and all the others spoke Spanish with their parents. I remember on one occasion, when the twins were about 10, they and a few other girls of similar age formed a circle in the water and proceeded to try out synchronised swimming, which was hilarious: we saw outstretched arms and pointed toes emerging from the water, but - not very synchronised! Every time they made another attempt, they would collapse in giggles, much to the adults' amusement.

A few years later, I took a two-day canal cruise north from Moscow to Uglich, west of Yaroslavl. It's a very relaxing experience - to move slowly and silently along Russia's waterways, seeing unspoilt villages on either side, people sometimes waving from the banks. Ancient white churches, their golden domes glinting in the sunlight, surrounded by white stone walls in every village. We stopped to bathe at one beach, and it was so pleasant to feel the sandy bottom beneath my feet and the warm lapping water with a gentle current.

As we went through one lock on the Moscow Canal, our ship was suddenly in the bowels of the deep lock before the water rose to allow us to emerge from the higher lock gates. I was on the lowest deck, looking out from a porthole in the side of the ship and seeing ourselves dwarfed by the immensely high walls of the lock, covered in algae, so close you felt you could almost touch them. I looked upwards and the top of the lock looked so far up that it felt like being in a deep, dark cavern with impossibly steep rock walls that you couldn't possibly climb up to get out. Eerie, even a little scary.

The Moskva-Volga Canal connects the Moskva River with the Volga. At 128 kilometres long, it was constructed during the industrialisation of the thirties. Thanks to this canal, Moscow has access to five seas: the White Sea, Baltic Sea, Caspian Sea, Sea of Azov, and the Black Sea. That's why Moscow is sometimes called *port pyati moryei* (port of five seas). The lock dimensions are 290 by 30 metres and there are 8 locks. It has several monumental statues along its length, including a 25 metre one of Lenin at Dubna, where the canal meets the river Volga. One of Joseph Stalin of similar size was demolished in 1961 during the period of de-stalinisation.[87]

The Moskva-Volga Canal is just one of the many huge and impressive industrialisation projects built during the decades of Stalin's leadership. At that time, science and industry were the most well-patronised and funded sectors of the economy. "By the time Stalin died on 5th March 1953, the Soviet Union boasted the largest and best-funded scientific establishment in history," claims one author.[88]

From a country in 1917 where industry was concentrated mainly in Moscow, St Petersburg and a few other cities, the USSR rapidly became an industrial powerhouse, with massive iron and steel plants like Magnitogorsk and Uralmash, huge hydroelectric power stations like the one on the Dnieper River, and the Chelyabinsk Tractor Plant, to mention just a few, all built in the twenties and thirties. And for all the criticism laid at Stalin's door during the Gorbachov years, the fact is that, due to this incredible pace of industrialisation in the early decades of the 20th century, the USSR was able to defeat German fascism with its superior tanks, machine-guns and other weaponry.

One of the most exotic trips I made during my years as a Moscow correspondent was to Nadym in the Yamal peninsula beyond the Arctic circle. It was early April, 1988, and the temperature there was -25°. It was so cold that my battery-operated camera would not work, so unfortunately I have few photographs from that trip.

I had read a damning letter in *Komsomolskaya Pravda* by a young geologist by the name of Bozhenko working in the Yamburg gasfields. It seemed like a cry from the heart:

> "I'm sick of hearing the word *"perestroika"* and not seeing any *perestroika* in practice. Come and visit us here beyond the Arctic Circle and see how we live......No proper work clothes, canvas boots and beachwear sweaters. Yet it's -48° C..... Worse provisions you'll not find

---

87 On Stalin's death in 1953, after a short period of collective leadership, Nikita Khrushchov became CPSU General Secretary and began reforms to eliminate the cult of personality around Stalin and dismantle the Gulag labour-camp system, denounced in Khrushchov's famous "Secret Speech" to the 1956 20th Communist Party Congress.

88 *Stalin and the Scientists*, Simon Ings, Grove Press, New York, 2016, page XV.

anywhere: rotten potatoes, practically no vegetables."

He goes on to slam the lack of any social facilities: "The young people – nearly a quarter of our settlement – return from work in the tundra and get drunk. What else is there for them to do?"

"Slovenliness, lies, favouritism. A management that's afraid of taking necessary decisions at the right time, waiting for instructions 'from above'," the letter went on. "Ordinary workers do an honest job....but hardly anybody cares about the conditions they live in or their health."

It was strong stuff. In the town of Nadym, though, where we stayed, things seemed a lot better than in Bozhenko's settlement, which was further north nearer to the gasfield. In Nadym there were blocks of flats, built in an ingenious series of curves, so as to give some shelter from the icy winds and snow for the triple-glazed innermost buildings - nursery, school, health centre and culture club.

Nadym's population in 1988 was 50,000. In the whole of the Yamal peninsula it was 80,000, of whom 2,800 were indigenous Nenets people, traditionally reindeer herders.

It was a memorable trip giving rise to conflicting emotions for me. On the one hand we met Russian and Ukrainian engineers and metallurgists who had pioneered a novel automatic electro-welding technique, which meant that sections of the giant pipes taking natural gas from Yamburg, Medvezhye and Urengoi to Western Europe could be welded in a fraction of the time manual welders could do the job; on the other hand we met Nenets people who complained that the gas industry was ruining the mosses on which their reindeer feed, as it takes 30 years or so for this delicate plantlife to regenerate.

"It used to be oil and gas production first, and people's needs relegated to the background," admitted Igor Shapalov, head of the Yamburg Oil and Gas Construction Board. "When we first started exploiting Medvezhye, it was detrimental to the ecology." Bulldozers had crushed huge numbers of trees and the heavy caterpillar tracks of lorries and jeeps had flattened the moss under the snow.

As you fly by helicopter over the tundra and the vast, blindingly white expanses of windswept snow, with not a tree or a building as far as the eye can see, you would be forgiven for thinking that there is plenty of untouched land for the 35,000 or so reindeer. But the Nentsy have to travel miles

with their sleighs, carrying their wigwam-shaped reindeer skin tents called *chum*, in search of new snowy pastures for their herds – their only livelihood.

We landed near a Nenets *stoibishchye* and were invited inside to meet the family inside their *chum*. A Nenets baby was rocking herself in a small cradle suspended from the reindeer-hide roof, and a couple of shyly smiling children were playing outside, well wrapped up in reindeer skin boots and fur coats and hats. Their mother spoke to us in quite good Russian, telling us that her older children were away at school, where they learned their own Nenets language, but also Russian and, later, another foreign language among the whole gamut of school subjects taught throughout the Soviet Union. They lived in their boarding schools during term time, returning during school holidays.

"The problem is that they're away so much that they lose the feel for the tundra," their mother told us. The result was that they often did not want to come back for good and work as reindeer-herders, as their ancestors had done for generations.

It is the age-old quandary: should indigenous peoples and tribes be left to live their lives as they have done for centuries, or should efforts be made to bring their living standards up to those in the more advanced regions and countries? Should their children have access to modern healthcare and education, even if in the process they lose something of their ancient cultures?

The Bolsheviks were sure that the social justice the new socialist society was going to bring should be afforded to *all* of the USSR's citizens. And just as they sent teachers into Central Asia, banning early marriage of young girls and undertaking mass re-education there, so they also sent people to the far-off northern regions of Siberia to bring literacy and healthcare to those indigenous populations and ensure that their children could enjoy the life chances that education and access to other cultures afforded them[89].

So the Nentsy children, boarding at schools from 7 to 15 years for most of the year, may be losing the 'feel for the tundra', but on the other hand, as the mother mentioned, they could call on a helicopter in case of illness – and through the education system they had access, not only to the rich culture of Russia, its literature, its music, its drama, its ballet, but to the cultures of all the other republics of the Soviet Union, each of them rich in their own cultures, languages, traditions and history.

As one friend once said to me: "We've got such a big and varied country, we don't need to go abroad for holidays; we can go to Samarkand, or Bukhara, or the Caucasus mountains or Altai, or Lake Baikal, or the Black Sea or Baltic coast – we have so many places to choose from!" It is true: I travelled a lot during my years as a correspondent, but still only managed to see a fraction of that huge country.

---

89 This is vividly described in a novel set in the far north, *Alitet Goes to the Hills*, by Tikhon Syomushkin, Foreign Languages Publishing House, 1947.

One evening whilst in Nadym, I went to the *banya* (sauna) with two local women and Olya, my assistant, who accompanied me on that trip. There was something a little surreal for me, sitting naked in that stifling heat, whilst outside the temperature was nearly -30° C. It turned out to be a fascinating evening, eating chocolates, drinking tea and later, *shampanskoye*. Soviet champagne was very popular and any celebration worth its salt in the USSR would be accompanied by *shampanskoye*.

One, Galina, had three daughters, the elder of whom was away studying dressmaking in Chelyabinsk. The other, Irina, had 2 daughters, the elder of whom was going to a *tyekhnikum*[90] in Tyumen the following year. Both women had had their children baptised in domestic ceremonies and celebrated Russian Easter at home. Galina joked that one of her daughters had unwittingly let this out at school – "You know what kids are like!" I asked if there had been any repercussions. "Oh no," she replied. "It's not illegal, of course, but it's something we tend to keep to ourselves."

After a few glasses of *shampanskoye* we got on to intimate topics, like *pederastiya* (paedophilia) and men who exposed themselves. I knew such things existed there, as a Swedish friend and I, living in Moscow at the time, had experienced an incident twenty years earlier. It felt good to be chatting with these Soviet women so freely and honestly; it was clear that such negative phenomena in society are not automatically solved under socialism and may take more than decades to disappear, if ever.

Once again, too, I was reminded of the hardships of life in the Soviet Union in the post-war years. Galina had come to the far north eight years earlier from the European part of Russia and had lived with her husband and daughter in one half of a railway carriage - 9 square metres - as they had to share it with another family. Now she lived in a 4-roomed flat in Nadym, which was bliss, she said.

There was so much to admire: the fortitude and stoicism of Russians, the feats of their engineers and scientists extracting oil and gas in such inhospitable regions. I asked one man why he had come to work up here. "Partly for my own professional development, and partly it's some kind of romanticism - you really get to test yourself here!"

In Nadym we saw swimming pools and gyms, schools, hospitals, cinemas, libraries and nurseries, as well as several *banya*. It was impressive. In Yamburg and Urengoi we saw their achievements in improving housing and social life and learned of their ambitious projects for the future. There was so much that was positive and the people we met seemed so practical and energetic, you felt sure that they *would* accomplish what they planned.

My Yamal trip reinforced my view that *glasnost* was all very well, and necessary, but that it should not blot out from view the immense achievements of Soviet society. Yet in the media and in speeches *only* the negative was

---

90 *Tyekhnikum:* something like our technical colleges.

highlighted. All balance had disappeared.

I sometimes felt a bit sorry for my fellow British correspondents: they had the unenviable job of concentrating mainly on the "dissidents", because that was what their editors wanted. The 1980's were still steeped in Cold War psychology, despite Gorbachov's new thinking and efforts to break down old stereotypes.

Whereas I had the opportunity to go on trips to exotic places like Yamal, in the pleasant company of other correspondents from the world's progressive media. We were often invited into local people's homes and, as Russian speakers, we could converse with people we met in Russian.

I tried to report, not only on all that was new in these *perestroika* times, but on cultural events and festivals and my chats with "ordinary" Soviet people as I went about shopping, or at theatres, on river boats, in parks or the grounds of what we would call stately homes, all of which were open to the public free of charge.

One day I went to the Blue Bird Jazz Club in Moscow, run by a young Armenian, Vartan Tonoian. It was in the basement of 23 Chekhov Street and jazz aficionados would crowd its tables every Wednesday to hear Soviet and visiting jazz players. Vartan told me it had only been going a year, and he was encountering a lot of problems.

"If I want to invite a superb musician or band that's not yet known, I can't legally pay them any fees," he explained, "because fees can only be paid to musicians on the Ministry of Culture registered musicians' list." To avoid the maze of paperwork, committees and officials that everything had to go through – like having entrance tickets printed – Vartan wanted to run it as a cooperative, but again, he had come up against problems.

"Nobody says it's impossible – but no one says 'yes' either!" he told me.

Over strong Armenian coffee in Vartan's flat, the yelps of his lively little dog Charlie interrupting the jazz playing on his stereo, he told me he agreed there should be financial control over coops so that people couldn't become millionaires, "because really rich people are beyond control and stop caring about music." He was scathing towards Soviet officialdom and "people who join organisations for the privileges and perks these offer."

"*Perestroika* means people doing things directly themselves, not having to wait for permission from someone 'upstairs'! If everybody is just going to continue waiting for instructions, it's not going to work. We need less control from bureaucrats!"

"Every government, whatever the system, has to believe in its own people." Whilst jazz was no longer frowned upon, Tonoian said, it still faced many obstacles.

Vartan's words struck a chord with me. There were many in the CPSU, I was sure, who had joined the Party for what they could get out of it, rather than anything else. Careerists exist everywhere, but it was a problem in a one-party system. As I had seen on my earlier visit to Uzbekistan, Party membership for some had meant special shops, better access to good polyclinics, sanatoria and holiday homes.

Gorbachov had announced that the CPSU would hold a special Conference – only the 19th ever held – between the five-yearly Congresses. And in the run-up to that June Conference, *Pravda* began to publish the views and ideas of many rank-and-file Party members.

"Better fewer, but better" had been Lenin's principle, scientist A. Zvezdin wrote, urging expulsion of all members unworthy of a Party card, such as drunkards, bribe-takers and those who abused their positions as officials. He attacked the present *nomenklatura* system by which management positions were filled by Party people. "Lenin in his day had demanded removal of Communists who were not up to the job," Zvezdin pointed out. "But we still mollycoddle mediocre managers: we move them into equivalent or even higher management armchairs!"

"*Nomenklatura*! Once a person gets into its orbit, he'll circle round in it till retirement!" he complained, urging a root-and-branch review of the system.

We may not have the exact equivalent here in Britain. But we do have the old school tie network, and when you learn that nearly half of the BBC's highest paid employees are educated at fee-paying public schools compared with only seven per cent of the nation overall – making someone who attended a public school six times more likely to become a highly paid BBC staff member – it is clear that we also have a "nomenclature" system, even if it is not given that name.

Oxford and Cambridge universities have special intake for pupils from the public schools, offering their own Admissions test for would-be applicants, either instead of or in addition to, the state A level examinations. I knew this from my own experience. When I was in my last year at our local grammar school (it was during the years of the 11+ exam), I attended a sixth form conference in Buxton at which I met a student from a big private school in Derbyshire. We met up a few times in the weeks that followed and, after we received our exam results, I discovered that he had barely scraped through his 'A' Levels, whereas I had got good results in mine. He wasn't worried though – his entry to Oxford was assured, he told me, as he had already been given a place through his school having reserved places.[91]

May Day in Moscow 1988 was a bright sunny day, and I took Martha and Liza with me, as I had taken Victor the previous year. We stood in the tribunes

---

91 "A decade ago, parents who handed over tens of thousands of pounds a year for the likes of Eton College, St Paul's School or King's College School in Wimbledon could comfortably assume their kids had a very good chance of attending Oxford or Cambridge, two of the best universities in the world. A 2018 Sutton Trust study showed that just eight institutions, six of them private, accounted for more Oxbridge places than 2,900 other UK secondary schools combined. When the headmaster of Westminster School boasted at an open evening that half the sixth form went on to Oxbridge, approving murmurs filled the wood-panelled hall. (I was there.)" From an article by *Financial Times* Business Editor Brooke Masters, FT magazine, July 2 2021.

next to the Lenin Mausoleum, among all the journalists and invited guests and dignitaries from other countries. That year there were posters celebrating the recent Afghanistan accords for the withdrawal of Soviet troops.

"More *glasnost,* more light!" came over the loudspeakers as that slogan came into view, carried by representatives of Soviet media workers, among the thousands of trades unionists and workers invited to that year's parade. "*Perestroika* of the economy: our aim is full self-financing! 45 factories in our district are now self-financing!" was another, not very catchy, slogan.

At the end of the parade, I caught sight of deposed Moscow Party Secretary Boris Yeltsin leaving the Square with his wife, and hurried to catch up with him. He had had a heart attack after his removal as Moscow Secretary, but was now back at work and looked well. "I'm from the *Morning Star,*" I told him breathlessly, "what are your hopes for the upcoming Conference?"

"The 19th Party Conference is very important," he said. "It's to discuss and resolve important issues of deepening democracy in the Party and in society."

"Democratisation of inner-party life is essential, for there to be progress." If it had been carried out earlier, he went on, his present situation might have been different. He was looking forward – if elected as a delegate, he added – to it resolving the central question of democratisation. Smiling at my daughters, he shook my hand, wishing us *s prazdnikom*! (Happy May Day)

I did not trust Yeltsin, since he had publicly revealed his differences with the rest of the Party leadership, which clearly went against the principles of democratic centralism. A genially smiling figure on that day, Yeltsin would become the divisive and back-stabbing figure who oversaw the disintegration of the USSR and the introduction of capitalism to Russia, which brought about mass poverty during the nineties.

One of the most interesting contributions to the pre-Conference discussion was by someone called Selivanov, from the Aviation Ministry. He traced the origins of the growth of bureaucracy in the thirties when "those who produced became fewer and fewer, whereas those who managed, and controlled - the go-betweens and pseudo-scientists - became more and more." Careerist tendencies took hold in the Communist Party, he argued, due to it being the party in power, and this led to mediocre yes-men being preferred to people prepared to speak out.

"Wherever Party membership – rather than personal qualities and qualifications – is the key to promotion to managerial posts, you're likely to get people joining who are thinking first and foremost of career advancement," Selivanov wrote. He argued for secret ballots and limited terms for First Secretaries of city and regional Party committees. More real power should be given back to the Soviets and there should be much less Party tutelage over their work.

The need for changes in administration to eliminate the vast bureaucracy had long been recognised. Moshe Lewin writes:

"Khrushchov's disbanding of more than 100 industrial ministries at the stroke of a pen was the most spectacular anti-bureaucratic initiative – the only one on such a scale. .....they were all reconstituted in 1965."

One of the problems highlighted by Gorbachov's attempted reforms was the duplication of government and Party in the economy, Lewin writes.

"...the transformation of the party into an apparatus ....entailed its de facto absorption by and into the bureaucratic realities of the state. The process started when the party became directly immersed in economic and other minutiae that were supposed to be handled by government ministries. Ministerial staff justly sensed that the party was duplicating their work, rather than concentrating on its own."[92]

Interviewing the Editor of *Kommunist*, Nail Bikkenin, I asked about this duplication of functions. The Party had to be relieved of many of its administrative and economic management functions, he said, "so that it can do its real job of political and ideological leadership." The administrative-command method of giving orders from the office chair had to go, he said, and be replaced by genuine work of convincing people of the worth of an idea.

Moves to cut Party privileges had been made, Bikkenin told me, e.g. cutting the numbers of functionaries allowed to use official cars. "It's easy to understand how special shops emerged when there are shortages in supplies, but they cause resentment in the population." Party workers had to be put under the strict control of society from now on, he said.

"Those against *perestroika* do not belong to one section of society alone," the *Kommunist* Editor explained. "They can be Party officials used to issuing orders, administrative functionaries accustomed to stealing, or workers used to getting paid regardless of the quality of their work."

The Soviet intervention in Afghanistan in 1979 was given enormous prominence in Britain and contributed greatly throughout subsequent years to the already strong anti-Sovietism and anti-communism of the Cold War years. It affected the British Communist Party and was one of the reasons for the split in the Party in the mid-eighties.

The mainstream British media, all owned by 'establishment' magnates, relentlessly hammered home the line that the Soviets had 'invaded' and was waging war on that country to impose Communism there.

The facts, as usual, are somewhat different. Afghanistan was a neighbouring country, sharing borders with the Soviet Central Asian republics of Uzbekistan, Tajikistan and Turkmenistan. Socialist groups had been active in Afghanistan since the sixties, but there had been a lack of unity in forming a united party capable of taking power. But in the seventies

---

92 Pp. 342 and 350, *The Soviet Century*, Moshe Lewin, Verso, London, 2016.

a socialist, Hafizullah Amin, became Afghanistan's President and began to introduce somewhat rash reforms, which caused a backlash, especially by religious traditionalists who felt they undermined Afghanistan's traditional Islamic culture. Foreign mercenaries intervened on the side of the opposition and, without proper equipment and training, the Afghanistan government was unable to resist them, eventually seeking help from the Soviet Union. Amid growing unrest and divisions inside the People's Democratic Party of Afghanistan, and no doubt fearing that this could lead to the overthrow of the socialist government, in December 1979 the USSR acceded to the request of the PDPA Government to intervene to help consolidate the progressive government under a less divisive figure, Babrak Karmal, who became President.

The United States and Pakistan backed, financed and trained the *mujahedeen* – the Afghan opposition forces who went on to wage war against the Soviet forces for the next 9 years. The Soviet Union lost 15,000 men in the war and 35,000 were wounded. The plight of the wounded *Afgantsy* veterans back home in the Soviet Union was a running sore for Soviet society for years after the troops' withdrawal.

My first visit to Afghanistan was to witness the initial stage of troop withdrawal in May 1988. I was part of a small group of correspondents, among whom was a Swedish journalist, Kerstin Gustafsson, of *Norrskensflamman.*

Kerstin and I had become friends soon after her arrival earlier that year. Her husband was a Chilean exile too, so we had that in common, and Kerstin, like myself, was a very active correspondent. We sat together on the plane to Kabul, and I'll never forget how, as our plane spiralled down to land in a corkscrew pattern in order to evade possible *mujahedeen* anti-aircraft missiles, Kerstin – who didn't like flying at the best of times – grabbed my hand in fright, digging her nails into my palm so hard it almost drew blood. She was terrified - yet later that trip, she accompanied the contingent of 1,200 Soviet troops in 300 armoured personnel carriers as they withdrew from Jelalabad, 80 km east of Kabul, which I dare say was just as dangerous.

Kabul, despite the destruction of parts of the centre from *mujahedeen* missiles, was beautiful in its way, with the snow-topped mountains of the Hindu Kush framing one's view. The people, too, going about their business at the busy street markets, seem to radiate a proud, noble presence, despite the years of war and hardship. After all, they were the descendants of a people who had never submitted to British efforts to conquer them, despite having been invaded three times from India (a British colony at the time) during the 19th and early 20th centuries.

Most of the women we saw in the streets and bazaars were dressed in the typical light blue *chadari,* all-encompassing flowing robes with a small rectangular mesh slit for the eyes, though we did see a few Afghan women dressed more like ourselves. The men wore turbans or the flat *pakol* caps and *payraan* tunics over loose cotton trousers. These were the clothes we mainly saw, but there are many different ethnic groups in Afghanistan each of which have their own traditional dress.

Was it right to have intervened to help the Karmal government introduce changes to drag the country out of its backwardness? In those few years, from 1978 until Soviet troops left, the government under both Karmal and later, Najibullah, introduced important changes such as education for both boys *and* girls, providing grants of 1,500 *afghanis* per month for the first five grades, so that poor parents could afford for their children not to have to work or beg.

It was never going to be easy in a country where men were allowed up to four wives according to Islamic law and where the educational level of the masses was very low; where subsistence farming was completely unmechanised and dependence on poppy cultivation for the heroin market had distorted the economy for decades. The Karmal and Najibullah governments had tried to diversify the economy, with Soviet help, and to the north there were some big economic projects, we were told, which provided half the country's national revenue. US financial and logistical backing for the *mujahedeen* opposition forces, together with anti-socialist islamist propaganda from neighbouring Pakistan and the USA, resulted in an exodus of some three million Afghans who left for Pakistan, to escape the war. There they became known as *taleban*, a Sunni Islamic fundamentalist political movement, but which originally simply meant 'students'. In exile they formed themselves into the military organization we know today, which ousted US and British forces in August 2021.

Obviously one of the main reasons for the USSR to intervene militarily was that of security for its southern border. The bordering Central Asian republics were also traditionally Muslim countries, though religion was not as powerful an influence there after seven decades of Soviet power. But to have a friendly, pro-socialist country on its southern border was obviously preferable to the Soviet Union, instead of a hostile, fundamentalist Islamic one, backed by the West.

Now, thirty or so years later, the West, in the form of NATO, has encircled Russia with bases, right up to its borders, despite promises to Gorbachov in 1990 that NATO would not expand eastwards. In the light of this, perhaps one can understand the Soviet point of view when it took the decision to intervene in 1979 to help Afghanistan consolidate what was then a friendly government.

The map below may be a joke, but it's not all that funny for the Russians:

"Proof that Russia Wants War": Look How Close They Put Their Countries To Our Military Bases!

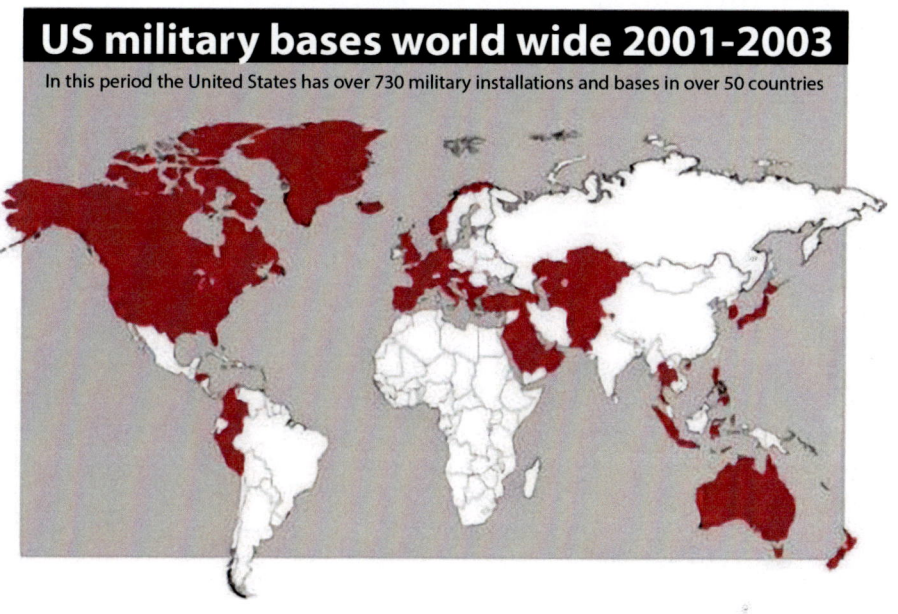

US military bases world wide 2001-2003

In this period the United States has over 730 military installations and bases in over 50 countries

Bad people are putting their countries closer and closer to our military bases!

The USA has 2,639 permanent bases in the USA and its territories, according to a 2005 Base Structure Report. And it has 737 permanent foreign bases and, since 1993, 98 temporary bases, according to Global Security.org.

A few days before our arrival in Kabul in May 1988, opposition forces in Pakistan launched 17 rockets on the capital, causing some 20 civilian deaths. Yet life went on: donkeys carrying baskets piled high with chilli peppers wove dangerously in and out of the traffic while wizened old men sat on pavements, their wares spread out on the ground in front of them.

We spoke to several Soviet officers and troops, who all said they felt satisfied with their mission to help the Afghan people against the most reactionary forces in Afghan society.

It was an exciting time to be there, witnessing the first phase of the historic withdrawal in accordance with the Geneva Agreement signed that April. I was interested to see how the locals reacted and was pleased to see that at least in Kabul and on the road from Jelalabad, the departing troops were met with smiles and garlands of flowers by local people and Afghan Government soldiers.

Exciting, but frightening too. Kerstin and I shared a room in a rather old-fashioned hotel in central Kabul and were chatting together before getting ready for bed when all of a sudden a deafening explosion rocked the old building. A shell had landed about 30 metres away. It was very scary.

"The opposition extremists always insisted Soviet troops must leave, but now that they are actually leaving, they are doing everything they can to disrupt the withdrawal," President Najibullah told us at a press conference the morning after. I found Najib very impressive. A well-educated, good-looking, moustached man with an imposing physical presence, he outlined the Government's two-year old policy of National Reconciliation, which was a partial retreat from his predecessors' socialist measures and an invitation to the opposition to share government on the basis of the country being declared an Islamic state.

"We Afghans are sick of war!" Najib declared. "War keeps our country in bondage to backwardness and starvation." Talks were going on with some 70 opposition groups and some of their leaders living abroad had now sought contact with the Government, he said. 50,000 of the armed opposition had laid down their arms, and 130,000 of the 3 million exiles had now returned. The Government had earmarked some 32m afghanis to cover the cost of resettling the 1 million Afghans they hoped would soon return.

Lt-General Boris Gromov, the sprightly 44-year old commander of the Soviet troops, told us the contingent's aim had not been military superiority, but to help the Afghan people to create the conditions for a peaceful life. The Afghan Army's combat readiness had increased greatly, he said, declaring that he was sure they would "be able to defend the gains of the 1978 April Revolution."

It was sad to see locals, among them children in school uniform, waving Soviet and Afghan flags as the armoured personnel carriers, tanks and other military hardware trundled past up the dry and dusty road northwards to the Soviet border. "Long live Afghan-Soviet Friendship!", "Thank you, Soviet internationalists!" some of the placards read. Sad, because the future was uncertain: would Najibullah's Government survive? And sad because of the many lives of Soviet conscripts lost and the many war wounded, left to live difficult lives ahead.

"Thanks to your valour, heroism and epic feats," Najibullah declared, "our children go to school, our peasants reap their harvests and our workers can work in the factories. We thank the Soviet soldiers for teaching our army not only how to defend their country, but also how to build and create, and risk their lives to provide what our people need – food for the hungry, clothes for the unclothed and medicines for the ill."

Afghanistan would remain a free, independent, sovereign, neutral and non-aligned country thanks to Soviet internationalist help, he declared. Up on the rocky brown hillside above Kabul, with the fierce sun beating down on us relentlessly, smiling retreating Soviet soldiers caught the flowers thrown by onlookers and punched the air with their fists.

As a mother, I found it heart-wrenching to visit a Kabul hospital where a 42-year old woman, Torpekai, was sobbing at the loss of her four-year old son, killed the previous night by a rocket fired by opposition groups operating from the hills around. They were well-equipped with all kinds of weaponry, including Stinger and Blowpipe anti-aircraft missiles, supplied by the West. Torpekai had been in her kitchen when tragedy struck, killing two other members of her extended family.

I met 12-year old Mohammed Hayad, badly burned when a bomb blast had set fire to a kerosene stove. A family of five had died. The father had owned a small cycle repair shop. Why bomb poor civilians like these? We were told that Afghan terrorists were getting paid big sums of money for carrying out such acts, and that the higher the rank of civilian killed, the higher the price paid.

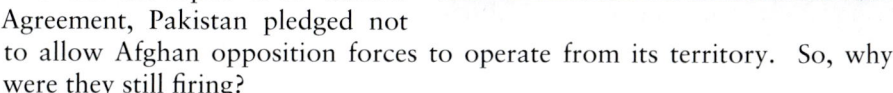

I asked Mohammed what he thought about Soviet troops leaving. "When they've gone, I think they'll fire more missiles," came his plaintive answer. What did he think of the opposition extremists who were prepared to do such things, I asked. "They're wicked, because they're killing a lot of Muslims."

Under the April 1988 Geneva Agreement, Pakistan pledged not to allow Afghan opposition forces to operate from its territory. So, why were they still firing?

We had fascinating meetings with former opposition exiles who had returned. Sitting cross-legged on a carpet, Mohamed Naim Ansori from Samangan province told us he had left his country in 1983, as "a lot of folk in that area were against the Government and they persuaded me to leave for Pakistan." Now, after hearing about the new policy of National Reconciliation, about 1,200 of them had decided to return. Ansori claimed he had been offered money by a French military adviser to go back to Pakistan, even after they had returned home.

The Governor of Jawzjan province, Gharib Hussen, told us: "Those fighting our Government at present are also our people, but they're being fed by those who want to crush our Revolution." The only people against the Government in his province, he claimed, were "those who want to live in great wealth and continue to exploit the people." Former opposition members had now been given posts in his province.

"Mistakes were made during Amin's rule," 47-year old Hussen said. "Many clergy and village elders were put in prison, under Amin, so people lived in fear of arrest." Now the new Constitution, passed last November at the Loya Jirgah (traditional assembly), had withdrawn Amin's Land Reform. Lands had been returned to the mullahs and private landowners, contributing to the National Reconciliation process, Hussen explained. The Constitution would guarantee a mixed economy, a multi-party system and recognition of Islam as the country's religion.

Another black-bearded and turbaned man, Kurban Shakh, told how he and others had for some time been prevented by their tribal leader from returning home from Pakistan. "Now the Government must go along with our national traditions and allow the people to practise their religion freely," he said.

Obviously in the course of a few days' visit one can only glimpse the reality of others' lives. But it was a privilege to talk freely to these men whom one would never normally meet, and hear their views about the present and the recent past. Apart from our Soviet interpreter, there was only our small group of Western journalists and we were free to ask anything. No one seemed reluctant to talk to us and we found a variety of views about the reconciliation process, the need as they saw it for Afghanistan to be an Islamic state, and the Soviet intervention. Some were glad to see the troops go, others less so and more appreciative of the economic help the Soviets had provided, in terms of new factories and schools.

The gains of the 1978 Afghan Revolution were tangible – the literacy campaign, free schooling, the 100 industrial projects built with Soviet assistance and encouragement for women to play a social and economic role in society. The National Reconciliation policy was a tacit admission that it had been a mistake to declare Afghanistan a socialist country before the people and objective conditions allowed for that.

Visiting the street bazaar on our last day, with Soviet soldiers guarding either end of the street, we spoke to the owner of a basement shoe shop, a father of eight, who told us that the state was now helping small private businesses like his. Why had so many of his countrymen left over the last 10 years, I asked him. "Some were from areas where the *dushman* enemy were fighting Government forces, so they left to avoid the war. Others were deceived by relatives who might have been with the opposition, and were persuaded to leave," he explained. "Now there's nothing to fear, even if they hold different views from that of the Government so I think most will come back."

As we left Afghanistan, I was filled with a mixture of feelings: admiration for the small advances that the Government had managed to implement, despite opposition from what I saw as reactionary Muslim clerics; admiration for President Najib, whose policy of National Reconciliation seemed intelligent and practical; but foreboding, as I feared American backing for the *mujahedeen* could tip the balance, bring down the Najib Government and wipe out those progressive gains.

After Soviet troops left, the Soviet Union continued to give economic assistance, but when the USSR disintegrated in 1991, this aid ceased. Najibullah's fragile Government collapsed a year or so later and he took refuge in the United Nations headquarters. In 1996, the forces of the *taleban* took Kabul and abducted Najibullah and his brother from UN custody, tortured them and hung their bodies from traffic posts. Only 49 when he was killed, a well-educated and cultured man, Najibullah was a man who could potentially have united Afghanistan's tribal population - a "truly national figure", as Gorbachov once called him.

Back in Moscow, there was no time to rest or recover my energy. There was so much going on. The new cooperatives were encountering resistance "from managers and Party leaders", according to Prime Minister Nikolai Ryzhkov speaking at a Supreme Soviet session in May 1988. I was particularly interested in what he said about the oldest type of coops – the *kolkhozy*.

These had accumulated debts of 88 billion roubles, Ryzhkov said, and in 3,000 of them, farmers were receiving more from the State than they actually earned. This could not go on, he said, and undermined the principle of cooperation. Since 1963 the USSR had had to import grain, despite having huge resources of fertile land. (This is in sharp contrast with today's Russia, which is the world's biggest grain exporter).

It was increasingly being highlighted that under socialism, where everything belongs to everybody, in fact this had ended up with a situation where nobody felt they owned anything. Was this due to the size of the collective farms, or the fact that managers had become divorced from the farmworkers, or that managerial methods were out-of-date, or that many farmworkers lived in blocks of flats, rather than in cottages with gardens and orchards?

I visited one of the new cooperatives in Moscow. It was housed in a dingy warehouse-like place with no windows and little natural light. The boss expounded all its virtues, the workers sat working diligently – but I was left with the distinct impression that such small coops could not possibly be the answer to the country's economic problems. What were the coop workers' pension rights, I asked. No straight reply. What were their holiday entitlements, sick pay? The same obfuscation. The country did need a better range and quality of consumer goods, it was true, but I couldn't see that this sort of small coop was the answer.

At the end of May 1988, US President Ronald Reagan came to Moscow – the capital of the country he had dubbed "evil empire" only a few years before. Earlier summits had managed to achieve some progress: the 1985 Geneva summit had agreed that nuclear war was unwinnable and should never be fought; the 1986 Reykjavik one showed that substantial cuts in strategic nuclear arms would be possible if weapons were kept out of outer space; and last year's Washington summit had ended with the signing of a treaty eliminating intermediate and shorter-range weapons.

Strategic arms cuts were much more difficult to agree on than INF, *Pravda* analyst Arkadi Maslennikov told me, partly due to the sheer numbers of missiles involved. "The aim is to bring each side's stocks down to 6,000 missiles each," he said. "70% of our strategic missiles are land-based, in silos, whereas the Americans have many sea-based long-range Cruise missiles, based on warships and submarines, and a large part of their air-based missiles on strategic bombers."

All that would be realistic from this summit, Maslennikov thought, would be a document registering progress and joint aims for the future.

Arkadi had been *Pravda*'s London correspondent in the years before I had come to Moscow. He was deeply intelligent and a kind, thoughtful and interesting man whom I grew to like and respect greatly the longer I knew him. He had a very good knowledge of our country, and much admired our peace movement, which he credited with having influenced world public opinion against nuclear weapons.

"The Soviet Union's merit is to have formulated "new political thinking" as our State policy, in putting forward our 1986 Programme of Universal and Complete Nuclear Disarmament by the year 2000."

The British Government's plans to "modernise" and compensate for the missiles due to be destroyed under the INF treaty were "dishonest and morally wrong", Maslennikov told me.

"If I were British, I would ask myself what my country's role is .... whether we should fight for peace, or whether we should go on building a new super-aircraft, which will probably be as costly as the Trident project," he went on. "In today's space-age and nuclear-age world, every nation and every people is involved in the planet's destiny – and Britain, as one of the world's five nuclear powers, has a bigger role than most."

It is depressing, as I write thirty or so years later, that Trident is still destined to swallow up vast amounts of money, as our Tory Government insists it is a deterrent that keeps the peace. CND has calculated that replacing Trident, Britain's nuclear weapons system, will end up costing at least £205 billion, though Ministry of Defence projects typically go well over budget.

To me it was sickening to hear Reagan, in a speech to students at Moscow State University, tell them what a wonderful place America was, how well the people lived, including native Americans on their reservations. He told them of the advances in democracy in Latin America, where in the 70's, he told them, only a third of the population had lived under democratic government – without, of course, mentioning Chile, where his country had been instrumental in snuffing out the one flame of democracy in that sub-continent at that time – the Popular Unity Government of the constitutionally elected President Salvador Allende.

His tone was smug and arrogant, but he was well received by the 750 students and staff who had come to hear him. Earlier in the week he had met with a group of dissidents, among whom was a former war criminal, Sasha Roshkov, who had worked as a *polizei* in territory occupied by the Nazis and had spent 25 years in prison after his conviction as a war criminal.

Reagan's lecturing on human rights didn't seem to have gone down so well among the students I spoke to afterwards. Hearing him say that now in the Soviet Union "the first breath of freedom stirs the air", one geology researcher, Tanya Kolchugina, told me: "Speaking for myself, I've never felt that our country wasn't free!" And those around her murmured their agreement.

Moscow State University is one of the seven "wedding-cake" buildings that tower over Moscow's skyline. It sits on the Lenin Hills, high above the river, with a great view over the city centre. Ricardo and I lived there during the academic year 1967-68, when we were studying Russian language and Phonology, Soviet and Russian history and literature, on a course for graduates of Russian from different parts of the world.

Students lived in small apartments for two, each of which had an entrance hall, with toilet and bathroom off it, leading to two small individual bedrooms, each with a double-glazed window at the far end. We used to put milk and perishables in the space between the windows to act as a fridge. Ricardo and a Colombian writer and literary critic, Jaime Mejía, shared the apartment opposite mine, which I shared with an Argentinian, Nancy Popenko, who spent most of her time playing loud tangos on her record-player and in deep nostalgia for her lover back in Buenos Aires. Our Swedish friend Ingelej - whom we have continued to see over the many years since - and three Finns, a few Italians, Belgians, French, Indians, Greeks, Japanese, Austrians and Sri Lankans lived further along the corridor.

Having known what British University halls of residence were like in England in the sixties, (single-sex, and visitors signed in for and out by 11pm), the halls at MGU (Moscow State University) were a refreshing contrast: they were mixed on every corridor and wing, with the only control being your University pass at the entrance. No one controlled who slept in whose room at all, which surprised me at the time, I remember. The only "control" was the *kontrol'naya komissiya*, made up of elected student members, whose job it was, very occasionally, to check on cleanliness and tidiness of the rooms. Poor Jaime, who had only one arm, the hand of which had four fingers but no thumb, lived in fear of the *kontrol'naya komissiya*, though at most they would have pointed out where more thorough cleaning was needed.

Back in Moscow in the eighties, we sometimes walked in the University grounds, now with our children, picking apples off the trees (all sorts of fruit trees grew there and people just picked them whenever they were ripe) and enjoying the views. We loved the new Circus nearby and were fortunate to see its world-famous clown, Oleg Popov, before he retired. Once, when we had gone as a family to the circus with English friends who were visiting, the clown invited me down into the ring, much to my embarrassment, and proceeded to make me the object of everyone's laughter!

Some of our friends preferred the old Moscow circus, which was a more intimate arena, but we found both of them equally impressive. Circus was taken seriously in the USSR: there were special Schools training circus artists, and the standards achieved by the trapeze artists, jugglers, weightlifters, clowns and animal trainers were first-class. The new Circus had the normal sandy arena for horse-riding and most of the acts, another one for ice-skating displays and yet another one with water, for sea animal performers - all of which were swiftly changed from one to another between acts. At this time, in the eighties, animals were still used in circuses, not only in the Soviet Union, of course. Most, under public pressure, have since phased them out.

The fourth summit between Presidents Mikhail Gorbachov and Ronald Reagan did at least see the signing of the INF Treaty. Gorbachov called it a "watershed political event", whilst at the same time condemning the American side for the missed opportunity to make real progress on cutting each side's strategic offensive arsenals by 50%, due to US intransigence on its SDI (Space Defense Initiative) programme.

A START treaty to cut strategic arms would have to wait for a future summit, he said, admitting that continuation of US-Soviet dialogue was the summit's main result.

"People are sick and tired of wars, tensions and conflicts," Gorbachov said, speaking after the summit, paying tribute to the important role of world public opinion, through the many peace and disarmament organisations.

Two people from a delegation of British peace organisations who met Gorbachov that June, 1988, were identical twins, Mary and Irene Brennan. When they came to see us in our flat, our twin daughters were keen to ask them what it was like for them growing up as twins. Irene was active in West Midlands CND and her sister, who was a nun, was there representing Pax Christi. Christian CND, Labour Action for Peace, London Centre for International Peacebuilding, CND and British Peace Assembly were some of the peace organisations who came to Moscow to meet the Soviet leader, who was given a tape of Christian CND peace songs.

There was much hope in those years, after Gorbachov's 1986 Declaration for a Nuclear-free World and ensuing US-Soviet summits, among progressive and peace-loving people in the West, tired of being constantly under the threat of nuclear annihilation. And Gorbachov himself was seen by many on the left as a leader who would breathe new life, not only into the peace process, but into the socialist system too.

1988 marked the millennium of Christianity in Russia, and commemorates the baptism by Prince Vladimir, ruler of the medieval state of Kiev Rus, of his subjects into the Christian faith in AD 988. From this event the Russians, Belorussians and Ukrainians all trace their religious heritage.

Celebrations began in Moscow on June 5th, with special gatherings and services attended by religious dignitaries from all over the world. The main celebrations on June 10th were at Moscow's beautiful Danilov Monastery, stunningly renovated in time for the millennium and paid for by the Russian Orthodox Church. Confiscated by the state after the Revolution, the historic thirteenth-century building was restored to the church in June 1983 and was once again a functioning monastery.

Russian Orthodox churches are invariably ancient and beautiful; inside you could see little old women in their typical Russian floral headscarves prostrating themselves in front of the altar.

Orthodox churches do not have seats, so the congregation stands throughout services, which did not seem very democratic. The bearded black-robed priests would intone incomprehensible chants in Old Russian, while their flock crossed themselves fervently. The priests were mostly middle-aged men, often looking rather self-important. Whenever we dropped in on any church, we saw that there were usually few, mostly elderly worshippers.

I interviewed Metropolitan Filaret of Minsk and Byelorussia just before the Millenium celebrations. He gave the impression of being rather bored as he told me that in his view, there was no contradiction between the Russian Orthodox church and the Soviet socialist state.

A new law on the freedom of conscience was being drafted, and the Church wanted 'legal representation' under that law, he said. They also wanted the right to carry out 'mercy missions' – visiting the sick in hospitals, for instance. I had to suppress the urge to laugh as I thought to myself that he'd be the last person I would want to see if I were in hospital....!

You have probably guessed by now that I am not a fan of the Russian Orthodox Church. Actually, being an atheist, I have little time for church establishments of any kind. The hierarchies of the big established religions seem to me to go against the essence of Christianity, and the only religious movements I can relate to are Liberation Theology and the Quakers. Before I went to live in Chile in 1969, I read the works of Latin American Liberation Theology priests like Hélder Câmara, who was a Brazilian Roman Catholic Archbishop during the military dictatorship. He is quoted as having said:

"When I give food to the poor, they call me a saint. When I ask why they are poor, they call me a communist."

One of the witnesses at my marriage to Ricardo in a Chilean prison after the 1973 military coup was a Spanish priest – José Luís Ysern - who espoused Liberation Theology and who had become a friend as a mature student of mine in English. So whilst I have no time for the hierachies of established religions with all their pomp and circumstance, I do acknowledge and respect honest Christians and people of all faiths who try to do good works. We have continued to meet with José Luís on recent visits to Chile.

The 13th century Danilov monastery comprises a number of churches and cathedrals ringed by thick whitewashed walls, and is the spiritual and administrative centre of the Russian Orthodox Church.

We headed over there for the Millenium celebrations, and on the way, as we approached the walls, a militiaman stopped our car, a white Lada 1700, asking for my credentials. I had not realised that I needed special accreditation on top of my normal Press Centre card, so presented that, hoping it would be enough.

"Hmm, all right, so this is you," he said, examining my photo on my Press Card, "but who is this?" nodding in the direction of Ricardo, who was in the driver's seat. "Oh, he's just the chauffeur!" I answered breezily. At this, the young militiaman turned towards our three children in the back: "All right, and so, who might they be?" At that point we all collapsed laughing, and fortunately for us, the militiaman laughed with us, and, still chuckling to himself, waved us through.

I have never lived that down: "Oh, he's just the chauffeur"! You can imagine how many times Ricardo has reminded me of that!

I wanted to visit the Baltic republics. The new independence movements that had been formed there were increasingly clamouring for independence; monuments to the victims of the deportations during WWII were being considered.[93]

I took the overnight train to Tallinn on 20th June and spent the next 3 days there. The old Estonian Communist Party leadership under Karl Vajno had been replaced. The new People's Front in Estonia had held a huge rally the previous week in the famous Lauluväljak song festival arena. Apparently some 150,000 Estonians had attended that rally.

In contrast with my previous visit to Estonia a year earlier, now I could sense the overt nationalism among People's Front members I met. During my trip I learnt that only 10% of Popular Front supporters were Russian-speaking. One Popular Front representative and Communist Party member, Edgar Savisaar, for instance, was reluctant to speak Russian to me, even though that was our best common language. I met the republic's President, Arnold Rüütel, who called the Front "normal, sensible and very positive". A delegate to the forthcoming 19th CPSU Conference, Rüütel explained that a parliamentary commission was looking at how to give justice to victims of repressions during WWII. "We must open up the whole truth and look at particular cases of people who suffered deportation," he told me.

The Estonian Communist Party delegation to the forthcoming 19th CPSU Conference was calling for economic matters to be decided within the republic, not through Gosplan or central ministries; for Estonia to have its own citizenship and for Estonian to be a state language, alongside Russian.

---

93 See Appendix I for information on the West's agenda vis-a-vis the Baltic republics.

At that time Estonian, like the languages of other non-Russian republics, was considered a national language, but not a state one.

"We propose that all that our republic produces should stay in Estonia," Dr. Rein Otsason, Director of Estonia's Institute of Economics told me. It sounded like a recipe for disaster – and likely to bring about the break-up of the Union, if all republics took a similar stance.

All the Estonian Party people I spoke to, including top leaders, economists and journalists, avowed their support for the Gorbachov reforms; as Rein Veidemann, Editor of the monthly magazine Raduga (Rainbow) put it: "We're not interested in separating from the Union, but in being the leading force for *perestroika*!"

A sociological survey held 5 years previously had shown that the majority of Estonians were worried about their language, whereas other nationalities did not have similar fears. This was partly due to the influx of Russian workers who came to man the new industries set up in Estonia. "In recent years we started to feel that if immigration continued at the present rate, then by the beginning of the 21st century the native population would be in a minority," Veidemann said. "We cannot allow this."

In 1979, only 13% of Russian citizens living in Estonia spoke Estonian. When I was there in 1988, I was told that 25-30% of Russians living there spoke some Estonian. This meant that the two communities led virtually separate lives. One can certainly understand that in such a tiny population as Estonia – 1.6 million, where only 1 million were ethnic Estonians, this could be seen as a problem.

I came away from Estonia feeling unsettled and concerned. I felt that there must have been many mistakes made over the years by the Party leadership there for so much to be questioned and rejected now.

Between meetings, I had time to look round the beautiful old town of Tallinn, with its narrow, cobbled streets and tiny bars and shops, which seemed well stocked.

From Tallinn I took a train to the neighbouring Latvian capital, Riga, which I had visited a few months earlier. Again I met the CPSU's Ideological Secretary, Anatoly Gorbunov, to ask him what the main issues were on the eve of the forthcoming and unprecedented Party Conference.

A few days before my arrival, Gorbunov had spoken in Latvian at a big open-air rally in the capital, organised by a committee of youth organisations under the auspices of the Young Communist League and the new Greens and attended mainly by the Latvian population, calling for them to support *perestroika*. He had spoken in honour of the innocent victims of the Stalinist repressions, he told me. Although the Latvian Party leadership had designated him to speak there, he came under fire for having done so at a subsequent Central Committee meeting. This was because provocative, nationalistic posters saying: "SS=KGB" and the flag of bourgeois Latvia had been seen at the rally.

"We haven't got any experience of rallies of this kind," Gorbunov told me somewhat ruefully, sitting behind his desk. "We've become too used to solemn, formal meetings in halls."

"But if we're to retain authority among the people," he said, "the Party has got to go out and talk to the people in this way."

Latvia's people were not doubting their choice of the socialist road, Gorbunov had told the rally, but excessive economic centralisation and diktat by central departments had rendered ineffective the republic's efforts to make its economy work better.

Gorbunov seemed intelligent and dynamic, someone who was not afraid to tackle what needed tackling, even if that made life difficult. He was more straight-talking than many I interviewed during my years as a journalist in the USSR. I felt some sympathy when he said he had respect for conservatives in the Party, because you knew where you were with them. It's those who say one thing one day and the next day something different – they're the ones I don't respect, he said.

The 19th Conference of the CPSU was fast approaching. It was unprecedented, as Party Congresses, held every five years, were the norm. But Gorbachov wanted this special conference to push the *perestroika* agenda forward. It was becoming increasingly evident that there were many Party officials who opposed the reforms, whatever they said in public.

Perestroika meant "the transfer of power from the Communist Party to those it should belong to according to the Constitution – to the Soviets, through free elections," Gorbachov writes in his memoirs. "It is obvious that the success or failure of reform, especially in the early stages, was wholly dependent on the attitude of the CPSU itself, which in essence had to give up voluntarily its own dictatorship. This ....was painful for millions of communists and especially difficult, one may say 'lethal', for the Party *nomenklatura*. 'Abdication of the throne' threatened the gradual loss of the privileges that the *nomenklatura* had enjoyed."[94]

Gorbachov would know about such privileges, of course, having himself come through the ranks of Party membership in Stavropol before reaching the top of the Party career ladder. Once when meeting ordinary people on one of his walkabouts, he told them that if it had been power that he was seeking, he would have left everything as it was before *perestroika*, since the Party General Secretary was pretty well all-powerful – which was undoubtedly true.

One of the slogans heard before and during the Conference was "More Power to the Soviets!" echoing the original slogan of the Russian Revolution in October 1917 "All power to the Soviets!"

Over the years the Soviets' role had to a large extent become usurped by the parallel powers of the CPSU, and legislation before any of the Soviets, at whatever level, had invariably been discussed and decided first within the CPSU.

---

94 Mikhail Gorbachov, *Memoirs*, Transworld Publishers Ltd, p.278.

"The important constitutional point about the Soviets is that, at least in theory, they always have had the legitimate right to control the executive ..... In practice, however, the Soviets have been very weak bodies and have not had the political clout to do so."[95] Lane attributes the Soviets' inefficiency to weak personnel (the deputies were part-time politicians with full-time jobs elsewhere, and the Soviets only met for a few days on two occasions per year) and to the lack of "independent financial means or powers".

To these reasons I think would have to be added the emergence of generations of "yes-men" from the thirties onwards, as the purges of independent thinkers and activists in the ranks of the Party from the top level down had the effect of silencing dissent and making people reluctant to step out of line. Added to this, the emergence by the early 1920's of the CPSU as the only party in a one-party state not surprisingly led to careerists and opportunists among the Soviets' deputies.

The layout of the hall inside the Kremlin where Supreme Soviet sessions were held was not conducive to real debate among deputies, as they sat in rows facing a raised platform, just as in a concert-hall. So 'More Power to the Soviets!' - if it meant turning them into more useful bodies which could debate and really examine proposals for legislation - would surely be positive for the country.

Like the slogan "More Socialism, More Democracy!" I applauded what I saw as attempts to improve the socialist system and make it more efficient and more accountable to the mass of the people.

For the first time, in the run-up to the 19th Party Conference, there was more than one candidate for each delegate to be elected, so some Party leaders who would have expected to be at the Conference failed to get elected. Another innovation was that many Party meetings were open to non-Party people. Some well-known and vociferous proponents of *perestroika*, like the sociologist Tatiana Zaslavskaya and historian Yuri Afanasyev failed to get elected as delegates.

The atmosphere in Moscow that June 1988 was one of excitement, anticipation and clashes of views, with new activists' groups and protest movements springing up here and there and holding street demonstrations.

Meanwhile some early Bolshevik leaders who had been repressed in the thirties were being rehabilitated: sentences passed over 50 years earlier on Zinoviev, Kamenev, Pyatakov and Radek[96] were repealed. They had been charged with forming an anti-Party bloc and complicity in Leningrad leader Kirov's murder in 1934 and were executed between 1936 and 1937; Radek died in a labour camp.

Many innocent victims of the repressions had been rehabilitated posthumously in the years after Khrushchov's damning denunciation at the

---

95 David Lane, *Soviet Society under Perestroika*, Routledge, 1992, p.60

96 All leading Bolsheviks who took part in the October 1917 Revolution.

20th Party Congress in 1956 of crimes committed under Stalin's leadership. But top Bolshevik leaders who had been convicted of anti-Party activity had not been part of those rehabilitations.

The 19th Communist Party Conference took place against a backdrop of growing political ferment. Many changes had already been introduced – the law making state enterprises self-financing, the law allowing new cooperatives, multi-candidate elections, so far just within the CPSU, the new atmosphere of *glasnost* prevailing in the media, which had led to worrying nationalistic outbursts. It was a heady mix, and all in less than three years.

The reasons behind the reforms were real enough: the need to make the economy work better so as to keep pace with people's expectations to have a better standard of living than the generation before them. Too many enterprises operated at a loss, kept going from the profits generated by the few, more successful enterprises. Food shortages - *defitsit* - whilst not extreme, neverthess existed.

Added to this, state finances were affected by the sudden drop in income from vodka sales, due to the anti-alcohol campaign, and the decrease in hard currency income due to falling global oil prices at that time.

"We're at the stage where we need another impetus to make the reforms produce tangible results," economist Dr Otto Lacis told me in an interview just before the Conference. "*Glasnost* and democratisation are very important to people, but if they don't see any improvement in their material standard of living, people will say *perestroika* is just so much hot air."

Why weren't "tangible results" being seen, I asked.

"One reason is what we call the administrative-command system of management which evolved in the thirties, resulting in over-centralised planning and the stifling of initiative and enterprise at local level," he explained. "Self-financing has begun to be introduced in factories, so *their* business has started to change – but the functions of the *ministries* has remained basically unchanged."

"Their functions have been taken over by the factories, which are now drawing up their own plans and getting supplies through the wholesale trade network on their own. This used to be the job of the ministries – of which there are over 800 if we include those at republic level. So these ministries are now basically redundant." he explained.

"The old administrative measures will still be needed in this transition period," Lacis said, "which I expect to last three years or so. We can only go as far as the majority of people will accept," he added. "Democracy is a difficult process even for those who support it."

Lacis's study of the Hungarian economy had led him to the conviction that the Soviet economy had to be more market-oriented. Price reform would be needed, to bring prices more in line with production costs, but "so far this is seen as unacceptable by the Soviet public, although the current situation of countless shortages is in fact worse."

212

It was clear that unless supply fully met demand, there would always be the temptation for speculators to make a quick buck by buying up goods in short supply and selling them off at higher prices, so depriving ordinary shoppers of the possibility of obtaining them.

Dr Lacis proposed cutting expenditure by ministries, reducing staff by a third, and putting a stop to big 'vanity projects' like the diversion of rivers for irrigation in Central Asia, which had already caused the drying up of the Aral Sea[97]. "The state has got to live within its means. At present we are living beyond our means."

In his opening Conference speech, Gorbachov hammered home the point: "We've under-estimated the extent and gravity of the deformations and the stagnation of the preceding period," he told delegates in the splendorous Palace of Congresses inside the Kremlin.

The Palace of Congresses, built in 1961, is a beautiful modern addition to the ancient churches and government buildings that comprise the Kremlin, which is surrounded by ancient, high red brick walls

"State expenditure is increasing more quickly than revenue," Gorbachov warned on the opening day of the Conference. In agriculture, he said, reform was being met in some regions with outright resistance by managements of state and collective farms.

And most intolerable of all, he went on, was the fact that ministries were still issuing enterprises with state orders for goods not wanted by the population.

Local Soviets should have the right to raise their own incomes through taxation of local enterprises, so putting an end to their reliance on central funds, Gorbachov said. And the chairpersons of the Soviets should have

---

97 By the late 1980s the Aral Sea had lost more than half the volume of its pre-1960 water. Increased salt and minerals made the water unfit for drinking purposes and killed off the once-abundant supplies of sturgeon, carp, roach, and other fish.

to stand in multi-candidate elections in secret ballots. "And if the Party candidate fails to get elected, the Party will have to draw its own conclusions!"

The Supreme Soviet should be enlarged to better represent working people through organisations like the trades unions, women's and youth organisations. He proposed a new, bigger parliament called the Congress of People's Deputies, convened annually and elected for a 5-year term. A new Presidential position would be elected by the 2,250 delegates to the Congress of People's Deputies. In between sessions, a reduced Supreme Soviet of 400-450 deputies, elected by the Congress of People's Deputies, would form a permanently working parliament.

In the CPSU, elected leaders should serve a maximum of two terms and multi-candidate elections by secret ballot should be the norm.

These announcements by Gorbachov at the start of the Conference represented enormous and far-reaching changes, yet they were being announced, one after another, as if they were minor changes that could be introduced quickly.

Many flaws in the proposed new Congress of People's Deputies became clear over the next few months – such as that representatives of All-Union organisations, i.e. the CPSU, Komsomol, trades unions, creative, women's and other organisations, might end up having two votes – one through their organisation and one territorial vote based on where they lived.

I had visited big plants like in Sumy, described earlier (p.81), where innovative economic methods had been introduced over recent years and proved viable and productive, which is why they had been incorporated into the new Law on the State Enterprise. That, it seemed to me, was the way to go – testing new ideas first before rolling them out wholesale. Whereas these sweeping new political reforms doing away with long-established structures of Party and State did not seem to have been discussed within the CPSU, much less tested anywhere.

My reports for the *Morning Star* bear out my fears. The famous saying coined by Chinese leader Deng Xiaoping - 'cross the river by feeling the stones' - to describe the process of pioneering new forms of business in China, was sorely needed in the USSR, it seemed to me.

To a sympathetic observer like myself, the Conference was of course very interesting. Many of the 5,000 delegates spoke about bureaucracy and interference by the ministries. A metalworker from the Urals, Veniamin Yarin, condemned this but pointed out that there was no strategy for tackling it in the Party's discussion document released before the Conference.

The famous eye doctor, Svyatoslav Fyodorov, called for a change from administrative-command methods to economic ones: self-financing in his institute had increased the number of eye ops from 24,000 to 100,000 annually and had given his staff good salaries on which they could live well.

Boris Yeltsin asked for his 'political rehabilitation', claiming he had "chosen the wrong time" last October, when he attacked the Politbuduro for slow progress in carrying out *perestroika*, resulting in his being sacked. "Leonid Brezhnev is not the only one to blame for the stagnation of the past," he said, criticising the Party's staff – *apparat* – for failing to tackle negative tendencies. But Politburo member Yegor Ligachov told the Conference there were "no grounds" for changing the Central Committee's evaluation of Yeltsin's actions as "erroneous".

The Soviet intervention in Afghanistan was questioned; ecological disasters were openly talked about; there was considerable discussion as to whether Party leaders should simultaneously hold top posts in the Soviets at their different levels.

Six resolutions were passed – on *perestroika*, reform of the political system, combatting bureaucracy, inter-ethnic relations, legal reform and *glasnost*.

It was clear from the Conference that there were demagogues like Yeltsin at one extreme, but also many entrenched *apparatchiki* interested more in preserving their vested interests than putting the reforms into practice.

Secret ballots and real contests for positions in the Soviets had to be the norm from now on, the political resolution said. Inside the Party itself, the Leninist vision of democratic centralism had to be adhered to, which meant free discussion at the stage when an issue is under consideration and concerted action after being passed by a majority. No more than five-year terms for elective Party positions should be the norm.

Essential measures to restructure the economy were being "paralysed by the bureaucratic moves of ministries .... and by the passivity of many Party and Soviet organisations," the resolution on bureaucracy said. The resolution on *glasnost* said every citizen had the right to obtain "exhaustive and authentic information on any issue of public life that is not a state or military secret."

The reforms were intended to make socialism work better and give people a higher standard of living. But I came away from the Conference worried that the *perestroika* process was escaping the control of the leadership.

Were the consistent attacks on the Party leaderships at all levels during the stagnation period justified, or, even if so, were they expedient, I wondered. It sometimes seemed as if the baby was being thrown out with the bathwater.

I spoke to several delegates; the only one that sticks out in my mind was Nikolai Travkin, who had been a rank-and-file building worker before rising to head an amalgamation of building trusts. I had visited Trust No. 18 at Volokolamsk in 1986, where Travkin had fought to introduce a team contract incentive scheme which had led to a 20% productivity increase. He had turned the trust from a loss-making one to a profitable one, resulting in 11% pay rises and a 12% drop in production costs. What was more, 80% of Mosoblselstroi Trust No. 18's management were workers.

Travkin was a tall, thin man who exuded energy and determination. "The essence of socialism is that those who produce all the goods should be the owners," he told me. "But here, distortions like the massive over-centralisation of the economy have resulted in social ownership becoming nobody's ownership."

The Law on the State Enterprise hadn't been able to operate properly, Travkin told me, because it couldn't work independently of the political system. "We need to emancipate the state enterprise and give it independence." The ministries might be needed for some areas, like education or defence, Travkin said, but not in industry, except to work out overall strategy. "They're certainly not needed in their present form, where they interfere with enterprises' work down to the smallest detail."

Immediately after the Conference, on 3rd July 1988, I had the chance to visit the Soviet chemical weapons facility at Shikhany, some 80 miles from Moscow in the Saratov region of Russia, on the Volga River. A British government delegation had just spent three days there. This included the director of Britain's chemical defence establishment at Porton Down, Graham Pearson, and Britain's Ambassador to the Geneva talks on chemical weapons, Tessa Solesby.

They had been allowed to choose whichever ten points they selected to inspect, seen from a helicopter flying over the Shikhany testing range - a reciprocal gesture after Soviet experts had earlier been allowed to choose two points for inspection at Porton Down.

Shikhany was a closed town, but an exception was made for Andrew Wilson, of the *Observer* and me, representing the *Morning Star*, to visit the secret facility. Andrew was a military historian, whereas I had little knowledge of chemical weapons except insofar as they had formed part of the talks between Reagan and Gorbachov at the recent summit in Moscow. We flew in a light plane to Saratov and from there by helicopter to the facility. It was an exhausting day – tiring after a busy week reporting from the 19th Party Conference and from flying there and back in one day in the searing heat of a summer's day.

Yuri Nazarkin, the Soviet Union's chief negotiator at the Geneva talks, said such random inspection requests could form part of a future convention on chemical weapons, which was what his country wanted. Speaking in a beautiful silver birch tree grove, against a backdrop of a row of different kinds of Soviet decontamination vehicles, Nazarkin criticised the lack of political will from Britain and the US at the Geneva talks.

Andrew and I watched national servicemen in their chemical weapons protective suits in the sweltering heat, first standing to attention, then doing a series of exercises, sprawled on the ground, firing dummy chemical weapons against imaginary targets. It was surreal, in the midst of the beauty and tranquillity of the unspoilt Russian countryside, seeing these monstrous dehumanised figures with their decontamination headgear and cumbersome breathing apparatus.

"Soviet chemical weapons are for defence, not attack," General Pikanov told us. "My cherished dream is a world without chemical weapons," adding that he was puzzled by the US's decision to start production of binary chemical weapons.

I badly needed a holiday, and that summer I and the children returned to Britain to see my family and have a well-earned break. It was very sad to see that my poor, dear Mum's speech had not improved, although she could walk, dress and look after herself pretty well without help. My father had learned how to cook, sometimes resorting to ready-made microwave meals.

Mum seemed very pleased to see us, and smiled a lot and watched the children play, getting obvious enjoyment from us being there. I felt the usual pangs of conscience that I would soon be leaving her to go back to work, so far away. Yet I knew she wholeheartedly approved of the job I was doing: she avidly read the paper when it arrived every morning through their letter-box.

We went camping with my brother Joe and family – that was the year we went to Devon and it rained the whole week.

Ricardo had remained in Moscow, so the plan was for us to have 10 days' holiday together with him at a Russian holiday resort near Gagra, on the Black Sea. It turned out to be one of the best holidays we have ever had. Situated high on a hillside above the sea, we had a luxury suite with three bedrooms, lounge and wide balcony running round two sides, with magnificent views over the vivid azure of the Black Sea and its white, smooth pebbly beaches.

The meals provided in the hotel's large dining room were delicious, with lots of fish and seafood dishes, even caviar, and with various salads and fresh fruit. We made friends with fellow guests from Czechoslovakia and Syria, who also had children, and went on excursions to Gagra and Lake Ritsa, 1000 metres up in the Caucasus mountains, to some deep caves where we took a boat into their furthest reaches, and by boat to Pitsunda where one evening we were treated to a concert given by Abkhazian dancers.

Lake Ritsa

The Black Sea is unbeatable for bathing, its waters warm and welcoming,

217

the large rounded pebbles smooth and clean beneath your feet, making the waters transparent right down to the sea bed. I had been to Bulgarian Black Sea resorts in my twenties, but this was our first visit to the Soviet Union's Black Sea coast. Gagra, and Kholodnaya Rechka (Cold Stream) - the resort where we stayed - are in what was an autonomous republic – Abkhazia - within the Soviet republic of Georgia.

Kholodnaya Rechka was also the site of one of Stalin's holiday homes, and one day we walked up the densely wooded hillside to the wartime leader's former chalet, where other guests were staying. We were shown around the chalet, and had a game of billiards in the big games room. Had Stalin played billiards there, with other Party comrades or relatives, we wondered?

Most days we took the spacious lift down from the steep hillside where the hotel was located to beach level, the sea a short walk away, and spent hours swimming, sunbathing, reading and chatting to our new friends. It was very relaxing, and a much-needed break from the vertiginous pace of change in Moscow.

Once we got back to Moscow at the end of August, it was time to prepare for the children to go back to school on 1st September. The flower kiosks were doing a busy trade, as children throughout the Soviet Union honour their teachers that day by taking them a bunch of flowers, often carnations, gladioli or crysanthemums. There is great excitement among the children as they make their way to school after the long summer break, when many of them will have been away at various Pioneer Camps, like our children.

Soviet workers were entitled to paid holidays, and most received *putyovki* (holiday vouchers) through their place of work for a sanatorium or rest-home somewhere in the countryside or at the coast. The problem was that the *putyovki* were usually just for that worker, not for his or her entire family. It was common, when you got talking to someone on holiday, to find that they were alone there, not with their families. So, instead of making use of their statutory right to a *putyovka*, many people would rent a small villa or B & B somewhere at the coast to have a family holiday. Those who had a *dacha* outside Moscow or other cities would spend the summer months there, parents travelling to work in the city on suburban trains during the weeks when they were not on holiday.

The *dacha* is a Russian institution. Everybody who can tries to obtain a *dacha*, either by inheriting, buying through their place of work or renting. Since most people live in flats in towns and cities, the countryside *dacha* is a way of getting close to nature and relaxing. People grow salads and vegetables in their plots, and the rest is usually left wild, with silver birch trees, long grasses and meadow flowers.

Summers in Moscow are brief but hot and sunny. June, July and August might see the occasional shower, but it is always warm, and bright, colourful flowers at last pop up cheerfully in the parks and gardens which have emerged, somewhat bedraggled and forlorn, from the snow, ice and sludge that have covered them for months. In June, however, the dreaded white *pukh,* the downy, woolly seeds of the city's countless poplar trees float and hover in the still air and give people like me hay fever. I was once told that it was Stalin who ordered the widespread planting of this variety of poplars in Moscow – I've no idea if this is true, or just one more sin to lay at his door.

In a sign of the times, an article in *Komsomolskaya Pravda,* the youth daily, carried an interview with the head of the Soviet State Education Committee, Gennadi Yagodin, who said that election of school heads and university rectors was now becoming the norm. Schools would also be allowed to fund-raise, enabling individual schools to hire extra teachers, pay higher wages or build extra school facilities for sport or leisure.

Wouldn't this lead to some schools becoming super-schools in "better" areas and sink schools in others, I wondered? Such possibilities were not discussed in the article, which presented the idea as entirely positive. I had also read that the first fee-paying school had recently opened in Moscow. It was disquieting that these initiatives seemed to be being put about as the solution for the problems of Soviet schools, instead of greater state investment across the board into all the nation's schools.

Later that year, the NUT's President, Malcolm Horne, told me he'd been impressed by the fact that Minister Yagodin had himself been through the Soviet education system which he was now in charge of. "None of our cabinet have gone through the British state education system," he pointed out. "They are busy reforming a system they know nothing about!"

It probably came as a surprise to Soviet educationists that most of the British Tory leadership had attended top fee-paying schools of the privileged and well-off elite – a situation no different as I write now thirty or so years later.

There was much that was positive about Soviet schools, but from what I observed, facilities were rather basic. Well-equipped gyms or sports fields were the exception rather than the rule. But what was good was the spirit of the class being a collective, together with the teacher, and the fostering of the collective spirit, whereby the whole class was expected to move forward to the next year, however badly individual pupils might have done during the year in schoolwork or tests. Our children seemed genuinely fond of their teachers, but from what I read in the press, this was not always the case, especially among older children.

In the summer, at the end of the school year, you could see lively groups of children with their teachers, walking by the river and down the boulevards, singing songs and linked arm-in-arm, celebrating the end of the school year.

In September 1988, after a conference in the Black Sea resort of Dagomys, the Pugwash movement[98] issued a declaration putting environmental destruction on a par with the nuclear threat. It is interesting that thirty

---

98 See Footnote 45.

years later as I write this, this matter is only now being taken seriously in the developed world after the rise of Extinction Rebellion and the school strikes begun by Swedish schoolgirl, Greta Thunberg. The Pugwash scientists were ahead of their time on climate change as well as the nuclear threat.

At this Pugwash Conference the renowned British scientist Professor Dorothy Hodgkin stepped down after many years as President and was succeeded by Professor Joseph Rotblat. During his tenure, Rotblat nominated Israeli nuclear technician Mordechai Vanunu for the Nobel Peace Prize every year from 1988 to 2004. Vanunu had disclosed the extent of Israel's nuclear weapons programme, consequently spending 18 years in an Israeli prison, including more than 11 years in solitary confinement.

The pollution and environmental degradation which concerned Pugwash scientists was also to be found in the Soviet Union, and in conditions of *glasnost*, citizens' concerns were increasingly being voiced. People linked arms along the Baltic coast to protest against marine pollution from pulp plants and phosphate mining. There were protests against the pulp and paper plant on the shores of the world's biggest freshwater lake – Lake Baikal, in Siberia. Articles in the national press highlighted the lack of attention by the authorities to pollution in areas of western Siberia where big chemical, iron and steel plants operated.

The drying up of the Aral Sea was always in the news, due to health problems in that region from increased soil salination. Dramatic pictures of the Aral Sea in an October 1988 edition of the popular illustrated weekly *Ogonyok* portrayed marooned fishing trawlers on a hard, sun-baked seabed and dead seabirds scattered on the parched ground. The sea had shrunk 46 kilometres from its previous coast line, *Ogonyok* reported, leaving desert-like soil "so salty that nothing can grow there." This had happened "because it had been deliberately sacrificed to cotton". As more and more cotton had been planted, to fulfil the plan, more and more water had to be taken from the sea's feeder rivers. Nearly two million hectares of exposed seabed sent up an estimated seventy million tonnes of salty dust into the air, the report went on. "Infant mortality has increased sharply: the Amu Darya's waters are virtually unfit for drinking, but they are being drunk by everyone living in the Aral area," the newspaper *Moscow News* revealed.

The dreadful statistics also served to condemn the previous Communist Party leadership in Uzbekistan, not only for the ecological situation, but as corrupt and incompetent.

The evident lack of care about the environment in the past seemed to indicate the need for campaigns which could draw attention to and put pressure on the government to improve air, sea and earth quality. It seemed that in the rush to industrialise, issues like environmental degradation had been put on the back burner. It was known about, but it was considered an inevitable by-product of heavy industry which was essential for the economy as a whole.

In September singer Paul McCartney told *Komsomolskaya Pravda* that he would soon be bringing out an album in the USSR and hoped to visit. The Beatles were immensely popular, especially for their songs with a peace message, like *Give Peace a Chance*, *Imagine*, and *All you need is Love*, but they had never visited the country. "With all these negotiations on arms reductions," Paul told the youth newspaper, "it has become easier to breathe." Changes for the better in international relations were reducing the threat of war and strengthening peace, he added.

Snova v SSSR (Back in the USSR) was released in October 1988, as a gesture of peace in the spirit of *glasnost*. An agreement was reached with the Soviet state record company Melodiya to license 400,000 copies of the album for release in the Soviet Union only. The first pressing of 50,000 copies contained 11 tracks and sold out almost immediately. A second pressing with two additional tracks was released about a month later.

I liked the Beatles, they were my age and I grew up with their music as a teenager. I admired the stance of John Lennon and Yoko Ono when they did their Peace sleep-in and was dismayed when John was shot dead in New York in 1980. I referred to this in a short story I wrote, published in the women's magazine *She* in April 1985, about a little Salvadorean orphan, Ramoncito, whose parents had been killed in front of him during the Civil War there.

I was told about Ramoncito by visiting Salvadorean trades unionists to the UK, for whom I was interpreting. My story linked his sad and troubled little life to John Lennon's son and my own son, who were all about the same age. When I interviewed Yoko Ono in Moscow in 1987, I gave her my feature. Here is a short excerpt:

"My thoughts again turned to the little Salvadorean boy with Indian features and straight stiff black hair, who screams in his sleep......... I went back into the kitchen. The nine o'clock news was on. John Lennon's little boy, Sean, was in Liverpool with his mother Yoko Ono. A boy of about the same age as my son and ....Ramoncito. I couldn't help thinking how strange and cruel that John Lennon was murdered – why him? His verses ran through my head: *No need for greed or hunger/ A brotherhood of man/Imagine all the people sharing all the world/Imagine all the people living life in peace....* As at the time of his death, I felt enormously sorry that he was gone, and especially saddened to think of his son, nearly the same age as my son and Ramoncito, having to grow up without his father.

......A little later, as I walked past his bedroom door, I could hear my son singing softly to himself in the dark, as he sometimes does before he drops off to sleep. It was good to hear him and know that he was happy.

But as I lay in bed later, the memory of that tuneful singing in my ears was drowned by the heartrending cries of a little Salvadorean boy who screams in his sleep...."

The struggles of Latin American peoples were never very far away in our household. Our friends in Moscow were exiles from the Chilean military junta; we knew Argentinian and Brazilian exiles from the military dictatorships in those countries, we supported the Sandinistas' victory in Nicaragua and the struggles of the Salvadorean FMLN (Farabundo Martí Liberation Front) and Guatemalan peoples who were trying to overthrow oppressive regimes.

The Soviet Union's help for Chile through daily broadcast of a radio programme *Escucha Chile*, produced by Chilean exiles in Moscow and beamed into Chile, played a big part in the final overthrow of the Pinochet dictatorship in 1990. In September 1988, after the lifting of a 15-year ban on political exiles returning to Chile, several exiled leaders left Moscow, including our friend Jorge Montes, a former senator, who had been severely tortured after the 1973 coup. Jorge related his experiences in jail in his book *La Luz entre las Sombras* (Light between the Shadows).

At a press conference shortly before leaving, Montes paid tribute to the immense international solidarity that had "fought constantly all these years for the right of Chileans to live in their own country."

Ricardo and I were close friends with several members of the Communist Party's Central Committee, so we were always well-informed and abreast of all the developments inside Chile. One friend was Volodia Teitelboim, who had been a senator before the coup and was Chairman of the Party. He was a distinguished author and cultural icon, who in 2002 was awarded Chile's National Prize for Literature. As a Party leader, he would sometimes be at the same official Kremlin receptions as I was, so I got to know him quite well. Ricardo and I met him in Chile for the last time in 2006, not long before his death, and I wrote an obituary for him, published in the *Guardian* 20th February 2008.

Inter-ethnic clashes continued that autumn in the disputed region of Nagorno-Karabakh. The Supreme Soviet's decision in July 1988 to leave that mainly ethnic-Armenian Autonomous Region where it was - within the Azerbaijan Republic - had not calmed the situation. The TASS news agency put the blame for the latest inter-ethnic outbursts on "anti-*perestroika* forces":

> "....the process of healthy improvements in Armenia and Azerbaijan are clearly disliked by those involved in corruption, bribe-taking and theft," it said. "Fearing exposure, they distract the people .... from the fight against negative phenomena by turning the public's attention to inter-ethnic issues. They won't stop at anything to stir up nationalistic passions."

Since both leaderships of Armenian and Azerbaijan's Communist Parties had recently been replaced, this could certainly have been a factor in the latest clashes. Those local leaders who had lost their high positions would have felt aggrieved and could have whipped up nationalistic tensions to cause problems for the new leaders. It is relatively easy, it seems, to prey on nationalistic feelings and use them as a scapegoat for economic or social problems.

Women's issues were at last being talked about. A *Pravda* editorial of 29 September 1988 revealed that about 4 million women workers laboured in conditions which contravened health and safety norms; 400,000 women were engaged in heavy physical work.

An earlier article entitled "*Why I can't be a minister*" by a shopfloor carworker, Ms Barulina, wrote that women couldn't rise to senior positions "due to their intolerable burden of hard work in production and excessive domestic drudgery." To add to their problems, she wrote, women were the first to be sacked in workplace cuts arising from the new Law on the State Enterprise, or found themselves having to agree to work night shifts to keep their jobs.

Conditions of women's lives were such that they could not even dream of a ministerial career, she complained. "Never-ending, totally unmechanised domestic work and constant chasing round the shops take up all our thoughts."

The Women's Councils – *zhensoviety* – had proved ineffective, managers had not listened to their grievances and the Communist Party's district committees and branches had shown indifference towards them, *Pravda* said. How had it become possible that women's rights had sunk so low, given their established rights under the Constitution and the law?

Re-reading my 1988 diary, there's an entry on a British Embassy press briefing in late November to which I hadn't been invited, but I was told about by Jonathan Steele, the *Guardian*'s correspondent. Apparently at that briefing, Ambassador Bryan Cartledge had asked my fellow correspondents whether they should just keep the briefings between themselves. Did he mean not to invite other Britons working for other agencies, one journalist asked. No, Cartledge had responded, rather embarrassed, apparently. "Do you mean Kate?" another correspondent asked him. "Yes!" he had admitted. Jonathan told me all the journalists present had said of course I should be invited in future.

Cartledge was soon to be replaced as ambassador by Sir Rodric Braithwaite[99], a likeable and knowledgeable man. It was gratifying for me to hear of this support by my colleagues, though I wasn't really surprised because they all knew how active I was as a correspondent and I had normal relations with all of them.

Jonathan Steele once did a nice *Guardian* piece featuring me as a good, persistent journalist during an interview we did together with a female Supreme Soviet deputy who was being quite evasive in answering my questions. Perhaps he wanted to make amends for the slanderous piece his predecessor, Martin Walker, had published about me in September 1985

---

99 His book *Moscow 1941 A City and its People at War*, 2006, Profile Books Ltd, London is well worth reading.

(see Appendix III). At press conferences I often exchanged opinions with Jonathan, and with Patrick Cockburn (*Financial Times*), Xan Smiley (*Daily Telegraph*), Christopher Walker (*The Times*) and others as well as Reuter journalists.

Now everything was coming under the spotlight, as *glasnost* became ever more widespread. At a doctors' Congress in October, 1988, the public health service came under fire. However, Soviet achievements were indisputable: life expectancy had doubled and infant mortality had dropped by 90.9% in the years of Soviet power. Our experience of the Soviet health system was very positive, both when our daughter Liza was hospitalised for gastritis and when Ricardo had to have a knee operation; routine care such as blood tests, minor health issues, X-rays and dental care were all excellent.

Wherever I travelled throughout the USSR, looking with a journalist's critical eye everywhere I went, I never saw any malnourished children or people without shoes or decent clothes, as you do in other countries like India or Afghanistan. Children everywhere I visited looked well fed and well dressed – a real credit to the nation.

The Baltic Popular Fronts were becoming increasingly emboldened; in Estonia the calls for Estonian to be the sole state language were described by *Pravda* as "not so much a means of communication between peoples as a means of antagonising neighbours." And calls for Russian nationals to be repatriated from Estonia were "extremist".

"Our union is a single and indivisible economic organism," *Pravda* wrote, "where the contribution of each republic is paid for by the labour contribution of all the others." To me as an internationalist, the increasing nationalistic fervour there was very unpleasant and went against our progressive ethos, as Communists, where the stronger helps the weaker. It was obvious to me, having seen the poverty and backwardness of a country like Afghanistan, which bordered Soviet Central Asia, that those southern republics could not catch up, in the course of one or two generations, with more developed parts of the Union, like the Baltic republics, Russia or Ukraine. But all together, they could make up a powerful and prosperous country which would benefit all. Calls coming from the popular fronts in Estonia and Lithuania seemed selfish, arrogant and frankly, anti-Russian.

At one Supreme Soviet meeting, I interviewed someone who herself embodied the sort of internationalist feelings close to my heart – Natalia Gellert, elected the previous February to full CPSU Central Committee membership, Supreme Soviet deputy, for 20 years a tractor-driver on a Kazakh state farm, married to a Kazakh and with two children who spoke Kazakh, Russian and German.

This wonder woman had time for her constituents, be it personal issues or problems arising from the new lease contracts at giant state farms like hers. Attractive, energetic, forthright, you could easily see why Natalia Gellert had risen to such prominence.

She told me of the problems women in agriculture face and that she was pleased that the "women's problem" had begun to be aired at last. As I wrote in a feature that October 1988, "While 400,000 Soviet women continue to do heavy manual work in industry and agriculture, others, in the *Komsomol* youth organisation, are busy amusing themselves organising beauty contests .... how did Ms Gellert react to that, I asked."

"I don't approve," she said forthrightly. "Perhaps I'm wrong, but I can't accept beauty contests. I'm definitely against!"

"Of course we women haven't achieved everything we wanted, but things are moving, both in mechanisation at work and in enabling women to improve their qualifications," she told me. In addition to all her other jobs, she was an extra-mural student in her fifth year of a six-year agricultural engineering course.

But at present, she added, it was very difficult for a woman doing the sort of job she did to take on leading posts. She seemed reticent when asked for her views on changes to the Constitution and electoral laws, which were supposedly being discussed nationwide.

At the Supreme Soviet session at the end of 1988, Soviet Finance Minister, Boris Gostev, told deputies of the scale of the Soviet budget deficit: losses of state revenue due to the fall in world oil prices and the anti-drink campaign, plus extensive state subsidising of 24,000 loss-making enterprises, to the tune of 11 billion roubles annually, and losses due to poor resource-saving. Whereas social spending had had to increase by over 18 billion roubles in the last three years, Gostev said.

Food supply was still erratic and light industry was still lagging behind. The shortfall in grain sales to the state over the last three years had been over 40 million tonnes. Shocking statistics given to me in an interview with Nikolai Shishlin, a CPSU Central Committee official, on the gains of the Great October Revolution: up to 50% of all fruit and vegetables and 25% of wheat go to waste, he told me, due to the inefficient system whereby *kolkhozy* have to go through state supply bodies to sell their produce.

The interview with Shishlin was interesting: Khrushchov's reforms in the fifties and sixties had not worked because the administrative-command system itself had not been tackled – Khrushchov had limited himself to destroying the personality cult that had grown up around Stalin. The command system's supporters had got the upper hand, he claimed, ousting Khrushchov and leading the country into stagnation.

In autumn 1988 the long-standing Foreign Minister Andrei Gromyko retired from the Politburo. He had had a brilliant career as Soviet Foreign Minister throughout the Cold War. I would have liked to interview him as I felt sure that behind his immutable, tough face would be an interesting personality. Shortly after my arrival as correspondent in 1985, I had been invited to a splendorous Kremlin reception where Gromyko was one of the hundreds of guests, but somehow I did not manage to get near enough to go up to him and introduce myself – one of my regrets as correspondent. Gromyko's memoirs are a fascinating read.[100]

I spent a few days in Oryol in early December 1988. Some 364 km south of Moscow, Oryol is a typically Russian town on the Oka river, in the rich Orlovskaya agricultural region. Its population at that time was 360,000. Founded in 1566, Oryol counted famous writers Ivan Turgenev, Nikolai Leskov, Fyodor Tyutchev and Ivan Bunin among its illustrious forebears.

Like all cities in western Russia, Oryol suffered greatly during WWII. It spent 22 months under Nazi occupation and 97% of the city was destroyed during the war. I discovered that mines still lay buried throughout the region, and every year unexploded mines killed and maimed children more than forty years later. That year alone – 1988 – 27 children had died from mines. "We can't plough 42 hectares of land around here because of this danger," local trade unionist Kapitalina Stroyeva told me. "If a tractor goes over a mine, it will explode." It was shocking to think that people were still suffering in this way after so many years.

I had gone to Oryol to look at the new kinds of farming initiatives that were being tried out there. I was with a group of journalists from China, North Korea, Mongolia and a few eastern European countries, who were all interested in the lease-farming and cost-accounting methods Oryol had been pioneering.

In the country as a whole, the situation in agriculture was far from satisfactory. Huge *sovkhozy* and *kolzhozy,* encompassing entire villages, had resulted in farmworkers feeling alienated from the land they worked on. In Oryol, several of these massive farms, with thousands of workers, had extended leases to a few of their farmworkers for them to go it alone – to run a small portion as their own family farms, with pigs and heads of cattle in the hundreds rather than the thousands.

One example was a man who, with his wife and son, took on an initial lease with 500 pigs. They had achieved good results, both in terms of animal weight gain and the family's monthly incomes. They had one tractor and were able to access the services of the *kolzhoz* vet. Whereas before the experiment in 1987, their wages had amounted to 160 roubles per month, now they were raking in 500 roubles. After one year, the family signed a 7-year contract with the *kolkhoz,* raising the number of pigs to 1,500, with commitments to sell 120 tonnes of pork annually instead of the 85 which had been the average before the lease-farming experiment. 22% of the family's income went on meeting lease payments to the *kolkhoz.*

We were told that the lease-farmers enjoyed the same rights as *kolkhoz* workers in terms of pensions and social insurance. But they would receive higher pensions than *kolkhozniki* because whereas a lease-farmer made produce worth 63,000 roubles, an ordinary *kolkhoznik* only produced on

---

100 *Memories*, by Andrei Gromyko, Arrow Books Ltd, London, 1989.

average 11,000 roubles-worth of goods.

What was clear to me after talking to several lease-farmers and to Party and trade union officials involved in these new initiatives was that they were certainly keen on what they were doing and confident about the future. Personal initiative and determination to succeed had replaced apathy and inefficiency which unfortunately was characteristic of many state and collective farms.

They were closer to the land and their animals and had a vested interest in succeeding. They had nobody bossing them about, they didn't have to await orders from above and enjoyed taking their own decisions, lease-farmer Nikolai Murtsanov told us. Now Oryol region was looking to expand the types of contract farming, including group lease-farmers, creation of small cooperatives for services and repairs and entire state farms going over to the *aryendny podryad* (rental contract) system.

Like the industrial experiments in Sumy described earlier, the Oryol agricultural experiments were designed to make the Soviet economy more efficient, but clearly, their promising results were a drop in the ocean in such a vast country as the USSR.

At the beginning of December 1988, at the United Nations in New York, Gorbachov called for a new world order, based on the United Nations. He also announced big troop reductions and withdrawal of six tank divisions from Eastern Europe. It was whilst in New York that news broke of the tragic earthquake in Spitak, Armenia. Gorbachov cut short his visit, which was meant to have been followed by visits to Cuba and Britain, and flew back home immediately.

Soviet TV showed the towns of Leninakan, Kirovakan and Spitak, where recently built nine-storey blocks of flats had collapsed like packs of cards, trapping hundreds of people. "Where were the seismologists, architects and overseers who designed and built those blocks that collapsed like matchboxes?" *Komsomolskaya Pravda* asked. In Spitak, not a single factory or block of flats remained standing after the quake, it was reported. It was the worst earthquake in that entire region for 80 years: some 25,000 people died, 21 towns and 342 villages were destroyed, leaving over 500,000 people homeless, according to the Armenian National Survey for Seismic Protection.

More and more questions were being asked. Gorbachov, visiting the affected area, announced a Government Commission to investigate why "in the reinforced concrete slabs, there wasn't enough concrete to make a cat laugh, as the saying goes, whereas the quantity of sand surpassed all measure." That meant cement had been stolen, Gorbachov said. "So who stole it?"

Two weeks after the earthquake I visited Spitak and saw the destruction for myself. It was a dreadful scene, with collapsed buildings everywhere and rubble all around. At the identification centre near the town morgue, heaps of coffins were stacked. As I rounded the corner of one building, I saw a corpse, stiff arm protruding from a coversheet.

I spoke to victims in the Sklifosovsky First Aid Scientific Research Institute hospital, who were immensely grateful for the massive help that had come both from other Soviet republics and from abroad, including 15 artificial kidney machines from Britain to treat the many victims suffering from crush syndrome. Cranes and other equipment arrived from all corners of the USSR, rescue teams from Donbass miners and volunteers from all over came to help.

I came across stories of luck amid the tragedy – like a fourteen year-old girl I spoke to in hospital, who had been trapped for days under the ruins of a building and had survived by eating snow.

"Spitak, 1500 metres above sea level, and surrounded on all sides by snow-capped hills, is today a ghost-town of mountains of rubble and empty shells of houses standing at crazy angles, washing hanging from balconies fluttering idly in the wind," I wrote in one despatch from the scene.

"The few people left, mainly men, huddle together in groups near the market-place, collars up against the biting wind. With drawn faces, they revise the pasted-up lists of survivors in hospitals, looking for relatives."

"Over 10,000 Spitak people, mainly children, women and the elderly, had so far been evacuated to trade union holiday centres outside Armenia, local Communist Party District Secretary Nurai Muradian told me. He had lost 11 relatives in the quake, though fortunately not his immediate family, and 8 of the Party's 60-strong District Committee had been killed."

"I did not see one building in Spitak left intact. Most are collapsed heaps of concrete slabs and rubble. Here and there a three-storey wall stands eerily against the leaden sky."

"A piano could be seen perched precariously near a TV set high up on one heap by the town's main street. A crushed baby's cot jutting out of the rubble told its own tragic story."

"It's thought that about 200 corpses remain under the ruins", Muradian said. "These will be got out before the new year. Only then will work begin on razing the town to the ground." The new Spitak would be built 5 kilometres deeper into the hills where experts consider firmer underground rock would provide a seismologically safer site, he told me.

I found the trip to Spitak and Leninakan depressing; not only the sheer scale of the destruction, but the apparent fact that builders had used inadequate materials, as the media was suggesting. And as a journalist, I was conscious of seeming like a voyeur of human misery, which made me uncomfortable.

I was glad to get back home to the safety and comfort of our Moscow flat and be with my family again. As always when I returned from one of my trips, the children flung their arms around me, all tripping over themselves to try and tell me something that had happened to them during the few days I'd been away. And we had the New Year holiday to look forward to. Christmas was not publicly celebrated in the USSR, but New Year was a big event in the Russian winter calendar. Children's *Dyed Moroz* (Grandad Frost) and *Snyegurochka* (Snow Maiden) parties were held at schools and at Pioneer Palaces and were great fun for the children who usually managed to get themselves invited to more than one, and would return home carrying a present or two they'd been given.

Two weeks off school – to go skating in Gorky Park, cross-country skiing at Izmailovo Park or to visit the attractions at VDNKh (the Economic Achievements Exhibition), where the different pavilions of the 15 republics comprising the Soviet Union had displays and national delicacies to offer. We tried to take the children to as many places as we could, even though I was not really on holiday since my newspaper wasn't. That was always a problem – I only had Saturday when I didn't have to file, since the *Morning Star* did not have a Sunday edition, and I certainly couldn't take the same holidays as the children.

We loved the Russian winter: it was often sunny, with clear blue skies, and the frost and snow would sparkle in the sunlight, crunching as you trod the freshly fallen snow.

On 8th January we held a New Year party at our flat, inviting our neighbours, Galina Gyorgevna and grandson Kirill, who was a year older than our son Victor, also Ricardo's younger brother, Jaime, who was visiting from Paris, where he was doing his Maths Ph.D, Professor Vic Allen[101], his translator Lynda and his friend, Cyril Ramaphosa, later to become President of post-apartheid South Africa, who happened to be in Moscow at that time. Our exiled Chilean journalist friends, Gaston and Valentina (not their real names) were also there. English, Spanish and Russian were to be heard all around the flat, and the jokes were somehow international. We were all comrades together, of different nationalities, of different skin colours, speaking different languages - but we were all, in our different ways, working towards a socialist society and a fairer, more peaceful world.

---

101 Leeds University Professor Vic Allen (1923-2014) was the author of "The History of Black Mineworkers in South Africa" a three-volume work that he was assigned to write on behalf of the South African NUM by its founding General Secretary, Cyril Ramaphosa, who was a close friend. In 1988, in the dangerous days of the end of apartheid, when the South African National Union of Mineworkers was a key player in organising resistance, Vic was invited to Cuba for a secret meeting between Fidel Castro and miners' leaders Cyril Ramaphosa and James Motlatsi. It was on their way back from this meeting with Fidel that Vic Allen told us about it at the New Year party at our flat. (See Appendix VIII for his account of that meeting with Fidel).

CHAPTER V

It was about this time – early 1989 - that I began writing articles for the *Scotsman*. I had met their Education Correspondent a few weeks earlier, he had asked me to write a piece about my children's Soviet school, they had liked it, and asked me for more. I wrote a piece on the Armenian earthquake, then the *Scotsman*'s Editor, Magnus Linklater, asked me if I would be interested in writing a weekly column for the *Scotsman* on the political changes in the USSR, from a personal and human interest point of view. So began my *Scotsman* weekly column, which was given great prominence in the paper, sometimes making up a whole half page, with photographs, and with my own byline. It lasted until I left Moscow in the summer of 1990. For diplomacy's sake (since I was the *Morning Star*'s correspondent) I used a pen-name – Tess Armand. I enjoyed writing it, as it was a welcome break from news reporting and gave me scope to talk about issues from a more human-interest perspective.

In January 1989 the Baltic republics passed laws giving precedence to their own languages over Russian, which had hitherto been the State language for inter-republic communication. It signalled the beginning of the end of their remaining within the USSR.

The campaign for the first multi-candidate elections to the new Congress of People's Deputies, due to be held in May 1989, began in earnest in March, and the media was full of information on candidates. Meanwhile, washing powder had disappeared from all the shops near us, and when I asked Lyubov' Sytnikova, the manager of our local supermarket on Taganskaya Square, why this was, I was told it was down to problems with suppliers, in turn due to the inter-ethnic problems between Armenia and Azerbaijan, which had led to irregular supplies of a chemical from a Sumgait factory in Azerbaijan.

But another shop assistant on the checkout told me she thought it was sabotage. "There are certain people who do not like our *perestroika*," she said, "they're deliberately creating problems."

The new Congress was to be made up of 2,250 deputies. One unusual aspect of the new structure was that a third of the seats were to be reserved for people elected from public organisations – like trades unions, the CPSU, the Komsomol, the Academy of Sciences, the *zhensoviety* (women's councils), veterans, cooperatives and professional organisations, like writers, artists and musicians.

I learnt that the Communist Party's Central Committee was putting forward 307 nominees for the 100 seats allotted to the CPSU in the new

Congress of People's Deputies, so for the first time ever, there would be competition for those seats.

It was becoming increasingly obvious from the rising ferment in the country that unless a tight rein were kept on the new processes - unleashed in quick succession - and unless tangible results in the economy started to show, the entire *perestroika* project would end in chaos. Whilst *glasnost* and new political thinking on the international scene were hailed as achievements, a January 1989 CPSU Central Committee address to the people acknowledged that "the economy is still not operating in the new way and people are not yet seeing results from *perestroika*."

With increasing inter-ethnic clashes in the Caucasus and calls for independence from the Baltics, problems were mounting. Special rule for the autonomous region of Nagorno-Karabakh was introduced in January in an attempt to calm tensions between the Armenian majority population there and the surrounding Azerbaijani population. But there would be no re-drawing of boundaries, as that could have opened a hornet's nest in many other regions of the Soviet Union.

Another factor, hinted at by leading *perestroika* proponents, was that tensions were being deliberately whipped up between the two ethnically diverse peoples by vested interests in those republics who wanted to stymie the reforms.

A friend of ours is the granddaughter of a famous revolutionary from the Caucasus region, and bears his name – Shaumyan. Her grandfather was a well-educated Armenian, Stepan Georgevich Shaumyan, who founded several newspapers and journals and led the Baku Commune, appointed by Lenin in March 1918 to work for the Revolution in the Caucasus. In those early days of the Revolution, there were numerous problems including ethnic violence between Baku's Armenian and Azerbaijani populations: Shaumyan had the task of defending the city against an advancing Turkish army whilst attempting to spread the cause of the Revolution throughout the region. Only three years before, the Ottoman Turkish regime had begun the massacre of some 1.5 million Armenians, recognised today as a genocide by most countries apart from Turkey, so there was deep hostility between Muslim Azerbaijanis and Christian Armenians during those years.[102] The Bolsheviks had a Marxist interpretation of those events, which lay the blame on the ruling classes, not the ordinary peoples of the region.

Shaumyan was made Commissar Extraordinary for the Caucasus and Chairman of the Baku Council of People's Commissars. The government of the Baku Commune consisted of an alliance of Bolsheviks, Left Socialist-Revolutionaries, Mensheviks and *Dashnaks* (Armenian nationalists).

When the revolutionaries in the Baku Commune lost power in July 1918, Shaumyan and his followers, known as the 26 Baku Commissars, attempted

---

102 See Page 82.

to flee across the Caspian Sea but were captured and later executed, on 20 September 1918, by anti-Bolshevik forces, with the connivance of the British, who at that time owned oil deposits in Baku[103].

The British journal *Near East* noted in 1918:

> "Baku has no equal in terms of oil in the world. Baku is the biggest oil centre the world over. If oil is a kingdom, then Baku is its crown."

The British Foreign Secretary, Lord Curzon (1859-1925), was one of the supporters of the capture of Baku, as the British Government was determined to increase its sphere of influence in the Caucasus region, both for oil-related and strategic reasons.

Baku's oil in Soviet times formed part of the country's total energy resources and was not a factor in the inter-ethnic problems that surfaced in the eighties. Whilst Armenians and Azerbaijanis had lived peaceably for decades since the early years of Soviet power, now, in 1989, old hostilities and deep-seated religious differences suddenly became topics that could be openly aired under the new regime of *glasnost*.

Stepan Shaumyan in his youth

In 1989, not only were people not yet seeing any improvement in their standard of living, but the state budget deficit stood at 35,000 million roubles, according to official statistics. Some economists, like Nikolai Shmelyov, put it at 100,000 million.

The State had to cut expenditure – both on expensive 'prestige' projects and on the military. Clearly the announcement of withdrawal of Soviet forces from Afghanistan can be seen in this light. My next trip was to Uzbekistan to witness the last stage of that withdrawal.

But before I left, I had an unexpected experience during a Labour Party visit to Moscow, involving Peter Mandelson, the delegation's spin doctor. The delegation arrived in Moscow on 30th January, and that same day I rang Ron Todd, General Secretary of the Transport and General Workers Union and honorary CND Vice-President, to request an interview. He seemed a bit cagey, telling me that it had been agreed by the delegation that none would speak individually to the press.

---

103 From 1903, twelve English companies were functioning in the Baku region. In 1912, Anglo-Dutch Shell obtained 80% of the shares of the Caspian-Black Sea Society "Mazut".

The following day, at a press conference at the Soviet Foreign Ministry, I bumped into Rupert Cornwell, the *Independent*'s correspondent, who mentioned a British Embassy briefing that morning having been "a waste of time". Apparently there had been a press conference with the Labour Party delegation and I had not been invited. I caught sight of Andy Tucker, the Embassy's Press Attaché, went up to him and asked him bluntly why I had not been invited. He blamed Peter Mandelson, the delegation's "minder", since he had given Mandelson the contact numbers of all correspondents, including me, he said.

I was furious at having been left out, and told Tucker I was lodging an official protest on behalf of the *Morning Star*, and told him to pass that on to Mandelson. "If there is one paper in Moscow that should have been invited because of its full coverage of Labour Party matters, it's the *Morning Star!*" I told Tucker in the presence of Rupert and the *Guardian*'s Jonathan Steele.

Mandelson phoned me early next day telling me delegation members were "giving no interviews". I rang the head of the delegation, Gerald Kaufman, who said that wasn't so, he would happily give the *Morning Star* an interview but I should arrange it through Mandelson.

I phoned Mandelson and overheard a conversation he was having with someone called Phil, which went like this:

"By the way, I thought I'd better tell you, Kate Clark of the *Morning Star* has bearded everyone in sight and complained of being left out. She's obviously going to be a nuisance, so we're going to have to admit her to the 6pm briefing at the Embassy."

Rupert Cornwall rang me that morning to let me know of the afternoon briefing, in case I'd been left out again, which was decent of him.

The background to all this was that the previous year's Labour Party Conference had backed the party's unilateralist defence policy – a policy the Party leadership was keen to reverse during the current re-drafting review of its defence policy. As I wrote in my diary:

"Kaufman was courteous and friendly enough in my interview with him. Not so Mandelson, who was rude, hostile and unpleasant and clearly intent on gagging the delegation. It gave a pathetic impression – that a high-level delegation consisting of elected members of parliament and Party leaders were not free to speak to the press unless they got permission from someone who is, after all, merely a salaried member of the Labour Party's staff."

"It's the only time in my nearly four years as the *Star*'s correspondent in Moscow – when I have interviewed many people from various parties, movements and countries – that I have been told that, to approach a member of the delegation, I had to go through the press officer."

In Moscow you can phone a minister or factory director and arrange an interview direct ..... isn't it an anachronism?"

The delegation had obviously come with the brief to prepare the ground for the Labour Party to ditch its unilateralist policy.

When *Guardian* correspondent Jonathan Steele and I went to see the Soviet Defence policy experts that the delegation had met the previous day, it was quite clear that the Soviet side had not indicated any preference regarding Labour's unilateral disarmament position: "It is the Labour Party's own business," they told us.

In fact, First Deputy Chief of Staff of the Soviet Armed Forces, Colonel-General Vladimir Lobov told us unilateral nuclear disarmament by Britain "would be an imaginative gesture." And if a future Labour Government were to take part in the multilateral disarmament process, that would also be positive.

"This could be by a freeze on present stocks, by unilateral cuts of one kind or another, by scrapping Trident or by a bilateral agreement on a weapon-for-weapon deal offered to Neil Kinnock four years ago."

On Sunday, 5th February I flew to Tashkent, the capital of Uzbekistan, to cover the final withdrawal of the remaining contingent of Soviet troops from Afghanistan, under the Geneva accords signed in April 1988.

The troops, numbering some 40,000 men, were due to cross the border at Termez, the southernmost town of Uzbekistan on the Amu Darya river. During the ten years of Soviet intervention in Afghanistan from 1979-89, Termez was an important military base and a road-rail "Friendship Bridge" spanned the river.

A Russian fortress and military border fortification had been built there in the late 19th century after the emirate of Bukhara had given the land to Russia's tsarist government. During the years of Soviet Uzbekistan, industrial enterprises were built and the town boasted a Pedagogical Institute and a theatre.

Crowds of relatives stood patiently under the hot sun as the first contingent of combat troops crossed. "By 18.00 hours on 15th February the last Soviet soldier will cross the border," Major-General Valeri Stripnin, of the Turkestan military region, told journalists who had flown there for the historic pull-out.

"The Soviet Union and Afghanistan are abiding strictly by the Geneva accords," he said, "whereas Pakistan and the USA are not."

"Our presence in Afghanistan was motivated by noble aims," Stripnin went on, "to help create better economic and social conditions for Afghanistan and prevent outside interference."

"History will judge," he added, "whether our decision to agree to the Afghan Government's request to intervene militarily was correct or not."

The nine-year war had cost over 15,000 Soviet dead, 35,000 wounded and 311 missing in action, he reported.

As the convoys of light tanks and armoured personnel carriers thundered across the wide bridge, clouds of dust filled the air in their wake. Sitting atop their military vehicles, the young soldiers waved and smiled broadly, catching bunches of flowers thrown up by the welcoming crowds.

"I can't wait till he gets back," Valentina Matveyeva told me. She had travelled two days and nights from Tyumen region in Siberia to meet her 20-year old son Sasha, whom she hadn't seen since he was called up two years ago.

At the welcoming ceremony for the returning troops, up on the dusty brown hillside overlooking the bridge over the Amu Darya, young Uzbek girls in typical national dress offered freshly baked Uzbek flat bread on a platter to the para troops' unit commanding officer.

I asked one private what his feelings were: "I reckon we've done our duty to the Afghan people," Vladimir Solomin from Leningrad replied. "The ordinary Afghan people related very well to us," he went on. "Not those up in the hills, of course."

Since the beginning of the Soviet phased withdrawal nine months ago, some 6,900 Afghan civilians had been killed by rockets fired by the opposition *mujahedeen* operating from the steep hillsides between Kabul and the Pakistani border, according to Afghanistan's Consul in Tashkent, Hasrat Hangar.

As ever, it is civilians, like the Afghan woman I spoke to in a Kabul hospital weeping over the death of her son, who bear the brunt of war. The Americans (and British) were embroiled in Afghanistan from 2001 till 2021 - and what was achieved? Nothing, except death, maiming and destruction. Since the start of U.S. military operations in Afghanistan from 2001 to mid-2019, nearly 2,400 American servicemen have died. 457 British soldiers died and over 300 were wounded.

In contrast, the USSR's intervention had given 170 factories to provide Afghans with work and backed a government that opened schools and universities for girls as well as boys. If the Najibullah Government had had more time, and if the Opposition had ceased being funded and backed by the US, the policy of National Reconciliation could have succeeded. After all, some 120,000 Afghan refugees did return to the country under that policy.

The Geneva accords bound the Soviet Union to withdraw its 110,000 troops. But they also bound Pakistan to dismantle the military training camps and Opposition bases on its territory – which was not done. The accords committed the US and the Soviet Union "to refrain from any form of interference and intervention in the internal affairs of Afghanistan and Pakistan." Yet US arms supplies continued to pour in for the *mujahedeen* entrenched in Pakistan.

The US was bogged down for 20 years in Afghanistan, suffering an ignominious defeat in August 2021 when the *taleban* took Kabul and established a government. If Afghanistan had been allowed to follow the policy of National Reconciliation, Najibullah could have been the leader to pursue that policy and bring his country into the modern era whilst respecting religious and tribal traditions.

Nowadays political scientists in Russia and the former Soviet Union mull over whether the USSR gave too much ground when it signed up to the Geneva Accords. Did Gorbachov's advisers know that the US side would be unlikely to keep to their side of the bargain? Or was Gorbachov simply seduced by the West's charm offensive in those years?

Back in Moscow from the temperate climes of Termez and Tashkent – where I managed to slip into a market and buy a traditional doll in Uzbek dress and a couple of other small gifts for the children – it was the depths of winter, with heaps of snow piled up on the sides of roads and pavements and grey slushy mush at the entrances to heated shops and offices.

Whilst the parks and countryside outside Moscow were beautiful, untrodden snow sparkling in the sunlight and tree branches heavy with icy snowflakes, the city centre tended to a grey-brown colour, as cleared-away snow, icy heaps, grit and mud combined to militate against the city's beauty.

The children got on with life, uncomplainingly trudging to school and back, their heavy satchels with textbooks needed for homework and sometimes encumbered with skis and skiboots whenever they had a PE class. Once every few weeks, they were also encouraged to take old newspapers and magazines to school for recycling. As I subscribed to several newspapers, magazines and journals, we always had piles of *makulatura*[104] for them to take. We would tie reasonably-sized piles up with string and the three of them would manfully carry them to school. I suppose they did not complain

---

104 *makulatura:* all newspapers and magazines were recycled in the Soviet Union, long before recycling became widespread in Great Britain. Recycling trucks would arrive in the neighbourhoods to collect glass bottles and other containers. Shops sold lots of products like sugar and butter, just wrapped in brown paper sheets twisted to form makeshift bags. In the eighties there was no plastic wrapping of any kind.

because that was the lot of all Muscovite children. Most parents didn't own cars, and all children walked or took a bus, trolley-bus or tram to and from school.

After school lunch, if any of the children had 45 kopecks they would go to the Institute across the road to buy a *bulka s makom* - a pastry with poppy-seeds inside - from the students' cafeteria. Delicious.

They uncomplainingly stayed at school for Afterschool Club *(prodlyonka)*, in winter returning home when already dark. But before starting on their homework, they would often snatch an hour's play with local children on the tree-filled slopes of our building's *dvor*. Despite their long school day and copious homework, our kids practically always seemed happy and cheerful.

In late February, Ricardo and our son Victor left to spend a month in Chile. The previous year, 1988, a plebiscite had been held there, under growing pressure from the Chilean people. 56% voted against Pinochet's continuing as president, which led to elections for the presidency and Congress, albeit within the confines of Pinochet's 1980 Constitution, under which terms he had made himself senator-for-life, as well as Commander-in-Chief of the Chilean Armed Forces.

Ricardo had not been back to Chile since being imprisoned and deported in March 1974, and now, after Pinochet had effectively been deposed, he was keen to re-establish links with his country and introduce our 14-year old son to his large family there. It was with some trepidation that we said good-bye at Sheremetyevo airport, conscious as we were of the still-recent crimes of the dictatorship, including disappearances of political activists.

In the event, all went well and they returned safely home. Ricardo was happy to have met his elderly parents and his five brothers and their families again after so many years, and for Victor, it had been a wonderful experience meeting for the first time his grandparents, uncles and cousins.

In the USSR, an unprecedented election campaign was underway to elect deputies to the new Congress of People's Deputies to be held at the end of May. On a February visit to Ukraine, Gorbachov listened to local people's complaints about food shortages and poor pensions.

Accompanied by long-time Ukrainian Communist Party leader, Vladimir Shcherbitsky, he heard people complain that pressure was being exerted to elect certain candidates favoured by the Party leadership. "It's up to you yourselves," Gorbachov told them, "if you don't like your bosses, you should get together, discuss things and elect someone else!" You can imagine how Shcherbitsky must have felt hearing that. Ukraine's economy was in many ways wasteful, Gorbachov pointed out – something that applied to the country as a whole.

One of the problems in Soviet society of the eighties was the alienation felt by many from the production process. "We say we have public ownership – but in practice, state property is nobody's in particular!" summed up Mikhail Bocharov, director of Butovo Brick Works, south of Moscow.

His works was engaged in an 8-year lease scheme, where the enterprise continued to be state-owned, but could spend its profits as the 500-strong workforce saw fit, once it had met its quota of sales to the state.

In its first year under the lease arrangement, Butovo works had achieved a nearly 30% increase in productivity. "Our aim is to become an independent firm – independent of any ministry or government department," Bocharov explained. "Our profits will no longer go to pay the salaries of ministry functionaries, since many of their jobs will be redundant once the factory is successfully running itself."

Bocharov called the new system at his works "collective ownership". From May 1988, the workers there could invest up to 5000 roubles in the firm, giving investors 6% annual interest – 3% more than the interest on state savings accounts. Workers without savings could opt to have a percentage of their wages deducted as part-investment in the firm.

Bocharov argued that this system resulted in better motivation among the workforce, "as they feel they are the real owners of their enterprise! Whereas before, people couldn't care less about anything: mismanagement, breakages, energy-wasting – people were indifferent."

The workforce's motto was "the more profit we make, the higher our wages!" However, in a socialist society, Bocharov said, there should not be huge differences in standards of living, as there is under capitalism. So no one should be permitted to hold as much as 50% of investment shares in any enterprise.

"We want to bring the workers closer to the means of production. People must become real stakeholders, real co-owners."

The problem of how to do away with all-union and republican ministries was one Gorbachov and his economists often raised. "We won't be able to solve our urgent economic issues unless we crush our bureaucratic management," he had told scientific workers last January. "But, how to do this? Not with reprisals, as in 1937! No, it will be by self-regulation, with the active participation of the people. After all, it was to gain power for themselves that the workers took to the barricades in 1917!"

Words like these served to bolster our confidence that Gorbachov's aims really were to improve socialism, not do away with it – as some of the more extreme reformers *did* want, even if they were not prepared to admit it openly. And what did the people think of all the rapid changes? Obviously, as a foreigner, even one who spoke good Russian, you couldn't hope to gauge public opinion in any scientific way. The people we met through our work and through the network of friendships we had with Russians gave us the impression that Muscovites in general supported the leadership at this stage, though there was a growing frustration that in terms of the economy, provision of food and goods, no visible improvement could yet be discerned.

I say "Muscovites", because in most parts of this enormous country, with their own distinct cultures, history and traditions, the fervour we saw in

Moscow – with demonstrations and angry discussion programmes on TV – did not exist in other republics, regions, smaller towns or in the countryside. In some of the republics, though, as we have already seen, *glasnost* had brought to the surface ugly nationalistic outbursts.

After the children had left for school, Ricardo and I would discuss the situation over breakfast, at our kitchen window overlooking the Moscow River and the Kremlin in the near distance. We had one of the best views in Moscow, high up on the ninth floor of our block of flats. We felt in turn exhilarated by the proposed changes to make socialist society more participatory and democratic, and worried that it was all spinning out of control when we read ever more critical articles in the press and ever more vociferous condemnation of practically every aspect of Soviet society. Not only the repressions of the thirties, but Stalin's actions as wartime leader – everything was being questioned and criticised.

As a journalist, I thought many of the editors were acting irresponsibly. I felt they should have been held on a tighter rein, because it was such an avalanche of negative reporting that all balance was lost. Instinctively I felt that a society used to one set of truths for decades could not be expected to reject so much of their society's past so quickly and without seeing clearly what future lay ahead. What was true and what was false?

Whether, if the reforms had proceeded at a slower pace (always supposing that was actually possible) the outcome for socialism in that country could have been more positive, we shall never know. Perhaps if they had been slower, they might simply have evaporated into the sand. Gorbachov's reforms *were* necessary, it seemed to us, though belated - they were at least 20 years too late - but they generated stiff resistance by vested interests within the Party and State. Could one expect enthusiastic support from the 800 ministries' staff, when the reforms meant doing away with their jobs? Or in the Party itself: could you expect Party officials at all levels to welcome new elections where they would now have candidates running against them, whereas before they had been elected unopposed?

We went to see a play called "Alive" at the Taganka Theatre, a 15-minute walk away from our flat. This was a play by Boris Mozhayev that had been banned in 1968 when the theatre's then young director, Yuri Lyubimov, had wanted to stage it. Now Lyubimov, resident in the USA, had been invited back to stage the play.

Topical in 1989 as it was 21 years earlier, the play criticised the distortions in collectivisation in the countryside. A Russian collective-farmworker, Fyodor Kuzkin, his wife and five sons, cannot make ends meet, so he tries to leave to find work elsewhere but comes up against a brick wall of bureaucracy shown in all its callousness. Without an internal "passport", which could only be given him by the collective farm bosses, he cannot move anywhere. He finds work as a forestry warden – only to find that if he took that job he would lose his family plot, since he would no longer belong to the collective farm. The system of *propiska*, which registered where a citizen lived, was now being criticised as an unnecessary means of control over the population.

Thousands of big collective and state farms were still operating at a loss, despite annual state subsidies of 10,000,000 roubles. Clearly something had to be done, and a March 1989 Party Plenum was called to address the problem.

"A large administrative-command machinery exists at the level of regions, republics and even the centre. What for?" Soviet leader Gorbachov asked at one agro sector meeting. "So that a high-ranking official who doesn't really know what's going on at collective farms can give all sorts of unnecessary and sometimes even damaging orders."

Productivity, he went on, was five times below that of seven leading capitalist countries and only 10% of that in the US, according to *World Economics and International Relations*, No. 12, 1987.

Results were promising from the new lease-farming methods being tried, but this was only on a small scale so far. As I wrote in March 1989, "lease-farmers are meeting considerable resistance from many farm and ministerial officials, and from other farmworkers not on leasing schemes."

"One state farm director in Oryol region put it this way: "If people had wanted to take out leases in earlier times, they would have been labelled 'anti-Soviet'!"

In early March a group of women journalists had a meeting with the Prime Minister, Nikolai Ryzhkov, a youthful-looking, business-like 60 year old. We met in the ornate gold and red Catherine's Hall in the Kremlin.

"For many years," Ryzhkov admitted, "we thought we had solved the women's question, but the new policy of *glasnost* has brought all sorts of problems to light, for instance, that too many women are still doing heavy, unmechanised labour."

I asked him about the increasingly frequent press pieces like one recently published in *Pravda - Zhenshchiny nye nuzhny na rabotye* (women are not needed in the workplace): didn't this sort of article go against the Communist Party's official policy of promoting capable women to senior posts, I asked?

It was important, Ryzhkov answered, to give women better promotion prospects. However, he added, some 500,000 Soviet women *did* at present occupy managerial posts, which represented a quarter of the total. He thought that the end of the "administrative-command" system would be good for women: "Women may not be as good as men at shouting orders, but when it comes to using their heads, they will come into their own!" he told the group with a smile.

Ryzhkov was one of the generation, like Gorbachov, who had come from a working class background – his father was a miner – and had started off as foreman at the giant Uralmash machine-building plant in Sverdlovsk (now Yekaterinburg). He now worked 12-13 hours a day, he confessed, made possible by his friendly and united family and his wife with whom he had lived "in love and accord" for 34 years.

The Prime Minister claimed that 40% of Soviet defence industries had gone over to civilian production, producing consumer goods and agricultural equipment; "plants that used to design missiles are now designing conveyor belts for producing spaghetti!"

Journalists always have an eye out for a scoop, and this *Morning Star* correspondent was no exception. I had two or three good contacts who were high up in the Party and in the press, and I made sure I kept in close touch so that I would be in the know when something was brewing. One day my friend Otto phoned me and said he'd got something for me. I could tell from his hushed tones that it was something important.

On the early evening of Friday March 10th 1989, he handed me a photocopy of the proceedings of the famous October 1987 CPSU Plenum, to be published the following day in the *Izvestiya TsK KPSS* No 2. The CPSU Central Committee bulletin was hardly a riveting read normally – but this was hot stuff, as it blew the lid on the fierce debates within the top leadership at that October 1987 Plenum when Yeltsin famously slammed fellow Politburo member Yegor Ligachov for holding back the *perestroika* process. Yeltsin was then replaced as Moscow Party Secretary, marking a definitive split in the top leadership.

Thereafter Yeltsin pursued his own leadership ambitions which were in part responsible for the demise, not only of the reform process, but of the CPSU itself and the disintegration of the entire Union of Soviet Socialist Republics.

My scoop didn't go unnoticed: Bob Evans, Reuter bureau chief, came round, eager to know how I'd got to know about this before publication. Good journalists never reveal their sources, I told him. My piece appeared the following day under the headline "Stormy Yeltsin Speech Published" (*Morning Star*, Saturday 11th March 1989).

The election campaign for the new Congress of People's Deputies was going on apace. 2,895 candidates had been registered in 1,500 constituencies, which gave a nationwide average of two candidates per seat. In a quarter of constituencies only one candidate was running. There were four Politburo members who were running uncontested, and only 16.6% of candidates were women – a much lower percentage than in the old Supreme Soviet. The number of worker candidates was also down. The fact that trades unions and women's organisations would have their own candidates, alongside constituency candidates, was meant to counter-balance these negative trends.

Despite filing every day and managing frequent features for the *Morning Star,* going on many trips to far-flung places and trying my best to cover everything that was going on at this febrile time, I received little encouragement from the London office. I had fairly frequent contact, by phone and telex, with the Foreign Editor but often found it difficult to understand from him what he wanted.

It was often disheartening, and if I hadn't had the support of Ricardo, I might have given up. As Ricardo often said, when I would complain to him that the paper hadn't published this or that piece I'd sent, "I don't know why they bother having a correspondent here if they don't want to know from you what is actually going on here!"

I understood the Star's dilemma: it had always highlighted the positive about Soviet socialist society, so now it was obviously hard to report that Soviet officials were saying the opposite – that practically everything in the past had been negative. But I always tried to write in a balanced way, with our readers in mind; now, thirty years on, as I re-read my despatches and features, I honestly think I did a pretty good job and deserved more encouragement from the editors.

So it was gratifying, on a visit to Edinburgh to meet with the *Scotsman* Editor, Magnus Linklater, Features Editor Bob Cowan and other journalists in April 1989 to hear them full of appreciation for my weekly column. Please, would I continue, and even write more, if I could, they said. "I thought your Armenia feature was brilliant," their Education Correspondent, Donald MacLeod, declared.

It was good to feel appreciated, since I often felt that I was neglecting my children to keep up with the demands of the job.

In London later that week, I met up with Kevin and Anita Halpin among *Morning Star* colleagues in a pub. I had known Kevin for several years and, together with an old friend who knew him well, had had dinner with him and his former wife Claire some years earlier. He was working-class through and through, originally from Preston, Lancashire, and had become a very well-known trades unionist in the car industry in Dagenham, later sacked for his militancy and blacklisted. He set up the Liaison Committee for Defence of Trade Unions, which did a lot of work to defend trades unions suffering the Thatcher onslaught against them.[105]

I went over to greet Kevin, but he was unsmiling, and from our ensuing chat, I could see that he was not at all happy with what was going on in the Soviet Union. He was worried that the USSR was going back to capitalism, he told me. I tried to explain that some reform *was* certainly necessary, as there were a lot of problems, as my reports had indicated. We parted friends, but I could see that to him, *perestroika* was nothing but a smokescreen for the destruction of socialism.

A two-day top meeting on agriculture – the brief considered a poisoned chalice given to Politburo member Yegor Ligachov after he became more critical of Gorbachov's reforms – had agreed that more lease-farming should be introduced: "Let the different forms compete," Ligachov said, "time will show which are more successful!"

That Plenum decided to do away with Gosagroprom – the state agro-industrial committee. This was an attempt to curb the ministry's interference

---

105 See Kevin's autobiography *Memoirs of a Militant*, Praxis Press, 2012.

in the day-to-day running of farms – something Gorbachov knew about first hand from his time as Party leader in the agricultural region of Stavropol.

"We must think of ways to promote leasing. Give people a chance to earn some money!" Gorbachov said. "In China people were simply given land and told: do what you want, and in spite of their poverty, production increased by 100 million tonnes of grain in only four years."[106] Whereas in our country, he said, it was all exhortation from above to produce more – which did not work.

Former Moscow Party leader Boris Yeltsin was very active in the election campaign. Speaking at the giant ZIL car plant, he slammed the recent agriculture Plenum for adopting "half-measures" to deal with the country's food problem. His demands for the abolition of all "special" privileges were met with resounding applause from shop-floor workers: "Let's eliminate all *spets*-this, *spets*-that, *spets*-the other!" Yeltsin told them, "and have equal access for all to food, goods and services!"

I didn't trust Yeltsin. It was clear that Gorbachov's reforms were meeting stiff resistance from entrenched Party leaders and ministerial officials, though so far he had managed to get them through within the top echelons by force of argument and personality. But they had been approved on paper only. The minutes of the October 1987 Plenum (my scoop mentioned earlier, p. 242) reveal how difficult it was for Gorbachov to carry the whole leadership with him in backing *perestroika*.

"At a time when the Gorbachov-led reforms are meeting resistance and even being actively countered by conservatives and people whose narrow group interests have been hurt by the reforms, Yeltsin's stand may be politically adventurist," I wrote at the time. "Whether his increasing tendency to set himself apart and above the Party, whilst remaining a Central Committee member, will operate in favour of *perestroika* or will act as a focus for an opposition, remains to be seen."

Results in these first multi-candidate elections for the new Congress were grim for many Party leaders at all levels. Leningrad's CPSU First Secretary, Anatoly Gerasimov, only got 15% of the vote, for instance, and Leningrad regional leader, Yuri Solovyov, failed to get elected even though he ran unopposed. Party leaders in many areas failed to get elected under the new system, losing out to previously unknown candidates. Yeltsin, however, won in Moscow by a huge majority.

The elections revealed the failings of Party leadership in many towns and regions of the country, and, as I wrote in March 1989, showed that "the authority the Bolshevik Party earned seventy years ago can decline if it is not merited."

As a welcome break from the febrile atmosphere of Moscow, I was invited to spend a week near Novosibirsk, in Akademgorodok (Academic Town). The students and postgraduates at this top science university had organised a

---

106 Gorbachov's *Memoirs*, p. 260, Doubleday, 1996.

week of events, discussions and exhibitions, and I was to speak at several of them, including the main May Day event in the town.

As its name suggests, Novosibirsk is in south-western Siberia, and a four-hour flight from Moscow. Ricardo and I left Liza and Martha, who were eleven years old, with our friend and fellow Russian-speaking journalist Ingela, a young Swedish woman, who stayed in our flat with them. They were fond of her and she was good company for them. Those were happy days, the twins have often told us, made even happier by the fact that the three of them – all cat-lovers – found an abandoned kitten and brought it to the landing outside our flat, cosily sheltered in a cardboard box, where we discovered it on our return to Moscow! Naturally we had to agree that the kitten, which they had called Kuzya, be allowed to live in our flat.

Novosibirsk was Russia's third biggest city after Moscow and Leningrad and one of its major industrial centres. Heavy mining equipment, metallurgical, food processing plants and other industrial factories were built during the rapid industrialisation of the thirties onwards, as well as a new power station.

During the Great Patriotic War many factories were relocated from western Russia to Novosibirsk in order to reduce the risk of their destruction. The city became a major supply base for the Red Army during the war and also received more than 140,000 refugees.

The big scientific research complex called Akademgorodok was built in 1957, about nineteen miles south of Novosibirsk. The Siberian Division of the Academy of Sciences has its headquarters there, and the town hosts more than 35 research institutes and universities, among them Novosibirsk State University, famous for Natural Sciences and Maths. We knew that, like Moscow State University, it was very hard to get into and thus had some of the country's best brains.

I was surprised to see, in one of the big foyers, an exhibition of my features both from the *Morning Star* and the *Scotsman*, displayed in prime of place. I got the impression that many of the students at the discussion workshops were looking to me for a lead, for approbation almost, which made me very uncomfortable. From the many discussions we had with students during that week, it was obvious that the atmosphere in Akademgorodok was no less febrile than in Moscow.

Students and postgraduates argued fiercely that *perestroika* was being stymied, and the only positive aspect of the Gorbachov period was *glasnost*. Russian friends had often joked that, yes, in the Soviet Union there *was* freedom – but around the kitchen table! Now the young people got up on platforms and spoke heatedly, denouncing those in the leadership they blamed for holding back the *perestroika* process. But what was the way out of the present difficulties?

Talking to many of the students there, Ricardo and I found that they did not decry the socialist system, but rather the conservative forces they blamed for holding back its improvement. The young communist organisation

(Komsomol) in particular came in for especially heavy criticism from the students who flocked to speak to us. "No one wants to be in the Komsomol nowadays," the University Communist Party committee secretary Mikhail Shelovsky confessed to us. "For years we educated our young people with slogans," Novosibirsk Komsomol First Secretary Aleksandr Morozov told us, "and this is the result."

The students we met were proud of their country's wartime past, very knowledgeable about the arms race and the dangers of nuclear war and firmly for peace throughout the world. Looking at their young faces, full of optimism and confidence, we felt sure that with students like these, the USSR would surely be able to sort out its problems and make the system work better for all citizens.

While we were there we met a shy young student, a Kazakh by nationality, who was studying physics at Novosibirsk University. I asked him how he had managed to get a place at this prestigious University. He had taken part in a republic-wide competition, he told me, and later, in a nationwide one.

He was from a poor peasant family, he told me, from eastern Kazakhstan. His parents had sent him to a Russian-language school there. "If they had sent you to a Kazakh-language school," I asked him, "do you think you would have got into this University?"

"No way," he answered in his quiet voice. "I am lucky to have the chance of such high-level scientific studies, with the further chance of a doctorate later, if I do well enough."

Was this an example of "russification"? This was often the mantra of anti-Soviet reporters during the years of the Cold War. Yet surely few can deny that in a case like that of this Kazakh student, Russian had opened up new horizons for him, which he would not have seen if he had not had the chance to be fully bilingual.

For Ricardo and myself, it was a wonderful week. The weather was mild – about 3 degrees below zero – and the snow was still crisp on the wooded slopes between the many blocks housing the different academic institutes. Our discussions had been stimulating and we made friends with Tatiana, a Latin America specialist, and Antonio, a Cuban writer. We knew our daughters in Moscow were in good hands, and it was one of the few times that Ricardo and I were able to go on a trip together. It was a welcome break from the never-ending stream of news and new initiatives that I, as a journalist for a daily newspaper, had to cover, absorbing nearly all my time and energies.

I tried to have as normal a family life as possible. We wanted the children to be able to swim well and learn new strokes. So I set about trying to arrange swimming for us as a family at a baths near the Press Centre. Unbelievably, I was told that we would have to provide samples of urine and faeces for all of us, give these in at our Polyclinic, plus I had to get certificates from the gynaecologist and dermatologist in order to obtain the necessary *spravki* to arrange for swimming sessions. Ricardo chickened out at this stage. I began the process on 14th April, making several trips to the Polyclinic with our three children, to see the various indicated doctors. On 18th April my diary entry says:

"Left the Polyclinic at 11.30am, with our 4 *spravki*. Total time wasted: 10 hours 15 minutes."

We *did* have a weekly swimming session at the baths, just for one term. I would have had to go through the whole process again if we had wanted to continue. I didn't have the time, so that was the end of our swimming.

It seemed to me that it was bureaucracy gone mad. It seemed to be more a way of actually *preventing* ordinary citizens from having access to such a simple thing as swimming. If you were a child earmarked as a possible future athlete, you would have all the facilities, but if you were just an ordinary schoolchild there was little or no sports provision. At our children's school, apart from some perfunctory exercise in the gym, and halfhearted trudging on skis through the adjoining park, there was nothing.

The only time they did any sport, including swimming, was at Pioneer camp every summer, when the children's days would begin with morning exercises.

That spring – 1989 - nationalism was on the rise in the southern republic of Georgia. A nationalist demonstration on April 9th had been dispersed using tear gas and 20 demonstrators died. A Parliamentary commission confirmed the government's claim that the deaths had resulted from trampling, but it condemned the use of tear gas by the military, which had caused the deaths in trying to disperse demonstrators.

The Georgian Communist Party First Secretary was forced to resign and Soviet Foreign Minister, Eduard Shevardnadze, himself a Georgian, was despatched there to try to calm the situation. As in other republics, *perestroika*'s failure to produce tangible results led to anger against the Communist Party leadership, and to the growth of nationalist feelings.

Historically the entire Caucasus region had been a hotbed of inter-ethnic problems. Tsarist Russia had conquered the Caucasus between 1800 and 1864, controlling all the area that is now Armenia, Azerbaijan, Georgia and the North Caucasus region of the Russian Federation. Given the different languages and cultures of the different ethnicities in that region, it was not hard to understand that there might be historical, linguistic, ethnographic and geographical reasons for the current unrest. Within the Georgian republic there was one part of a different ethnicity – Ossetia - the other part being within the Russian Federation; also within the Georgian republic there was another ethnicity – Abkhazia - which had the status of an Autonomous Soviet Socialist Republic.

Russia's great poet, Alexander Pushkin, wrote about the troubled region in his narrative poem *Captive of the Caucasus*, published in 1822, in which a Russian officer disillusioned with life decides to seek adventure in the Caucasus, is captured by local tribesmen but then saved by a beautiful local girl.

Later, in 1872, Lev Tolstoy wrote a novella of the same name - *Prisoner of the Caucasus*. Based on a real incident in his life while he was serving in the Russian military, the story relates how two soldiers are kidnapped for ransom and kept prisoner by locals. The Russian soldiers try to escape, are recaptured and finally manage to escape. From these works by two of Russia's greatest writers you get an impression of 19th century Russia's attitude towards the Caucasus region – as a lawless, fierce and proud region, unwilling to submit.

The existence of so many diverse ethnicities in a relatively small geographic area was a recipe for disaster in the growing climate of nationalism during the late eighties. Georgian nationalism had history - in the nineteenth century, when Georgia was part of the Russian empire, and again during the Civil War following the 1917 October Revolution, there were flare-ups of "Great Georgian" nationalism with incidents of what today we would call ethnic cleansing.

As always, history plays a big role in events and attitudes centuries later. During the early years of Soviet power, it had not been considered a priority to redraw boundaries, as the entire region would now be within the same nation – the USSR. The young Soviet nation devised an intricate Nationalities policy comprising a complex web of Soviet constituent republics (the 15 Soviet Socialist Republics that made up the USSR); Autonomous Soviet Socialist Republics (like North Ossetia and Abkhazia); Autonomous Regions (like South Ossetia and Nagorno-Karabakh); and Autonomous Administrative *okrugi,* e.g. Chukotka, Yamalo-Nenets, which are vast, but sparsely populated, areas in the far north and east; and the *krai*, e.g. Kamchatka. Krasnoyarsk, Krasnodar. The aim was democratic self-government; and the policy did allow for a considerable amount of self-government in the vast regions and ethnicities of such a huge country.

It's hard for us to realise how vast the country is: I was once in the Urals city, Sverdlovsk[107], and needed to interview someone who lived "nearby", I was told. We set off by car, and when I asked how long it would take, my Russian friend said breezily: "Oh, it's not far - about 300 kilometres!"

On my very first visit to the USSR, in 1963, I had attended a seminar on the Nationalities question, held in Baku, Azerbaijan. I admired the way the complex system worked to give each ethnicity considerable control over matters in their own patch. What other country with so many different ethnicities and languages had their own parliaments and administrative structures serving these diverse ethnicities? Unlike the USA, where all immigrants were expected to merge into the Anglo-Saxon dominant majority, becoming simply "American", here the indigenous peoples of this vast country ran their own affairs, with media, schools and culture in their own languages, and elected their own leaders, who in turn participated in the All-Union structures of power. To me it seemed a good system, and although *glasnost* showed up the failings there may have been, I still think that the Soviet Nationalities policy had much to commend it. After all, 130 ethnicities, each with their own languages, had lived in considerable harmony for 70 years in the USSR.[108]

In May 1989, President Gorbachov was due to visit Beijing on a State visit. The Soviet press was reporting that student protests supporting Gorbachov's reforms had started in Tiananmen Square. We knew that there was a great deal of interest in the forthcoming Gorbachov visit.

I consulted with my Foreign Editor, who was keen for me to cover the visit. It was arranged that an occasional contributor to the *Morning Star* – an Englishman who lived in Beijing - would put me up if I could make my own way there. So it was that on Saturday 13th May I left for China, arriving in Beijing at 1.20am local time. I made my way to the so-called Friendship Hotel, which was a big complex of buildings comprising hundreds of flats. In the fifties these had housed the 3000 Soviet workers and their families, who had gone to China to help build bridges and reconstruct the country after the destruction of the Civil War, which had ended in 1949 with the triumph of the Chinese Communist Party under its leader Mao Zedong.

---

107 On a research job for Jeremy Isaacs' *Cold War* TV series.

108 See *National Languages in the USSR: Problems and Solutions*, M.I. Isayev, Progress Publishers, 1977.

Friendship Hotel where I stayed, about 15km from the city centre

This was the first visit by a Soviet leader in 30 years. After Soviet leader Khrushchov's 1956 denunciation of the crimes committed under wartime leader Stalin, the Chinese Communist Party leadership had denounced the revelations as revisionist. Ideological differences sharpened, leading to a split in the communist movement worldwide. There were also constant border disputes along the 7,500 kilometre Chinese-Soviet border.

In the eighties, the Chinese leadership under Deng Xiaoping had introduced significant market reforms. Agriculture was de-collectivised, foreign investment encouraged and limited private enterprise allowed, although most industry remained state-owned.

Limited market reforms within the bounds of a socialist society were of great interest to the Gorbachov leadership. The growing student demonstrations in Beijing on the eve of the visit acclaimed the energetic Soviet leader as a modernising role model, with many of their slogans supporting Soviet *glasnost* and *perestroika*. Observing him at a press conference, I could see that Gorbachov felt uplifted, even flattered by all the attention and admiration. Yet a sober analysis would show that, whereas the Chinese reforms had actually already borne fruit, Soviet *perestroika* so far had nothing to show for it except words, resolutions and pledges.

The British comrade, who had been asked by my editors to put me up, met me when I finally found Friendship Hotel, which was some way from central Beijing, and took me to his flat. His wife was away looking after her elderly mother, he explained somewhat shamefacedly, as he showed me the untidy bedroom. Given the small size of the flat, I realised that he would have to sleep on their sofa. The following day I met Corinne, a Frenchwoman living in the same block, who invited me to stay at her flat, where there was more

250

room. I was glad to accept, and spent several very interesting hours with her, talking about China, her job and what she thought of the new developments there. Single, with a wonderful zest for life and a large circle of friends, she exuded confidence in China and its future.

The next day I made my way down to the protest occupation of Tianenmen Square, named after the Gate of Heavenly Peace which separates the Square from the famous Forbidden City.

I mingled with the young students, many of them wearing red headbands or white kerchiefs with handwritten slogans on them in Chinese script. A surprising number of them spoke English and gathered round me excitedly, telling me they wanted an end to corruption, more freedom of speech and a dialogue with the authorities.

In a letter to Ricardo, dated May 16th 1989, I wrote:

"Beijing in summer is lovely, trees everywhere, flowers and shrubs lining many streets. But the city is alive at present with the incredible student demonstrators – you can see hundreds of them on bicycles riding into the centre, day and night, in a never-ending stream, carrying flags and banners and sometimes singing the Internationale. And their hunger strike has spread – over 3000 students have now joined in. Many are fainting because the heat of the square is so intense, with no shade anywhere. Surely the Government will have to do something to defuse the situation. So far the students are very calm and restrained. They are not asking very much – only that their movement be considered democratic and patriotic and that the Government should dialogue with them."

On the Monday – 15th May – I spent much of the day in the square, talking to students. A 26-year old medical student, Liu Feng, told me: "We welcome Gorbachov's visit and want him to speak at our University. We're not trying to get rid of socialism, we just want more political freedom, and to get rid of corrupt leaders!"

"We also want the Government to acknowledge that these demonstrations are not trouble-making – so we want them to apologise for the accusations levelled at us earlier."

Another, a 20-year old girl, Li Naxin, from the University of Economic Law, said: "We should allow different people to express their views in the papers, without being checked first by the authorities."

Their movement was not organised by the official Students' Union, she told me, but was a spontaneous new movement, supported by most students, and the population too, she thought.

A student of English, who did not want to give me his name, told me: "The Government must change the way it works. The reforms need to go further, especially the political structures. The main task is to build up democracy, science and the legal system."

In the blazing sun, milling round sitting on the paving stones in groups, with no shade, you had to admire their perseverance. I had a long talk with one group who had managed to find a little shade under trees to the side of the square. "We don't want private ownership of the media, we just want fuller and more truthful reporting of our movement!" one earnest young man told me. "We don't want to bring down the Government or change the socialist system; we just want to make it work better!"

They were young, impulsive, naive probably, earnest, well-educated and well-meaning. I wondered how the authorities were going to deal with them, especially with the hunger-strikers. No doubt Gorbachov's visit, which was evidently widely supported by these students, had severely embarrassed his Chinese hosts.

After a few hours in the square, I made my way to the big Shangri-la hotel, where my other British colleagues were staying, to file my copy to the *Morning Star*. The first thing that struck me on entering the Press Centre was how well equipped and modern it was, compared with similar facilities in Moscow and indeed everywhere I had ever filed from in the Soviet Union. There were telex machines, faxes, telephones, enough for all of us to use, service was efficient and the Chinese staff extremely helpful.

I realised yet again how backward the USSR had become in some areas of the economy, that even a comparatively poor, developing country, as China was at that time, had better electronic facilities than in Moscow.

I had always found filing from places outside Moscow difficult – during the trial of the Nazi war criminal Fedorenko, for instance, I had found it nigh on impossible to file daily as the trial was progressing, and the same from Kiev when I went to cover the Chernobyl story.

The next day, Tuesday 16th May, was to be the day of the main press conference Gorbachov would give during his stay. My friendly host, Corinne, invited me to go with her by bus down to Xinhua news agency, where she worked, and walk to Tianenmen Square from there. On the streets leading to the Square there was an endless stream of students and groups of technicians in white coats – one such group from an electronics factory. I made my way over to the southern entrance of the Great Hall of the People, with its giant picture of Mao Zedong adorning the front façade, where journalists had been told the previous evening that Gorbachov would be likely to enter. I met up with a Swedish journalist, Harold, whom I knew slightly from Moscow, who was with Steve Handelman from the *Toronto Star* and Steve Goldstein of the *Philadelphia Enquirer*. We swapped impressions and news whilst walking up the steps to the southern entrance to try and persuade the Chinese officials to let one of us phone the Soviet Press Centre to find out if the venue had been changed. They let Harold in, and he emerged shortly telling us that so far it had not been changed – which seemed unlikely, in view of the fact that the Square and surrounding area was thronged with chanting crowds of students. We couldn't see how Gorbachov's car could even approach the Hall.

A big group of journalists gathered and we were allowed in, ready for the much-heralded press conference. The Great Hall is an enormous building, "not at all impressive or beautiful without or within," I wrote in my China diary at the time. We waited for about 45 minutes, then an announcement was made that the press conference had been transferred to the Government's Diaoyutai Guest Residence on the outskirts of Beijing. So began a mad rush to hand in the translation equipment and earphones and get our accreditation cards back.

It was each journalist for him/herself then as we all tried to get a taxi to the new venue. I was in that desperate search when I came across Conor O'Clery, the *Irish Times* correspondent, who was in the same predicament. We decided since there were no taxis, we'd hail a rickshaw to take us to his hotel from where we'd hopefully be able to get a taxi.

(From my China diary): "It was a fascinating half-hour ride on this two-seater rickshaw, through the back streets and alleys, as the rickshaw cyclist tried to avoid the crowds of demonstrators on the main street. Fruit stalls, mend-anything stalls, little backyard cafes full of men playing Chinese table games and cards. And people on bikes riding precariously through the narrow, twisting back alleys, between old ramshackle houses which contrasted so sharply with the many modern high-rise hotels along Beijing's main thoroughfares."

We made it to Conor's hotel, found a taxi and arrived just in time for the press conference. It was in a low, quite modern building, one of several set in beautifully kept gardens and across a lake from the pagoda where I was told Gorbachov was staying. The hotel complex had been built in 1959 for the 10th anniversary of the People's Republic of China.

Gorbachov had to field some difficult questions about the student demonstrations – what did he think of their demands and had he talked to any of them? The *Daily Telegraph* correspondent Xan Smiley asked him what he would do if Red Square were filled with students the way Tianenmen Square was. Gorbachov looked ruffled at that, answering that Smiley was trying to get him to make judgements or impose a single model for every situation "which had been the mistaken practice in the past".

Conor had paid the taxi-driver 100 yuan to wait for us. We met up with Jonathan Steele, the *Guardian*'s correspondent (who, inexplicably, had a bike with him) Rupert Cornwall, of the *Independent* and Xan Smiley and his wife Jane. Unbelievably, we all squeezed in the taxi, Jonathan's bike in the boot, Conor in the front with me on his lap and Jonathan, Rupert and Xan at the back, with Jane on Xan's knees. A comfortable ride it was not, and our jocularity revealed our huge relief at having made it when it had seemed nigh on impossible.

Back at Conor's hotel, Xan invited us to have dinner (on the *Daily Telegraph*, of course), so since I had barely had anything to eat all day due to being down to my last 200 yuan, I accepted. Then I went down to the Business Room, which, like at the Shangri-la and the Beijing International where I had filed on previous days, was well equipped, so I was able to write my report on the press conference and fax it in good time to the *Morning Star*.

It had been a long day, and now all I had to do was manage to get home to Corinne's flat at Friendship Hotel. I hailed a taxi and sat back, almost starting to relax as I enjoyed the night-time sights of the capital. The driver took a ring road so as to avoid the centre which had been closed to traffic since Monday. Not far from Friendship Hotel we came to a junction where about 200 demonstrators were blocking the road. They immediately swarmed round our taxi, their young faces up against all the windows, and others banging on the bonnet and thumping the roof. All I could see from the darkened windows was a sea of Chinese faces pressed up against the windows on all sides. Their faces were not menacing, but the sheer numbers and the thumping was really scary. The driver wound down his window and tried to reason with them to let us through. I couldn't understand a word of course, but the driver suddenly switched on the light and gesticulated towards me in the back, as if arguing that, since I was a foreigner, they should let me through. After what seemed an eternity, after more arguing, the young men let us through. My heart was thumping. I really thought at one moment that they were going to turn the car over.

The driver, almost as shocked as I was, I think, was muttering to himself the rest of the way and when we got inside the Friendship courtyard, he stopped the first driver he saw and recounted with gestures the whole frightening episode. It had obviously unnerved him. He demanded four more yuan, presumably for having got me out of a sticky situation. I wasn't going to argue.

That night, safe in Corinne's flat, I stayed up late, writing my diary and a letter to Ricardo to post in the morning. I was missing him. The desperate scramble to get to the important press conference had shown me once again that in the world of competitive journalism, it was very much each for himself. I did not really belong in that world, but I was determined the *Morning Star* would get the best coverage I could provide and that way compete with the big, well-financed newspapers like the *Telegraph*.

Xan and Jane Smiley had asked me if I'd like to go with them to see the Great Wall of China – at their (or the *Daily Telegraph*'s) expense. I jumped at the chance. We set off about 12.30 and after a one and a half hour drive got to the nearest point of the Wall to Beijing, north-east of the capital. It had been slightly misty when we set off, but now it was distinctly foggy and was starting to drizzle. We ate the sandwiches Jane had asked their hotel to prepare for the three of us, then caught a cable-car up the steep hill to the Wall itself. By the time we reached that amazing structure it was raining quite hard and was so misty that we could only just make out the wall at a few metres distance!

We had to laugh at the absurdity of it all – our only chance to see the Great Wall, and we could barely see from one side of the wall to the other, three metres or so away! Let alone see the Wall snaking over the hills in the distance, or the view down the hillside we had come up. There was nothing for it but to walk back down and put it down to one of life's experiences.

I really enjoyed staying with Corinne. She was knowledgeable and clearly loved China and her people. I learnt the Chinese custom of mass distribution of hot water in big thermoses, delivered to your door every morning. What organisation! Corinne would open her front door, bring in the thermos and we would have breakfast together.

I also met other foreigners who lived in the same complex of buildings that comprised Friendship Hotel. It was very pleasant in the evening to meet up at the restaurant and learn more from them – who were all resident in Beijing – about what was going on and where it would all end.

Paul White, the *Morning Star*'s occasional correspondent, took me to meet Israel Epstein, English Editor of *China Reconstructs,* a man of about 75 who had known Chou en-Lai and had met Mao Zedong. I found out in the course of the conversation that he had also known a friend of my mother's, Rose Smith[109], a founder member of the Communist Party of Great Britain, who had lived in Chesterfield for a few years when I was a child, before going to China, where she worked on *China Reconstructs* and then at Xinhua News Agency. She left China during the Cultural Revolution, returning to Chesterfield for a few years, later going back, apparently at the personal request of Chou En-Lai. She remained in China till her death in 1985.

I have very clear memories of Rose Smith in her little terraced house on Whittington Moor, Chesterfield, where my mother and I would have tea with her while she recounted tales of her years as a trades union leader and organiser. I remember her upright frame and somewhat distinguished demeanour, and the wide-brimmed hat she wore out of doors - when nobody else wore hats like that in Chesterfield. She had been National Women's Organiser for the Party for several years, but in the years when I was taken to visit with my mother, she was already elderly. She must already have been 71 when she accepted the offer to go and work in China. Whilst there, she adopted the Maoist line during the Sino-Soviet split of those years.

After chatting to Israel Epstein about his memories of Rose Smith, I asked him what he thought about the current sit-in by students in Tianenmen Square. "Basically positive, I think," he replied, "though it could get out of hand." The situation was very different, he went on, from that of the Cultural Revolution, which had been a power struggle between different factions within the Party –

109 Readers can find more information about Rose Smith from *Chesterfield's Remarkable Women*, by Janet Murphy, Bannister Publications, 2021.

"pure Marxists" as against "bourgeois revisionists", for example.

Deng had achieved popularity, he went on, due to his role in combatting the Cultural Revolution, during which time his son had tragically been thrown out of a window, as a result of which he was now a paraplegic. Epstein himself had spent five years in prison, he told me, with a wry smile: "my interrogators refused to tell me what I was charged with – they said I must know and should confess."

He thought the Chinese economic reforms had worked quite well; workers, especially peasants, had done well out of them, whereas intellectuals had not. Far more products were now available in shops and markets, he said, but there were still problems of inflation, unemployment and landless peasants coming to the cities to find work.

Students I spoke to in the Square complained that some of their textbooks cost about 5 yuan, whilst their student grants were only 58 yuan per month and a doctor's salary was between eighty and a hundred yuan.

"There has been no corresponding political reform," Epstein told me. "That is what the students want, because the entire leadership is discredited, as are the "official" student leaders." The protesters call Chinese Premier Li Peng "the Prince", he added, and accuse him and other Government and Party officials of enriching themselves at the expense of the people.

Party leader Zhao Ziyang was considered more progressive, Epstein said. "It's difficult to know what's going to happen in terms of leadership changes – the Chinese don't go in for conflicts, it's not their style."

I found it interesting that both in China and in the USSR, privilege and corruption were so vehemently denounced by protesters. As I reflected in one of my despatches from China:

> "Capitalist society's innate injustices of rich and poor coupled with large-scale tax frauds and all sorts of corruption do not bring the people out on to the streets in protest.
>
> "It seems that socialism, by eliminating basic economic exploitation, engenders a new scale of expectations from the people – of social justice. And therefore any deviations from socialism's claim to be an inherently more just society meet with opposition and resentment."

On a bilateral level, Gorbachov's State visit could be considered a success. As Gorbachov put it at his press conference: "It's as if those thirty years of hostility had never existed."

But his visit had been the unwitting catalyst for unprecedented, million-strong student demonstrations, sit-ins and a 3000-strong hunger strike in Tianenmen Square, increasingly encompassing wider sections of the population.

The Chinese students were seeing in the USSR a process of democratisation and increased freedom of speech – and they wanted the same for China. For them Gorbachov's visit was the ideal time to make their demands heard.

The Chinese authorities' reaction was interesting: for weeks it seemed to be 'sit it out and wait for it to blow over'. But just as the student protests were restrained and disciplined on the whole, so their will became stronger in the face of the authorities' seeming lack of response.

After differences within the leadership as to how to deal with the crisis, finally the State Council declared martial law on May 20 and mobilized some 300,000 troops. The troops advanced into central parts of Beijing on the city's major thoroughfares in the early morning hours of June 4. Some demonstrators, bystanders and conscripts were killed in the process.

Estimates of deaths range from 200 or so to many thousands and it is hard to establish the truth of many claims. It was, of course, a tragedy and I wondered - from my talks with many students over the week I was in Beijing - whether the authorities could have moved further to meet their demands and avoid bloodshed altogether.

Some Western reports of a "massacre" on June 4th 1989 seem to conflict with the report of a Chilean diplomat who personally witnessed events on the Square on June 3rd and 4th.[110]

My trip to China had been a stimulating and exciting one. I had made some new friends, witnessed those turbulent events, talked to some interesting and knowledgeable people - and on my last day even managed to snatch a couple of hours to look round the Forbidden City, which, once seen, is unforgettable. I came away from China on 19th May exhilarated and impressed with that society's dynamism.

As always my family were overjoyed to see me and we enjoyed a lovely but brief weekend together before the next event in the relentless calendar of earth-shaking changes in the USSR. No sooner was I back in Moscow than the new Congress of People's Deputies opened in the splendid Palace of Congresses inside the Kremlin walls.

There was huge interest in the new-style Congress, which was televised live. From its 2,250 deputies a smaller standing parliament would be elected which would operate for eight months of the year.

Since these parliamentary structures were completely new, many of the Congress Deputies themselves having been elected in multi-candidate contests for the first time, there was much debate around whether major decisions should be taken by the annual Congress, or by the new Supreme Soviet. A poll showed 87% of the public preferred the Congress to take the major decisions.

Attending the Congress, I watched the angry, fierce interventions from

---

110 Chilean Embassy Second Secretary Carlos Gallo: "Although gunfire could be heard, apart from some beating of students, there was no mass firing into the crowd of students at the monument." When (told of) eyewitness accounts of massacres at the monument with automatic weapons, Gallo said that there was no such slaughter..... From what he could see, Gallo claimed 'most of the tents on the Square were empty when the armoured vehicles rolled over them." However, the diplomat did concede that there were casualties.

speakers from the floor. It was as if all the pent-up emotions and resentments against the Party leaderships of the past had been unleashed in a tsunami of accusations and recriminations of all kinds. Delegates queued at the microphones, shouting and gesticulating, proposing alternative motions from the floor. It was totally unprecedented.

One of the issues was over whether Gorbachov – as CPSU General Secretary – should also serve as President of the Supreme Soviet. He managed to get this passed, as too that the Supreme Soviet should be elected at the start of the Congress, not at its end, as Academician Andrei Sakharov proposed.

The Supreme Soviet was to have two chambers – a Soviet of the Union and a Soviet of Nationalities. How should these two chambers be elected? The Congress Praesidium proposed that all deputies should be able to vote for any of the candidates to the Soviet of the Union, not only for candidates from their own republics. This vote was carried by a big majority.

Former Moscow Party leader, Boris Yeltsin, at first narrowly failed to get elected to the Supreme Soviet, subsequently scraping through when a Siberian deputy stepped down to let Yeltsin take his place.

Gorbachov's handling of debate was generally fair, though he gave lengthy replies whilst delegates' interventions were strictly time-limited. In his keynote speech, Gorbachov announced further cuts in the military budget and plans for more arms conversion to peaceful purposes. The release of these funds would help solve the country's economic problems, he said, pointing out that over forty million people lived on low incomes.

The consumer market was unbalanced, which led to shortages in the shops, he told the Congress. Expenditure on managerial posts had to be cut, he said, as it cost the country 40,000 million roubles a year. The Party's new economic policies were encountering opposition from State and Collective farm directors who were reluctant to introduce the lease-farming methods the Party was advocating.

As long as workers were not exploited, nor alienated from the means of production, different forms of farming could exist alongside each other, he argued.

Every speaker professed to be fully behind the reform process, but it was clear that behind the scenes many Communist Party leaders in the republics and regions were ploughing their own furrows – saying the right things, but with the intention of keeping the status quo.

Dmitri Likhachov, chair of the Soviet Culture Fund, told me he thought it was great that delegates were saying exactly what they wanted. "It's a great step forward. Of course," he added, looking at me, "you can't remember what it was like in Stalin's times...."

One speaker who caught my attention was a young scientist, Ilya Zaslavsky, a disabled deputy from Moscow's Oktyabr constituency. He spoke of the 'crying need' for better quality artificial limbs, telling how he had taken part in settling a strike at a prosthetics factory. "The workers said they weren't going to carry on producing the rubbish they had been churning out for decades!" They were in favour of lease forms of production so that they themselves could decide what needed to be produced, not be dictated to by the relevant ministry.

There were five disabled deputies at the Congress, two of whom represented the bloc of public organisations which had seats reserved for them for the first time in a Soviet parliament. One was from the Society for the Disabled and one from the Association for the Blind.

It was about time provision for the disabled was discussed. I never saw a wheelchair in the six years we lived in Moscow. What we did sometimes see, which was shameful and an indictment of Soviet society, were legless disabled men seated on little wooden platforms on tiny wheels which they propelled by pushing with their hands along the pavements.

It was one more indication of the stagnation afflicting society and the economy, the low priority given to anything which would have meant shaking up the way things were done to introduce essential new changes. The need was urgent – all the Soviet *afghantsy* returning home, wounded, some limbless – yet provision for the disabled had until now been dismal.

It was encouraging that now at least their voices were being heard.

One of the most thoughtful interventions came from the writer and historian, Roy Medvedyev. He argued against Yeltsin's ultra-radical agenda, arguing that some compromise was necessary at the present time. "Yeltsin is supported by several radical groups," he said, "but 'radical' is not the same thing as 'progressive'." Many of them were far from progressive, Medvedyev argued, and are demanding rapid economic transformations the country isn't yet capable of. "If they won, it would probably be a catastrophe for the country!"

"Yet on the other hand, the conservatives want to leave everything as it is, or even go backwards, and if they were to win, it would be no less of a catastrophe."

Medvedyev had had his Party card restored after expulsion twenty years earlier. His books critical of Stalinism were now being published.

Leaders from the various republics argued for more autonomy, even on foreign policy, as Latvia's President advocated. And the thorny issue of what to do about loss-making farms was raised, with ideas of transferring land to the local Soviets for them to lease land to rural coops or individuals.

Women's issues were raised sharply by the Chair of the Soviet Women's Committee, Zoya Pukhova, who pointed out there was no integrated state policy for improving women's status. More women were doing night shifts, heavy manual work and harmful types of production, she told Congress in a hard-hitting speech.

"Yet in the recent elections, in many constituencies no women even got nominated, let alone elected!"

Former Moscow Party leader, Boris Yeltsin, claimed that anti-perestroika forces were gaining ground in the country and proposed an extraordinary CPSU Congress to elect a new Central Committee, since the present one "had failed". He also proposed a law to regulate the role of the CPSU. This was code for scrapping Article 6 of the USSR Constitution, which stipulated:

> "The leading and guiding force of Soviet society and the nucleus of its political system, of all state organisations and public organisations, is the Communist Party of the Soviet Union. The CPSU exists for the people and serves the people."

The calls for a multi-party political system, heard during the Congress, began to gain traction, although it must be said, more in Moscow and the Baltic republics than elsewhere. Article 6 was eventually removed from the USSR Constitution in February 1990, giving rise to the formal establishment of other political parties.

"Initially, Gorbachov believed that the Party could play a major role in *perestroika*," Gorbachov's interpreter, Pavel Palazhchenko, recalled two decades later. "But the Party was such a big and difficult bureaucracy that it soon became a hindrance to *perestroika*."

"By that time, within the Communist Party, within the Central Committee and the Party apparatus there were all kinds of people and all sorts of tendencies and even different ideologies. There were traditional communists, social democrats, and those who later became liberals," Palazhchenko told RT. "The problem and challenge for Gorbachov was initially to integrate those groups and find a way to make decisions, given those conflicts and dividing lines. But then he concluded that it was no longer sustainable and that those groups should basically go their separate ways into different political parties and organisations. So he came to believe in a multi-party system."

It had been two weeks of unprecedented debate and revelations of the myriad problems besetting the Soviet economy at the time – 40 million living in relative poverty, murderous inter-ethnic clashes in Uzbekistan and other parts of Central Asia and the Caucasus, poor health and safety (during the Congress there was a horrific gas explosion from a leaking pipeline involving two trains near Chelyabinsk, resulting in 575 dead), ecological disasters such as the drying up of the Aral Sea and a host of other problems.

The two standing parliamentary chambers – the Soviet of the Union and the Soviet of Nationalities – had been elected, and the rift between the pro-*perestroika* forces and the 'conservatives' had become clear for all to see. The population had been energised during live-time transmission of the proceedings, but – everyday problems of shortages in the shops continued and nothing had changed for the population at large.

In my final despatch from the Congress, I wrote:

> "But what did the Congress actually achieve? Firstly, it laid down a practice whereby different views and positions are not the exception but

the norm. .... Such an active feeling of involvement and identification with the Congress's work must now be channelled into constructive participation in decision-making at all levels, from shop-floor to local councils.

"Then we might see a real people's democracy in the making – a democracy where people govern themselves and their own lives.

"Lenin's dream of true self-government by the people could still come true. It's still a long way off, but the just-ended Congress allowed a chink of it to shine through the clouds of bureaucracy and inertia."

It had been an exhausting two weeks. Prime Minister Nikolai Ryzhkov's report putting the country's foreign debt at 34,000 million roubles and the annual cost of the nine-year Soviet presence in Afghanistan at 5,000 million roubles was sobering, as were reports of the dire living conditions of miners in Siberia and the far north. I had already arranged to go to the Donbass, in Ukraine, to see for myself what conditions were like there, and so, straight after the Congress had ended, with barely a day to spend with my family, I found myself on a flight to Donetsk.

A Dutch photographer, Bertien van Manen[111], accompanied me on this trip. From a mining family herself, the main focus of her photography is on working people, with a special interest in mining communities. She was keen to document the lives of Soviet workers in this time of rapid transformations. For both of us, women of similar age, it was a fascinating insight into the lives of miners of the famous Donbass region. We stayed in the surprisingly attractive city of Donetsk, where a million fragrant roses grow in all the central gardens to beautify the city.

The Donbass was the biggest producer of coal in the USSR at that time, but production costs were high due to many seams being very difficult to work. The quality of coal, however, was excellent and the coalfield extensively exploited, since, compared to coalfields in the far north and Siberia, the Donbass was more conveniently located in an industrialised and urbanised part of the country.

It turned out that my Donbass trip was on the eve of the first-ever strike in that coalfield just a couple of weeks later, in July 1989.[112]

During the week we spent there we had many meetings with pit

---

111 Bertien van Manen has published several photographic books, such as A *Hundred Summers*, A *Hundred Winters* (1991) from her travels in the former Soviet Union, and *Moonshine* (2014) with photographs of mining families in the Appalachian Mountains. She has exhibited at London's Photographers' Gallery.

112 My timing sometimes seems uncanny: Reuters chief Bob Evans met Bertien and myself at a party on our return from Donbass, just as the strike was breaking out there and commented on our good timing. Then on hearing from me that I had arrived in the USSR just 2 weeks before Gorbachov took over as Party leader, and that years before, I had arrived in Chile just before Salvador Allende was elected President of Chile, Bob remarked: "Incredible timing! Can you please tell us where you're going next, Kate?!"

managements and trade union officials, saw some of the excellent health and holiday facilities, went down a mine and crawled along an incredibly low seam that was being worked, and generally had free rein to talk to miners wherever we saw them, coming up off their shift or relaxing in the city's bars of an evening.

My impressions after all our meetings and conversations was that conditions in the mines we visited were good, but that the geology was difficult, making many seams hard to work.

Valeri Kalmykov, a member of the Miners' Union Central Committee, told me that it was hard being a trade union rep. "You have to work your shift and then on top of that try and deal with union problems."

He was in favour of the new multi-candidate elections for Trades Union posts, he told me, saying it would ensure that the unions defend workers' rights better than hitherto. At 26, his wages were 300 roubles per month, his wife worked, and they had a three-year old daughter at nursery.

Yuri Mazhan, 18 years at the coalface, had for the last four years been Vice-Chair of the trade union committee at Kirovskaya pit, elected unopposed as was usual back then. The Chair and Vice-Chairs were exempt from their work as miners for the period of their election (2 or 3 years), Mazhan told me. Kirovskaya employed some 3,500 workers, all except two of whom were members of the Miners' Union.

I asked Mazhan whether Soviet trades unions had become discredited. In the West, trades unions had the clearly defined role of defending and improving workers' rights and conditions at work. But in Soviet society, where the state was meant to be a workers' state, was their role different?

"You're right," Mazhan admitted. "For a long time the trades unions have not lived up to their job. They have spent too much time on managerial problems. Trades Union committees have been controlled by and responsible to Party organisations, whereas now they will be independent."

He insisted, however, that he himself was well respected by the miners, explaining that the Trade Union Chair was third in the hierarchy, after the Director of the mine and the Secretary of the Communist Party Committee.

But the Trade Union Chair was elected by the Trade Union committee – some 20-30 people – not by the workforce as a whole. Usually, he explained, people who already had some sort of leadership role, like for instance, a *brigadir* (team-leader), would be put up for election, unopposed.

Dressed in suit and tie, Yuri Mazhan, who had been a *brigadir* for five years before becoming a trade union official, seemed a long way from the miners we met later, in their blackened overalls and helmets. But then, it would be the same in Britain, I think – elected union officials work in offices, after all.

It was ironic that he was denying that the workers were engaged in any sort of struggle to improve their conditions, when only a couple of weeks later, the miners there came out on strike. He insisted that their main tasks were how to improve health treatment, to get more places at sanatoria (holiday and rest homes), nurseries, pioneer-camps – and to solve the perennial shortage of housing. At Gorky mine, we were told that there were 900 miners on the waiting list for a flat.

All of which were, of course, valid and essential tasks, and the facilities we saw for the miners during our week's stay showed the tremendous progress that had been made over the decades since the end of the Great Patriotic War.

One morning we saw a group of miners at the pithead, waiting to go down for their shift. A tall, well-built 37-year old miner with a broad smile, Georgy Tarasenko, stayed back to talk to us. I discovered that the men worked in units, or links (*zveno*) – four of them 'coal-extracting' and one 'repair' unit. In each *zveno* there were between 10-12 men.

"The more coal we get out, the more we earn," Tarasenko told us. "The seam we're working at present is coming to an end, so we're getting about 1000 – 1200 tonnes a day, which earns us between 450-600 roubles a month, depending on qualifications and years worked.

Brigadir Ivan Manyekin butted in to tell us that there were 130 men in his team and that their wages were calculated using a complicated system of coefficients. I asked how much of their labour was manual. "A lot", came the reply, "especially when we're working some of the narrowest and lowest seams where it's practically impossible to use a pneumatic drill."

Tarasenko got 27 working days annual leave, plus 1 day for every two months down the mine – called 'heat' days, given for working in temperatures above 26°C, making a total of 33 days. For *prokhodchiki* (shaft sinkers) holidays are even longer - 39 days, Ivan told us.

What do you do if there is too much dust or it's too hot, I asked. "We complain to the trade union rep, of course," came the reply. "So ventilation might be improved, new air-conditioning installed... But we've known worse conditions than this – once we worked when it was above 40°C," Ivan said, grinning broadly.

It was unprofitable for management to have to pay miners the extra money they would be entitled to in such temperatures, he went on, so they always tried to solve such problems.

I asked Tarasenko straight out if he was satisfied with the work of the trade union at his pit. "Why not?" he replied. "We've got sanatoria, holiday homes, sports and recreation facilities. Of course demand is always more than supply!"

At another pit, named after the writer Maxim Gorky, we met Trade Union rep Anatoly Marinov, who stressed that the main problem for miners and their families was food supply. "We (Gorky mine) have a farm which provides the miners with pork. Last year the farm owned 5,500 pigs, this year we've got 6,000, which means more than 69 kg of pork per miner can be sold in the pit shop. We also have greenhouses where we grow cucumbers, tomatoes and other vegetables and salads." Mushrooms were grown in worked-out areas of the pit, he told us.

It was in talking to Marinov that I realised the relative lack of priority given to health and safety issues. "We've had quite a lot of injuries," he admitted. "We work at great depths – 1200 metres – so proper ventilation at such depths is difficult." Training was always given to starting miners: they were taught what to do in the case of sudden gas discharge - a particular danger, he added, at Gorky pit.

Price rises were of concern, Marinov said, drawing my attention to an angry article in the trade union newspaper, *Trud* (labour) by national Trade Union leader Stepan Shalayev. "Our Prime Minister, Nikolai Ryzhkov, promised at the recent Congress of People's Deputies to stop these price hikes."

Do you ever consider striking, I asked Marinov. "Yes," he answered, "one pit has already had a strike - over stagnant wages when prices are going up." It hadn't happened at his pit, as wages were generally higher. "But in the Kuzbass, Siberia, and Karaganda (Kazakhstan) the problems are really serious – wages might be as low as 100 roubles, yet a coat costs 250 roubles."

Another new problem, Marinov said, was that some miners were leaving to set up coops, now that these were allowed, citing a group from his pit who had left to set up a car-servicing coop in the centre of Donetsk, where their income would be a lot higher and the work easier.

At that time there were 120,000 mineworkers and 21 pits in Donetsk. Women had worked down the pit until 1966, but were now doing only pithead work. Work often went on at 1,300 metres depth, where temperatures could get to 40°C, whereas officially the limit for workers was 25°C. How often that was ignored we couldn't tell, but I suspect quite often. Some seams were as low as 60cm.

We had asked to see conditions for ourselves. Oktyabrskaya mine was established in 1975, replacing an older one from 1955. We got to the pithead and entered the cage, operated by women, to descend to the seam. With a tremendous clang, the cage door opened at a depth of 1,200 metres and we got out, fitted out in white miners' helmet with lamp, loose black cotton jacket and trousers, cloth mitts and what looked like wellington boots – which was the normal gear we saw the men were wearing. Then we got into an open-top mini-train which clattered and jerked its way for over two kilometres, at a pace of 12k per hour. We could see workings on either side of the track. It was very warm, especially in our borrowed work gear. All of a sudden I felt a rush of fresh air through the open metal doors of the train as we passed a ventilation shaft. It was very welcome. The temperature of the surrounding rock was 41°C, I was told. Our rattling little train would suddenly go uphill up a slope, or even backwards.

All the miners wore a measuring device to check for gas. We were told it was 0.5% methane in the tunnel we were in. Roughly hewn rockfaces of black, glistening coal shot by. Our faces caught drips from the roof as the pit train rattled onwards.

At some points the arched steel roof supports holding the roof back with long wooden planks had bulged, I saw, and one or two of the wooden planks had broken with the pressure. "This section is due for re-propping," chief engineer Yuri Denisov said cheerfully. I hoped to God it wouldn't collapse while we were there.

We got out at the seam being worked and had to crawl on our hands and knees along where the roof was in places only 1.4 metres high, with hydraulic roof supports holding the seam roof up. There were moments when it felt really claustrophobic, as the roof was only inches from my face and my body could nearly touch the sides. I tried to breathe calmly and tell myself it would soon be over, as I inwardly paid heartfelt tribute to mineworkers all over the world for the horrendously difficult and dangerous work they do.

The men were working with pneumatic drills in some places and with picks where it was tighter. We saw men shovelling coal on to a moving conveyor belt. A mechanised coal excavator cut coal with its big toothed wheel, spraying the air as it worked to dampen the dust, the extracted coal sparkling a rich black as the machine worked its way along.

Our faces blackened by the dust, I confess I was glad to get back into the lift and to the surface, with the blessed blue sky of a gorgeous sunny Donetsk day. We showered and dressed before meeting with *brigadir* Anatoly Alekseyev, Section head Mikhail Mosyakin, Chief Engineer Yuri Denisov, Oktyabrskaya Director Vsevolod Morzak and Miners' Union Chair Viktor Zakharovich.

Our pit visit had been pretty exhausting. The heat, the crawling along what seemed like endless tiny tunnels and the information overload had all contributed to my feeling whacked. But I got the feeling that they were all decent, hard-working and dedicated men, doing their best for their industry and their fellow men. There may have been careerists and yes-men among them, I suppose, but that was not the feeling I got from any of the mine officials at any level that I met during that week.

We saw kindergartens with their classes of beautiful, healthy-looking children; we saw health centres run by the different mines; we went round sanatoria where miners were given exotic, health-

Back at the top, Oktrabrskaya mine,
after my visit underground
(photo courtesy B. Van Manen)

265

giving treatments like mud baths, oxygen inhalations, vacuum massage, electro-treatment, high-pressure "Scottish" showers (alternate hot and cold, we were told!), hydrogen sulphide baths for arthritis, underwater massages....

"Our miners are much healthier than 20 years ago," Anatoly told me. He had been a miner for 20 years. "Then we had a lot of silicosis, pneumoconiosis, but now there's very little of such diseases. Our machinery is better, we have decent respirators and ventilation is more powerful. And we have more automatic monitoring for dust and gas."

But at A. F. Zasyadko mine earlier, Miners' Union Chair Nikolai Sipyenko told me about some of the health and safety aspects of his job. "With difficult conditions of heat and sometimes poor ventilation, miners have to look out for themselves."

"Our mine is very dangerous: we often used to work at above 40°C, so if you didn't take care, you could get injured. But since 1988 there's been a sevenfold reduction in work accidents after *brigady* (teams) signed labour safety agreements with management - which mean that miners get a 100 rouble reward if the number of accidents goes down."

"There used to be cases of men coming to work drunk. Now they get sacked," Sipyenko told me.

In general, my impression was that health and safety at work was taken less seriously than in Britain. Several of the miners we saw underground had taken off their jackets and shirts due to the heat, which was against safety regulations. And I was surprised that the boots the miners wore had no toe protection, nor did I see any knee-pads being worn, which I would have thought were essential in such narrow seams.

There is a certain pride I often came across in the Soviet Union in being 'hard' – *zakalyonny*. From our children being told that their vaccinations HAD to hurt, otherwise they wouldn't do any good, to Ricardo being told the same in hospital when he had painful daily injections after a knee operation, to the dentist telling my daughter Martha not to be such a baby when she reacted to the pain of dental treatment without anaesthetic, to the *morzhy* (walruses) – men and women who delight in plunging into freezing holes in the ice in the midst of winter, there is definitely something in the Soviet or Russian psyche that admires toughness.

I put it down to the harshness of life under tsarism, the exile of dissidents to Siberia, the harsh northern climate; the period of *smuta* (time of troubles) after the October Revolution and through the ensuing Civil War, and, most of all, to the sufferings endured during the Great Patriotic War by soldiers and civilians alike, both in occupied territory and throughout the country, where citizens worked at full tilt to make arms and tanks for the front and ensure that production carried on to feed, clothe and supply the whole country.

Before we left the Donbass, we had the chance to visit Gorky mine's holiday camp in Novoazovsk on the Azov Sea. It was a beautiful setting, the calm blue sea lapping gently at the sandy beach a short walk from the *baza otdykha* – an attractive building with chalets among the pine trees. You could not fail to be impressed by all the facilities, but I knew from our many conversations with the miners that there were not nearly enough places for all who wanted to holiday there.

No sooner had I got back from Donetsk than the children were due to go to Pioneer Camp, as their school year had ended at the end of May. It was a bit of a rush to get their summer clothes and pioneer uniforms ready for them to board the buses to take them to *Orgres* Pioneer Camp, some 50 kilometres from Moscow. This was primarily a camp for children of energy industry workers and was a little less formal than the Pushkino camp they had been to in previous years. It was in beautiful countryside, with good facilities including a swimming pool (but they complained that they were only allowed to swim for a half hour at a time!)

While they were away at camp I joined a journalists' trip to Moldavia[113], and for only the second time in our six years' stay, Ricardo came with me, representing the Chilean cultural magazine *Araucaria*.[114]

I knew little about Moldavian history before I went. I knew it had the same language as Romania and that it shared some common history with that neighbouring country, but little more than that.

The Soviet-German non-aggression pact of 24 August 1939 contained a secret protocol which gave the province of Bessarabia, at the time controlled by Romania, to the Soviet "sphere of influence." On 2nd August 1940 the Moldavian Soviet Socialist Republic was formed and was formally incorporated into the Soviet Union. There already existed an Autonomous Moldavian republic within Ukraine, so this now became part of the new Moldavian constituent republic of the USSR.

In the summer of 1941, Romania joined Hitler's forces in invading the Soviet Union, and thus won back Bessarabia and northern Bukovina, as well as occupying the territory to the east of the river Dniester. Soviet partisans were very active in those regions and by the end of the Great Patriotic War, the Soviet Union had reconquered all of the lost territories, reestablishing Soviet power there.

Since then, Moldavia (population just over two million) had been one of the fifteen full constituent republics of the USSR, with equal constitutional rights as the bordering republic of Ukraine, which had a much greater population (42 million).

Gorbachov's policies of *glasnost* had created conditions for Soviet republics to demand greater independence from the central government. As we were

---

113 I use Moldavia as the name of the republic and Moldavian as the language, which were the terms in common usage in 1989. Nowadays, the country is known as Moldova and the language Moldovan.

114 *Araucaria* is the name of a southern Chilean tree. Printed abroad, the magazine was a top-quality publication with contributions from leading Chilean intellectuals, most of whom had been forced into exile after the 1973 military coup.

to see in the days we spent in Kishinyov, as the Moldavian capital was called in Russian, Moldavia was no different. (Chişinău is the name in the Latin script).

Not long after our visit, on 31 August 1989, the republic's Supreme Soviet adopted Moldavian as its State language, and the return of the language to the pre-Soviet Latin alphabet. We were party to very heated discussions on this topic at a meeting we had with Moldavia's Academy of Sciences.

All the people we met on our visit spoke good Russian and Moldavian. Street names were in Russian and Moldavian. Moldavians made up 64% of the population, Russians 13%, Ukrainians 14%, Gagauz 3%, Bulgarians 2%, various other nationalities the remainder.

It was so obvious to us outsiders that if Moldavian were to be adopted as the republic's sole State language, this would inevitably discriminate against other nationalities living there who would have to know their own language, plus Moldavian, plus Russian. The change from the Cyrillic script - in use throughout the Soviet Union - to the Latin script would inevitably set Moldavians apart and result in children in Moldavian-language schools growing up with a poor knowledge of the Cyrillic script - essential to be able to read Russian and communicate with the other 14 republics of the USSR.

We learned that there had always been a Moldavian-language TV channel, Moldavian schools and nurseries, theatre and cinema in that language. We saw street kiosks with newspapers, magazines and books in Moldavian, albeit in the Cyrillic script. Street names were in both Moldavian and Russian. Moldavian could be heard everywhere on the streets of Kishinyov, spoken by people of all ages.

I met a farmworker at a state farm outside Kishinyov who turned in an instant from chatting to a colleague in Moldavian to fluent Russian as he answered my question, explaining his support for the proposed language law by complaining that when he finished his Moldavian-language secondary school, his subsequent electrical engineering studies had had to be in Russian.

I pointed out to him that if you lived in the USA, you wouldn't expect to be able to study electrical engineering in, say, Italian, even if you were part of the American-Italian community there. And in the UK, would you be able to study that subject in Welsh, or Gaelic, at higher education level?

In a feature for the *Morning Star*, I wrote:

"Moldavia's language demands might seem to an outsider as somewhat impracticable in today's technologically advanced and increasingly integrated world, where only a handful of languages dominate world research and development.

"But they clearly form part of a deeper political and social movement whose more extreme elements are right-wing separatists.

"These are able to capitalise on economic and social discontent throughout the Soviet Union at a time when the economic reforms have still not produced the goods, whilst *glasnost* continues to expose all that is negative."

The separatists had formed a *fronto populare* – and in response the non-Moldavians living in the republic formed an "inter-movement". There were Communists in both movements, yet the positions of each were fast moving poles apart. On the eve of the 49th anniversary on June 28th of Bessarabia's unification with the rest of Moldavia, the complex history of the region was coming under review by the *fronto populare* and calls were being heard for Moldavia's separation from the USSR and unification with Romania.

At our meeting at the Academy of Sciences the interventions of some of the Moldavian academics were more passionate than rational. Cooler heads were needed, I thought, for anything good to come of all this.

Whilst in Moldavia we went to the *Biruinza* (victory) state farm to taste some of their excellent wines. We lunched in a huge wine cellar six metres underground, with lofty ceilings and subtle lighting. The farm produced far more than wine – fruit and vegetables, meat and milk, we learned. The 1,200 farmworkers produced 10,000 tonnes of grapes annually and were 85% profitable in all agricultural produce. The *Aligote* white wine was delicious and we also enjoyed their Cabernet, which they told us was given to Soviet cosmonauts and submariners, as it helps eliminate strontium from the body. Yuri Gagarin had enjoyed a visit to *Biruinza* just after his heroic space flight, our hosts told us.

Our visit to Moldavia gave Ricardo and me much food for thought. It seemed to us that everything was getting out of control and that some of the demands were unreasonable and would not have been accepted by any government anywhere.

Article 70 of the 1977 Constitution reads:

"The Union of Soviet Socialist Republics is an integral, federal, multinational state formed on the principle of socialist federalism as a result of the free self-determination of nations and the voluntary association of equal Soviet Socialist Republics.

"The USSR embodies the state unity of the Soviet people and draws all its nations and nationalities together for the purpose of jointly building communism."

After listing the 15 republics, Article 72 reads:

"Each Union Republic shall retain the right freely to secede from the USSR."

The Soviet Constitution, in my opinion, was inherently democratic and whilst there may have been deficiencies in the ways in which it was applied at different times, the fact is that that right of secession *was* guaranteed legally precisely because it was based on the democratic principles of self-determination.

Many people might question the concept of "the Soviet people" in Article 70, but when you consider that at that time, some 60 million USSR citizens were living outside the republics where they were born, it becomes easier to understand the concept of many peoples merging together to form one new entity, for the benefit of all – the USSR.

Ricardo and I, on our return to Moscow, drove out to see our children in the Orgres Pioneer Camp. We took them their favourite fat round biscuits – *pryaniki* - and *ponchiki* (small doughnuts) and the delicious flat, crunchy almond cakes, perhaps some *blinchiki* too. And of course some *borodinskiy* (Russian black bread) or *rzhanoi* (rye) bread and various types of cooked sausage or *wurst,* as I knew from their letters that they were sometimes hungry, especially Victor! Parents weren't expected to enter the Camp, but we could take the children out for the afternoon. So we would collect them, drive to some local beauty spot and have a picnic with them for an hour or two. It was lovely to hear them tell us all about their new friends and activities, and we were relieved, as always, to hear that they were having a good time. I remember one afternoon when we found a small lake surrounded by fields and woods where people were bathing. We enjoyed a lovely swim under the hot Moscow sun, before it was time to take the children back to the Camp.

They usually spent five weeks there of the 3-month summer holidays from June-August. Once or twice we were asked if they'd like to stay on a few weeks more, which we agreed to, since they themselves wanted to. If not, they played at home with friends in our block or with schoolfriends, invited their friends round to our flat and Ricardo and I got on with our work as best we could whilst keeping an eye on them. Victor would mainly go to his friend Artyom's flat or meet up with him and other schoolfriends near *Ploshchad' Nogina* (a Square named after a famous Bolshevik, Viktor Nogin), whereas Liza and Martha usually played in the flat or in the *dvor* outside.

I did not have much time to give the children, as I had my hands full trying to keep on top of all the changes going on. The *Morning Star,* being a newspaper run on a shoestring, did not have the sort of fully equipped office other British newspapers had, with their secretaries, couriers, drivers and nannies at home. The *Morning Star* was me, with a bit of volunteer help from one or two students from time to time, plus my ancient telex machine and the non-stop TASS wire feeding through in a tiny vestibule next to my little office.

It was becoming the norm for candidates for ministerial posts to face a gruelling question and answer session, broadcast on one of the TV channels, some failing to get the requisite endorsement. During the course of these sessions, some interesting facts were revealed, such as that 60% of Soviet exports were raw materials and that 44 million tonnes of grain would have to be imported in 1989. Prime Minister Nikolai Ryzhkov justified the raw materials sales as essential at that time to pay for imports of priority goods, mainly food.

Once again, as I watched from the sidelines, I had the feeling that everything was being destroyed before anything substantial was ready to take its place. Would the new-found "democracy", where accusations and vilifications of ministers and long-standing Party leaders were rife, be enough to satisfy the economic and social needs of the people? Obviously not. Economic achievements had to come first, it was clear. As the weeks went on, the future of socialism in the Soviet Union looked increasingly shaky. Leaders' speeches all talked of the *perestroika* process being intended to *strengthen* socialism, not weaken it. Yet the facts on the ground seemed to be increasingly pointing the other way.

Pravda commentator Arkadi Maslennikov wrote:

"Our people have too long been starved of information for all the 2,250 deputies they elected to be equally capable, in a qualified and knowledgeable way, of making judgments on all the highly complex and neglected diseases of society."

So it was not surprising that immature political discourse often took the place of respectful, considered and rational dialogue on the public stage, since *glasnost* had given everybody the right to say anything and everything.

I interviewed *Pravda* Editor Ivan Frolov and other leading comrades, including Nail Bikkennin, the Editor of *Kommunist;* I expressed my disquiet at the stream of negative features and reportage, and at the extremist tone of some articles, even in sober newspapers like *Pravda* or *Izvestiya*. I was assured that this was democracy in action, that the public had thirsted for. The sceptic in me wondered whether what the public had thirsted for was plentiful food in the shops and a bigger selection of good-quality consumer goods.

July 1989 saw miners' strikes in Siberia and in the Donbass, where I had so recently been. Prices were rising whilst wages stagnated, I had been told then. In the west Siberian town of Mezhdurechensk, miners at Shevyakov pit staged a sit-in and the strike encompassed some 12,000 miners protesting about empty shops and the poor amenities at their pits. The demands were pretty basic - better packed lunches, round-the-clock canteen service, warm winter work gear; 800 grams of soap and a monthly towel per miner.

Miners and their families sat for hours in the town's main square, demanding the resignation of local leaders. I've lived among mining communities and I knew that such protests must have had a valid basis - miners are not the sort of people who act on a whim. It was worrying, as up till then, the workers seemed to have been in favour of the reforms and the whole *perestroika* project.

At the same time as these unprecedented strikes, Leningrad Regional Party

First Secretary, Yuri Solovyov, had to resign after failing to get elected to the new Supreme Soviet. I wrote that July: " How come he was so discredited in the eyes of his constituents that he didn't even get 50% of the votes cast, even though he ran unopposed?"

Gorbachov, on a visit to Russia's second-biggest city, denounced the conditions of the mainly women workers at Leningrad's Izhorsky factory:

"It's like in Peter the Great's time! Dreadful dusty atmosphere, intolerable conditions. It's shameful! Where are the trades unions? Where are the Party organisations?"

I was glad to escape the febrile atmosphere of Moscow for a three-week break in Britain, to see my parents and my brother Joe and family. That year – 1989 – we went to our favourite Northumberland spot - Bamburgh - to stay with our friend Mary Cowan, who had a cottage opposite the castle, and to St. David's, where we had a week's camping on a clifftop in glorious sunny weather. It wasn't as luxurious as our Black Sea holiday the previous year, but just as enjoyable.

Unfortunately my mother had not improved much since the previous year, I was sad to see. My father did his best, taking over the cooking, shopping and general upkeep of the house, with the help of a weekly cleaning lady. It was good to see her happiness at seeing us, and the affection she showed for her grandchildren. She tried to ask questions of us, but it was hard to glean what she meant to say. Strokes can be devastating, and certainly my poor Mum had to live the last five years of her life with that disability. As usual, I felt terrible as I prepared to take my leave of her. The only saving grace was that I knew that she thought I was doing an important job for the *Morning Star*.

Ricardo had not accompanied us on this holiday back home, so he was overjoyed to have us back again. It was 10th August, and in the heat of the Moscow summer we spent a lovely few days together as a family, taking the *raketa* out to various picnic spots on the Moscow-Volga canal. We loved those beaches, the water was warm, and we would spread our picnic blankets among the fragrant tall trees in the dappled sunlight, Ricardo and I either resting, playing ball or bathing with the children.

Moldavia's contentious new Language bill was to be decided at the republic's Supreme Soviet soon. A mass nationalist demonstration in Kishinyov called for the bill - making Moldavian the sole State language - to be passed. On the eve of the crucial vote, *Pravda* sent its correspondent there, who called the bill a "vote for national discord, the isolation of Moldavia and destruction of her links with other fraternal republics."

I agreed, having met some of the most vociferous proponents during our recent trip there. To me it was heartbreaking to hear that slogans such as "Moldavia for Moldavians!" "No to the Russian language!" and "Russians go home!" had been voiced on the demonstration. Given what I had observed about the state of bilingualism in Moldavia, and knowing that Moldavian

272

nationals made up 64% of the population, it seemed unfair and unjustified.

Meanwhile the situation in the three Baltic republics was similarly heated and society sharply divided. A CPSU Central Committee statement in late August 1989 accused 'separatists and anti-Soviet elements' of having taken over the popular movements there. The mass action of holding hands across the three small republics had caused much concern, the statement said, calling on the working class, intelligentsia, women, people's deputies and CPSU members to work for concord and consolidation.

Ethnic Russians went on strike in several Moldavian cities against the proposed Language Law which would relegate Russian to second-class status and force all non-Moldavians not only to learn that language but the Latin alphabet too, but to no avail - Moldavia's parliament voted to make Moldavian the republic's "state language".

These arguments may seem somewhat peripheral to readers, but the issue was of supreme importance. If every republic decided to outlaw Russian as the "state language", you could have a situation where Central Asian republics reverted to Arabic script, Armenians and Georgians to their distinctive scripts and there would no longer be a language of common intercourse among all the republics making up the USSR.

The children went back to school on Friday 1st September, Liza and Martha wearing their crisp white aprons over their chocolate brown dresses and Victor looking very smart in his new white shirt and light navy school uniform, all with their bright red pioneer scarves. Victor, I noted in my diary, "very unwilling" to start school again, whereas the twins were happy at the prospect of seeing their friends and teachers again after their 3-month break.

We had a family meeting that weekend about the idea of Victor going back to Britain to start his GCSE course - which would mean accepting my brother Joe's offer for him to stay with them. We looked at all the arguments, and decided we should go along with what Victor himself so obviously wanted, which was to go and study back in Britain, even though he would know no one at his new Derbyshire school.

I "blame" a comrade, Irene Brennan, for Victor's decision! She had been to see us together with her sister Mary, of Pax Christi, the previous year. Irene and Victor had had a chat in which she told him that the GCSE course was two years long, so he would be better starting at the beginning rather than halfway through.

Having decided, after weighing up all the pros and cons, I moved very quickly to buy a flight and Victor flew out a couple of days later, starting school in Old Tupton, Derbyshire, a mere two days later. His best friends Artyom and Roma came to the flat to say goodbye. It was sad in many ways, and at the airport I felt torn between needing to stay in Moscow because it was where both Ricardo and I worked, and unhappiness at the thought of our family no longer living together as a unit. The only comforting thing was that Victor seemed sure that this was what he wanted. It turned out to be a good decision, Victor was really happy at his new comprehensive, after a few initial teething problems and his absence spurred us to seriously think about our own return.

The daily barrage of fault-finding continued unabated. The Trades Unions met, delegates telling of local strike committees having forced new elections in trades union organisations. The Government daily newspaper, *Izvestiya,* wrote that Soviet trades unions had been "converted into a meek appendage of the administrative-command system". "Our trades unions have become part of the management," said one Donbass miners' union branch official, Yuri Mazhan. "In practice they've been controlled by local Communist Party organisations."

Was this true? I'm sure it was, although that is not to say that there weren't many good, honest people defending workers' conditions in lots of factories and workplaces around the country. It was also true, as I had seen for myself on many trips round the country, that trades unions did much for the welfare of members. They built flats for their workers, polyclinics and sanatoria, holiday homes, pioneer camps, sports halls and other leisure facilities.

As Professor David Lane points out, writing in 1990: "the working class has high job security and the worker is cushioned by overfull employment and a labour shortage. ....mass unemployment has been unknown. The Soviet regime has maintained very high levels of paid work for men and women. There has been a slow but constant rise in wages coupled with low price inflation."[115]

The introduction of *khozraschot* (self-financing) was already resulting in some unemployment, the development of coops was leading to rising inequality among workers and full-blown *glasnost* meant that previously hidden grievances were made public. It was a dangerous mix.

Strikes were becoming commonplace, from Azerbaijan, where even defence establishments went on strike, to many of the country's coalfields - the Kuzbass, Donbass and Karaganda among them. Workers' Committees were being set up in parallel to existing trades union bodies. Meanwhile Uzbekistan's former Communist Party First Secretary, Unman Khodzhayev, was sentenced in September 1989 to nine years in prison for bribery. It was clear that a lot had been going wrong for a long time.

Gorbachov, at a Central Committee meeting called to discuss the nationalities issue, denounced secessionist tendencies in some of the constituent republics, arguing that the solution to their problems lay in *perestroika.* Their rightful autonomy had become overly restricted, he said, due to the prevailing administrative-command system and an over-centralised economy.

He held out a vista of far greater rights for all national formations, including the smallest peoples, but rejected any redrawing of borders. The

---

115 *Soviet Society under Perestroika,* revised edition, by David Lane, Routledge 1992, p.160.

Soviet Union's economy was integrated, he pointed out - just one big auto works in Latvia, for instance, depended on supplies from 400 factories elsewhere. He criticised Party leaders and members in those republics where secessionist tendencies were most evident for failing to combat their excesses. "What we're about is to reveal the potential of socialism and give socialism its second wind!"

As always, Gorbachov's words sounded good. Reform *was* clearly needed, but was it wise to trash the country's history, overturning seemingly every "truth" the country had known up till then? Most people were more concerned with the bread-and-butter issues of life than wholesale revision of history.

Polarisation of society was more and more evident by 1989. Certain media were more and more openly pro-Yeltsin (as opposed to simply 'pro-*perestroika*') and others were increasingly taking a 'conservative' stance. *Pravda* printed a defamatory article about a recent United States visit by Yeltsin, reprinted from the Italian paper *Repubblica,* claiming he had spent his time there drinking and shopping.

Yeltsin supporters saw this as an attack on their hero, whom they saw as valiantly trying to push forward the reforms against the dead weight of conservatives in the Party and ministries. Once Yeltsin had broken with the rest of the Party leadership in October 1987, the stage was set for *him* to be seen as heading the reform agenda, rather than Gorbachov.

That year - 1989 - was the year of the unravelling of the socialist system in the countries of eastern Europe. Back in July, Mikhail Gorbachov had declared that the nations of the Warsaw Pact (set up in May 1955 in response to NATO's formation in April 1949) were free to choose their own road to socialism, giving the green light to anti-government forces to press for change. In August a non-Communist Government took over in Poland and in September Hungary opened its borders with the West.

In October 1989 Gorbachov told crowds in East Berlin "life punishes those who fall behind" - a clear reference to his host, the elderly GDR leader, Erich Honecker, who was replaced soon after. A month later the Berlin Wall came down. It was soon followed by the Czechoslovak Government's resignation.

These momentous changes obviously had an effect on the public in the Soviet Union. The Soviet leadership seemed to approve the changes in eastern Europe, at the same time giving the impression that they thought it inconceivable that such an unravelling could ever happen in their country.

By late September 1989 I had already decided that I wanted to go back to Britain to live. It had been clear to Ricardo on his visit to Chile that it would be extremely difficult for him to find work in Chile, so we both thought that we would stand a better chance of finding jobs in Britain. I missed Victor, now living there in my brother's family, and gradually that feeling, plus the accumulated tiredness due to the exhausting job as a Moscow correspondent during those fast-changing years, convinced me that we had to think of our return the following year.

Psychologically I was at a low point. My mother seemed worse; on my weekly phone calls, I could hardly make out anything from her slurred speech, and I got the feeling that she was deteriorating. I decided we should make the effort to go back for Christmas and gauge for ourselves how she and my father were, and how Victor was faring.

I needn't have worried about Victor: he had fitted in well at his new school and seemed very happy there, with a group of new friends who had soon accepted him. Some of the kids called him "Russki" and "KGB" when they found out that he had come from a Moscow school, but he had not met any outright hostility.

The little cat we had taken in, which we called Kuzia, died, apparently attacked by one of the big hunting dogs who lived in a different part of our block and often exercised in the interior grounds. It had been my fault, in the sense that I had let her out (she always clamoured to be let out) just for the short time it would take me to pay our rent at an adjacent office. I had not realised that Muscovites, like many Europeans who live in flats, do not let their pet cats out at all.

It was an upsetting experience for us all, especially for our 11-year old daughters, who were very fond of Kuzia. Even Ricardo, who was not a pet-lover, had grown fond of her, as she was such an affectionate little cat.

Together with friends Baira and Masha, Ricardo, Martha, Liza and I took the dead Kuzia in a small cardboard box up to the shady copse which formed part of our *dvor*. Ricardo dug a small hole among the silver birches and buried her, saying a few heartfelt words in a little ceremony to comfort the four friends who had so enjoyed playing with her.

It seemed like another omen telling me that it was time to think of leaving Moscow and the job of correspondent.

Victor came back to Moscow during his first half-term at his new English school, full of his recent experiences there. Many years later, when looking through memorabilia, letters and cuttings, in preparation for writing this book, I came across a letter from Victor to his cousin telling him how during his October holiday week back in Moscow, he had visited his old Moscow school where his former classmates and teachers had welcomed him with open arms. I found it funny that he had spent the whole week back in class together with his Moscow pals!

At the autumn session of the new parliament, the new coops were held up as an example to follow. Soviet coops were taking the first practical steps in forming a socialist market, top economist Leonid Abalkin told delegates, and had produced "many businesslike, enterprising people." Yet black marketeering was a big problem, as some cooperatives were simply buying up great quantities of goods in short supply and re-selling them to the public at grossly inflated prices.

"People are indignant," Gorbachov told the Supreme Soviet, "that soap,

Moldavian folkdance, Kishinyov, Moldavia, June 1989

Miners voting, Novokuznetsk Conference, November 1989

Q & A session, Novokuznetsk Conference, November 1989

Miners debate
in front of bust
of Lenin

Andrei Sakharov lying in state, December 1989

Flowers for those killed in ethnic unrest, Baku, Azerbaijan, Feb1990

Interviewing Bihojal Rakhimova (Tajik) - Dep. Chair of Supreme Soviet's
Women, Family, Maternity and Childhood Committee, Feb 1990

Street scene, Ashkhabad, Turkmenia, Feb 1990

In ancient city of Merv,
Turkmenia, Feb 1990

Carpet-weaver,
Turkmenia, Feb 1990

Women hoping to conceive hang cradles from
tree branches, Turkmenia, Feb 1990

In front of The Hermitage, Leningrad, March 1990

With war veterans and former partisans, Gorky Park, May 9th 1990

With writer Daniil Granin at his *dacha* outside Leningrad, summer 1990

With engineering workers, Uralmash, Sverdlovsk, 1991

"Memorial for the victims of Stalinism!" demonstration, Moscow, 1990

Yeltsin is the people's candidate!"; "It's not the people for socialism,
but socialism for the people!"; "Hands off Yeltsin!" were some of the slogans
at this demo, Moscow 1990

Selling off uniforms and *matryoshki*
(nests of dolls), Moscow 1991

Soft drink can on
riflewoman statue,
Revolution Square Metro
station, Moscow 1991

Collage of Kate's press passes, to 27th CPSU Congress (Feb 1986); and to Red Square for 70th Anniversary of the October Revolution (Nov 1987); for May Day 1988; and for Victory Day on 45th anniversary (9th May 1990)

ПРОПУСК № 11953

тов. Кларк

Кейт

на Красную площадь
В ДЕНЬ 70-й годовщины ВЕЛИКОЙ ОКТЯБРЬСКОЙ
СОЦИАЛИСТИЧЕСКОЙ РЕВОЛЮЦИИ
7 ноября 1987 года

Трибуна ДК

Действителен при предъявлении документа

1917 **1987**

ПРОПУСК № 14228

тов. Кларк

Кейт

на Красную площадь
В СВЯЗИ С ПРАЗДНОВАНИЕМ ДНЯ
МЕЖДУНАРОДНОЙ СОЛИДАРНОСТИ ТРУДЯЩИХСЯ
1 Мая 1988 г.

Трибуна ДК

Действителен при предъявлении документа

1 МАЯ

ПРИГЛАСИТЕЛЬНЫЙ БИЛЕТ

№ 17024

тов. КЕЙТ КЛАРК

"Морнинг Стар" (Англия)

на Красную площадь
9 Мая 1990 года В ДЕНЬ 45-летия ПОБЕДЫ
СОВЕТСКОГО НАРОДА В ВЕЛИКОЙ
ОТЕЧЕСТВЕННОЙ ВОЙНЕ 1941—1945 годов

Трибуна ДК

(Действителен при предъявлении документа)

9 МАЯ

MOSCOW DAYS
by Tess Armand

Food, glorious food: the problem eating away at the hospitable hostess

IT IS one of the curious paradoxes of life here in the Soviet Union that though people are forever complaining that there is no food in the shops, whenever you go for a meal with Russian friends, the table is bound to be absolutely groaning with food.

Nothing of your slim starter so typical of Britain's more spartan hospitality — here, if you're invited round for a meal, don't eat anything from at least lunchtime, or you won't be able to do it justice.

Invited round to our neighbour's recently, I couldn't help but marvel at the sheer variety and splendour of the many dishes — and wonder at the work and effort our hosts must have gone to to get it all together.

A lot of the first-course dishes were home-made: marinated squash, pickled garlics and *cheremsha* — a long green stalk typical of Caucasian cuisine; home-made cheese and ham sausage, salamis, salted herrings, delicately spiced and marinated aubergines, Russian salat, beetroot grated with garlic and walnuts in mayonnaise and many more.

All this is put on the table at once, and everybody spends a long time trying out all the various dishes, which are handed up and down the table several times. Usually, people are so full after the 'first' course that it's quite common to leave the table for a while, talk and wander and then go back to the table for the main hot meal.

Russians love making toasts and if there's anybody there from the Caucasus region, he traditionally a man) will be appointed *Tamada* — a sort of unofficial master of ceremonies who calls on different guests to make the next toast, either in vodka, champagne or wine.

Even in more modest homes, the traditions are much the same. Until about a year ago when she finally got a three-room flat, one of our friends, a teacher, lived in a shared flat with two other families. About 18 per cent of Muscovites still live in shared accommodation because of the housing shortage. Though she, her husband and daughter only had one room to themselves, they would extend the dining table to its full extent whenever they had guests and the spread would be equally impressive.

It's a sort of standing joke here that "there's nothing to buy in the shops, but everybody's got everything". And, to a large extent, it's true. But *how* they get it, that's the question. "We go to enormous lengths," one friend said simply when I asked her. "And we spend a hell of a lot of time doing it."

Mind you, people can get weekly food orders through their work, you can get orders made up at local shops, people ring friends who might have better access to special delicacies, or they might foster special relationships with foodstore staff. But mostly, people — and it's usually women who do most of the work — simply go round the shops and buy what is there, then prepare the exotic dishes themselves by sheer skill, time and effort.

Actually, to say there's nothing in the shops is an exaggeration. But it is true that there's little variety in the state shops. You won't get good salami or ham from your state grocer, but you can get them quite easily from the new consumer co-ops specialising in wurst, salamis and hams.

It is the same with salad and fruit — you can get a big variety of these at any of the big private markets where country people bring their own produce to sell. But since prices are higher at co-ops and the market, this is an expensive luxury for many Soviet people, reserved for special occasions.

Bon appetit: gastronomic delights at a plush Moscow restaurant, and despite apparent food shortages many Muscovites offer similarly lavish meals for their guests

The food problem is something the authorities have been talking about for long enough. It's nearly a decade since a special food programme was drawn up under the then leader, Brezhnev.

Under Gorbachev, the Soviet Communist Party has agreed new measures to increase farming efficiency. Last March's central committee special plenary meeting on agriculture gave the green light to lease-farmers — individuals or families prepared to take a number of acres of livestock on lease for anything from five to 50 years, under contract to produce an agreed amount to the local state or collective farm.

But as one Moldavian lease-farmer commented to me a few weeks ago, taking land on lease from state or collective farms was not the solution because "they hem you in with such restrictions that you wonder if it's all worthwhile".

Now the Supreme Soviet, in its present session, is proposing beefing up lease-farmers' rights, enabling them to lease land direct from local councils, not only from existing farms.

There are clearly differences within the leadership on how far to go with lease-farming and private property in the countryside.

The man in charge of agriculture for the party is Yegor Ligachov, who stresses the advantages of existing state and collective farms. There are those in the party who fear that lease-farming could open the door to privatisation of land and a return of the *Kulaks* (well-off peasants considered enemies during the collectivisation of agriculture).

But most ordinary people would probably agree with former dissident Roy Medvedev, now Supreme Soviet Deputy, who told me last week: "I wouldn't mind seeing, perhaps not *Kulaks*, but good, hardworking peasants come back to our countryside, hiring say two or three helpers during harvest-time. Their output will be higher, and I can't see anything to be afraid of in that."

Revolutionary tidal wave reaches the shores of perestroika's homeland

THE TIDAL wave which has rolled and thundered with increasing force across Eastern Europe has now reached the shores of the country whose earthquake first set it in motion. Moved by the swift events in practically all its western neighbours, the Soviet Union, whose perestroika revolution was launched from the top, is now at last seeing some of the characteristics of people's revolution here.

On Thursday, Leningrad communists decided to expel their former regional first secretary and erstwhile politburo member, Yuri Solovyov, who is still a central committee member. He may no longer be, though, after today, when the Soviet Communist Party central committee meets in the building with the red flag on Old Square for what may well prove a watershed session.

Solovyov is accused of violating party ethics by having bought at an apparently nominal price through the state-owned commercial network a Mercedes car. To people in the West, Solovyov's crime may not seem very serious. But here, where the very cornerstone of the socialist system is meant to be that of social justice, any abuse of this principle by leaders is resented by ordinary people, who have long since cast out of the window all pre-revolutionary notions of the poor accepting their station in life.

Removal of privileges enjoyed by functionaries of the *nomenklatura* and their families was one of the main tenets of the election platform of the former Moscow leader Boris Yeltsin last year, and no doubt responsible for much of his 90 per cent of the poll.

"The German Democratic Republic has done in five weeks what it has taken us five years to achieve," a friend of mine complained to me a few weeks ago. His frustration at the slow pace of change was typical. But the signs are that people's patience has now already run out in some places.

In a Latvian resort, people have organised a squat in smart holiday homes which otherwise go empty most of the year. In Moscow a high-quality block of flats destined for the families of Party City Committee functionaries has been handed over to large families, as a result of public pressure.

And the list doesn't stop there. In Volgograd, Tyumen and Chernigov the entire party leaderships have been forced to step down under pressure from grass roots. All this has happened since the last central committee plenum, and will obviously have a bearing on what happens there today and tomorrow. For the conservative majority, they will provide extra grist for their mill in blaming Gorbachev for causing all this disorder.

With the most serious crisis to date in Transcaucasia, threatening to develop into full-scale civil war, and increasing moves towards independence in the Baltic republics, this won't be hard to do. But there is growing understanding that the "half-measures" the radicals accuse the leadership of and the indecision to which it often seems prey, are precisely due to the power the conservatives in the party still hold in the central committee and in the regions.

Today's plenum has the job of approving the party's platform for next October's 28th party congress, which was brought forward by six months, but many critics insist it should have been held sooner. They may well be right, as the party's prestige continues to decline.

The other main question to be discussed at today's plenum is that of the rebellious Lithuanians, who have declared their communist party independent of the Soviet communist party. Gorbachev's recent televised visit to the republic may have proved more useful for central committee members than for himself, as those used to laying down the law actually saw for themselves the strength of feeling in the republic and the party's popularity there.

As the hard-line central committee statement on the situation in the Baltics, issued last August when Gorbachev was on holiday, showed, the Soviet leader has always had to keep looking over his shoulder for their reaction. As yesterday's mass demonstration in Moscow underlined, the time has surely come when the progressives in the leadership can afford to ignore the conservatives, whose power is fast waning in the face of growing public consciousness and the imperatives of the multi-candidate election contests in March.

"Many of the present central committee would even vote for restoration of the monarchy, if you assured them they would still be *boyars*," a leading party theoretician, Eduard Arab-Ogly joked in conversation with me last week. "But they no longer have the power to hold Gorbachev to ransom." The Soviet leader had "huge" support in the country and at all levels, he assured me. Similarly, a miners' leader from the big Kuznetsk coalfield told me on the phone recently: "Here all the lads will come out on strike if there's any attempt to shift Gorbachev."

People await today's plenum with more-than-usual anticipation. Will it be televised? Will there be a show-down? Will arch-conservative Ligachov be sacked? But above all, will it lead to real changes?

Boris Yeltsin: wants privileges removed

The pioneer spirit of a Russian summer

4.6.90

SUMMER is here at last. Soon the pavements will be covered with white fluff from the poplar trees, which every year about the beginning of June float about in the warm air, drifting through open windows and making your nose tickle, and chased along the ground by gentle breezes. The white *pukh* annoys everyone and makes you wish for a gale to blow it off the trees once and for all.

Someone once told me it was Stalin who was fond of this particular poplar and had so many of them planted in the city.

It's a nice story, but then who can the summer mosquitoes be blamed on? Even high in our skyscraper block of flats (another of Stalin's works . . . one of the seven wedding-cake-shaped huge buildings that dominate Moscow's skyline) the mosquitoes fly in to find their victims during the warm summer nights.

June is the first month of schoolchildren's three-month summer holidays. You can hear sirens wailing — a rare sound in Moscow — as fleets of buses ferry hundreds of children off to pioneer camps outside the city. And notices hang on bus stops to explain that normal schedules might be interrupted due to buses being used for this purpose.

Last Wednesday we, like many Soviet parents, said goodbye to our two daughters, leaving for a pioneer camp for a month's holiday. Amid all the dizzying changes in Soviet life these past few weeks, the excitement of the Russian Congress of People's Deputies and last week's election of Boris Yeltsin as its chairman, at least there are a few constants that remain.

With our doctor's notes from school certifying that the girls were well, we took them to another, fairly cursory, medical examination and they were given the *putyovki*, the vouchers giving them the right to go to the camp. At present everything here is submitted to the harshest criticism and pioneer camps are no exception. Yet there's a lot to be said for them and I am sure many a working mother in Britain would welcome something similar for the summer holidays, to know that the kids were being well looked after and enjoying the company of children their own age.

Of course there are good camps and not-so-good camps, and it is true that not all Soviet children like going to them. But our three children have been to camp each year and thoroughly enjoyed their month in the country.

A lot of Muscovites have *dachas* — country cottages — and usually spend the entire summer there, parents travelling into work by suburban electric train or car and carrying back provisions not available in remote villages. Often children spend the summer at the *dacha* with the grandparents, rather than going to pioneer camp, which is voluntary.

The first camp my children went to was a big one for about 1,000 children, set in a forest of pine and birch, the children sleeping in wooden chalets dotted here and there in clearings. It had an excellent sports ground, the food was so good that they all put on weight and there were all sorts of activity clubs, run by a big team of instructors and pioneer leaders.

But it was all very organised, from the moment they were woken by a bugle call at eight in the morning, to the enforced two-hour sleep in the afternon. So then we found a smaller camp, where the discipline is less strict and there's more freedom to do what you like, when you like, which suits our children better.

Pioneer camps are run by many different organisations — factories, ministries, teachers etc. All have a wide network of camps at seaside resorts and countryside beauty spots.

They are financed by the trade unions and parents pay only a fraction of the cost. We paid 14 roubles (about £14) for each of our daughters for the month's stay, whereas the real cost per child is something like 65 roubles.

For the 300 children, aged from seven to 15, the camp has a staff of 70. A few are trained for work with children, but most are young men and women, either students or employees of the organisation whose pioneer camp it is.

The camp, which is 30 years old, is about an hour's drive from Moscow. Wooden chalets, where children sleep four to a room, are set among tall and slender silver birch trees, so typical of the Russian countryside.

They have a swimming pool, football and volleyball pitches and a small athletics ground, a library and activity rooms for when the weather is poor. All built and financed by the trade union.

Heading off: Pupils leaving a Moscow school for summer break

Winter bliss as another socialist achievement goes up in steam

WHILE the world is transfixed watching events in Soviet Transcaucasia teeter on the brink of civil war, life in Moscow goes on much the same.

Though people are worried about the situation there getting out of control, the southern republics are far enough away for most Muscovites to carry on with their normal lives. Concerts and theatres are packed as usual, with people badgering you for a spare ticket as you go in, cinemas are still a favourite haunt of young people, and ice hockey rinks and swimming pools attract their usual numbers.

I suppose I can safely bet that you've never been swimming in an outdoor pool when it's 20 degrees below zero. Well, it's quite an experience. When I went the other day, the water was 30 degrees centigrade, and if you kept your shoulders covered, you didn't feel the cold at all, unless you stayed still for more than a minute or two.

On a frosty day you will see clouds of steam rising from the circular Kropotkinskaya outdoor swimming pool in central Moscow and the trees round about clad in a particularly thick hoar frost. When you're in the pool, you can see only about a yard ahead, but nobody seems to bother in the muffled silence of the warm, enveloping steam.

I remember having a discussion once with a minor Soviet diplomat, who had recently returned from working abroad and who, not having quite got into the swing of perestroika's new, self-critical approach, was boasting that the Kropotkinskaya pool was one of the achievements of socialism. "But it's so wasteful," I protested, "all that heat going up into the freezing air." "Ah, but the people like it," he retorted.

The funny thing is, we were both right really. Swimming outdoors in winter is truly magical, yet like so many aspects of life here, it is so extravagant. As Mikhail Gorbachev told a meeting of workers in the Kremlin last week, "Our riches have, so to speak, corrupted us." Speaking of traditional Soviet wastefulness he pointed out that the Soviet Union uses 25 per cent more energy than in developed capitalist countries.

I remember on one of our early visits back to the UK after we came to live here, how shocked my two daughters were, when , after one had had a bath and washed her hair and the other

MOSCOW DAYS
by Tess Armand

was just about to rinse her hair, she found to her horror that the hot water at Gran's house had run out. "How can it run out?" my seven-year-old expostulated. "How come in Moscow it never runs out?" Talking to a Russian friend shortly after, I asked her how she managed without washing-up liquid which you can't always find in the shops. "Oh, we just wash the pots under hot running water from the tap," she answered, "Most things come clean that way."

Unlimited hot water, which is not paid for separately, but just as part of the normal monthly rent, explains the reason why most Russians don't use plugs in bathrooms: running hot water is a so much cleaner way of washing oneself than sitting in a bathtub of water. Hot water radiators in your flat are on day and night in winter, whether you're at home or away, and you don't pay any extra for the luxury.

As Mr Gorbachev was exhorting Soviet industry to be more thrifty, proposing that factories which save resources should be rewarded and spendthrift ones penalised, a thousand or so scientists, politicians, religious and arts people from 80 countries of the world were gathered here in Moscow to discuss the problem of resource depletion.

The "Global Forum on Environment and Development for Survival" was addressed by Mr Gorbachev and by the United Nations secretary-general, Perez de Ceullar. Both stressed the need for a global programme to tackle the growing ecological crisis worldwide.

When the Brazilian president, Jose Sarney, was in Moscow a year or so ago, Mr Gorbachev called the vast forests of both their countries the "lungs of the planet." Yet last year one and a half million hectares of Siberian forest was consumed by fires, environmental campaigner Alexei Yablokov said last week. And how much longer will Brazil's tropical rain forest be one of the lungs of the planet?

"We have to think not only in terms of nation patriotism, but world patriotism, the UN secretary-general said: "We must not only love our own country, but the world."

It was a week when a senior United States official rejected the Soviet Union's proposal for a joint US-Soviet pledge that neither country would ever be the first to use nuclear weapons, whereas Mr Gorbachev — amid all his troubles in Transcaucasia — offered to stop nuclear testing "at any moment" if the US did likewise. A nuclear test ban would make good sense for the world's environment and for development — and wouldn't it be a nice way of showing love for the world?

Gorbachev keeps trying but Baltic party's almost over

Scotsman

Monday 15 Jan 1990

MOSCOW DAYS
by Tess Armand

"LET THEM go if they want," my Russian acquaintance said, with just a trace of bitterness. "Who needs them anyway, they're only, what, three million people?"

We were talking about the Lithuanians and their calls for independence and secession from the Soviet Union, calls which have pursued President Gorbachev at nearly all his meetings during his three-day visit to this Baltic republic.

My acquaintance's attitude of disdain towards the rebellious Lithuanians is not an isolated one; it's the gut reaction of representatives of a great nation — Russia, with its 150 million people, who are used to being told that they gave the other peripheral peoples of the Soviet Union their freedom and development.

This is not untrue, in most cases, if you think of the backward areas of Central Asia, or the many nationalities inhabiting Russia who did not even have a written alphabet before the revolution in 1917.

However, it is far less true in the case of the three Baltic republics, whose historical development, while rarely independent of foreign masters, was more on a par with their European neighbours before their incorporation into the Soviet Union in 1940.

"The native population know that they had their own traditions, history, culture and developed economy," an Estonian literary editor, Rein Veidemann, once told me. "So you can understand their feelings when they are constantly told that only after the Russians came did their land start to blossom . . ."

Veidemann blamed the "Stalinist, totalitarian administrative system" for this. It was this system, he said, that made many Russians feel like "representatives of some liberating mission" when they migrated to the various republics. "It's a very dangerous Stalinist ideology."

The increasingly vociferous calls for independence and even secession from the USSR emanating from the Baltic republics and spreading to the Caucasus and Moldavia have produced the inevitable backlash Gorbachev himself referred to in Lithuania last week when, with some humour, he held to ridicule the claim by Russian nationalists that if Russia were to secede from the union (*sic*), it would soon become the most flourishing nation on earth.

Watching his spirited performance on television, as he put his political reputation on the line in urging the Lithuanians not to secede and Lithuanian communists to think again about breaking away from the Soviet Communist Party, one could not help admiring his ability to show up weaknesses and contradictions in the Lithuanians' argument and his touches of humour.

With his announcement on Thursday night that a bill defining the mechanism for republics to secede from the USSR would soon be put to the country's parliament, Gorbachev has once more shown that he means what he says about turning the USSR into a truly law-governed state.

While it may seem on the surface an amazing gesture of the freedom of nations' self-determination, it is actually simply putting flesh on the bones of the declared right long since enshrined in the USSR constitution, whose Article 72 says: "Each union republic shall retain the right freely to secede from the USSR."

Until now, it has never been necessary to spell out how to secede: glasnost has forced it on to the agenda — but that doesn't mean, as Gorbachev indicated in Lithuania, that secession will be made easy.

And why should it be? What state on earth would stand idly by and let any of its territory slip away without a fight? Even the Scots' long-standing pressure for a cautious measure of devolution meets with stiff resistance from Whitehall. So financial compensation and intricate defence considerations are just two things likely to enmesh the legally fleshed-out right to secede, the Soviet leader hinted last week.

Gorbachev is at his best when he is up against it and utterly convinced of his cause. In Lithuania he argued, lectured, hectored, but also listened, chatted and was his genial self whenever possible. Perhaps he was there doing what the Lithuanian party leaders ought to have been doing all along — arguing all out for a line which might not be the most popular, but could be the one necessary to preserve the union.

However one looks at it, it seems a remarkable paradox: that while that "bastion of the free world," the United States, invades tiny Panama on the flimsiest of pretexts and grinds its fragile sovereignty into the dust, the country that former President Reagan once called the "empire of evil" prepares a law which will allow any of its 15 republics, large or small, to secede from the Soviet Union.

Gorbachev: lectured, hectored, but also listened

MOSCOW DAYS
by Tess Armand

Mon. 16 October 1989

Shock sharp shots of life in a land of black snow and poisoned skies

WHEN I first saw the black and white photograph, I thought the white winding strip coming from the distance down to the foreground must be a river, its waters catching the light. In fact, as the author of the photograph explained to me later, it was the fresh track of a tractor that had driven through black snow.

I was at a remarkable photographic exhibition in Moscow called "Region". The region of the title is that of the Siberian mining area of Novokuznetsk, the scene of the long miners' strikes last summer.

Black snow in the long winter and permanently polluted skies are among the features of this exhibition and partly why permission for it was withheld on a couple of occasions this year.

"It was the strikes in the Novokuznetsk coalfield last July that finally made the authorities give permission," the tall, tousled, fair-haired Vladimir Vorobyov told me.

Even then practically no publicity was given to it, though it was held only a few steps from Red Square in one of those lovely forlorn little churches along Razin Street which are dwarfed by the huge square block of modernity that is the Rossiya Hotel.

So little publicity did it receive that I would have missed it had it not been for a photographer friend from Kazan, Lyalya Kuznetsova, who rang me and insisted that I go and see it, even though it was closing the next morning. "I'll ring the lads and ask them to keep it open for an hour or two, OK?" she said. "You can't possibly miss it, these lads' work is something really special."

What might be called social photography is something entirely new in the Soviet Union, as Lyalya explained. "We have no proper schools of photography here, so practically all photographers have up till recently been the sort like Tass or official press agency photographers."

But photographers interested in showing the reality of life in the deprived areas had a hard time getting their work shown. Vorobyov and a younger colleague, Volodya Sokolayev, were working in the steel industry in Novokuznetsk at one of the two big works in the heart of the city.

At first they took photographs of the "best workers", whose portraits would be put up on the "board of honour" that adorns all Soviet factories and farms. But even then they were criticised because the portraits showed the workers in their

Art in a cold climate: The exhibition showing life in the deprived areas of the Siberian mining area of Novokuznetsk included these rare photographs. Above, a tractor leaves white tracks in the black snow and, right, a miner comes up for air

working clothes and environment, "without any smartening-up tricks", Vorobyov grinned.

So in 1981 they were both sharply reprimanded for such "experiments" and, shortly afterwards, "We just happened to be included in redundancy cuts."

Despite that setback both found other jobs in the area and continued their photography semi-underground, without any hope of their work ever being shown to the public.

"It was an inner urge that kept us going and moral support from similar people doing social photography in Moscow, Kazan, Leningrad and Kharkov," Vorobyov explained.

The new climate of glasnost enabled their exhibition of photographs ranging from the 1970s to the 1980s to be shown in Novokuznetsk just over a year ago. "The photographs for which we were persecuted ten years ago were now occupying the place of honour and were praised all round," Vladimir said.

The authorities decided to term it an "Ecological Exhibition", which was not strictly correct, since their art is wider than that, but it allowed it to be shown.

One photograph, River Ob in the Barnaul area, shows a half-broken pipe spewing filthy industrial effluent into that majestic northern river.

But there are also remarkable indictments of privilege: photographs of affluent-looking women in furs and fox collars in black limousines in which high-up party and council officials travel.

In fact one wonders how on earth they got away with taking some of the photographs, so damning are they. "It wasn't easy," Sokolayev said. "The workers themselves usually didn't want to be photographed in dirty clothes and surroundings. They were just as suspicious of our motives as the authorities in the past, even though they knew us as fellow workers."

Several photographs show maternity homes, one a shockingly skeletal new-born baby; others portray disabled children and youngsters from children's homes in a state of disrepair.

Did they think their work was objective? "Probably not," Sokolayev conceded. "Being banned for so long, we've probably gone to the other extreme. But we feel that our exhibition should be an eye-opener for Moscow people who don't know Novokuznetsk; we want our work to help expose reality."

That reality, they insisted, was one of shocking pollution, with two steelworks in the city centre and pits all round. "The steelworks between them belch out one-and-a-half tons of pollutants per capita per year," Sokolayev said.

"The river which flows through the centre of Novokuznetsk is the colour of black oil (mazut) and stinks permanently of it," added Vorobyov.

"One in five children born develop allergies or other Sokolayev said. photographs are of children in the city's psychoneurological children's home.

In many there is satire — little broken-down huts with a picture of Lenin, arm outstretched, painted on the side, and a brilliant portrait of a worker behind stacks of sacks containing highly toxic chemicals with a notice on the wall above which reads: "Work in protective goggles. (Or respirators and so on)."

"Despite everything, I'm an optimist," Sokolayev said. "Of course our exhibition in itself is not going to solve any problems, we know that. But it might help. The problem in the Soviet Union at present is that the top want changes and those at the bottom want changes — but the bureaucracy in the middle don't.

"But if some of these bureaucrats can get shifted, replaced by the new leaders who emerged during the recent strikes, that would really be a step forward in starting to tackle some of the problems our photography depicts."

THE WEEK AHEAD

WEATHER IN SCOTLAND

which has disappeared from state shops, can be found on the shelves of the new coops."

A new law on cooperatives, other bills on land and land usage, lease-holding, the taxation system were all in the pipeline in an attempt to give more security and a firm legal basis for those prepared to take the risk of opening cooperatives.

The country's budget deficit would be 60 billion roubles the following year - 1990 - parliament was told. The USSR continued to import "huge volumes" of grain, fodder, metal and raw materials for light industry.

Defence spending would be cut by 12 billion roubles the next year, to help fund social spending. But, as one deputy pointed out, the existing minimum monthly income of 78 roubles was already "useless" due to inflation and the disappearance of cheaper goods from shops. She argued for ration cards to help those below the poverty line.

The new-style parliament was a much more active body than the old Supreme Soviet. There was real debate now, and various commissions were working on different stages of the new bills before being presented to the full parliament. The issues to be solved were real and urgent and the atmosphere was more businesslike than the first meeting of the new parliament - but was it all too little, too late?

Was the Communist Party in danger of losing power? At a meeting of the Ukrainian Party leadership in early October 1989, Gorbachov warned that the Party either worked with the masses to win their support, or risked becoming isolated.

Ukraine's former First Secretary, the elderly Vladimir Shcherbitsky, had held the position for 17 years. Ukraine, the second biggest republic in the USSR, with huge industrial and agricultural wealth, had been "slow to introduce the changes mapped out by *perestroika*," Gorbachov told the meeting.

In parliamentary elections held a few months earlier, Ukraine had a bigger proportion of seats where candidates ran unopposed than anywhere else in the country, he said. But the recent formation of a Ukrainian Popular Front (*Rukh*) had forced the Party there to reexamine many old positions.

Forces of an anti-socialist nature were posing as champions of working-class interests and even demanding the Party disband itself, Gorbachov warned. "No Communist should sit on the fence and avoid taking an active social stand or succumb to ... defeatism," the Soviet leader warned.

"*Perestroika* means renewal but not dismantling of socialism", Gorbachov told parliamentarians. "It is a revolutionary transformation, remedying deformations of socialism, but not for the restoration of capitalism."

It was clear that Gorbachov was conscious of the calls for precisely that - restoration of capitalism, or at least, knew that the anti-Party movements, including the new nationalistic ones, were directed towards that end.

Alongside the lack of positive economic and social improvements, Gorbachov's verbosity began to irritate. What had seemed so refreshing on those early walkabouts in 1985 when he first became leader and started talking of his reforms, using the new word *'perestroika'*, now sounded verbose.

What also irritated people was to see Gorbachov's wife, Raisa, in the spotlight, as if she were "First Lady", like Nancy Reagan. In beautiful fur coat and hat, Raisa's presence in the limelight jarred on many Soviet women struggling with inflationary prices.

Perhaps that was mainly due to seeing them when abroad, at summit meetings, for instance, when they were filmed by Western TV. Raisa Maksimovna had every right to be at her husband's side, of course. She had done research on Collective Farms in the Stavropol *krai* and knew the problems of rural life. But Soviet people were not used to seeing wives elevated to the status of celebrities, and were unforgiving.

Could the setting up of a few new coops save the economy based on a system of centralised planning which had worked, if imperfectly, for decades? I was reminded of the words of our friend Otto Lacis, Deputy Editor of *Kommunist*, when he told me a few months earlier that Gorbachov's reforms should have been started years ago, that they should have followed on from those Khrushchov had tried to introduce. "If we had started then, instead of the stagnation of the Brezhnev years, our economic reforms would have stood a chance, as the people were still behind us."

He didn't need to voice the rest: *'now it's too late, the people no longer believe in the Party's leadership....'*

This may well have been Otto's view, although he would never have confessed as much to me, a foreigner. He was always strictly loyal to the leadership and the Soviet Communist Party. But the Party was now riven by internal contradictions between those who were certain that reform was the only way to save socialism and those who, divorced from the 'common people', wanted to preserve the status quo.

From my daily conversations with people - parents at our children's school, neighbours, cafe attendants, cleaners, *dezhurnye* and the many people I met on my various trips outside Moscow, I got quite a mixed picture. But nowhere, except in the Baltic republics, did I come across voices calling for the end of the system. In fact, especially outside Moscow, I found much genuine belief in socialism as a fair and egalitarian system and pride in everything they as a society had achieved.

Which was considerable. When you think that 27 million people, the majority of them men, were killed during the Great Patriotic War and that the housing stock and industrial infrastructure in the Nazi-occupied territories was mostly destroyed by bombing, and the fact that the Soviet Union, unlike West Germany, did not benefit from any Marshall Plan to help them rebuild, and only received reparations from the least industrially developed part of Germany - which became the GDR - Soviet achievements were indeed remarkable. Whenever I visited Soviet people in their flats and saw their pride in their new two-bedroom flat, after having lived for years in a *kommunalka*, I always felt moved, remembering the huge sacrifices the whole country had made during the war and the reason many people still did not live as well as they might otherwise have done.

The new-style Supreme Soviet held that October debated bills intended to introduce a mixed economy. Cooperative and individual property would be recognised as equally valid as state property. Land was to remain public, not allowed to be sold or mortgaged. Enterprises would have the right to decide how to use their profits.

But, as the session was going on, Azerbaijanis, inflamed by ethnic tensions, were blockading the mainly ethnic-Armenian enclave of Nagorno-Karabakh by road and rail. Airlifts had to be organised to ensure supplies to the besieged enclave. A decree was passed to send Interior Ministry troops to break the blockade.

A new law on the settlement of labour conflicts was passed which not only enshrined the right to strike but also recognised the newly-formed unofficial strike committees. I had a chat with a very active deputy from Oryol who had a big hand in drafting the new law. Youngish, moustached, with a flock of straight brown hair falling over his brow, Vladimir Samarin argued strongly for the right to strike, as "the socialist system does not yet provide security against bad management."

But he was firmly against the new strike committees being set up as parallel organisations to the established trades unions. The new leaders thrown up by the strike committees should be put forward for trades union posts, he argued. "We don't need *parallel* organisations, but to infuse new blood into *existing* trade union and local government bodies."

The thorny question of pricing was also debated. Workers' representatives argued that the prices of basic foodstuffs should be regulated, otherwise wages would not keep pace. Top Trades Union leader, Stepan Shalayev, argued for an across-the-board price freeze. Prime Minister Ryzhkov, took a middle position - against a price freeze but against allowing market forces full rein in the economy. "If we orient ourselves only to supply and demand," he warned deputies, "this will lead to uncontrolled inflation." He argued for state control over certain prices whilst allowing the market to regulate contract prices.

Economists I interviewed during this period always highlighted the pricing problem. Goods in state shops had prices which did not reflect their true cost, as they were subsidised by the State. The *perestroika* economists argued that prices had to more closely reflect the actual cost of production. Whilst it was true that foodstuffs and many Soviet-made consumer goods were very cheap, imported goods like winter coats and boots were expensive, as foreign currency had to be spent on their importation.

The most important new bill under discussion was that on property. Should private property be allowed? Prime Minister Ryzhkov reminded deputies that it was the USSR that had ended private ownership over the means of production, based on the exploitation of one person by another. "But the great potential inherent in socialist ownership has not been tapped," he pointed out. "State ownership by the whole people - public ownership - has become excessively centralised and bureaucratic."

So instead of 88% state ownership of the country's economic assets (from land, and giant hydroelectric stations, to small repair shops), Ryzhkov explained, the new bill envisaged "socially-owned property." This meant that not only the state, but coops, civic organisations, joint-stock companies and other economic entities could own property.

One Deputy, Vladimir Desyatov, argued strongly that industry should remain state-owned. "If we allow enterprises to offer shares, and private individuals buy them up, then we shall be restoring capitalism," he pointed out. It was a prescient warning.

As so often during this period of momentous change, one proposed reform ended up changing much more. The change in parliamentary structures - the new Congress of People's Deputies and the smaller working Supreme Soviet elected from its number - entailed restructuring all the 15 constituent republics' parliamentary bodies too. So the Russian Federation (the biggest of the 15) would need a two-tier parliament like that of the USSR as a whole. Thus two equal chambers were proposed for the Russian Federation - one called the Soviet of the Republic and the other the Soviet of Nationalities. This, it was explained, should ensure better representation for the 31 autonomous republics, regions and areas which existed on the territory of the Russian Federation. And likewise, two new chambers for each of the other 14 constituent republics where Autonomous Republics, Regions and Areas existed on their territories.

If we take the Russian Federation, for instance, this includes diverse nationalities which had their own Autonomous Republics, like Bashkiria, Dagestan, Kalmykia, Yakutia, Komi and Chechnya-Ingushetia to name just 6 of the 16 such republics. Then there were the Autonomous Regions like Gorno-Altai, the Jewish Birobidzhan, Adygei; there were also what were called Autonomous *Okrugi* (areas) - territories with sparse population but covering large areas, as in northern Siberia and the far east, such as the Chukchi, the Yamalo-Nenets and Evenki to name just three of the ten Autonomous *Okrugi*.

Each of these administrative and linguistic formations had their own constitutions and political structures, such as Supreme Soviets and Councils, which were elected every five years. These were intended to give all citizens of the USSR, with its 130 languages and ethnicities, a say in self-government. It may not have been a perfect system, but it had many good features.

The USSR Constitution states:

"Citizens of the USSR of different races and nationalities have equal rights. Exercise of these rights is ensured by a policy of all-round development and drawing together of all the nations and nationalities of the USSR, by educating citizens in the spirit of Soviet patriotism and socialist internationalism, and by the possibility to use their native language and the languages of other peoples of the USSR.

"Any direct or indirect limitation of the rights of citizens or establishment of direct or indirect privileges on grounds of race or nationality, and any advocacy of racial or national exclusiveness, hostility or contempt, are punishable by law."

Formerly illiterate northern peoples had the same rights as educated Russians, Ukrainians or Georgians. From what I saw on my visits to the Nenets people on the Yamal peninsula or the Yakut and Evenki people I met in eastern Siberia, those rights had been achieved. Decent housing, education, health and cultural facilities were very similar wherever I travelled in the Soviet Union.

The debate over 'denationalisation' – selling off enterprises by means of issuing shares - and the benefits of lease-holding, especially in the countryside, continued throughout the rest of 1989. One economist, a member of the Academy of Sciences by the name of Laptyev, referencing Lenin, slammed the selling off of state enterprises as "total renunciation of socialism." There was no evidence that this would be the solution to current problems anyway, he argued.

In early November the Supreme Soviet approved a State Budget significantly amended from that originally proposed. The Deputies, now elected in constituencies contested by more than one candidate, voted for 40% more social funding to improve people's standard of living.

This meant that 1990's budget deficit would be 60,000 million roubles, to be covered by the issue of state bonds for certain enterprises.

Increasing social tension could be felt, as ordinary people failed to see their expectations materialise. There were miners' strikes in the far north and lightning stoppages in other coalfields. New demands were voiced for successful pits to be given autonomy and to be allowed to sell their coal on the open market. Yet the geology of the different coalfields was different: older coalfields, like the Donbass, where some pits were worked at depths of 1000 metres and in seams of 60 cms, could not possibly compete with other, opencast mines.

As the Soviet Miners' Union President, Mikhail Srebny, once told me: "If many of our pits were run by the British Coal Board, they would have been closed long ago and the miners would be out of work!"

New concepts like "unemployment" started to be bandied about - something entirely new for Soviet workers. Economists like Nikolai Shmelyov argued openly that a certain amount of unemployment wouldn't be a bad thing - to act as a stimulus for people to work better.

As I wrote in one of my reports to the *Morning Star*, "it has to be admitted that one of the problems in Soviet society is that job security and the same-wages-for-all mentality have led to low productivity."

Yet one of the great strengths of Soviet socialist society had always been that there was virtually no unemployment. I have often thought to myself: 'why *shouldn't* people have the right to permanent employment?' Having myself found it difficult to find work in Britain in my speciality, after a B.A. Honours and a Master's degree, I applauded the USSR's policy of full employment.

With likely cuts in ministerial posts, due to the new policy of independent, self-financing enterprises, there would be many redundancies. Already 3 million people had lost their jobs since 1985, when *perestroika* began, and one forecast I saw said a further 15-16 million jobs would go over the next fifteen years.

On the eve of the November 7th celebrations, I interviewed Professor Yuri Krasin, rector of the Soviet Communist Party's Social Sciences Institute, for a prominent *Morning Star* feature. Looking back on the October Revolution, he argued that, due to the low level of economic and social structures in Russia in 1917, what the Revolution had achieved was an early model of socialism, a form of "state socialism."

That early model, whereby the whole economy was nationalised, did not develop into the next necessary stage in time. If Lenin's intelligent, flexible policies had been followed, Krasin told me, the early state socialism model would have been transformed.

"An authoritarian-bureaucratic variant of state socialism was established, which in the thirties actually led to Stalin's despotism," he said. It was *despite* Stalinism, not *because* of it, that socialism had been able to give a great impetus to the Soviet Union and to the international democratic movement as a whole.

Krasin's view was that the current acute problems did not prove that the reforms had been a mistake: "No, *perestroika* was an objective necessity. Our difficulties have not been caused by the reforms; they are the price we are paying for the years of Stalinism and stagnation."

Warning that success was by no means guaranteed, since there was a struggle going on between opposing forces in society, he argued that there was no going back, because that form of administrative-command socialism was no longer viable.

Democratisation had come into conflict with low political culture and lack of tolerance. Decentralisation had caused very strong centrifugal tendencies, especially in the republics. Economic incentives towards a more market-oriented economy were being countered by people used to similar levels of wages for all.

"Nobody wants anyone else to live better than himself, even if all of us together have a low standard of living."

I was surprised by what followed: "This mass levelling psychology has its

282

roots in the mentality of serfs in feudalism. This was a factor which enabled collectivisation of agriculture to be carried out in the twenties - an impossible task if it had not been supported from below."

Krasin reflected soberly that part of society felt that *perestroika* was proceeding too slowly, and part that it was too fast. "If we move too rapidly, the fabric of social relations in our society, already stretched to the limit, may not withstand the strain."

"But if we move too slowly, *perestroika* will get stuck in the silt of conservatism. This is what happened to the reforms of the fifties and sixties," he explained. "Those reforms did not go deep enough - it was thought then that things could be changed without changing political structures. But they cannot - as we have come to realise."

On new economic methods being introduced, Krasin claimed these corresponded to Marx's original concept of socialism, as a "society of freely associated producers". "We are seeking a modern model of socialism where people will not feel alienated from public property and power, as they have come to feel under the administrative-command model we have had up to now."

"As Marx put it in his *Communist Manifesto*, the free development of each person is the condition for the free development of all."

Krasin ended the interview insisting that those who looked forward to the demise of socialism, due to the difficulties Soviet society was going through, would be disappointed. "The cause of the Great October Revolution will live forever!"

It had been a thoughtful interview, not one full of empty slogans and glib forecasts, which I sometimes endured when interviewing Soviet officials. But I came away feeling far from sure that the reforms would succeed.

November was a busy month. A friend had invited us to Tallinn and we spent a relaxing long weekend touring the old town, sampling the city's modern bars and restaurants and chatting with our hosts. It was one of the few times we had visited other parts of the Soviet Union with Liza and Martha, as their school and homework and my busy schedule never normally allowed for it. They enjoyed their break and were surprised how different Tallinn looked from Moscow, with their very different historical and cultural traditions.

We walked down the narrow cobbled lane with a long black metal boot projecting from the wall near the top end - *Pikk Jalg* (Long Boot Lane) - and along Katariina käik (St. Catherine's Passage) and all around the picturesque Old Town. We looked in at a few shops, which my daughters remarked had more fashionable clothes than Moscow shops. We passed the unusually-shaped historical clock-tower and the lovely cobbled central square bordered by colourful, tall and narrow terraced buildings. The modern architecture and design we saw was also very different - bolder, more innovative than that seen in Russia. Our friends were very proud of their city and took much

283

pleasure in showing us round.

When we got back to our flat in Moscow the phone was ringing. The Berlin Wall had fallen. I had filed my weekly column to the *Scotsman* without that knowledge, of course - and my piece musing on the November 7th Red Square demonstration seen from the dark red granite Mausoleum housing the embalmed body of Lenin suddenly seemed somewhat irrelevant.

Meanwhile Estonia's parliament branded the republic's incorporation into the USSR in July 1940 as "illegal", and the Estonian Duma's decision at that time "null and void". Whilst Estonian Communist Party leaders were at pains to explain that this was not a declaration of intent to secede from the USSR, it was obvious that this would be their next step.

Whilst in Tallinn I had interviewed the leader of the Russian-speaking 'Inter' movement - Yevgeny Kogan, also a Deputy in the republic's Supreme Soviet. He condemned a recent electoral law whose residence requirements would bar most non-Estonian immigrants from voting in elections.

I also interviewed Estonia's Minister of Labour and Social Issues, Juhan Sillaste, who explained that the high percentage of non-Estonians now living there had not been the result of any deliberate 'russification' but simply that after WWII factory sites with the best infrastructure were chosen where construction would be cheaper.

Estonia had good roads and communications and was, overall, better developed than other parts of the USSR, especially when so much of the country had been bombed mercilessly during that war. "But what it lacked was a sizeable workforce, so labour was imported from other parts of the Soviet Union," Sillaste explained.

He told me an interesting story: once on the overnight train from Tallinn to Moscow, he had shared the compartment with a Russian managing director of an enterprise in Estonia. That person had lived in Estonia for five years, yet knew only eight words in the Estonian language and could name only five Estonian towns!

"While ever managers of enterprises belonging to national, All-Union ministries know that they are answerable only to Moscow, they will not take the trouble to learn Estonian, of course," the Labour Minister told me. Whereas he, Sillaste, was fully bilingual.

At a meeting with students, Gorbachov warned that, on the pretext of discussing Article 6, which specified the CPSU's leading role, attempts were being made to decrease the Party's authority. A multi-party system did not necessarily mean more democracy, he argued. But since the media were present, it was a surefire way of giving the issue publicity.

Miners in Vorkuta in the far north were on strike again. I suspected that their main concerns would not be Article 6, but bread and butter issues. I had the chance to find out for myself: I had been invited to a crucial conference of miners' strike committees in Novokuznetsk in Siberia's massive Kuzbass coalfield. I flew there on 19th November 1989, covering the nearly 2000 miles in four and a half hours.

In a feature for the *Scotsman*, I wrote that the atmosphere at the Kuzbass conference reminded me of the ferment characteristic of those early Congresses of Soviets, when Lenin strode the platform arguing for the Bolsheviks' positions as against those of other parties.

In a piece entitled *"Miners' demands forcing the pace of change in Siberia"* I wrote that the slogan from 1917 - "All Power to the Soviets!" - could be seen here, as fiery delegates from pits all over that vast region got to their feet to demand real power be transferred to local bodies. "Only if the soviets once again become the real organs of power in the Kuzbass, regionally financed and with genuine decision-making powers will the people's living standards improve," delegates argued.

Driving round Novokuznetsk, a city of 590,000 inhabitants, I saw some old black wooden houses, which the locals called 'barracks'. These had no individual running water, an ex-miner and workers' committee leader called Andrei Belov, told me. I noticed a slogan painted on one of these 'barracks': *"Thanks be to our city authorities for our happy childhood!"* The sarcasm was a cry from the heart of the residents of these temporary wooden houses, Andrei explained, the slogan a parody of the sort of slogans common in the Soviet Union on Pioneer Palaces, schools or cultural centres.

Belov was typical of the new sort of workers' committee representatives: brash, angry, determined. "For too long we've been treated like a colony," he told me bitterly. "All these years, it's been 'Give, give, give!' And we've had practically nothing in return!"

Kemerovo's rich natural resources - coal, gold, oil and minerals - had been endlessly swallowed up by the centre - Moscow - he went on, whereas the region itself got poorer and poorer. Local councils had no teeth, everything was highly centralised, and people's living standards had fallen.

The workers' committees in the vast Kuzbass were by then a force to be reckoned with. Organised in practically every mine and works throughout the Kemerovo region, they had grown out of the strike committees set up in July 1989.

"In many ways we are now doing the work of local authorities," another young miner, Yuri Komarov, told me. "People come to us with all sorts of problems they want solving, because they trust us more than the Party or local councillors."

The febrile atmosphere of the conference was exciting but the angry and headstrong speeches did not augur rational analysis and decision-making. I found widespread support for Gorbachov, but increasing impatience and mistrust of local Party and Soviet officials and ministerial management, who were blamed for holding back the economic, political and social reforms he had initiated.

The delegates voted for a 24-hour strike throughout the Kuzbass unless the Government unfroze the bank accounts of the Vorkuta miners currently on strike, as the miners there had lost out on wages since their strike began on October 25th.

Much time at the conference was spent on discussing whether the new Union of Kuzbass Working People should be classed as a "social" or "politico-social" organisation. Why was this important, I asked a delegate sitting next to me. "We're preparing to found a new party," he replied. Why was this necessary, I asked.

"For many years we've had an authoritarian state," another miner, Aleksandr Bir, from Dimitrov pit, butted in. "Despite all the nice words about the role of the working class, in practice our class has been alienated from politics and from the distribution of material benefits."

"Now *perestroika* has opened our eyes, and shown us that it's the working people who must be the real masters, not the privileged managerial stratum that has grown up here over the years."

His smile revealing several gold-capped teeth, Bir told me he thought Gorbachov was "a brave man" for initiating the reform process, but stressed that so far nothing had improved, and in fact, Gorbachov's anti-alcohol campaign had actually made things worse.

I spoke to one local official trades union delegate, Nikolai Alamov, who told me that all the miners from his pit (named after Bulgarian anti-fascist, Georgi Dimitrov) had backed setting up the strike committee four months ago. He denied that the strike committee in any way challenged or competed against the official union structures. "Let them co-exist," he said.

"The workers' committees' demands are correct," he went on. "They're fighting for a better life for us, and we all support them!"

So it seemed that the official trades unions would continue looking after holiday and sick leave, housing and benefits, and the new workers' committees would take on the role of defending workers' rights and wages. I didn't detect any animosity towards the trades unions, but a general acknowledgement that they had become too closely identified with the management.

One of the demands the Kuzbass miners had was that their mines should be self-financing and independent of the mining ministries.

"The ministries are afraid of mining associations and entire regions getting economic autonomy, because then nobody will need them any more!" Aleksandr charged. His Dimitrov pit had made two million roubles profit last year, he claimed, "but we've seen nothing of it. It all went to the mining association to cover losses at other pits." (Mining associations were conglomerates encompassing several mines in a given region).

In theory, mining associations, each comprising dozens of mines, now had independence from the mining ministry. But in practice, since the price at which they could sell any surplus after fulfilling their obligations to the State was little above cost-price, they were doomed to operate at a loss.

It was interesting that the majority of delegates were Communist Party members, although few of them had ever played a leading role before July

1989. At the conference there was none of the formality of traditional CPSU meetings - and few suits, collars and ties either.

The Conference was capably chaired by a young open-cast coalminer, Vyacheslav Golikov. He recognised that strikes in a socialist society did harm the whole country, since the industry was state-owned. "But it's also true that if agreements are made during a strike they have to be met."

Some of the Vorkuta miners' demands had become overtly political - such as direct elections for the position of USSR President. The Kuzbass Conference did not agree with such demands, Golikov said. And Kuzbass miners had heeded Prime Minister Nikolai Ryzhkov's call not to strike so as not to inflict more damage on the economy.

"We've lost 8,000 million roubles due to strikes and other disruptions throughout the country," Gorbachov had told Kemerovo TV on the eve of the Conference. "Where are we going to get that amount to make up for these losses?"

The 1989 miners' strikes were a clear signal that time for *perestroika* was running out. All the workers I spoke to during the three days I spent in Novokuznetsk stressed the urgent need to dismantle the administrative-command managerial system and hand over real power to working collectives and the local soviets.

"The majority of people here are for the socialist path of development," stressed Aleksandr Bir, his gold-capped teeth flashing. "But we've found ourselves up a blind alley because those methods have proved no good, and big mistakes have been made by previous leaderships."

I have covered this Conference at some length here, because I know my readers will be interested to know how ordinary working people were thinking at that crucial time. It was a great opportunity to speak to many new workers' leaders, 'official' trades unionists and local Party leaders and officials to find out how they saw the issues. It had also been an opportunity to see a little of the housing problems still too prevalent in one of Siberia's big industrial cities. I'd been able to see for myself that living standards in that harsh climate had indeed been falling behind and that the workers' grievances were well-founded and real.

Back in Moscow, I read a long article by Gorbachov in *Pravda* and a TV interview with Politburo member Aleksandr Yakovlev dealing with the CPSU, the opposing forces within the Party itself, falling Party membership and careerism.

One of the problems of a party in power, particularly if it is the country's sole party, is that all sorts of people join it for careerist and opportunistic reasons. People like this were the least able to defend the Party line against other, non-Communist forces, Gorbachov wrote.

Glasnost continued to give voice to incendiary material hardly conducive to national harmony, and seemingly unchecked by editors at any level. Anti-semitism, for instance. Since the 1950's, when wartime leader Stalin had coined the word "cosmopolitans" to accuse Jews - due to some having relatives abroad - of anti-Party activity in show trials, anti-semitism had been banned and you would not find it in any publication anywhere. Many well-loved arts people were Jewish, although this fact was not alluded to normally. Neither would it be if a person had an Armenian or Uzbek surname, for instance.

As in Britain, anti-semitism had deep roots, long before the Soviet period. On re-reading Pushkin's classic tale *The Captain's Daughter* recently, I came across the following: ".....(billiards) is quite essential to us soldiers," he said. "On a march, for instance, one comes to some wretched little place; what is one to do? One can't be always beating Jews, you know. So there is nothing for it but to go to the inn and play billiards..." Shakespeare's depiction of Shylock in *The Merchant of Venice* can also be considered anti-semitic, through our 21st century eyes.

According to verbatim extracts of speeches at a November 1989 meeting of the Russian Federation Writers' Board, published in the popular magazine *Ogonyok*, terms like "russophobia", "zionist" and "cosmopolitan" were bandied around, befitting the worst years of Stalinist repressions.

Several speakers referred to Jewish writers as "Russian-speaking" - a clear insult to people born and bred in the Soviet Union. It was another example of the fast-increasing polarisation of positions in the country, with the openly Russian-nationalist organisation *Pamyat'* at one extreme.

Even writers of the calibre of Valentin Rasputin supported this tendency during the above-mentioned writers' meeting. He was reported as saying "we certainly cannot stand by and let the national minority (i.e. Russians, K.C.), that remains in Leningrad, be sacrificed."

The Russian nationalists who dominated the leadership of the RSFSR Writers' Union wanted to oust the editor of the Leningrad literary journal *Oktyabr* - Anatoly Ananyev - for publishing previously-banned work by the exiled writer Andrei Sinyavsky.

Soviet literary journals, such as *Znamya, Novy Mir* and *Oktyabr* played an important part in the nation's cultural life, and have no real equivalent in Britain. They were thick, monthly publications in which new, innovative and sometimes controversial novels were serialised. The editors sometimes found themselves in trouble with the authorities over their decisions to publish works by previously-banned writers, such as George Orwell, Joseph Brodsky and Vladimir Nabokov.

In November 1962, for instance, *Novy Mir* (New World) (monthly circulation circa 150,000 copies) had become famous for publishing Aleksandr Solzhenitsyn's *One Day in the Life of Ivan Denisovich*, about life in the Gulag.

I was always impressed by the depth and extent of knowledge of Soviet and Western literature that many Soviet people had at that time. I have talked to miners and shop floor workers in engineering plants who, I discovered, had read English novels in translation. I used to think to myself, how many British workers (or intellectuals, for that matter) would be able to say they had read any Russian or Soviet literature?

From time to time I would be asked to address meetings, of students, parents, children and once, even Soviet diplomats. I was one of the few correspondents who spoke good Russian. On one occasion I had been asked to address a class of students at some academy, whose name I was not given before agreeing to do the talk. Students, I thought, that meant 18-22 year olds, they usually like Western pop music, they want to know about life in Britain, so I'll talk to them about issues often featured in the pages of the *Morning Star*, i.e. unemployment, the fight for better wages and conditions, and I'll play them Peter Gabriel's *Don't Give Up* which was popular at the time.

I made a few notes, looked out the lyrics of the song and took a tape-recorder along with the taped song at the appointed time and place. On being ushered into the room, I saw about 50 or 60 grey-suited middle-aged men, not students at all! It turned out that the person who had invited me meant to tell me that my talk was for diplomats on a refresher course, not "students" as such. I don't know what they thought of having to listen to Peter Gabriel, instead of a serious lecture on the stage of monopoly capitalism in contemporary Britain....

Calls to remove Article Six from the Constitution were ever more frequent. Gorbachov did not seem able or willing to tackle the extremists within the CPSU, simply limiting himself to saying that its removal at this stage would be detrimental. Lithuania's parliament voted to remove it and the republic's Communist Party voted to become independent from the CPSU.

At a CPSU Central Committee meeting early in December 1989, warning against extremes within the Party, Gorbachov argued that Article 6 was not an obstacle to holding free elections. He called on the Party to put forward as candidates for the forthcoming republican and local elections "the best representatives of the working class, peasantry, intelligentsia, women and youth", whether Communists or non-Party members.

He also welcomed the changes the world was seeing throughout Eastern Europe, saying that these were the natural outcome of a certain stage of development there. Did the beleaguered Soviet leader believe what he was saying, I wondered. Was this an example of his naivety in not realising what he himself had set in train three years earlier?

The Second Congress of People's Deputies was to be held for 10 days starting December 12th, only 6 months or so after the First. With no real improvements in the economy in sight, I feared it would be little more than a talking shop - and one riven by polarised, sometimes extremist, views.

It was clear that the future of the entire reform programme was at stake. As one well-known deputy, Nikolai Travkin, a former building worker now in charge of a big construction trust outside Moscow, put it: "the most important thing is to prevent a counter-reform movement."

Dissatisfaction with results so far were leading some to call for a return to the past, whilst others, he said, were turning to nationalism in the search for scapegoats. In an article in *Moscow News,* Travkin wrote that trying to reform the existing system was pointless. Those in the administrative-command system are particularly afraid of radical economic reform," he wrote.

The Congress was to be televised throughout, which was no doubt intended to show the public who was for what, among Party leaders and deputies. I wrote at the time, "This week's Congress is unlikely to be able to bridge the increasing gulf between reformers and anti-reformers, but it may produce much-needed clarity by bringing more out into the open and consolidating all those genuinely for reform."

Differences among the CPSU leadership became clear at this Congress. Whilst journalists had known this for some time, the population as a whole had not, since all speeches tended to toe the same, "official" *perestroika* line. At this Second Congress of People's Deputies, while Gorbachov argued for radical economic reforms, Prime Minister Nikolai Ryzhkov urged caution, warning of mass unemployment and social crisis if market mechanisms were introduced too soon.

Ryzhkov took a veiled swipe at Gorbachov over his failed anti-alcohol campaign, saying that it had done "not only economic, but moral damage" to the country. Present shortages were partly due to rumour-mongering, he said, but the fact was that too few goods were being produced to satisfy demand. The previous year had seen a mere 2% production increase, whereas wages had gone up by 12%.

Even the pro-reform economists were warning against proceeding too fast: Leonid Abalkin, for instance, slammed speakers like Boris Yeltsin and Gavriil Popov for urging faster reform without taking account of the current mood in society.

During the Congress, the famous physicist Andrei Sakharov, "father of the Soviet hydrogen bomb" and Congress Deputy since April 1989, died of a heart attack at 68. Thousands of Muscovites filed past his open coffin where it lay in state at the Palace of Youth. Like so much else in those times, part of the population admired Sakharov and part regarded him as an anti-Soviet dissident.

In a tribute to Sakharov, fellow academician and People's Deputy Roald Sagdeyev claimed the nuclear physicist had never repented his contribution to the creation of the hydrogen bomb. "Until his last day he thought that the bomb was needed to help restore strategic parity at that moment." But, he added, Sakharov had fought tirelessly to end policies based on the balance of fear and mutual intimidation with weapons.

The Second Congress solved nothing. Positions were more polarised than ever. It ended by facing two ways - backing the Government's economic reform programme whilst at the same time allowing much of the current administrative-command system to remain intact.

The 'radicals' (Yeltsin and co) attacked this programme as a postponement of reform, whilst the 'conservatives' regarded it as dismantling the centralised planning system and leaving the door open for private ownership.

Years later, reading the *Guardian* of 11 July 2020, I learned that Ukraine's richest man, Rinat Akhmetov, "whose fortune is estimated at £5.2bn, recently bought a £176m villa ...on the Cote d'Azur to add to a portfolio that includes a £137m flat in London's One Hyde Park...."

The creation of obscenely rich billionaires like Akhmetov, many of whom are former Komsomol and Party big shots, was indeed the result, intended or otherwise, of the reforms set in train by the Gorbachov leadership. Whether it could have been otherwise, I shall attempt to analyse later.

I was glad to escape Moscow's heated political atmosphere to return to England for Christmas. I had realised from phone calls home that my dear Mum had deteriorated since the summer when we had last visited. So we decided we should all go back, no matter the cost.

We arrived in London on 22nd December and went straight up to my parents' Derbyshire home. My mother was worse, hardly speaking and more bent over than before. But she was downstairs, and was still able to walk. We spent the next few days together and it was very nice to see her come alive in the presence of the children. We had Christmas Day together, trying to include Mum in the conversation, and watching her with the children, when she managed to smile and speak a little with them. The next morning - Boxing Day - I took a cup of tea up to her in bed. She was facing me and was asleep, so I took it back downstairs. When I went back half an hour later, she had turned over. I went round the bed and saw from her face that she had died. Her body was warm, she had obviously just died. I was sorry that I hadn't stayed with her when I first took the tea up. I could have held her hand as she passed away.

I knew that she had somehow "waited" for us to come back, and had then let go of life. It was peaceful, she was not in pain - and she had had the satisfaction of seeing us for a few days, which I knew would have made her happy.

It was a sad time then, seeing my Dad so upset, and having to get down to organising and planning Mum's funeral. She had been a stalwart of the local Communist Party branch, very active in CND and the Women's Coop Guild and well loved by all who knew her. It was important to pay tribute to her at her funeral.

My brother and sister-in-law and all the family, who had loved her and been with her much more than I had over the years, felt that her death, at the age of 82, was a release from what had become an intolerable life. My father had looked after her as best he could. But for someone like my mother, a sociable person and avid reader, her disability was a heavy burden.

After the funeral I went up to Edinburgh to meet the *Scotsman* Editor, Magnus Linklater. He was fulsome in his praise for my columns, which, he said, gave a real insight into what was going on and what ordinary people in the Soviet Union were thinking, amid such momentous changes.

We returned to Moscow in early January 1990. It was to be our last year - and near the end of an era.

CHAPTER VI

When I got back to Moscow and our daughters started back at school, I fell ill with full-blown flu. My mother's death and the organising of the funeral had taken its toll. The Polyclinic doctor came and told me very sternly that I had to stay in bed and rest up, which I was glad to do.

It wasn't only physical, I think. Obviously it had been a stressful trip back home, but it was also the situation in the Soviet Union that was depressing. I had had hopes that Gorbachov would improve socialism, yet what we were observing was increasing chaos and the collapse of the socialist societies in Eastern Europe.

For us as a family, too, the outlook was not rosy. Ricardo had wanted to work in Moscow mainly because it was a job that he knew he could do, despite his deafness. But neither of us had jobs to go back to in Britain.

A couple of times on visits back to London, I had had lunch with Ken Gill, who was on the Management Committee of the *Morning Star*, and talked things over with him. He was very sympathetic to the problems I faced in reporting the changes, and was keen that if we did decide to leave Moscow, I should return to the *Star*'s London office. But the Editor had already warned me that the paper's finances made this highly unlikely.

In mid-January the situation in Azerbaijan was extremely serious, with clashes between Azerbaijanis and Armenians resulting in dozens of deaths. There were reports of pogroms by Azerbaijani youths using firearms. Ships with Armenian refugees docked in the Turkmenian port of Krasnovodsk. Refugees! In the USSR! It was literally unbelievable.

A silent Armenian protest vigil was held at the headquarters of the CPSU Central Committee on Ploshchad' Nogina. One banner read: "The corpses of Armenians lie on the conscience of the country's leadership." I knew our readers would be finding it very hard to understand these inter-ethnic clashes and tried to explain some of the underlying issues:

"Ethnic problems in the region have deep roots. The Armenians were traditionally Christian, whereas the Azerbaijanis were Muslim.

Armenia, which after centuries of Arab and Turkish domination finally became part of the Russian Empire after the Russian-Iranian war of 1826-28, has not forgotten the horrific Turkish genocide of 1915, when over 1.5 million Armenians were deliberately killed."

A leader in *Pravda* of 17th January 1990 blamed the Stalin and Brezhnev eras, which, it said, had fomented strife between nationalities by deciding "to expel entire peoples from their native lands" and then declaring officially that the "national question" had been solved.

Only now, under extreme *glasnost*, were problems, once deemed solved, coming to the fore, like those of the Crimean Tatars and Volga Germans, uprooted and rehoused far away during WWII. The Armenians had never accepted the administrative decision to transfer Nagorno-Karabakh to Azerbaijan in 1923 and had continued to ask the central authorities to review the decision.

When shop shelves are empty and life becomes more expensive, the temptation is to look for scapegoats, I wrote at the time. I went to the Azerbaijan mission in Moscow for a press conference, where apparently there were no official Communist Party, Government or state officials present, only activists from the nationalistic Popular Front, who openly called for independence from the USSR, burning of Party cards and "Islamic solidarity".

I talked to one Azerbaijani poet there - Ilkham Bagalbeili, who was scathing about Azerbaijan's recently deposed leader, Abdul Rahman Vezirov: "He's a criminal - all he wanted was to keep the Party in power, he didn't care a damn about the people." It was people like Vezirov, Bagalbeili told me, who were holding back *perestroika*. The 200,000 Azerbaijani citizens who had recently fled their homes in Armenia due to inter-ethnic killings had added to the already explosive situation in Azerbaijan, which had 300,000 unemployed of its own.

It was frightening to see how quickly the situation had got out of control. The parents of one of our daughters' friends had taken in one of the refugee families - a young Russian woman, with three young children, who was married to an Azerbaijani. Sanatoria, holiday camps and pioneer camps in many areas were being used to shelter the thousands of refugees.

In *Voices from Chernobyl*, one woman, Lena M., a refugee from Kyrgyzstan, now housed in the Chernobyl area, put her feelings like this:

> "We had a motherland, and now it's gone. What am I? My mother's Ukrainian, my father's Russian. I was born and raised in Kyrgyzstan, and I married a Tatar. So what are my kids? What is their nationality? We're all mixed up, our blood is all mixed together. On our passports, my kids and mine, it says "Russian", but we're not Russian. We're Soviet!"

And the K. family from Dushanbe, Tajikistan, tells how Tajiks and Russians used to live in harmony before the war there: "We drank beer together, ate *plof* together."[116]

Yet now in the Baltic republics and parts of Central Asia, anti-Russian feeling was being whipped up and repressions began against Russian nationals.

---

116 *Voices from Chernobyl*, Svetlana Alexievich, Picador, 2005.

Many people throughout the USSR suffered as a result of the increasing nationalism and inter-ethnic clashes, which were virtually unheard-of before 1986. 'Friendship of the Peoples' was not just a slogan: it was a reality for decades, and the population's mixing was testament to that.

Gorbachov was becoming increasingly unpopular in the Soviet Union, as people failed to see any improvement in their standard of living. But in the West, "Gorby" continued to be the most popular Soviet leader ever.

A World Environmental forum held that January in Moscow showcased his concern for the environment, which endeared him to Western delegates from over 80 countries. There Gorbachov reiterated the offer to stop all nuclear testing for good, if the USA did likewise.

But environmental concerns were the least of the country's worries at that time. In Volgograd (formerly Stalingrad) the entire Communist Party's regional leadership resigned, in the wake of protests after revelations of irregularities in allotting municipal flats.

In Odessa, Party leaders warned of 'ethnic trouble-makers' circulating inflammatory leaflets in the Black Sea port, home to many nationalities, including many Jews. The beautiful Ukrainian city is famous for its 19th-century architecture, including the Odessa Opera and Ballet Theatre. Readers may remember the long, wide flight of steps leading down to the sea, immortalised in Eisenstein's classic film *Battleship Potemkin*.

Early in February Moscow saw an estimated 200,000-strong demonstration, stretching all along the ring road and down Gorky Street to a rally on Manezh Square. Announced beforehand by the popular TV programme *Vzglyad*, the rally was addressed by Boris Yeltsin, and organised by a radical group within the CPSU calling themselves "Democratic Platform", together with some other *informaly*.

Yeltsin, still a CPSU Central Committee member at the time as well as parliamentarian, declared that this was the last chance the Party had "to remain a credible force for change"; other speakers called for the Party to give up its "leading role", enshrined in the Constitution and allow other political parties.

The weekly *Moscow News* had a centre page spread outlining the sharp differences between Gorbachov and Politburo member Yegor Ligachov, whose brief was Agriculture, accusing him of being anti-reform. Meanwhile former Leningrad leader Yuri Solovyov was expelled from the Party for abuse of power, and Party leaderships in Tyumen and Chernigov had resigned due to public pressure.

The CPSU Central Committee held a plenary meeting, to which a delegation of miners who had gone on strike the previous summer were invited by Gorbachov, who clearly wanted them to see who was who in the Central Committee. As had become customary with Gorbachov, a number of new proposals were made - concerning the post of General Secretary, the size and composition of the Central Committee, and the need to bring forward the

28th CPSU Congress to the summer, rather than the autumn. Factions with differing political platforms would be allowed within the CPSU. The sheer number and frequency of such new proposals were dazzling and seemed to indicate a lack of serious consideration. One thing was clear from the Plenum: that the two opposing sides in the Party - for reform or for the status quo - were now fully out in the open. The gloves were off.

The third session of the new Supreme Soviet was to begin in mid-February, 1990. Among the most controversial issues was that of private property and ownership. At the recent Plenum, Yegor Ligachov had come out categorically against privately-owned farms and had not even mentioned lease-holding, the new initiative being tried out in several places in an attempt to improve productivity and alleviate the crisis in food supplies.

I remembered a conversation I had had nine months earlier with the Deputy Editor of a Novosibirsk journal, *Eko*. An economist himself, Yuri Voronov told me that if the Soviet Union had the same amount of private ownership in farming as there was in the German Democratic Republic, some would say that was already capitalism.

Everything in the USSR, down to the last corner cafe or cobbler's, was state-owned and run. Having seen how these shops and services were often run (see Pages 29-30 for an example), I personally would have favoured a bit of private enterprise.

I had an interesting conversation with a Tajik Deputy, Bihojal Rakhimova, representing the Women's Councils in Tajikistan. Her official title was Deputy Chair of the Supreme Soviet's Committee for the Affairs of Women, Protection of the Family, Maternity and Childhood. Ms Rakhimova's mother had been illiterate at the time of the Russian Revolution, she told me. At that time, Tajik women wore the veil and were often given away in marriage at fourteen or even younger.

But, she said, despite the huge strides Central Asian women had made in emancipation since the Revolution, serious problems still existed, the terrible instances of women committing suicide by self-immolation among them. Last year alone there were 200 cases of this in Tajikistan, Ms Rakhimova told me, though fortunately not all were fatal.

"Illness, excessive child-bearing, malicious gossip in societies which pride themselves on women being faithful to their husbands - these are some of the stresses behind such tragedies."

Ms Rakhimova's colleague on that Supreme Soviet's Women's Committee, Leningrad Deputy Valentina Matviyenko, told me of urgent problems women faced: 3.5 million women working in harmful production, 3.7 million on night shifts, shortage of maternity homes, high rate of abortions, infant mortality and deaths in childbirth. In light industry, mainly staffed by women, only 31% of managerial posts were held by women, and only 21% in the textile industry. "Looms are still being produced which are at the wrong height for most women, despite many complaints," Ms Rakhimova told me.

Their Committee was proposing important legislation to improve the situation, imposing better maternity benefits, forcing managements to provide lighter work for pregnant employees, enabling shorter working days, better family allowances and other improvements.

Pravda carried a feature by two feminists, Natalia Zakharova and Natalia Rimashevskaya, which actually admitted for the first time that "a patriarchal view which puts women's place 'in the home' exists in our society", going on to attack the lack of career and promotion prospects for women[117].

As I was interviewing Ms Rakhimova, disturbances were going on in the Tajik capital, Dushanbe. Soviet TV showed the Communist Party headquarters there being attacked by hundreds of stone-throwing youths, shops looted and set on fire.

What did it all mean? Had everything been so dire that the whole of society seemed to be erupting? Or was some of it deliberate stoking of flames by sectors who wanted to keep the status quo?

A new Tajik People's Committee demanded urgent measures to tackle unemployment, that week's *Rabochaya Tribuna* putting it at somewhere between 70,000 and 200,000, and to ban the sale of pork, which Muslims in the Republic did not eat.

How was it possible, Ricardo and I often asked each other, that this great multi-ethnic, multi-cultural and multi-lingual country could have descended to this, after more than 70 years of Soviet power which had at its foundations the equality of peoples and which had done so much, as I had seen on my many travels, to bring the less-developed republics and regions up to the level of the historically more developed ones? No one could deny the achievements that had been made in Central Asia and the Caucasus. Women in higher education, in parliament and in the Party, not veiled as in neighbouring Afghanistan, freely walking in the streets; proper housing, not adobe shacks or makeshift shelters such as I'd seen when I lived in Chile in the seventies, in the *poblaciones callampas* (shanty towns)..... Theatres, arts and leisure centres, schools, colleges and universities, libraries - all these could be found everywhere in the Soviet Union, whether in the depths of Siberia or in Central Asian cities. Was there really such dissatisfaction that people were prepared to smash up shops and set fire to buildings?

Both Ricardo and I were fearful for the future. We both felt that there was so much that was good in the Soviet Union, there were so many achievements and that, whilst the standard of living might not be as good as middle-class families in Britain enjoyed, it was not so bad as to warrant such disturbances.

We had not done much socialising of late, and I was due to go to Azerbaijan to report on the inter-ethnic problems there. On the eve of my trip, we invited

---

117 For more information on Russian feminism, see *Women in Russia*, Verso, 1994, for which I wrote a Preface. The book, which I translated, is a collection of essays from an original idea by Ruth Steele.

some of our closest friends to dinner and enjoyed an evening exchanging opinions on the situation amid the usual jokes, anecdotes and banter typical of Chilean humour. Gaston and Valentina were journalists, working for the Mexican News Agency; Kerstin wrote for a Swedish weekly and went on to publish several books back in Sweden, her husband Juan studied medicine and later went on to become a child psychiatrist in Stockholm; and Pablo and Cristina worked in a Soviet trade organisation.

We had known Pablo since the early seventies, when, after his studies at the Patrice Lumumba University, he had returned to Chile, where we were living at the time, with his Soviet wife Lyudmila and their little boy, Yuri. Years later, all of us again finding ourselves in Moscow, we had been invited to her parents' flat on the outskirts of the city, where we were treated to a simple but wholesome meal, on a table covered with newspaper in place of a tablecloth, I remember. Then tragedy struck when Lyudmila lost her life in an accident at work. Pablo brought Yuri up on his own for several years until he married Cristina.

I left for Baku the next day, with a slightly sore head, after a little too much Bulgarian *Gamza* the night before.

On my way to the hotel from Baku airport, I could see a big poster of Lenin and the slogan: "The CPSU is the leading and guiding party of the Soviet Union!" Our group of journalists met representatives from Azerbaijan's Popular Front, Communist Party leaders, Interior Ministry troops spokesmen, artists and writers and members of the republic's Academy of Sciences. During many meetings and press conferences, accusations came and went, reasoned voices were few. Historical grievances were aired, truths, untruths and half-truths voiced.

The Popular Front press conference was held in the same old-style Intourist hotel room where, as a student in 1963, I had attended a seminar entitled: "How the Nationalities Question has been solved". I remembered the wide balcony overlooking Baku bay and the passageway encircling the central hall down below. How different, how optimistic Soviet society had seemed then! How ironic that I should find myself in the same room, now hearing the opposite - that the Nationalities Question was far from "solved".

Outside, I could almost imagine I was in the Baku I had loved then, on my first visit, feeling the constant warm breeze on my face. But now I could see military patrols and armed soldiers stopping and searching cars, requesting documents.

The January 1990 pogroms against Armenian residents, resulting in over 50 deaths, were quickly quelled by Soviet troops brought in to restore order. But over 100 Azerbaijanis were killed when tanks moved in to break up street barricades, and a State of Emergency had been imposed.

"The situation was becoming intolerable," a grim-faced military commander, Vladimir Dubinyak told us. They had had to intervene to restore calm, keep the peace and defend innocent people, he explained, and had helped evacuate

16,000 Armenians by sea.

"If it had been Azerbaijani lives at risk, we would have done the same," Dubinyak stressed.

From the conversations I had with locals, it seemed the Popular Front had considerable support. The Front claimed 200,000-300,000 members, but out of a population of seven million in 1989. My impression, after my two-day visit, was that ordinary Baku citizens, especially women I talked to in a nearby market, were distressed at the entire turn of events which had so quickly spiralled into such violence.

After several meetings with a number of local leaders, I could not detect any willingness to look for a way out of the impasse, let alone to compromise. All were unanimous in demanding that the Armenian side had first to give up all claim to Nagorno-Karabakh.

A member of the Editorial Board of the CPSU's theoretical Journal *Kommunist* - Eduard Arab-Ogly - claimed that Azerbaijan had for many years refused any autonomy for Nagorno-Karabakh, despite its constitutional status as an Autonomous Region, and had actually pursued a policy of deliberate assimilation of the population, not allowing education or TV channels in the Armenian language.

Whereas Eldar Salayev, President of Azerbaijan's Academy of Sciences, gave us his somewhat unscientific explanation for the conflict: "The Armenians are a difficult people to get along with, and this is why they have been oppressed!" We heard all sorts of theories as to who had been behind January's anti-Armenian pogroms - from the KGB, to the Azerbaijani criminal mafia, to the Popular Front, to gangs of criminals let out of Russian jails for the purpose..... As I wrote in my despatch from Baku, "it was impossible to get at the truth in so short a time and with such conflicting views."

"Perhaps it is too early for courageous people on both sides of the conflict to be prepared to swim against the tide of current nationalistic feeling and be prepared to talk of compromise," I summed up. "Yet without such willingness to compromise even a little, it is difficult to see how this conflict can be settled in the interests of the ordinary people in both republics."

It was becoming increasingly clear that the current nationalities problem and inter-ethnic strife was closely linked to the pro- and anti-reform tendencies within the CPSU. It was not inconceivable that such conflicts were being deliberately stirred up by conservatives in the Party who, used to certain perks and privileges, were determined to preserve the status quo. The Vezirov Party leadership had been the continuation of previous corrupt leaderships in Azerbaijan, Arab-Ogly told journalists. "The entire Party leadership there has taken no real measures to clean up the clan corruption that existed under (former leader, K.C.) Aliyev, who was still a Politburo member as recently as 1987."

Vested interests tend to be firmly entrenched wherever they exist, in my experience, whether in Britain, where the ruling class are definitely keen to hang on to their privileges and power, or in the Soviet Union. The question of vested interests was a tantalising one which began to haunt me more and more over the coming weeks and months.

During this short trip, I became friends with a Canadian journalist, Julie O'Neill, who represented Southam News of Canada. Just before it was time to leave, we headed together to a local market and both ended up buying colourful Azerbaijani rugs, without much thought of how we would carry them through the airport and on to the plane.

We still have ours in our Derbyshire home, and when I look at it, I prefer to remember my first exciting, exotic, 1960's trip to Baku rather than the 1990 one when everything was falling apart.

Back in Moscow the system continued unravelling. In local elections held throughout the country, pro-independence candidates won in the three Baltic republics; in Moscow and Leningrad official Party candidates failed to win. Such was the speed of change that the idea of demanding secession from a State consisting of 15 republics - the USSR - which had existed since 1922 no longer seemed incredible or fanciful.

The Supreme Soviet, followed by the Third Congress of People's Deputies, voted for increased presidential powers, amid a new demand by the most radical elements - that the Presidency should be directly elected by the whole country, not by Congress. At a rally held on the inner ring road near the "wedding-cake"-style Ministry of Foreign Affairs building, some speakers called for the CPSU Politburo and entire Central Committee to resign. Gorbachov's image was shown as if he were one of the 'conservatives' under attack.

On the wall at the entrance to our block of flats there appeared a poster with 20 or so photographs and resumés of the various candidates contesting our "Proletarian" constituency in elections for the Russian Federation parliament. One of them was the well-known TV presenter of the controversial current affairs programme, *Vzglyad*. It seemed obvious that someone like him would have a big advantage over a less well-known candidate.

One Supreme Soviet deputy from the industrial city of Novokuznetsk told me that local Party officials there were busy finding constituencies to stand in where there was little or no competition. "How can conditions be equal for all candidates, when Novokuznetsk's Party First Secretary is always on air telling us what he has done?" Viktor Medikov asked. Whereas the new Workers' Committee candidates were having to fight for every inch of space in the local, Party-controlled press, he complained.

A rank and file Communist himself, Medikov was scornful of Party leaders, both local and national, whose "only concern is not to lose their cushy jobs". "Most of the present Central Committee are that sort!" he declared.

He was very hopeful about the Workers' Committees, seeing them as an effective force which could breathe new life into the Soviets - parliament, regional and local councils - which should be the real power. "Power has got to be transferred back to the Soviets," he insisted.

Medikov's enthusiasm and optimism were encouraging, but in the current ferment where everything, every institution, every shibboleth, every historical truth, every certainty and belief was under attack or being challenged, I did not share his optimism. It seemed to me that nobody had control of anything any more. It was like a massive show of fireworks, with individual fireworks shooting off in all directions.

In late February 1990 I went to Turkmenia for a few days. I had not been to that Central Asian republic before, so was keen to find out how people there were faring in the current turbulent times. I landed in the capital, Ashkhabad, (now written Ashgabat) in the early afternoon, after a 3 hour 40 minutes flight. As always, travelling within the USSR, one marvelled at the distances and time zones.

I always felt safe on Aeroflot: Soviet planes could land in any kind of weather, on any kind of frozen runways, it seemed. I was always impressed at the national airline's efficiency - timetables were kept to, whatever the weather. The food on board was pretty good, too. In all the flying I did during my six years living there, I never had cause to feel dissatisfied.

Turkmenia is a fascinating country, and I would have loved to spend longer there. 88% of its territory is taken up by the huge Kara-Kum desert, crossed by camel caravans traversing ancient routes, like the Great Silk Road. And though hit by devastating earthquakes in 1929 and 1948, Turkmenia had clearly made huge strides towards modernity. Industrialisation, mechanised agriculture, a well-educated population, the preservation of national culture and traditions were all in evidence on my visit, and, knowing the feudal state of the country before Soviet power, which was finally established there in 1925, you couldn't fail to be impressed.

Turkmenia had been part of the Russian tsarist empire since 1886, but had experienced very little development. It was only as part of the Union of Soviet Socialist Republics that the population of Turkmenia became educated and women granted equal rights under the law. For me, it was a joy to speak to educated and confident Turkmen women wearing their colourful patterned dresses, some with headscarves tied at the back of the neck. Women made up 42% of Turkmenia's workers, I learned, and 40% of its scientists.

I knew tremendous strides had been made, but I also knew from the press that there were problems. We learnt that two new mosques were being built to replace former prayer-houses. We learnt that the birth rate was among the highest in the USSR, but that many young people (about 358,000) neither worked nor studied. While I was there, Turkmenia's Government announced a programme to develop light industry and food processing, and build new electronics and tool-making enterprises in the north of the republic in an attempt to tackle this problem.

At a meeting in the Council of Ministers building, we were told that of the population of 3.5 million, 80% were ethnically Turkmen, approximately 12%

were Russians and 8% Uzbeks. Altogether some 100 nationalities, including Kurds and Germans, coexisted peaceably: "We haven't got problems of nationalism," an official told us, "and we're trying to prevent any."

A nomadic tribal country before the Revolution, at that time only seven in every 1000 people were literate, when the script was Arabic. A Latin alphabet Turkmen script was then used until 1940, when Cyrillic, the script used throughout the Soviet Union, was adopted.

"You can't compare Turkmenistan with the Baltic republics," Deputy Prime Minister Tubak Bibi Amangeldyeva told our group of journalists, "they didn't start from where we started." To see this slim, dark-haired woman dressed in a mid-calf red and grey checked dress, and realise that she had reached such an eminent position, it was indeed impressive. If it had not been for Soviet power, would a woman have been able to rise to such a position? Yet now she was one of three female ministers - occupying Foreign Affairs, Health and Education portfolios.

During our visits to the capital and to the smaller town of Mary (formerly Merv), further east, we met women chief engineers, academics, power station staff, workers, farmers and carpet-weavers. In the streets of Ashkhabad, many women wore the traditional brightly-coloured, loose, ankle-length dresses. Men were dressed in European-style clothes, although in the countryside, we met white-bearded elderly men in their traditional striped gowns. Some wore sheepskin *telpek* hats, which they tend to wear summer and winter, to protect their heads from the searing desert heat.

Water, or rather the lack of it, was one of the main problems facing Turkmenia. The ambitious Kara-Kum canal, which was begun in 1954, runs some 520 miles from the river Amu Darya along the Kara-Kum desert. In the 1970s and '80s the canal was extended to the Caspian Sea coast, making the total length 870 miles (1,400 km). Water from the canal, which is navigable for 280 miles, has transformed 2% of the desert into fertile land.

However, this had brought its own problems; Turkmenia's Academy of Sciences President, Agajan Babayev, confessed: "Nobody thought about the consequences when scientists decided to take water from the Amu Darya. Ashkhabad needed water," he told us, justifying the decision he admitted he had a part in. "Those who object to the canal - and distort the facts - are people who do not live here."

On the road from Ashkhabad to Mary, the earth looked white in places, as if with a fine powdering of snow. It was salt which had come up from the lower soil to the surface.

Speaking to the head of the "Socialism" collective farm, Myalik Mukhammet Khummedov, we heard how irrigation had transformed rural people's lives for the better: "We used to live as nomads, in *yurta*[118], before the Revolution," he said. "Now look at our collective farm cottages built of

---

118 *yurta*: a kind of felt tent.

brick, each with their own garden!"

Many farmers had their own cars and motor-cycles nowadays, he said with pride. Asked about his attitude to the new reforms favouring lease-farming, Khummedov said he was not in favour of disbanding collective farms.

"Our people fear exploitation! They fear that the *bai*[119] will come back if private property is allowed again."

Local people I spoke to were proud that Turkmenia had not experienced outbursts of nationalism, attributing this to the ruling Communist Party's firm hand and the Party's reputation among the masses.

88.8% of recently elected Supreme Soviet deputies in the republic were Communist Party members, so clearly the Party bore most responsibility for the state of affairs there. We spoke to one of them: Sapar Nuryev, director of a power station in Mary. Discussing the question of whether or not Turkmen should be the "state language", his view was that it should, but alongside Russian, which was the language for inter-republican and all-Union affairs. "People should not lose their native language," he said, "but I'm not going to *force* the 28% of non-Turkmen staff at our power station to learn Turkmen!"

Permanent residents should be encouraged to learn the native language, he said, but the present practice of bilingualism should continue.

I spoke to several Turkmen-nationality technicians at Mary power station; they had studied at Turkmen-language schools but had learnt Russian at technical college and spoke it well.

Nuryev was proud of what the socialist system had given his formerly under-developed people, contrasting Turkmenia with what he had seen on a visit to India: "That's poverty for you," he exclaimed, "there no one bothers about the poor!"

Like other leaders we spoke to during our four-day visit, Nuryev was against republics' "exclusivism", recognising that whilst Turkmenia had oil and gas, it received meat from Kazakhstan and diverse products from other USSR republics.

I raised the problem of female self-immolation, which the national press had highlighted. There were over 100 cases a year, we were told. Deputy Premier Tubak Bibi Amangeldyeva told us that the Government was trying to operate through the republic's spiritual leaders, since the Koran forbids suicide of any kind.

The tradition of young women, on marriage, going to live with their in-laws' family, and the typical houses with high walls surrounding the property, making social contact harder; and traditional families discouraging young women, once married, from furthering their education, were all likely contributing factors, she said.

---

119 *bai*: rich landowner before the Revolution.

303

The traditions of *kalym*[120] and men taking on a *nalozhnitsa*[121] still existed, one woman, Maya-guzel Amanova, explained. "I might suggest a future wife for my son, but he will make up his own mind," she said smilingly, adding that many parents do not pay dowries these days.

After dinner one evening, I went for a stroll and sat on a bench in a nearby park. Across from me on another bench sat a dark-haired girl and a blonde girl chatting and laughing together. They looked about fifteen. We got talking, and I discovered that they went to the same *spetsshkola* specialising in English, so they were happy to practise speaking the language with me. Mekhri was of Turkmen nationality, Lena was Russian. "There are some nationalist youths around who want women to go back to the past," Mekhri told me. "If they see girls with short hair, like mine, or wearing tights and knee-length skirts, they call you names." But they were a minority, she said, brushing it off, "they're mainly youths who have done time!"

We chatted about their school and friendship. They seemed optimistic about their futures. When they got up to leave, Mekhri took a ring with a tiny ruby off her finger to give me. I still have it and it reminds me of that pleasant meeting in an Ashkhabad park.

I wished I could have stayed longer in Turkmenistan. Though it had only been a short visit, we had had many enlightening conversations and I had seen so much of interest, including the ancient ruins of Merv and the Kara-Kum canal. It was good to see women, many in national dress, confident and enjoying the status that having an education and a worthwhile job give.

I was truly impressed with what I had seen and learnt in Turkmenia: 100% literacy, compulsory secondary education; 1,647 secondary schools, 101 vocational colleges, nine higher educational establishments with nearly 40,000 students, for a population of a little over three million; and 16 scientific and research institutes under Turkmenia's own Academy of Sciences.

Long after we had left Russia, browsing in a charity shop one day I happened upon a booklet called "Turkmenistan Cultural Directory". Seeing that it was printed after the demise of the USSR, I bought it out of curiosity. It was produced with the help of the British Embassy in Turkmenistan.

There I read: "Jeren Durdieva opened a theatre for puppets following the independence of Turkmenistan. Such folkloric traditions had been discouraged during the days of soviet occupation" (sic). But then the writer had to admit that Durdieva had studied puppetry in St Petersburg (sic) (it was called Leningrad then, K.C.).

Elsewhere I read: "Since independence there are 60 music schools in Turkmenistan, three colleges and the National Conservatory which was set up under the Directorship of Rejep Allayarov in 1993." Are we really to understand that those "60 music schools" and "3 colleges" were set up *since*

---

120 *kalym*: dowry.

121 *nalozhnitsa*: mistress.

independence?

I mention just these two excerpts, but the whole booklet is full of inferences of this kind - as if during the Soviet period there had been no Turkmen flourishing of the arts at all. Yet the contemporary building pictured here had housed Ashkhabad's Conservatory and Music Academy since 1972!

The British Embassy publication was a travesty of the truth. Folkloric traditions? They were everywhere on my visit. Traditional music? *Bakhshi*[122] songs were frequently performed in theatres, with national instruments like the *dutar,* a sort of long-necked 2-stringed lute.

And when I read the CV's of the artists included in this British Embassy directory, you can see that they had had the opportunity of studying at the best conservatoires, theatre and film schools in the Soviet Union.

Turkmenia's National Conservatory

This was typical of all artists from the different republics: they had the opportunity to study classical music and opera as well as traditional, national art forms.

Readers, forgive my digression. I cannot help but feel annoyed when I read such lies about the Soviet Union. No one is saying that it was a perfect society, but repression of national folklore and cultural traditions was certainly NOT one of the things it can be blamed for.

Back in Moscow after my fascinating Turkmenia trip, I met TV producer, Norma Percy, who wanted me to work on a big project they were calling "Second Russian Revolution" for BBC2. It was an intriguing prospect, but I could not think of adding to my already overloaded work schedule at that time. I did, however, join their team later, after I had left the *Morning Star* and returned to London.

The third, extraordinary session of the new Congress of People's Deputies began on 12th March 1990. As always during such events, I had the chance to chat with deputies, some formally in interviews, others informally. One of the people I remember meeting was Georgian filmmaker Tengiz Abuladze. He told me he was writing the scenario for a film based on Günter Grass's

---

122 *bakhshi* - oral story-tellers.

novel "The Rat", published in 1986. "Humankind has relapsed into living like rats, only concerned with their own foul-smelling wellbeing," Abuladze said. Did he see parallels in today's world, I asked him. His reply was non-committal.

This Congress was going to discuss whether the USSR should have a presidential system as in the USA or France. And if so, should the 2,250 Congress deputies elect the President, or the public as a whole? At that time, Gorbachov was president of the Supreme Soviet praesidium.

Some of the deputies argued that a strong presidency would have more powers to deal with civic unrest and ethnic disturbances. A 'presidential council' and a 'council of the federation' were also proposed, to be appointed personally by the President.

One of the most zealous 'reformists', Politburo member, Aleksandr Yakovlev, argued that the present Soviet leader's powers were "very limited" and that a new-style presidency was needed to contribute to separating the powers of Party and State, which would be even more essential under a multi-party system.

The wider powers envisaged, he said, would give the president the right to remove people in high places who were boycotting the reforms. The reasoning went that, whilst in other hands such powers might well constitute a danger, in Gorbachov's hands, such powers were needed to force the *perestroika* programme through against the many local and national Party leaders who were resisting it.

Lithuania did not send delegates, having declared independence from the Soviet Union on the eve of the Congress, a decision Gorbachov called "alarming". In what other country would one of its constituent parts be allowed to simply declare independence, without facing judicial measures or force to prevent it?

You could say it was precisely *because* the USSR Constitution was essentially democratic that secession *was* allowed (Article 72). However, more could surely have been done, under provisions of Article 73, to prevent or at least hold back this decision by Lithuania.

One wondered what would have happened in the UK, for instance, if, say, Scotland or Wales had simply declared independence, without permission from the central UK Government and without even holding a referendum.

The Third Congress voted to renounce the Communist Party's leading role in Soviet society by changing Article 6. Economic reforms had been "running on the spot" for the last five years, as one Congress Deputy put it. But it seemed doubtful that President Gorbachov, now elected USSR President by this Congress, would be able to unblock the reform process and stem the tide of popular discontent.

The food problem was severe, with rationing in many areas and a quarter of agricultural produce lost before it even reached the shops; everyone agreed that something had to be done, but there were widely divergent views as to *what*. Even among the pro-reform people there was little unanimity.

Gorbachov, under his new presidential powers, issued a decree to protect USSR sovereignty, after Lithuania unilaterally declared secession on March 11th 1990. A new bill on secession submitted to the Supreme Soviet envisaged calling a referendum requiring a two-thirds majority among permanent residents of any republic before it could secede. It was like shutting the stable door after the horse had bolted.

Interior Ministry officials started to confiscate weapons in Lithuania, rejecting that republic's setting up of "volunteer border detachments". This was an attempt to create parallel formations, said KGB (State Security Committee) Lieutenant-General Valentin Gaponenko, in charge of border troops there.

The Lithuanian Communist Party split between Communists of the republic's independent Communist Party and those loyal to the Soviet Communist Party platform. Whilst Lithuania was a republic of only 3.5 million people, its actions and declarations were having an inordinately unsettling influence on the entire multi-nationality nation.

In an article at the time I wrote:

"Sajudis's (Lithuanian nationalist, pro-independence movement) argument is that, since the republic was "annexed" and "occupied" in 1940, the new bill on secession going through parliament does not affect Lithuania.

"Whatever the circumstances of the republic's incorporation into the Soviet Union - and the world situation on the brink of a major war cannot be ignored in this context - their argument takes no account of present realities. Neither does it take account of the need to preserve European stability based on post-war realities.

"No state can let itself be dictated to by one of its territories, no matter how these territories came to be part of that state - whether annexed by war, as Texas and California were, from Mexico - or however.

"Sajudis-dominated parliament should retract its March 11th UDI[123], on the understanding that talks follow on establishing new relations between it and the rest of the Soviet Union.

"Such new relations are obviously needed to meet the will of the majority of the Lithuanian people. But they need to take into account the interests of other nationalities in the republic, USSR state economic and defence interests and the interests of world security."

The Soviet Communist Party was due to have its next, 28th, Party Congress in July 1990. Some members started calling for dissenting platforms and factions to be allowed within the CPSU. A Central Committee open letter to

---

123 UDI: Unilateral Declaration of Independence.

members accused "Democratic Platform" and its spokesman, Boris Yeltsin, of wanting "to turn the Party into a loose association with complete freedom for factions and groups, i.e. in practice, to destroy it."

"Some reject *perestroika*, seeing it as the "liberal-bourgeois degeneration of society and the Party," the Central Committee's Open Letter said. "Others, joining up with anti-socialist forces, proclaim the October Revolution a tragic mistake and call for the restoration of capitalism."

One could sympathise with the Party's General Secretary, Mikhail Gorbachov, as he tried to democratise the Party without bringing on its disintegration. But by this stage, the damage to Party unity and to unity in the country as a whole had already been done: the leadership's questioning of every facet of society over the previous seventy years, from centralised planning to historical events, and from collectivised agriculture to parliamentary structures, had undermined many citizens' faith in their system.

The Soviet Communist Party, like the majority of communist parties in the world, was based on a system, devised by Lenin, called democratic centralism. Broadly speaking, it enabled widespread debate at the discussion phase, but once motions were passed at congress, all members were expected to argue for that line - now "the Party line". It did make for an effective, organised party; in the British Party's case, one able to punch far above its weight.

In the USSR, the difference was that the barrage of criticism of the Soviet Union's entire history was that *it was coming from the ruling party itself - the CPSU!* Emanating as it did from the leadership, the veritable onslaught of historical revision during the *perestroika* period inevitably proved unsettling and destabilising.

After an exhausting week of reporting on the Third Congress of People's Deputies, Ricardo and I and our two daughters, Liza and Martha, made a trip to Leningrad. We were conscious of the fact that, although we had once holidayed on the Black Sea with the children and had explored Moscow and environs, they had not seen anything of the Soviet Union, apart from one short trip to Tallinn.

The best way to go to Leningrad was to take sleepers on the night train, arriving there well rested and ready for a day's sightseeing. Russian trains are famous for their comfortable cabins and for the endless supply of tea, brewed and brought to your door by the stewards from their little cabins at the end of every coach.

We stayed at the Moskva hotel at the end of Nevsky Prospect, which was quite a luxury for us, unused as we were to staying in hotels. We explored the centre on foot, visiting the famous Hermitage, with its world-famous art collection and the Winter Palace square where in October 1917 the Bolsheviks had stormed the high wrought-iron gates of the tsar's palace. Readers may have seen that unforgettable scene in Eisenstein's famous film *Oktyabr*.

We toured Peter and Paul Fortress, the original citadel of St. Petersburg, founded by Peter the Great in 1703. Between the first half of the 1700s and early 1920s it had served as a prison for political prisoners, and we shuddered, seeing the tiny dank cells where Dostoyevsky and Gorky, among other important cultural icons of the day, had been imprisoned.

Leningrad's (now St Petersburg) picturesque canals crisscross the city centre, their bridges adorned with statues and wrought-ironwork. On the embankment of the River Moika is a museum in the writer Aleksandr Pushkin's flat, near Nevskiy Prospekt. It was here that Pushkin died in 1837, after being mortally wounded in a dramatic duel. I had been to this museum on a previous visit, but on this occasion we were unlucky – when we arrived, it was closed *na uchyot* (for stock-taking). You could be unlucky for various reasons: shops, museums and offices could be closed for lunch, or for one day a week, for repairs or for stock-taking. It was always frustrating after you'd trekked halfway across the city to find your destination was *zakryt na remont* (closed for repair). (These were the days before you could look a place up on the internet to find opening hours).

We had to laugh - above the theatre poster the notice
read: *Zakryt na uchyot* (closed for stock-taking)

Pushkin is perhaps the most revered poet in Russia, both in Russian and Soviet times. In the nineteenth century, Pushkin had gradually become committed to social reform and emerged as a spokesman for literary radicals. His "Ode to Liberty" was found among the possessions of Decembrists exiled to Siberia and the poet publicly recited his poem, which was enough for Tsar Aleksandr the First to order the poet's exile in May 1820.

In his *Message to Siberia*, Pushkin wrote:

Deep in the Siberian mine,
Keep your patience proud;
The bitter toil shall not be lost,
The rebel thought unbowed.

The sister of misfortune, Hope,
In the under-darkness dumb
Speaks joyful courage to your heart:
The day desired will come.

And love and friendship pour to you
Across the darkened doors,
Even as round your galley-beds
My free music pours.

The heavy-hanging chains will fall,
The walls will crumble at a word;
And Freedom greet you in the light,
And brothers give you back the sword.

(Translated from the Russian by Max Eastman)

Pushkin is perhaps best known in Britain for his narrative poem *Eugene Onegin,* of which there are film versions, and his play *Boris Godunov,* turned into the eponymous opera. His love poems are rightly celebrated throughout the world.

We managed to squeeze in a visit to the famous Kirov Opera (now known by its former name Mariinsky), where we saw *Lucia di Lammermoor* from seats in the upper balcony. Liza and Martha were very excited to be in the beautiful and rather opulent theatre and to try dainty caviar sandwiches and *kompot* during the intervals.

Our other visit was to the Piskaryovskoye War Memorial Cemetery,[124] which Ricardo and I had both separately visited on previous occasions, and wanted our daughters to experience. Once seen, this moving Memorial is never forgotten, and is a fitting tribute to the millions who died in the Leningrad siege during the Great Patriotic War.

We left on the night train back to Moscow, tired but very happy with all

---

124 Described on page 58.

that we had managed to see and do during our four-day stay. I was only sad that Victor couldn't have been with us, as it was the first time we had ever been away without him. But he was coming back soon to spend his Easter holidays with us.

The next few months were ones of increasing division and disunity in the country and in the CPSU, as two distinct tendencies emerged within the party - one called Democratic Platform (pro-reform) and the other Marxist Platform (status quo). The recent Central Committee 'open letter' appeared to give the green light to local party authorities to expel members who supported Democratic Platform positions.

I wrote at the time: "...in a party with little tradition of active pre-congress discussion and acceptance of different views, the Central Committee recommendation may well be interpreted otherwise in the regions." Obviously, if pro-reform members *were* expelled in the run-up to the July 28th CPSU Congress, this would affect the composition of delegates.

Lithuanian independence forces continued gaining ground and nationalist *savanorial* volunteer units[125] were being formed there. Units of that name, of anti-communist orientation, existed in 1918-1919. Soviet news agency TASS reported a Lithuanian lawyer as saying that the father of the nationalist President of Lithuania's Supreme Soviet, Vytautas Landsbergis, had been a *savanorial* member who, in 1941, had signed a greeting to Hitler, calling him "the liberator of Lithuania and saviour of European culture".

At times you almost had to pinch yourself to believe what you were seeing: on the last May Day parade I attended, in 1990, alongside slogans reflecting trade unionists' worries about unemployment and higher prices in a more market-oriented economy, at the end of the official parade, a whole host of unofficial organisations joined in, holding slogans like: "the CPSU is the Exploiter and Oppressor of the Workers!"; "Party of Lenin - Out!"; "72 Years - to Nowhere!" Gorbachov's face looked grim as he watched for a while before leaving the Mausoleum rostrum.

On 29th May 1990, Boris Yeltsin was elected President of the Russian Supreme Soviet - in effect, President of Russia. On 8th June, the Russian parliament declared that Russian laws would henceforth take precedence over Soviet laws. It was the end of decision-making at an All-Union level. Henceforth, it was to be each republic for itself.

My last despatch as the *Morning Star*'s Moscow correspondent was 31st May 1990. It talked of the Government's plans for a "regulated market economy" and Russia's new President Boris Yeltsin's call for the Government to resign. Here was someone who had long been urging deeper and faster market reform; yet now when the Government actually began raising prices on many basic products - an essential part of market reform - he opposed the measures. Yeltsin was a master of demagoguery.

---

125 translated from the Lithuanian: National Defence Volunteer Force.

Our friend Otto Lacis, Deputy Editor of *Kommunist* and a doctor in Economics, was one of the foremost advocates of market reform, as the only way out of the deepening economic crisis.

"Yes, prices will go up," he admitted in a long interview in *Izvestia* that week. "But the market will start to fill with goods - and if goods are available, the black-marketeers will disappear."

Lacis debunked some of the myths about stable low prices, which, fixed by the state, have remained unchanged for decades. "What's the use of a bar of soap at the fixed price of 10 kopecks, if I can't find it anywhere in the shops?"

When there are constant shortages - *defitsit* - items of daily necessity cost more *in practice,* Lacis argued, than the fixed price, because they can only be obtained through the black market.

The Soviet budget deficit would be 80-90,000 million roubles in 1990, Lacis pointed out. State investments, defence spending and management costs should be cut back to reduce the deficit to no more than 2-3% of GDP, i.e. not more than 20-25,000 million roubles.

"No bank in the world would do what the Soviet Government regularly does," Lacis pointed out, "which is to continually give credit to loss-making enterprises, knowing that those loans will never be repaid."

The economy's distortions were self-evident: "if prices are lower than the supply and demand balance, shortages are the result." Studies had shown that the lower a person's wages, the more he/she ends up paying for meat and conversely, the more a person earns, the cheaper he/she could buy meat.

This was because higher wage-earners could get state-subsidised meat through their places of work, whereas pensioners, students, non-working mothers etc, could not find meat in the state shops and were therefore forced to pay high, 'market' prices.

The transition to a market economy, Lacis argued, would entail both price rises and redundancies. But the first would be softened by the Government's proposed compensatory measures, by means of index-linked wage increases. The second issue was more of a problem. Re-training, re-distribution of labour resources and job-finding programmes would be needed.

As I wrote in my last piece: "It is doubtful whether the Government or trades unions have the necessary re-training programmes ready to absorb the likely influx of workers from loss-making production facilities."

"The transition to a regulated market economy is *perestroika*'s last chance," Deputy Premier Leonid Abalkin warned on 30th May. "The question is," I wrote in my final piece, "will the Soviet people be willing to pay the price to give *perestroika* that 'last chance'?"

I had not wanted to leave the *Morning Star*, but we did want to leave Moscow to return to Britain. Our son was already there, and we badly wanted to be reunited as a family once more. I was grateful that Brian Lapping and Norma Percy had offered me work as a researcher on their project *Second Russian Revolution*, which would mean working mainly in

London and travelling back to Moscow to do interviews with the key figures of the *perestroika* period.

At least we would have an income for a period on our return, though we knew it would probably be unlikely that Ricardo would be able to find work, as he was severely deaf by this time and in his early sixties.

The rest, as they say, is history. That year, 1990, the measures hastening the end of the USSR followed each other in quick succession: Russia asserted that its laws took precedence over Soviet, All-Union laws; a separate Russian Communist Party was founded; Gorbachov ended Party control over the media; Ukraine declared sovereignty (codeword for independence) in July; Foreign Minister Eduard Shevardnadze, a Georgian by nationality, resigned, warning of impending dictatorship.

In August, Armenia, Turkmenistan and Tajikistan declared sovereignty; in November attempts were made to set up a new Soviet government with representatives of all fifteen republics; the Congress of People's Deputies approved new executive powers for Soviet President Gorbachov - but it was all too late.

1991 saw even speedier unravelling of the state's structures and institutions. Yeltsin, who was now Russia's President, assumed more and more popularity as Gorbachov's economic reforms stalled and became discredited. In August a half-hearted coup was staged whilst Gorbachov was on holiday, it failed and two of its self-named "Extraordinary Committee" committed suicide[126].

Gorbachov resigned as General Secretary of the CPSU, the USSR Congress of People's Deputies dissolved itself; Yeltsin banned the CPSU and the Russian Communist Party; in December Russian President Yeltsin together with the Presidents of Ukraine and Belarus declared the USSR dissolved.

Thus by the end of 1991 this once great nation had ceased to exist. The USSR had been the first country to abolish the ruling capitalist system and to implement a socialist system where the working people would rule. It had lasted 74 years. Whilst many in the West gloated at its demise, I, like many Communists and socialists worldwide, was saddened and dismayed.

In my final chapter I attempt to summarise the Soviet Union's undoubted achievements and its shortcomings, and examine what could have been done differently to introduce necessary reforms without destroying the entire edifice.

---

126 See Jonathan Steele's reports at the time in The *Guardian*.

CHAPTER VII

The rapid unravelling of the USSR and the dissolution of that once-powerful nation in 1991 caused heartache, consternation and puzzlement among Communists and progressive people worldwide. How could it have happened, so swiftly, so easily, without bloodshed or fightback?

Theories abound. That Gorbachov was a traitor, knowingly introducing reforms destined to destroy the system. That the "conservatives" - those against the reforms - stymied the whole *perestroika* project, leading to its failure. That the policy of extreme openness and transparency - *glasnost* - destabilised society and led to the emergence of nationalistic tendencies. That it was the *nomenklatura* class itself which in the end voted to destroy the socialist system, as they envisaged becoming the new capitalist class.

In this final chapter, I attempt to analyse what happened, from my point of view as a longstanding Communist and someone who witnessed the entire process from beginning to end. The foregoing chapters will, I think, have given readers an understanding of the problems that definitely *did* exist in 1985, when Gorbachov became CPSU General Secretary.

What could have been done differently? Was the demise of the world's first truly multi-national and multi-ethnic socialist state, which had lasted 74 years, inevitable? Did the majority of Soviet citizens at that time actually want their country to disintegrate?

Many books have been written since 1991, some of which genuinely try to analyse the causes of the collapse, from a progressive, even pro-socialist stance. But among socialists and Communists there is no consensus as to the reasons behind this world-shattering event.

One thing is obvious, however: that the reforms begun under Gorbachov were carried out at the height of a Cold War against the USSR, which had been ongoing ever since the birth of the world's first worker state in 1917, with a temporary hiatus during WWII, when Britain and the USSR were allies. We shall never know how the country might have developed over the decades since the Revolution, had it not been for foreign intervention, Soviet losses in WWII and then an unrelenting decades-long Cold War.

As Bahman Azad says: "...it would be a grave mistake to forget that the Communists' subjective errors, regardless of how grave and critical they may have been, occurred within the framework of an extremely difficult and unequal struggle against world imperialism and its intrigues; that they have occurred in the course of traversing a completely uncharted historical path for which there does not exist any pre-established guidelines."[127]

This unrelenting ideological struggle by the capitalist world against the world's first socialist state cannot be underestimated, when analysing reasons for its downfall. Diversion of huge resources into a futile arms race, in order to ensure the nation's security, was certainly one of the reasons for the economic problems the country was increasingly experiencing by the 1980's.

What is clear from history is that capitalist societies, or rather, the ruling class of those societies, will always try by whatever means possible to prevent and crush socialism, wherever it emerges. The ruling class has its own interests - private profit - which would be eliminated in a socialist society. This is the reason why, throughout the 20th century, all attempts by different countries to introduce a socialist system have met with intransigent opposition by the ruling capitalist class and their backers in the major imperialist powers. We can cite Jacobo Arbenz in Guatemala (1954), the massacre of Communists in Indonesia (1965-66), Salvador Allende in Chile (1973), the decades-long imprisonment of Nelson Mandela and others by the apartheid regime in South Africa, the 1992 coup attempt against Hugo Chavez in Venezuela and against Bolivia's Evo Morales in 2019 as some of the most notorious attempts by the ruling elites of those countries, with the aid, overt or covert, of the United States, to stem the socialist tide and prevent it from ever re-emerging.

Could socialism have developed and progressed successfully, if it had not been for this undeclared war against the first socialist nation? Cuba, for instance, has long been a beacon of hope for a socialist society for the peoples of Latin America and beyond - but Cuba has been subject to a cruel economic blockade by the USA which has lasted decades and has crippled Cuba's economy and blighted its society in many ways. What would Cuba be like today if it had not been subjected to such entrenched economic and political warfare waged by the USA? We can never know, of course.

Consequences of the USSR's collapse for world peace and security

The USSR was, as many have realised since the country ceased to exist, the main bulwark against imperialism's aggression. However critical many on the Left were of the Soviet Union, its disappearance from the international scene has emboldened imperialism like never before. Thus we have seen the encroachment of NATO's forces right up to the former Soviet Union's borders (despite the promise given to Gorbachov in February 1990 by US Secretary of State James Baker that NATO would "not move an inch" eastwards).

We have seen the US establish bases in the former Soviet Union's Central Asian republics; we have seen the US invade Afghanistan in 2001 and engage

---

127 *Heroic Struggle Bitter Defeat, Factors contributing to the dismantling of the Socialist State in the USSR,* Bahman Azad, International Publishers, New York, 2000.

in a war that has cost at least 170,000 lives, on the pretext of hunting down those responsible for the September 11th 2001 attack on the New York Twin Towers; we have seen the US and the UK invade Iraq in March 2003, resulting in some half a million deaths from war-related causes, according to one academic study.[128]

We have seen the US and its allies, including our country, invade Libya in March 2011, leading to the assassination of that country's leader, Muammar Gaddafi, without any pretence at a trial, and bringing in its wake absolute chaos and anarchy which continue to this day.

It is doubtful that the US and its allies would have done any of the above had the USSR still existed. Like it or not, the USSR - the second most powerful nuclear-armed state after the USA - would have deterred such actions on the part of imperialism - and the world would be a safer place as a result.

Suicide-bombers, terrorist organisations such as Al-qaida and Isis, vast numbers of displaced people, huge numbers of refugees trying to reach a safer life - most of these are as a result of the US-led invasions and wars, which have destabilised the Middle East in particular. Even in countries not at war, in the Americas, for example, the long caravans of Central American families seen in recent years, walking hundreds of miles to escape poverty in the hope of a better life in the USA, prove that capitalism in the countries of Central America cannot guarantee citizens even the minimum standard of living.

Why reform was needed in the USSR in 1985

Gorbachov was not alone in his desire to reform the system. There was a whole school of economists and sociologists in the USSR who had come to the realisation over the previous 20 years that the Soviet economy had to reform in order to feed, clothe and satisfy the burgeoning aspirations of a well-educated populace. Great hopes had been invested in the Yuri Andropov leadership (1982-4) which had managed to put the brake on the slide to stagnation the country saw under the previous leader, Leonid Brezhnev (1964-82). But Andropov died less than 2 years into the job, his place being taken by the elderly and infirm Konstantin Chernenko, who himself died after barely a year in office. So that by the time it came to name a new General Secretary of the CPSU, it had become clear to most in the Party leadership that not only would the country need a younger leader, but that that person would have to tackle the evident economic problems that had accumulated over the previous two decades.

---

128 The study - by researchers from the University of Washington, Johns Hopkins University, Simon Fraser University and Mustansiriya University - covers March 2003 until June 2011, six months before the US withdrawal.

What were these problems?

One big problem concerned the role of ministries and the Party in the economy. There were over 800 ministries, replete with functionaries. There were ministries for every possible branch or sector of the economy, and not only at national, All-Union level, but also at the level of the fifteen constituent republics of the USSR. It can easily be imagined that this would lead to duplication and unnecessary bureaucracy. In essence, the system was that Gosplan - the State Planning Committee - devised each industry's targets, according to the national 5-year plan, and the ministries told the enterprises under their remit what their production should be under that plan. So there was practically no leeway for individual enterprises - be they factories or farms - to make a profit to use to plough back into their social and housing programmes, for instance. Whilst good, successful enterprises *did* make a profit by over-fulfilling their quotas, they did not stand to benefit much, if at all, as their profits went to the ministry to which they belonged - which could then use those profits to prop up unprofitable enterprises elsewhere. So the system did not foster initiative, either at individual worker level, or at the level of works management. Why bother, if you would be given the same budget to achieve a particular output, whether you innovated and introduced incentives or you didn't?

Not only were there too many ministries, with central, all-Union ministries and the constituent Republics' ministries inevitably overlapping, but the CPSU, at all levels, national, republic, regional and local, had also, since the thirties, played a role in production targets and productivity drives - resulting in yet another layer of bureaucratic control over the production process. Instead of playing a political role, the Party had gradually come to form another part of the management, seen in many places as just another of the bosses.

This situation is in marked contrast with that described by the US Ambassador to the Soviet Union, in a report dated March 5 1937, to President Franklin D. Roosevelt, which lauded the achievements of Soviet industry at the time:

> "The plants and equipment which I saw are first-class, the result of the synthesis of the best engineering judgment of the capitalist countries. ..... But the communistic principle here has in fact been abandoned. ....The profit motive and self-interest are the mainspring. .....The plant itself is required to make a profit and does, generally, ranging from five to thirty percent, which goes to the Central Government. This system, they found, was necessary for success. It is a socialistic enterprise based upon capitalistic principle of profit and self-interest, which they had to come to, to make the machine function."

318

The Ambassador concludes his report with the words: "...granted five or ten years of peace, extraordinary results will be developed by this industrial programme."

So in 1937, whilst centralised planning already existed, individual enterprises still had to operate on a profit basis. They could not expect, if loss-making, to be propped up by the relevant ministry, as was the case by the eighties.

At some stage, between the late thirties and late eighties, ministries began to proliferate beyond reason and the CPSU's political role turned into one of overseeing, even interference in, commercial and industrial matters at every level.

Centralised planning

Centralised planning has often been considered one of the advantages of the socialist system. Rather than 'the market' deciding what is available, through the system of supply and demand, it was considered by Marxists that a centralised planning system would be more efficient, as it would mean that the country would only produce what was needed (which would be decided centrally), thus eliminating the over-production of goods and the plethora of unnecessary products we see under the capitalist system, where enterprises fight for a share of the market, the least successful going to the wall.

When thinking of the benefits and drawbacks to a centralised planning system, it has to be admitted that in some parts of the economy, that system appears to have worked well: the achievements of the Soviet space programme testify to this. And in the sphere of arms production, centralised planning apparently managed to achieve high levels of technological progress. Which leads to the question: if centralised planning was effective in these areas, why was it ineffective in other parts of industry, in particular in the production of consumer goods, and in agriculture?

Professor David Lane sums up the Marxist criticism of a market economy like this:

"Traditionally, Marxists have shared a deep suspicion if not an outright opposition to the market. They believe that the market is not only uneven or unequal in the relationship between buyers and sellers of commodities, but also that the exchange involves "exploitation." For Marxists the market may be defined as the mechanism through which labour power is exploited because the worker's labour creates a profit for the entrepreneur and shareholder. In so doing, capitalist exploitation gives rise to anarchy in production. It leads to slumps and to unemployment, which in turn gives rise to poverty."[129]

This partially explains the resistance by many Soviet workers and shoppers in the late eighties to their Government's first steps towards a more market-

---

129 *Soviet Society under Perestroika,* by David Lane, Routledge,1992, p. 27.

oriented economy, as they saw prices of basic goods rising, while wages failed to keep pace and the variety and quality of goods stayed the same.

The question of "exploitation" which Lane mentions above was less convincing, I would say, to most Soviet workers, judging by extremely critical letters in the press during the eighties concerning workers' conditions. It seems that many of those in unproductive and old-fashioned plants felt "exploited" by their managements in a way that was not very different to the exploitation Lane describes as a feature of capitalism.

Referring to the planning system that existed in the Soviet Union before *perestroika*, David Lane points out that "production has not been carried out for profit. ..... Goods and services have to be produced, but selling them has not been a criterion of success. In practice, the planning system gives people what it wants to produce, but the needs of people are incompletely fulfilled. Consumers have to take what comes out of the system even if the material and human products do not meet their needs. This has led to the criticism that the planners have exercised a "dictatorship over needs."" (op. cit. Page 30)

The problem with centralised planning in the USSR, in addition to the surfeit of ministries dictating from above, was that the Plan, worked out every five years for the oncoming 5-year period, did not necessarily correspond to what the public wanted and needed. Because of the lack of any real need - on the part of enterprises - to introduce changes to their products, make them more modern, introduce innovations, make them more stylish - most enterprises simply continued producing the same items that they had been producing for decades. So lorries, as my 10-year old son pointed out a few days after our arrival, looked like WWII lorries you can see in old films; living room furniture, though of good quality, tended to be made of dark wood and similar in style to everybody else's, and it was difficult to find good-quality *and* attractive, fashionable clothes and shoes. Soviet people who travelled abroad or who watched foreign TV stations knew that they were falling behind, and they called it 'stagnation'. The economy was stagnating.

Centralised planning did, though, have some advantages, both during WWII and subsequently. As Kotz and Weir say,[130] the system "achieved a very high rate of investment, which made possible the rapid creation of a whole set of new industries. It was able to rapidly educate and train the population for industrial work and rapidly shift the population into better-paying, more productive urban industrial jobs.

.....The highly centralised planning system also proved effective at the process of building at least the first stages of a modern urban society, with a reasonably high level of amenities and consumer goods for the population. Soviet central planning proved able to rapidly build urban infrastructure (transportation, communication, power, etc.), construct new housing, and manufacture new consumer goods."

---

130 *Revolution from Above: the Demise of the Soviet System*, Kotz, David M and Fred Weir, 1997.

But to work well, a centralised planning system must have a mechanism for ensuring that the public's demands and needs in terms of manufactured goods and products can be met. That is, it must be flexible enough to cope with the population's new requirements and wishes. This was not the case in the USSR by the second half of the eighties, when consumer goods were inadequate for people's needs and food supplies were erratic.

As Carlos Martinez[131] says, "an economic framework that was appropriate in 1928 was not necessarily appropriate a quarter of a century later, in significantly changed circumstance." I would say, it almost certainly never would be, anywhere. That is what *zastoi* (stagnation) meant: fossilised systems that prevented advances to newer systems and practices. What was acceptable to older generations, who had suffered the unbelievable hardships of war, was no longer acceptable to their children and grandchildren who had grown up in peacetime, with enough to eat, conditions of stability and prospects for the future.

I remember once interviewing a group of elderly women seated on benches outside their block of flats in Sverdlovsk (now Yekaterinburg). One said, talking of the future: "*Vsyo budyet normal'no*: there is milk, there is butter, everything will be all right!" Even at that time - 1990 - that was *not* enough for younger people in the Soviet Union. They wanted plentiful supplies, they wanted good-quality consumer goods and fashion items, many wanted to be able to travel abroad...

If Gorbachov's economic reforms had been limited to gradually curbing the numbers of ministry officials, and boosting and extending the experimental programme of introducing the self-financing (profit and loss) system which had been shown to be successful at Sumy[132] and other key enterprises, and had not been accompanied simultaneously by such a ferocious pace of political and media change, most likely the system would not have collapsed. The question is, why were those economic experiments which had proved successful at certain big enterprises not introduced more quickly and more extensively, *before* introducing a wholesale, nationwide programme of sweeping political reforms, as was *perestroika*?

From 1987 onwards, the pro-*perestroika* media began to describe the Market as a panacea that would solve all the Soviet Union's economic ills. At the same time only shortcomings in the Soviet system were highlighted, with none of its positive features and achievements. It was disheartening for those who had been involved in the economic experiments at various enterprises, and who had witnessed good results in terms of profitability.

Is the Market the only economic driver for success? Here in Britain we have the magnificent example of our National Health Service which is a state-run

---

131 *The End of the Beginning, Lessons of the Soviet Collapse*, Carlos Martinez, Leftword Books, 2019.

132 described earlier p 81.

and state-financed system giving the whole populace good-quality healthcare from cradle to grave, and is the envy of other countries' healthcare systems the world over. The present Conservative Government's creeping privatisation - allowing British and foreign private firms to take over ever more parts of the NHS - has not improved the system, but is certainly a lucrative business for firms like Virgin Care and Care UK.[133]

It is simply not true that not-for-profit services, like the NHS, are less efficient than privatised systems, as in the USA, for instance, where people who do not get health insurance through their place of work are forced to pay huge amounts of money to get healthcare. And where people who are unemployed are simply not covered for healthcare. Or in Chile, for instance, where patients have to pay for every injection, every tablet given, every orthopaedic sandal provided during and after hospital operations.

Our NHS and many other not-for-profit services, such as state education, library services, rubbish collection, road upkeep and many other services historically provided by local councils have been run efficiently and well for years in the interests of consumers and residents.

Whereas farming out private contracts to cleaning firms for NHS hospitals led to the emergence of MRSA and other super-bugs on hospital wards.[134] Prior to this, cleaning had been an in-house service run by the hospitals themselves.

Market economy and the Voucher scheme

In the USSR, the reform-minded economists and sociologists were certain that the market was the only solution. So under Russian President Boris Yeltsin, from 1991 onwards vouchers began to be issued to the workforces of plants and factories. These vouchers supposedly represented a share in their enterprise.

I interviewed leading market economy advocate, Anatoly Chubais, in 1991, and asked him what he envisaged would happen after the issue of vouchers. Smiling, Chubais blithely told me that most workers would no doubt sell their vouchers to keen buyers. He did not spell this out, but it was clear that he envisaged that this process would result in a new class of capitalists. Publicly the issue of vouchers was proclaimed as a measure that would give the workers more say over the enterprises where they worked. In actual fact, workers had the wool pulled over their eyes in what can only be called a massive scam. In this way, under Boris Yeltsin as Russian President, the oligarchs made their money without any personal talent (except for making money) or effort (since

---

133 The *Guardian*, on 29 November 2019, reported that almost £15 billion had been awarded in NHS contracts over the previous 5 years.

134 "Outsourcing cleaning services increases MRSA incidence. Evidence from 126 English Acute Trusts", *Social Science and Medicine*, February 2017.

they themselves had not built up those industries). Who were these new oligarchs? In many cases, they were the former managements of industries, since those individuals had more knowledge and experience than those on the shop floor as to how systems work. Many so-called Communists - members of the CPSU - suddenly became the new capitalist class. Many of the old *nomenklatura* accepted and welcomed the change, since they were the ones who would benefit.

After the mass issuing of vouchers and their purchase by the minority who had savings and the ambition to become owners, there began, by the early 90's, a rapid impoverishment of the population; the metro underground passes began to fill with elderly people standing pathetically trying to sell whatever they could to survive - household belongings, clothes, vegetables and fruit from their village plots. Many young people, especially young women, were lured to the West by new Russian "entrepreneurs" to work as dancers or waitresses, only to find themselves tricked into prostitution. On several visits to Russia in the early and mid nineties, I found the situation heartbreaking. What had been a proud and independent nation was reduced to poverty and despair among those left unemployed by the factory closures and lay-offs and the elderly, whose savings were reduced to a pittance by raging inflation.

A British Medical Journal paper published in October 2003 states that "an extra 2.5-3 million Russian adults died in middle age in the period 1992-2001 than would have been expected based on 1991 mortality. Although Russian adult mortality was relatively high in 1991 compared with levels in western Europe, it increased rapidly in the immediate period after the break up of the Soviet Union, with a more marked increase among men."

Glasnost and nationalism

Did *glasnost* lead to the increasing emergence of nationalism after 1987? How was it possible that after decades of the state encouraging friendship among the peoples and harmony among the many ethnic groups of this most diverse nation, increasingly ugly nationalistic outbursts could occur and spread?

I have talked earlier about the problem of Russian-nationality workers being brought in to Latvia and Estonia, for instance, to work in new industries there, and that they tended not to learn the local languages. But what I saw almost everywhere on my trips outside Moscow was that there was considerable mixing of nationalities in the workplace, which was considered natural in a country with so many nationalities, languages and ethnicities. Everywhere I found that people I met could all speak Russian, but you could also hear native languages in the street and in the countryside in the different republics.

It seemed to me from my observations that the majority of people *did* feel "Soviet"; perhaps less so in the Baltic republics, but certainly in the far north and in Central Asia, where it was obvious to anyone that the standard of living had improved enormously since those regions - formerly under the tsarist yoke - had been incorporated into the Soviet Union in the early twenties. The statistics speak for themselves, in terms of life expectancy, live births, housing, education (both in the national language and Russian), cultural life, women's rights, sport and many other facets of life. Those republics had literally been brought from feudalism to advanced societies in a matter of decades.

Anyone who has seen the wonderful 1965 film *"The First Teacher"*,[135] directed by Andrei Konchalovsky, based on a novel by famous Kirghiz author, Chingiz Aitmatov, will know of the problems faced in Central Asia in combatting feudal ideas and traditions which held women in particular in bondage.

Travelling in the republics of Central Asia in the 1980's, you could not help but see how far women had come since the feudal attitudes prevalent in the twenties, as shown in that film. I saw no veils covering faces and instead found women in responsible positions in industry, education and politics; everywhere you could see young women chatting in groups, on park benches and in the streets and cafes, just as everywhere else in the USSR. I was always shocked on my visits to neighbouring Afghanistan to see the contrast with the position of women there, many of whom wore the ubiquitous and all-enveloping pale blue burkhas with only a mesh oblong slit for the eyes.

The Referendum

The feeling of being "Soviet" and belonging to the Soviet family of republics is borne out by the results of a referendum on the future of the Soviet Union, which was held on 17th March 1991. This referendum is hardly ever mentioned when discussing the disintegration of the USSR, yet it clearly shows that the vast majority of Soviet citizens did NOT want the end of their country. In this referendum, practically 78% of voters (with an 80% turnout) voted for the preservation of the USSR, "as a renewed federation of equal sovereign republics in which the rights and freedoms of an individual of any ethnicity will be fully guaranteed". It is true that the authorities in the small Baltic republics, Armenia, Moldova and parts of Georgia boycotted the referendum. These were republics with very small populations. But in Ukraine 71.48% voted for the preservation of the USSR, in Uzbekistan, 97.6% and in Azerbaijan, 94.12%, to give a few examples. By population, the overwhelming majority of citizens were for preserving the USSR.

The "renewed federation" never came to be. In June 1991 Boris Yeltsin

---

135 Described on p. 186.

was elected President of the Russian Federation; in August a coup ousted Gorbachov; by December the leaders of Russia, Belorussia and Ukraine declared the USSR dissolved. Yeltsin banned the CPSU and the Russian Communist Party; Gorbachov resigned as CPSU General Secretary and advised its Central Committee to dissolve itself.

The once-powerful state had unravelled at an unprecedented rate, to the delight of its enemies. In his State of the Union address in 1992, US President George H. W. Bush said: "By the grace of God, America won the Cold War." The end of the USSR was undeniably a victory for imperialism and all anti-Communist forces, and certainly a huge defeat for socialists and the common peoples of the world, for whom socialism was and still is a beacon of hope for a more just society, one ruled, not by a wealthy capitalist class, but by the people, for their benefit.

Was *glasnost* to blame for this "End of the Beginning[136]", as Carlos Martinez called his interesting book on the lessons of the Soviet collapse? The Soviet Union had been a "beginning", in the sense that it had charted a new, distinct path in the evolution of societies in the 20th century world. My conclusion is that *glasnost*, as it was introduced during the *perestroika* period, was, at least partly, to blame for the USSR's end.

It is naive to think that complete transparency in political, social and historical matters can be introduced suddenly. Is there is any country in the world where complete transparency exists? Every state chooses what to reveal, what to admit to and what to conceal. The 1956 Khrushchov revelations at the 20th Party Congress concerning the crimes committed during the Stalin years were devastating, but were limited to that particular historical period and did not cause major societal upheaval.

But the *glasnost* Gorbachov began to introduce from 1986 onwards was much more wide-reaching and unbalanced. A free-for-all began among mass media editors - almost like a competition as to who could publish the most sensational revelation. All caution was thrown to the winds. Everything that was negative was suddenly there for all to read and see on TV. It was unbalanced, because anything positive - the undeniable gains since the 1917 Revolution - was omitted. Whereas before 1985 the media highlighted the positive and talked of plans for the future, now the negative took precedence. Dreadful housing conditions, corruption and nepotism in Central Asia, crime among young people, Communist Party officials divorced from people's needs, forced removal of Crimean Tatars and others from their homelands during WWII - to mention just a few. It was like an avalanche of bad news stories, starting in a more measured way but gathering pace as it hurtled onwards.

There had always been criticism in the Soviet press. In the sixties, when I first visited, I remember being surprised by critical letters in the newspapers. The difference during the *perestroika* period was that it was the Party

---

136 See Footnote 131.

leadership *itself* which was behind the avalanche of criticism; it was *the Party itself* that was directing and guiding the whole process.

Already by 1987, certain top leaders were worried by the effects on society of so much sudden *glasnost*. Yegor Ligachov, for instance, who was reform-minded and an ally of Gorbachov's in the initial period, wrote:

"Abroad and in some places in our midst there are attempts to call into question the whole course of the construction of socialism in the Soviet Union, to represent it as a chain of never-ending mistakes, to disregard the historical feat of the people that created a mighty socialist power, and to do all this by referring to the facts of groundless repression. .... After all, in the thirties the country reached second place in the world in industrial output, agriculture was collectivised and unprecedented heights were reached in the development of culture, education, literature and the arts."[137]

Laqueur makes the point that actually outside Moscow and the big cities, there was no great clamour for *glasnost*. This accords with what Ricardo and I observed - that, despite the problems there were in daily life, such as shortages in the shops - Soviet people were not unhappy with their lives in the mid-eighties. A factor in this is probably that Soviet society was not consumerist, there were no ubiquitous advertisements for exotic holidays, beauty products or stylish clothes or cars. There were no magazines or tabloids incessantly writing about the rich and famous, to make people feel dissatisfied with their lot. There were, however, many magazines for hobbies and sport, nature and the arts, among others. What there *was* was friendship and long chats around the humble kitchen table, with family and neighbours. What there *was*, or at least, what was fostered, was pride in one's place of work, in one's team or brigade. There was an emphasis on *the collective* at places of work, whether that be in your factory, publishing house, mine or engineering works or your classroom, and there, the better pupils were supposed to help those who struggled.

It may seem to readers that I regret *glasnost* and the revision of historical events. No, my view is that transparency over historical events *was* necessary, but that it was all too much, too soon for a population unused to it.

Let me make an analogy: suppose our media in the UK were suddenly to talk non-stop about British colonialism's crimes in Africa, or how many of today's wealthy aristocrats enriched themselves with the slave trade, or how in 1953 the British secret services carried out a coup to overthrow the democratically elected Prime Minister Mohammad Mosaddegh in order to install the pro-British Shah of Iran.... There are so many examples of Britain's nefarious dealings and role in history. These are known about in academic circles, but they are not widely known about by our population and certainly do not figure in our daily news fare.

---

137 *Pravda*, August 27, 1987, quoted in *The Long Road to Freedom, Russia and Glasnost*, Walter Laqueur, Unwin Hyman, 1989.

A more recent case is the Black Lives Matter movement in Britain today: even the tentative moves towards a different, anti-colonialist interpretation of Britain's role in Africa, India and the Caribbean are criticised in the media as simply "woke" culture, i.e. not valid. Despite this, many thousands of especially young people have learned that there are different interpretations as to empire's role, and are increasingly unwilling to accept the establishment's interpretation.

Looking back on the period of *perestroika* and reflecting on the historic collapse of a nation, one cannot but reflect on the importance of stability in society. Mass media editors have a great responsibility to report and comment on stories and issues in a measured, responsible way, always conscious of the effect their output may have on society.

In capitalist countries, the majority of editors approve of the capitalist system in which they and we live. You will not find an editor of a major, mass-circulation newspaper or magazine who is in favour of a socialist system. The British ruling class is careful to pick people who have been to the "right" schools and to Oxbridge to fill such positions in the mass media here.

In the Soviet Union the CPSU, which, according to the country's Constitution, was the guiding force in socialist society, should have made sure that those in charge of the mass media were equally loyal to the ideals and aims of Soviet socialist society.

What actually happened was that Gorbachov appointed new editors who were in favour of total transparency, total *glasnost,* without enough thought, it seems to me, as to the consequences of this being introduced in such a short space of time. Of course it was understandable that Gorbachov, elected CPSU General Secretary by the Party Central Committee on a reform ticket, would want to have editors who were in favour of the *perestroika* line. But he, as the person ultimately in charge of the entire Party machine, should have seen to it that editors and mass media journalists kept a sense of proportion and balance in their reporting.

Vested interests

Another problem *perestroika* faced was the backlash by disgruntled Party leaders and officials who found themselves replaced after Gorbachov came to power. In any society vested interests do exist. In capitalist society, for instance, those who own big capital, industries and the banks have a vested interest in perpetuating that system, so that they - the owners and shareholders - can continue to make handsome profits and live luxurious lifestyles. In the Soviet Union it was different, but among Soviet Communist Party personnel, inside its various levels of leadership in the republics and regions, vested interests *had* formed over preceding decades - and those vested interests were determined to keep the status quo. They now saw themselves adversely affected by the changes, by new personnel imposed from the centre, and, to a greater or lesser extent, these disgruntled former leaders worked to undermine the *perestroika* project.

In the Central Asian republics, replacement of former leaders who had often been in power for a long time, took on a nationalistic hue, as those replaced were able to whip up nationalistic sentiments against those they saw as being imposed from outside. And whereas before *perestroika*, the media would never have uttered a word against another nationality, now, under conditions of *glasnost,* accusations and exaggerations became increasingly rife.

Gorbachov knew of the dangers and risks a leader would run in trying to introduce substantial change. He was already a rising star in the Party when, in October 1964, General Secretary Nikita Khrushchov was ousted by the Central Committee of the Party. In the 11 years since the death of previous leader Josef Stalin, Khrushchov had implemented both economic, social and cultural reforms, usually referred to as the "thaw" (*ottepel'*) as well as denouncing the crimes committed under his predecessor. Whilst it may have been true that Khrushchov's economic reforms were at times erratic and ill thought-out (such as the drive to plant wheat in northern regions not suitable for grain), the real reason he was deposed was that he had trodden on too many toes of Central Committee members, republican and regional Party leaders who preferred to carry on doing everything the old way.

So, being aware of Khrushchov's fate, Gorbachov almost certainly took the gamble of attempting to introduce changes in a more wholesale way, throughout the country, in the hope that they could be implemented and up and running before any backlash would emerge. Some readers may think that Gorbachov's aim all along was to destroy socialism and introduce capitalism. I am not of this view: certainly all his pronouncements from the very beginning indicate that he wanted to reform, not destroy, the system. "More democracy, more socialism" was one of the slogans, and a call to return power to the soviets, echoing the revolutionary slogan "All power to the Soviets" of seventy years earlier, when the soviets really were the new seats of workers' power.

It would not be a dialectical approach for Marxists to argue that no reform was needed, when manifestations of that urgent need were all around, for everyone to see. The question is, *which* reforms, *how* they should have been introduced, how *fast*, and how *extensively*, given the very different conditions in the different parts of the country. And, of course, it is easier to see more clearly with the benefit of hindsight.

The mass of the people in the Soviet Union did support *perestroika* for the first 2-3 years. But as there was no visible improvement in the economy or people's standard of living, many people became disheartened and turned to supporting Boris Yeltsin, who appeared to offer really radical action. Entrenched vested interests, whilst publicly supporting the reform programme, in fact stymied it, and the demagogue Yeltsin, by his divisive actions inside the leadership, hived off a section of the people who were in favour of reform but who were getting impatient with the lack of tangible results.

Gorbachov was certainly guilty of too much change, some of it ill thought-through, too soon. The economic experiments described earlier, based on profit-and-loss accounting, should have been gradually extended to other key enterprises, and a start made on cutting the ministries. The wholesale shake-up of the political structures of the country should only have been introduced *after* improvements in the economy began to be seen. Whereas in fact, all the political structures of Soviet power which had existed for decades were swept aside by the new reforms of *perestroika,* at breathtaking speed, and *before* any substantial improvements to the economy.

Gorbachov

The personality of the leader undoubtedly also played a part. After decades of Soviet isolation by a hostile West during the Cold War, with the negative consequences in terms of scientific and cultural collaboration and exchanges, the new reform-minded leaders relished the acceptance and welcome they were now, under *perestroika,* getting in the West. President Gorbachov travelled the world with his elegantly-dressed wife Raisa, feted and welcomed wherever they went. Gorbachov was surely naive in believing that foreign leaders like Margaret Thatcher and US President George Bush were welcoming him as the leader of a *socialist* nation and that their hand of friendship was genuine. In fact, these and other Western leaders clearly had their own agenda in showing Gorbachov so much warmth and approval.

By contrast, the USSR's long-time Foreign Minister, Andrei Gromyko, who had supported Gorbachov as the new CPSU General Secretary back in 1985, was famous in the West for being "Mr *Nyet*", when in international fora he would reject initiatives which he knew were against the USSR's interests. His book *Memories* is a very interesting read, covering his Foreign Ministry career under every leader from Stalin to Gorbachov. He clearly knew the wiles and tricks of the major Western nations and knew that their overall strategy was to bring down the system of socialism, as they had tried to do during the Civil War when they intervened militarily on the side of the Whites. Gromyko knew that for them, socialism presented a threat to capitalist societies everywhere, based as they are on the system of private profit and exploitation of labour.

Gorbachov was from a different era, and he thirsted for international recognition. He was tired of his country always being painted as the enemy, and no doubt genuinely wanted to make the world a more peaceful and less dangerous place for future generations. Did he capitulate too much in his negotiations with US President Ronald Reagan? Was withdrawal of Soviet troops from Afghanistan seen as a weakness by NATO and the West? At the time, such moves seemed like genuine breakthroughs in a nuclear stand-off that had existed since the first use - by the USA - of the atom bomb in 1945, on Hiroshima and Nagasaki. Some historians think this was actually aimed as a threat against the Soviet Union, devastated and weakened by its 27 million war dead and widespread destruction of infrastructure, factories and housing left by the Nazis' invasion during the Great Patriotic War. It will be for historians in the former Soviet Union to determine the place of Gorbachov during the *perestroika* years, and so far, studies have been far from laudatory. And certainly, with the collapse of the USSR, world peace has *not* been achieved, and many would argue that the world is in a far more dangerous state today than it was in the 1980's.

The man who was key in ousting Gorbachov in the end - Boris Yeltsin - played a classic Judas role. Seeing the people's dissatisfaction with the reforms' lack of concrete results, Yeltsin positioned himself at the head of those who wanted to see swifter progress, causing disunity within the leadership of the CPSU. There was already disunity between those who backed Gorbachov's reforms and those whose vested interests were being affected - often called 'conservatives' by Western journalists. Now Yeltsin's actions ensured disunity among those backing *perestroika*. It was a recipe for disaster.

That Yeltsin became the darling of the West is hardly contentious. The extent to which the USA was invested in him becoming Russia's leader is revealed in an article by a US journalist, Walter Pincus.[138] Pincus writes that the Bush administration gave intelligence support to Boris Yeltsin at the time of the August 1991 attempted coup against then-President Mikhail Gorbachov, which helped Yeltsin emerge as a hero from that event.

"American officials in Moscow, with access to US intercepts of Soviet defence communications, were ordered by the Bush White House to tell Yeltsin that Soviet military units were not responding to calls by the coup leaders, Defense Minister Dmitri Yazov and KGB Chairman Vladimir Kryuchkov", wrote Washington journalist Seymour Hersh, quoted by Pincus. "An American communications specialist was sent to Yeltsin's headquarters in the Russian parliament office building "with communications gear and assigned to help Yeltsin and his followers make their own secure telephone calls to the various military commanders.""

This is evidence of clear interference by the USA in the affairs of a sovereign state, no matter what was going on in the USSR at the time in terms of its domestic political turmoil. Boris Yeltsin was the man the US identified as the person who would destroy the Union and introduce full-blown capitalism to the world's first socialist state. That state was the world's first experiment in organising a society without a capitalist class that owned the means of production, distribution and exchange. It was a society run for the first time

---

138 Walter Pincus in *The Atlantic Monthly*, May 15, 1994

ever by representatives of the working class and peasantry, elected to bodies called the *soviets,* the people's parliaments and councils.

Yeltsin was instrumental in destroying the Union of the fifteen constituent republics, in Belovezha, Belarus[139] declaring the dissolution of the USSR, together with the leaders of Byelorussia and Ukraine, in December 1991.

Secession

It is interesting (but largely ignored by Western sovietologists) that it was precisely the democratic nature of the Soviet Constitution that allowed for constituent republics to secede (Article 72). Whilst there may have been deficiencies in the ways the Constitution was abided by at different times, the fact is that that right of secession *was* guaranteed legally precisely because it was based on democratic principles of self-determination.

In a book review[140], historian Sheila Fitzpatrick makes a similar point when debating how to think about the Soviet Union, now that it has gone. "…was it, perhaps, a multinational state in which the leaders of its constituent republics *acquired so much freedom of action that in the end they could just walk out of the union and declare themselves presidents of sovereign nations?"* (My italics, K.C.). Further in this review, Fitzpatrick points out that the new Party programme adopted in 1961 under General Secretary Nikita Khrushchov talks of the emergence of a "Soviet people" with a common purpose, ideology, economic system and psychology. This new identity could be considered a complement to each republic's own national or ethnic identity, it was thought. Fitzpatrick mentions that during the 1961 drafting of that new Party programme, in the endeavour to guard against any manifestation of Russian "great nation chauvinism", any suggestions that special mention be made of Russia's leadership role in the Union, especially during WWII, were voted down.

Lenin had warned against what he called "great Russian chauvinism" as early as 1914:

> "No nation can be free if it oppresses other nations," said Marx and Engels ..... And, full of a sense of national pride, we Great-Russian workers want, come what may, a free and independent, a democratic, republican and proud Great Russia, one that will base its relations with its neighbours on the human principle of equality, and not on the feudalist principle of privilege, which is so degrading to a great nation.
>
> …The proletarian revolution calls for a prolonged education of the

---

139 At that meeting, a so-called Commonwealth of Independent States was set up including the majority of former republics, with the exclusion of the three Baltic republics and Georgia.

140 London Review of Books, *Get your story straight*, by Sheila Fitzpatrick, 2 December, 2021.

workers in the spirit of the *fullest* national equality and brotherhood. Consequently, the interests of the Great-Russian proletariat require that the masses be systematically educated to champion—most resolutely, consistently, boldly and in a revolutionary manner—complete equality and the right to self-determination for all the nations oppressed by the Great Russians. The interests of the Great Russians' national pride (understood, not in the slavish sense) coincide with the *socialist* interests of the Great-Russian (and all other) proletarians. Our model will always be Marx, who, after living in Britain for decades and becoming half-English, demanded freedom and national independence for Ireland in the interests of the socialist movement of the British workers.[141]

Vestiges of what Lenin called great-nation chauvinism may have remained in the mentality of some of Russia's citizens, though I must say, I did not perceive it on any of my travels. It was such a mixed population, where people of different nationalities and ethnicities could go to work in far-flung parts of the USSR and frequently did so - in the harsh regions where gold and other precious metals and coal were mined, engineers, metallurgists, geologists and other specialists worked side by side, whichever nationality they were and wherever they were originally from.

It is interesting that Krista A Goff[142], speaking of the nationalisms of the non-Russian republics vis-a-vis their own minorities, concludes that the "big brothers" that minorities in Azerbaijan, for instance, resented were the *Azeri authorities*, rather than the All-Union authorities in Moscow. It was the Azeri republic authorities, Goff maintains, who were guilty of assimilation drives over the years, deliberately squeezing out minority languages and cultures and essentially forcing minority populations to assimilate to the main nationality of that particular constituent republic.

In conclusion, though it is obvious that ethnic and nationality problems did exist at various times and places during the seventy years of Soviet power, the CPSU had an admirable nationalities policy and worked hard to achieve harmonious relations and deal quickly with any problems that arose over the decades. It is hard to think of another country with so many nationalities where mixing was so prevalent and largely successful for so long, and where each nationality's language, culture and history was so well promoted throughout the entire Union.

Here you will see the front cover and title page of a little book I bought in Moscow. It is just one tiny example of the millions of publications intended to spread the cultures of non-Russian peoples throughout the USSR: a book

---

141 *On the National Pride of the Great Russians*, V.I.Lenin, in *Sotsial-Demokrat* No. 35, December 12, 1914.

142 *Nested Nationalism: Making and Unmaking Nations in the Soviet Caucasus*, by Krista A. Goff, Cornell, 2022.

of Selected Poems by a 19th century Uzbek poet, Berdimurat, published in the Russian language by the Uzbekistan Communist Party press, Tashkent, in 1984.

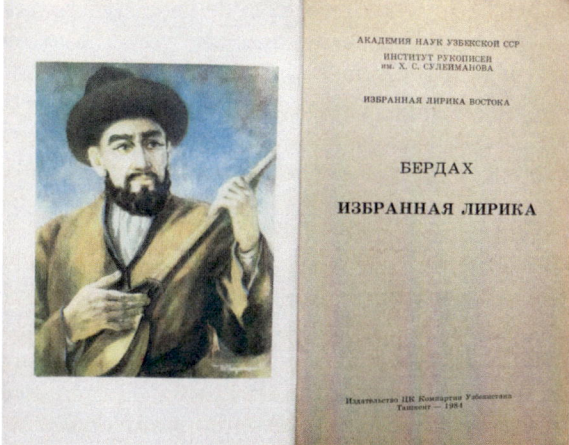

Likewise works of Russian literature were translated and published in very many languages of the republics and autonomous republics and regions throughout the USSR, as well as being available in the original Russian, which most citizens could read even if it was not their native language.

Why then, in view of these positive nationality policies, didn't the peoples of the Soviet Union defend their country when it was at the point of collapse? The answer is that they *did*, partially, by their massive majority vote in the nationwide referendum held in March 1991 for the preservation of the USSR. Practically 80% voted in favour on that occasion.

Many people on the Left, and especially in the world's communist parties, ask how it was that the Soviet Union's working people did not go out on to the streets to defend the gains that the Revolution had undoubtedly given them; why, they ask, were there no mass protests against this seemingly overt money and property grab by the oligarchs?

I hope that my book will have provided some of the context to enable readers to answer the question posed above. The CPSU was the *only* political party, and the one written into the country's Constitution as the "guiding force" in the building of communism - which was the aim of the 1917 Revolution and all the Party programmes since. The *perestroika* reforms had been initiated and propelled *by that very Party leadership*, and initially welcomed by the majority of citizens who wanted the system to work better. This majority welcomed *glasnost,* too, as something natural for well-educated citizens, many of whom had come to resent censorship of certain books, films and plays. And because it was the *country's leadership itself* which was introducing the reforms, and then later, because the reforms were not producing tangible results quickly enough, it seemed to much of the population that the only solution was to keep along the same *perestroika* path, even when it seemed that the process was starting to spin out of control.

So that by the time of the divisions emerging - between those in the Party leadership who became unhappy with the manner and pace of the reforms, and the pro-reform people around Gorbachov - and then, *within* the pro-reform movement itself the divisions between the adventurist wing around Yeltsin and the more moderate wing around Gorbachov, the majority of the working people took positions or simply adopted a wait-and-see approach.

In this way, because of the fact that *perestroika* - which seemed to be much needed by the mid-eighties - came *from above, from the Party leadership*, which by the eighties was probably still trusted by the majority of citizens, by 1991, the working people were disarmed and confused. Yeltsin had seized power, outlawing the Communist Party - this from a man who had been the CPSU's First Secretary of Sverdlovsk region until Gorbachov brought him to Moscow to head the Party's City Committee - and Gorbachov virtually overnight became a leader without any power or prestige. It is not surprising that in the end the people, the masses, did not know what to do, how to defend themselves against this sudden and overwhelming power and property grab.

Gorbachov himself at a certain point in the process found himself unable to stop the reforms even if he had wanted to, as they and *glasnost* had developed their own momentum. By the time of the attempted "coup" against Gorbachov in August 1991, it was too late - and Yeltsin was able to seize the initiative and pose as popular hero, standing atop a tank to denounce the putschists whilst simultaneously wresting from Gorbachov, who was held captive in his holiday villa, what little remained of his power.

It is also true that, because the voucher system had been publicised as something positive for working people, as they would ostensibly become shareholders with a real say in their workplaces, few people could foresee that the issue of vouchers was basically a trick to hoodwink the workers, or that it would result *so swiftly* in the emergence of a new class of proprietors.

These new owners, who had the initial capital to buy up large quantities of vouchers from workers prepared to sell (since they could see that their individual vouchers did not have much value and, with inflation rising, they might be better off selling them) became known as the oligarchs - owners of lucrative oil and gas companies, diamond and nickel companies and vast areas of land.

The oligarchs

In today's Russia, the oligarchs are resented by much of the population. According to a poll by the Levada Centre - an independent Russian polling body - taken in March 2020, 38% of those polled saw President Putin as championing oligarchs' interests. Twenty years earlier polls had shown that Putin represented the so-called *siloviki*, i.e. the military and secret service echelons. Third on the list in Levada's most recent poll are government officials and bureaucrats, with 28 percent of respondents saying Putin represents their interests. The middle class, heads of large enterprises and ordinary people have hovered in the middle of the pack since 2000, with 18 percent, 17 percent and 16 percent, respectively, in the most recent poll. Directors/CEOs of large enterprises rank fourth on the list of groups Putin represents, according to the March 2020 poll. The share of Russians who hold that view has declined from 25 percent in 2017 to 17 percent in 2020, but it is still higher than the share of Russians who believe Putin is representing the interests of all Russians. The view that Putin is a champion of all Russians "without exception" has waned over the past three years. That view peaked at 17 percent in 2016-2017, but then shrank by more than half to a mere 9 percent in 2020. While Putin is now seen more as a champion of the oligarchs than the *siloviki*, most Russians still believe Putin relies most upon the latter in his rule.

It is interesting that in 2020, Levada polls showed that 75 percent of Russians believed that the Soviet era was the best time in Russian history. In an interview in May 2021, Lev Gudkov, head of the Levada Centre, said that "idealization of Soviet life and Soviet times in Russian society is a condition for criticizing the present. People have no other means to evaluate and articulate their dissatisfaction with the current state of affairs and the regime's policies."

"Soviet ideological slogans get reborn in the mass consciousness, but are mistaken for a reality that never existed. Soviet myths about free public healthcare, free education, guaranteed jobs, low housing costs, trade union vouchers, good pensions are quite persistent. When a market economy was introduced to Russia, the country's impoverished population was not given any idea of the future or development goal. The reformers were later discredited, the liberals and the very concept of democracy vilified, and people had no other option but appeal to the past as an ideal. This coincided with the general traditionalist trend, the perception that our life, our country's greatness were in the past, so they must be restored. Over the past 25 years, 55-60% of respondents in our polls have repeatedly said that the reforms made them feel like losers, that it would be better if nothing had changed during *perestroika*."

Why the Cold War did not end with the end of the USSR

When thinking of how the West consistently opposed socialism during the years of the Cold War, the question arises: did the USA always have the aim of defeating the USSR because it was a *socialist* nation, or because any big country with vast natural resources presents a challenge to US hegemony, and must therefore be constrained and weakened?

One only has to look at the number of capitalist countries (Britain, the USA, France, Japan, the Czech legion) which invaded the young Soviet Union in support of the Whites - the army which opposed the 1917 Revolution - to understand their determination to crush the new Soviet power of the masses. The ruling classes of those interventionist armies knew that if the 'toiling masses', or, as Churchill called it, the "red menace", once took power anywhere, it would sound the death knell for the capitalist system.

Confrontation between the two major powers, the USA and USSR, continued throughout the decades since, with a brief hiatus during the Second World War when we were allies in the fight against Nazism. As early as 1961, President Eisenhower had defined the supreme objectives of US foreign policy in the Single Integrated Operational Plan (SIOP): a U.S. strategic war-fighting plan for the use of nuclear weapons in a surprise nuclear attack on the urban centres and industrial targets of Russia and China.

According to Heinz Dieterich, director of the Centre for Transition Sciences (CTS) at the Autonomous Metropolitan University in Mexico City, and coordinator at the World Advanced Research Project (WARP), "when Soviet Socialism imploded in 1991, Washington decided to use two major political stratagems to 'finish off' its potential global rivals Russia and China: first, to expand its NATO war organisation towards the east, as close as possible to Moscow, to dominate Russia militarily; second, to prevent the Russia-China strategic alliance from being reborn, because it would form an invincible regional power bloc."

President Dwight D. Eisenhower and other top officials believed that the first SIOP went too far because it called for multiple nuclear strikes against military and urban-industrial targets (i.e. "counter-value" targets) in the Soviet Union, China and their allies. Since then SIOPs have changed based on new thinking about nuclear strategy. The plans focused on counterforce strategy from the early to mid-1960s, deterrence and more-flexible responses with limited nuclear options in the mid-1970s and early 1980s, and again on counterforce strategy in the mid- to late 1980s. The number of targets dropped dramatically after the collapse of the Soviet Union in 1991. The SIOP is one of the most highly classified of all U.S. government documents, and many details about it remain shrouded in mystery. From the beginning, a special information category—extremely sensitive information (ESI)—has been attached to the SIOP.[143]

The US and its NATO allies have been enlarging their military bloc towards Russia's borders for almost 30 years, Professor Dieterich points out, despite Washington and other Western European states' commitment to the Soviet Union not to expand it either formally or informally to the East. These

---

143 SIOP information can be found on the Britannica website.

pledges were put on paper, as shown by the latest revelation by German magazine *Der Spiegel* and the Washington-based National Security Archive's 2017 publication of declassified documents.[144]

Within weeks of the end of WWII and the defeat of Nazi Germany, Winston Churchill instructed the War Cabinet to draw up a contingency plan for a massive attack against the Red Army leading to the "elimination of Russia", according to a top secret file released in 1998 at the Public Record Office. Entitled *Russia: Threat to Western Civilisation*, the plan, which had the code name "Operation Unthinkable", envisaged tens of thousands of British and US troops - supported by 100,000 defeated German soldiers - turning on their wartime ally in a surprise attack stretching from the Baltic to Dresden.

"The overall or political object is to impose upon Russia the will of the United States and British Empire," said a report given to Churchill by Lt. General Sir Hastings Ismay, chief of staff on May 22, 1945.

These and many other indisputable facts in this top secret file were revealed in an article in the *Guardian* of October 2, 1998. It shows, as do some more recent statements about the aim of the West being to "weaken Russia" made by occasional top politicians in unguarded moments, that the battle is still ongoing, to crush every vestige of socialist ideology wherever it might be found. Russia today is by no means a socialist country, but Russia's Communist Party still polls about 19% of the vote in Russian elections, so it is obvious that Communist ideology is not dead and still represents a force to be reckoned with.

The collapse of the Soviet Union was a bitter defeat for all who wanted a more just, more equal and peace-loving society, both those living in the former USSR and the millions throughout the world who yearn for a more equitable society. "Another World is Possible" has yet to become reality, but millions of poverty-stricken workers and their families everywhere, especially in the global south, are desperate for it. This is why the dream of socialism will not die, no matter how maligned it is by the rich world's media. This is why, despite thirty years of capitalism in Russia, a majority of people (75% in 2020, according to the Levada Centre) still look on the Soviet period with nostalgia and regret at what was lost, in terms of free healthcare, education, full employment and happiness.

---

144 A formerly classified 1991 document retrieved from the British national archive shows Western states did commit to the non-expansion of NATO eastward, Germany's *Der Spiegel* reported in its February 11, 2022 edition. The document depicts the talks between high-ranking officials from the United States, the UK, France, and the Federal Republic of Germany (FRG) in Bonn on March 6, 1991. *Der Spiegel's* article provides evidence that the Western states agreed that membership of Eastern European states in the NATO alliance was unacceptable. "We made it clear during the talks that NATO will not expand beyond the Elbe. Therefore, we cannot [offer] membership of NATO to Poland and others," FRG's Foreign Ministry spokesman Jürgen Chrobog reportedly said in a statement cited by *Der Spiegel*. US career diplomat, Raymond Seitz, who was at the talks, reportedly agreed with Chrobog, saying, "We made it clear to the Soviet Union that we will not [capitalize on] the withdrawal of the Soviet troops from Eastern Europe...NATO must not expand eastwards neither officially, nor unofficially."

There will continue to be attempts by different peoples of the world to do away with capitalism and introduce socialism, seen as a more equitable and peace-loving society and one which favours those who have nothing to sell but their labour power - i.e. the working people. Progress towards this more just society will be uneven and suffer setbacks, but no doubt the day will come, as envisioned by the English poet Shelley, when he exhorted the people to:

"Rise like Lions after slumber
In unvanquishable number,
Shake your chains to earth like dew
Which in sleep had fallen on you -
Ye are many - they are few."[145]

In capitalist societies, the "few" run society in their interests, and the working people can achieve more or less happiness and fulfilment according to their standard of living, education, and status. Many people in Great Britain may consider themselves happy and content with their lot, since, compared with many countries, our standard of living is relatively high. But how much of that standard of living is due to Britain having been a colonial power, which still hugely benefits from unequal trade terms with the poorer ex-colonial countries? A poor brick kiln worker in India, whose children are born into bondage to pay off his "debt" to the kiln owner, is not likely to have a happy life. According to Anti-Slavery International, hundreds of thousands of people - men, women and children - are forced to work as bonded labourers in this way, today, in the 21st century. In much of the global south, many work from childhood to the grave, eking out an existence in unequal societies in hock to the International Monetary Fund and World Bank.

Maximum happiness for the world's citizens should surely be the goal of successful societies. To what extent are capitalist societies achieving this goal for their own citizens, and for the citizens of the poorer global south?

THE END

---

145 Final stanza of *"The Mask of Anarchy"*, by Percy Bysshe Shelley, 1792-1822.

APPENDIX I

US interference in the USSR during the decades of the Cold War

Project Camelot was the code name of a counter-insurgency study begun by the US army in 1964. The full name of the project was *Methods for Predicting and Influencing Social Change and Internal War Potential.* This project was carried out by the Special Operations Research Office (SORO), a Psychological Warfare unit whose particular work "centered on ideas and doctrine." Its mission was to "manage global politics and usher in gradual, stable change toward an American-led world order" through research on "communist-threatened countries."

Project Camelot was ostensibly disbanded in 1965, after South American academics revealed its military funding. However, its aims and funding have continued under other guises.

The nonsite.org website[146] reveals much interesting information on the extent of US interference in the USSR, using, among other mechanisms to provoke change, Gene Sharp's[147] theory of Neoliberal Nonviolence.

"Sharp's was a theory of state transformation easily compatible, philosophically and practically, with neoliberal free market fantasies and programs of vast privatization—as demonstrated by the course of the USSR's collapse and the Color Revolutions, where Sharp's ideas were pivotal."

"AEI's (American Enterprise Institute[148]) first dramatic success came at the end of the 1980s, when Sharp and Ackerman met and began corresponding with the leadership of nationalist separatist movements in the Soviet Union, namely those of Lithuania, Latvia and Estonia. Here, the NED (National Endowment for Democracy) was also at work. For example, the nationalist Lithuanian front with which AEI was working, Sajudis, was getting NED money. The funds were channeled through Lithuanian Catholic Religious Aid, a U.S. NGO led by bishop Vincentas Brizgys. According to Holocaust historian Raul Hilberg, during World War II under the Nazi regime, Brizgys had forbidden his clergy from aiding Jews."

"In March of 1990, riding on the momentum of *glasnost* and *perestroika*,

---

146 described as an open access, peer-reviewed quarterly journal of scholarship in the arts and humanities. affiliated with Emory College, USA.

147 According to the nonsite.org website, "Sharp was .... one of the most important U.S. defense intellectuals of the latter twentieth century, who furthermore possessed surprisingly neoliberal politics. Sharp developed his core theories about nonviolent action between the 1960s and 1980s, with Department of Defense funding, at the elite Cold War institute, the Center for International Affairs at Harvard. "The CIA at Harvard," as it was cheekily termed, was co-directed by Henry Kissinger and future CIA chief Robert Bowie."

148 Founded in 1938, the AEI is a rightwing US think tank that researches into government, politics, economics, and social welfare. It is in favour of private enterprise, a limited role for government and advocates what it calls "democratic capitalism".

Lithuania became the first soviet (sic) to assert its independence from the USSR. Predictably, Gorbachev refused to recognize the secession, and tensions escalated. In mid-1990, Sajudis member and director-general of the Lithuanian Department of National Defense Audrius Butkevicius "had Gene Sharp's *Civilian-based Defense: A Post-Military Weapons System* translated into Lithuanian for use by government officials." In January 1991, in effort to quell the Lithuanian rebellion, Gorbachev deployed tanks to Vilnius. The plan backfired, per Sharp's political jiu-jitsu. Eleven civilians ended up dead, and by April 1991, Estonia, Latvia, and Georgia, had also announced their secession from the Union."

"At the end of April, in the midst of the power struggle, Sharp and Ackerman made a personal visit to the Baltics. There they consulted with members of the new secessionist Lithuanian government—including the president, defense minister, military personnel, religious leadership, and Sajudis movement leaders—regarding use of nonviolent action as a weapon against the Soviets. Sharp even drafted a study guide on nonviolence for the Lithuanian defense department. It worked. The Soviets were forced to withdraw, and by September, conceded Baltic independence. According to Butkevicius, AEI's help had been decisive in the victory: "I would rather have this book [*Civilian Based Defense*] than the nuclear bomb.""

"Baltic secession was highly destabilizing to the USSR. The chaos was exacerbated by a "carefully planned assault against the ruble in 1989-1991" via a "worldwide operation by currency speculators and professional money launderers involving several Western banks." The result was a severe and legitimacy-eroding economic recession in the Union."

"In November and December 1991, with the USSR in political and economic tailspin, Sharp and Ackerman conducted another three-week consulting trip to Russia and the Baltics. There they coached the anti-Soviet activists of Boris Yeltsin's camp who wanted the USSR totally destroyed and its economy pried open for private capital penetration. Yeltsin was leader of the Russian soviet, but his was a minority position: in a 1991 referendum, over 75% of the Soviet citizenry had affirmed they wished the Union to remain intact. The preference of the majority would not be heeded. AEI wrapped up its trip to Russia and the Baltics on December 7. The next day, Yeltsin and other Soviet leaders signed the Belovezha Accords, formally dissolving the USSR."

APPENDIX II

The Soviet School today

By Ricardo A. Figueroa, Ph.D

Recently I attended a parents' meeting at the school my children go to in Moscow. I couldn't help being struck by the attitude of the teaching staff complaining about the bad behaviour of the children, especially the boys. Among these, unfortunately, was my son, as one of the candidates to become a hooligan. A whole number of escapades had come to a head when the group of "hooligans" had thrown a home-made stink bomb at a group of girls. The meeting had been called to "take measures".

I couldn't help wondering why so much urgency to impose discipline, but no initiative towards solving the problem in a positive way, or drawing any pedagogical advantage from this unhappy experience. It seemed to me that the teachers had an excellent opportunity here to teach and to educate, thereby awakening a consciousness rich in humanistic content.

To my surprise, I suddenly found myself addressing those present not because I had to defend my son – he wasn't implicated on this occasion anyway – but more because the incident in itself was a good enough motive to arouse my professional interest and cause me to reflect on this strange case.

It seemed ironic that we were witnessing the opposite of the promising and brilliant start of our son at this school, and above all, it seemed ironic that this mess should have occurred in a system whose educational philosophy – as it was being shown in practice anyway – contradicted the highest objectives of its humanistic content. A system which had once been the object of our sincere admiration for very specific pedagogical reasons, and because, even after many years of deterioration, the system was capable of forming the enormous human capital the Soviet Union has at its disposal.

The country has a well-educated population and a wide range of top specialists – scientists, technologists, artists and intellectuals. There are so many of them that it constitutes a problem for the State to put them to full and suitable use. Thus, one of the ways of understanding the concept of "the human factor" – about which so much is said here – is related to the role this priceless intellectual capital is called upon to play in the challenges which Soviet society has set itself.

But at that moment, there in the classroom, I was once again feeling the effects of the intellectual and emotional collision with a reality whose countenance was quite different from that which I had always conceived of from a distance. ....they were practically classifying the children into those who belonged to organised society and those "predestined" to remain

341

outside it because of their being mere 'hooligans', i.e. anti-social elements. ..... nowhere was there so much as a trace of the heritage of the great Makarenko,[149] author of "A Pedagogical Poem".

Perhaps in view of this we should not be surprised to hear the First Secretary of the Komsomol (Young Communist League) informing the organisation's leadership that crime is increasing, that it has risen by 33% over the last nine months and that young people and adolescents are responsible for a third of that increase.

Of course it is not the school which is the cause of this phenomenon, although the school is part of the sum total of circumstances which have to do with it; but, having said that, the school, by its present characteristics, does not contribute to combating a social ill which has other causes.

The problem of youth, it seems, is a reflection of the crisis Soviet society is going through: the rise in the indices of juvenile delinquency is a by-product of *perestroika*. Because just as the educational system in the past achieved its aims thanks to an iron discipline based on boundless respect for the principle of authority, so too the social behaviour of the Soviet citizen was kept subject to parameters which were not only similar, but in fact paradigmatic for the entire sphere of institutional and social life. *Perestroika* has come to replace the old rules of the game with a permissiveness which has begun to liberate not only the creative spirit and initiative in taking action, but also, initiative in thinking and in critical judgement; but together with this, it has lifted the barriers which formerly caused people to repress certain tendencies, and these are now spreading. A certain hidden expression of protest, or at least of frustration, can be seen. Because if you add to the anxieties normal for young people all those others that derive from the disillusionment which the revelations of *glasnost* have left behind like an inevitable scar, and then, on top of this, you add those of the nuclear age with all its problematic, with a big question mark hanging over the survival of civilisation and of the human species itself – which is nowhere perceived more sharply than here, especially among the young, as a result of that very same political and educational system – you will have an approximate idea of the reasons for the problems of Soviet youth today. It would seem that *perestroika* and *glasnost* are likely to leave behind a negative mark too.

In practice the authoritarianism which *glasnost* is today denouncing so repeatedly as the origin and cause of all the ills which afflict socialism, actually begins at school. And as might have been expected, just as has happened in society as a whole, this authoritarianism bore fruit in its time in that it rapidly raised the intellectual, scientific and cultural level of this multi-national country. But just as it's an ill wind that blows nobody any good, the reverse can also happen, since that very, alas, already past, excellence ended up being immobile, giving shape to an education system which at the present

---

149 See Footnote 83.

time does not respond to the requirements of the age. This incongruence is all the more notorious since the educational reform launched before *perestroika* has up to now shown no perceptible progress. And it could not be otherwise, since it is not education which will carry out the changes Soviet society needs, but the latter which will generate the educational system which can harmonise with its activity and its aims.

The process is, it seems, going on: at my children's school, a group of teachers organised a parents' meeting to tell them about some new points of view and their new way of conceiving the function of education. But this big meeting, as well as demonstrating that the parents are also interested in the issue, at the same time showed that this is no easy matter. Near the end of the meeting, one of the parents got up to speak, only to refute the new ideas and proposals which had been put forward by the young and enthusiastic teachers, with no better argument than his own scepticism, with no other horizons except the collective pessimism much in fashion at present, and without any other proof except to enumerate the failure of other similar initiatives. To my great surprise, the reaction of those present was to give him loud applause. But if the noise of the applause created the impression that pessimism was in the majority, the significant silence of those who did *not* applaud was almost audible. For me, the situation was clear: there was *perestroika*, in action, in one of its many facets, with its common denominator which is the struggle between those who are for *perestroika*, and those who are against *perestroika*, though the latter never actually say so aloud.

I was among those "for", because the earlier meeting had demonstrated that the Soviet school needs profound reform, and needs it urgently. If in the process the virtues – and only the virtues – of the old system can be preserved, there is no doubt that such a reformed education could surpass its former excellence.

4 November 1989

APPENDIX III

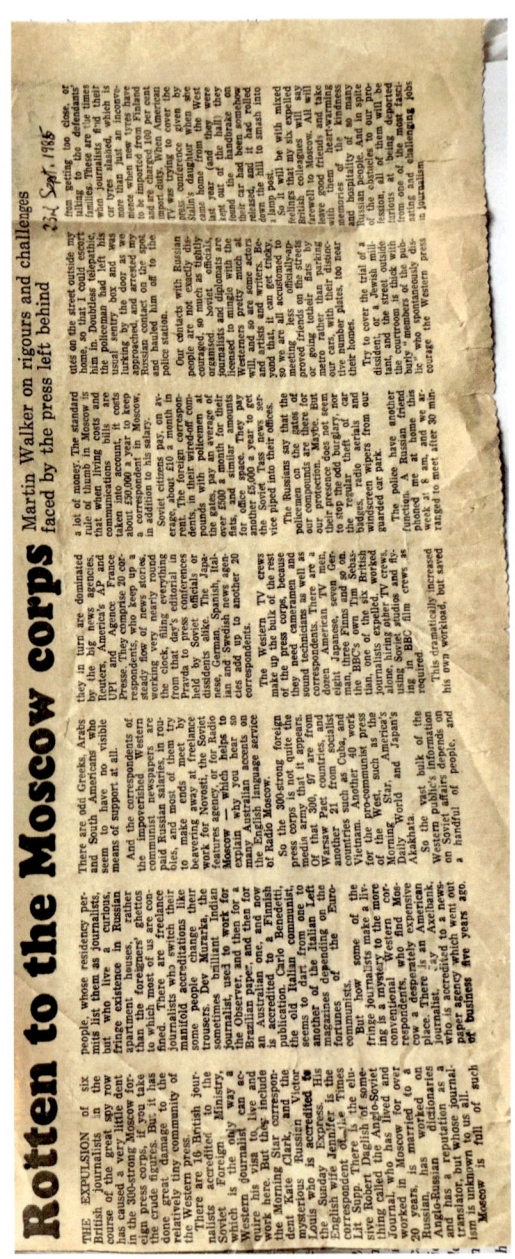

The *Guardian*'s Martin Walker's letter of 23 Sept 1985

Getting to know Soviet Union outside in

Sir, — As Morning Star Correspondent — one of the people apparently living a "curious, fringe existence" in Moscow — perhaps I will be allowed a few comments on your article, "Rotten to the Moscow Corps," (September 23).

It is nothing new to read articles on the Soviet Union characterised first and foremost by their crude anti-Sovietism. And in the present artificially whipped-up anti-Soviet hysteria, I suppose it is not so surprising that the Guardian has fallen into line with the rest of the "free" Press. But I must object to my name and that of the Morning Star being used for such purposes.

The implication in Martin Walker's article is that I and certain other people "listed as journalists," are somehow less than journalists because we live among Russians instead of in 'foreigners' compounds.

The Morning Star, and its predecessor the Daily Worker, have had a correspondent in Moscow for more than 40 years. Our aim as a Communist newspaper which defends the interests of the British working class is to give informed, sympathetic, and supportive information about what is going on in the Soviet Union.

I and other Communist journalists working in Moscow are fortunate in enjoying certain respect and trust on the part of the Soviet people and authorities, which enables us to get to know Soviet reality at first hand, to talk to people in factories, on farms, in ministries, in trade unions, and in their homes.

Of course, journalists of other British newspapers work at a severe disadvantage in that respect. They are supposed to present the Soviet Union as some sort of totalitarian dictatorship. This is what their editors and newspaper-owners expect. That is why they mingle with the tiny circle of so-called "dissidents" rather than the millions of ordinary Soviet workers and their families who are proud of the achievements of socialism.

Kate Clark.
Moscow.

My reply, published in the *Guardian*

APPENDIX IV

Tamara from Ukraine

This is the article I wrote about Tamara, which was published in *Radyanska Ukraina,* (Ukrainian Communist Party daily newspaper) on 20th September 1986. Notice that the newspaper is entirely in the Ukrainian language, despite frequent Western claims as to the "russification" of the non-Russian republics of the Soviet Union. You can see my byline "Kate CLARK, English journalist" at the end

Tamara's story:

It happened like this: Ricardo was returning to Britain by train to see us, as we hadn't been able to join him in Moscow - his job had already started so he was living on his own there for a few months until I arrived with our children. On the train, he had made the acquaintance of an elderly woman from a rural backwater in Ukraine who was making the journey, on her own, to see a long-lost sister whom she had not seen since the Second World War, when the Nazis overran Ukraine. Tamara had been forced to leave her Ukrainian homeland to work as a servant for a Nazi family in Germany, leaving her sister behind. That sister had married a Yugoslav, and after the war they had come to Britain as refugees. Tamara managed to return from Germany to her home village, far from any town or city, where she had lived a solitary and hard life during those very difficult post-war years in the Soviet Union. She had never married or had children, but had never forgotten her sister. She had been looking for her for years, contacting the British Embassy to try to find out what had happened to her sister and where she was living now. After many years, she finally managed to trace the sister, and when Ricardo befriended her, she was on her way. A simple woman of very modest means, Tamara had never even been to Kiev, let alone Moscow, much less anywhere abroad. She had an address for her sister, had managed to communicate with her by post, and was sure that her sister would be at Victoria station to meet her.

Ricardo helped her off the train with her little brown case and cloth bag and stayed with her until he caught sight of me and the children waiting on the station forecourt. After all hugging him by turns, Ricardo introduced me to his travelling companion. She was nervous, not speaking a word of English. We set about trying to find her long-lost sister among the crowds. She was nowhere, and poor Tamara was at a loss. This was long before mobile phones, of course. We went to an office at the station to see if there might be a message for Tamara, but there was nothing.

Ricardo and I consulted with each other and decided to offer for her to stay the night with us in our north London home, and the next day to take her up to Bradford, where her sister lived. We were due to go up to Chesterfield to see my parents, so Bradford would not be too much further for us to drive.

Tamara was very grateful, and the next morning, after she had slept on the bottom bed of our children's bunk beds, we were touched by her gesture of gratitude. It turned out that her little brown suitcase contained, not clothes or pretty gifts, but small green apples, which she was taking as a gift for her sister. She insisted on sharing half of them with us, and we could not refuse, as we saw it would have seemed like an insult or rejection.

Next day we took her to Bradford, found the address, and delivered Tamara to her sister. She had not been able to travel to London to meet Tamara, she explained, because her husband had become unwell.

We bade our farewells, after a cup of tea, and exchanged telephone numbers, in case she might need us again for her return journey to Moscow. A couple of weeks later, I received a call from Tamara, who told me she was returning by plane, not train. We arranged to meet at Heathrow before she boarded her flight. She was sad, disillusioned even. She told me that she and her sister were like strangers and she had not felt at home in their house. It was sad, after so many years, after so much hardship and suffering during the war and all the effort Tamara had made over so many years to trace her only living relative - yet now they had met, they were like strangers, with little in common, apparently.

There must be so many stories like Tamara's resulting from the Second World War. So many people get displaced and lives disrupted and ruined during all wars.

APPENDIX V

Besse took place in a Montparnasse street at 7.25pm.

Sainsbury's, British Caledonian and Smiths Crisps. aspects of party publicity. Alliance choice, page 4

...ing at the White ... between President Alfonsin and President Reagan.

BBC in new row over diplomats film

From Christopher Walker, Moscow

Nov 18 '86

The BBC is at the centre of a new controversy as the result of a documentary about the lives of British diplomats and journalists based in Moscow, which is thought by senior figures in the Foreign Office to have deliberately shown the work of the British Embassy in an unfavourable light.

British sources told *The Times* yesterday that the British Ambassador, Sir Bryan Cartledge, planned to write a personal letter to the BBC complaining about the film, *Caviar and Cornflakes*, and its director, Mr Richard Denton, who was given unusually wide access to Embassy facilities as part of an arrangement reached before filming began last May.

Because of the anger among many diplomats at the treatment given to the Embassy's work, pressure is growing inside the Foreign Office for any similar access to be denied to the BBC in future films it may seek to make about embassies abroad.

It is understood that the Ambassador and leading members of the Embassy staff are unhappy about what they consider to have been the failure of the BBC 1 documentary to show a fair picture of the Embassy's work. Some diplomats have complained privately that Mr Denton, formerly producer of the series *Comrades*, had deliberately set out to denigrate them.

During the filming, which lasted for almost a month, members of the BBC team, including Mr Denton, complained to British journalists at the end of last month, with some British papers contending that it reflected poorly on the Embassy.

Much of the footage concentrated on emphasizing the remoteness of the life lived by diplomats from that of ordinary Soviet citizens, and much emphasis was laid on a petty squabble with journalists over Press passes to accompany a British delegation into the Kremlin.

The film has been dogged by controversy from the outset. When Mr Denton first arrived in Moscow, where he has a Soviet wife, he was unable to begin shooting immediately. His original camera crew refused to fly to the Soviet Union because of what they claimed were dangers posed by the Chernobyl nuclear disaster. A substitute crew was eventually found.

Mr Richard Denton: The producer under fire.

who were also taking part, that despite the agreement with the Foreign Office, much of the Embassy routine was out of reach of the cameras for "security reasons".

The film received mixed reviews when it was screened

Insular freedom

The Maclaren of Maclaren, Press Attaché to the British Embassy in Moscow, lives in a foreigners-only department block with a Sloaneish wife who has long abandoned her early inhibitions at knowing their bedroom to be the object of electronic eavesdropping. Downstairs lives Patrick Cockburn of the *Financial Times*; he and The Maclaren attended the same school (not, one imagines, a comprehensive).

Across Moscow, in a Russian apartment block, the *Morning Star*'s correspondent sends her children to a Russian school and — uniquely, it seemed — speaks the local language.

TELEVISION

Filmed in the aftermath of Chernobyl, *Caviar and Cornflakes* (BBC1) had the makings of a farcical soap-opera: on the one hand, a microcosm of British insularity peopled with anachronistic remittance men who have only tangential connection with the high octane of international politics; on the other, a conveyor-belt of visiting British journalists who fretted to be let into a press conference which lasted all of two minutes and at which sound-recording was not permitted.

It is, as Mrs Cockburn observed with dry understatement, "a slightly colonial existence" — and one that could be done justice only by the comedic talents of an Evelyn Waugh. Somewhere outside these cushy enclaves, of course, dissidents are being harassed and enormous fibs promulgated. BBC Radio's Moscow correspondent palliated his ignorance of Russian on the grounds that the average comrade in the street, if canvassed in his native tongue, would simply parrot the received wisdom of *Pravda* or *Tass* — quite forgetting that the average democrat in the street might well get his knee-jerk opinions from the *Daily Beast* or (let us say) the BBC. Freedom of choice should never be confused with independence of thought.

In this context, it was significant that the only overt censorship on display came from the British Embassy. The KGB, huddled under umbrellas in groups of three ("one can read, one can write, and the third is there to keep an eye on the intellectuals") were simply present for light relief.

Martin Cropper

The *Times* reviews of *Caviar and Cornflakes*,
a TV film in which I featured

APPENDIX VI

My article *Women in the Russian Revolution*, published in the Society for Cooperation in Russian and Soviet Studies Digest, No. 3, 2017. (1917 Russian Revolution Centenary Issue)

This centenary year gives us the chance to reflect on the significance and effects of the Revolution on the whole world – workers' rights and the struggle for women's emancipation foremost among them.

What was the situation of women in Russia and Central Asia before the Revolution? The vast majority of women were from rural peasant households, living a life of drudgery not very different from that under serfdom, which was only abolished in 1861.

In March 1916 The *Times*, in its *Book of Russia* wrote: "..... poverty and ignorance are widespread, and it is the women of the lower classes who feel most keenly the effects of the social and economic backwardness of the country."

Autocratic tsar Nicholas II took Russia into the First World War, which served as a catalyst for the momentous changes three years later.

Women working in industry, many replacing men at the front, were becoming politicised both due to exploitation by the factory owners and the war, as they saw their menfolk killed and wounded; women increasingly joined in demands for peace, land and bread.

Women in Central Asia, then part of Russia's tsarist empire, were living in feudalism, with practically no political, social or economic rights. The veil was ubiquitous and girls could be married off even before puberty.

In Russia there had been a feminist movement since the beginning of the twentieth century, with the formation in 1905 of the League for Women's Equality, and a number of very committed and capable Bolshevik women, among them Konkordiya Samoilova, Nadezhda Krupskaya, Alexandra Kollontai and Inessa Armand, were active among working-class women in opposing the war. The more upper-class part of Russia's feminist movement, just as in Britain, supported Russia's participation in the war.

The Bolsheviks (Majority) were so called after a Congress of the Social Democratic and Labour Party (RSDLP) split due to irreconcilable political differences, the Mensheviks (Minority) forming a more social democratic party as opposed to the Bolsheviks, who were fighting not only to bring down the tsarist government, but to establish a socialist government in its place.

As well as opposing the war, Bolshevik women leaders worked to get factory women to join trade unions which had recently become legal and to spread the ideas of socialism which they thought would be a prerequisite for women to achieve true equality with men.

They published magazines focussing on women's issues, such as *Rabotnitsa*

(Woman Worker) which came out as early as 1914. And they organised industrial action - between 1912 and 1914 some 9000 strikes were recorded and Bolshevik trade unions and influence increased significantly.

In February 1917 the Provisional Government was formed after the collapse of the tsarist government. But the Petrograd Soviet was in many ways more powerful and better organised, taking advantage of the lifting of press censorship. Kerensky's Provisional Government did not really carry out any major reforms and, worse, it continued the hugely unpopular war. So the Bolsheviks' slogan: 'Peace, land, bread!' was increasingly taken up by women and men alike.

International Women's Day 1917 saw mass demonstrations by women and strikes among many sections of the female workforce.

Unlike the working women feminists, the educated upper-class and upper middle-class feminists supported the Provisional Government, and threw their lot in with the warmongers.

These were heady days, prior to the October Revolution. The Bolsheviks were represented in the Soviets – councils set up all over Russia since 1905 among workers, peasants and soldiers – but did not form a majority in many of them. The Bolsheviks argued for these local and regional councils of workers' deputies to take power from Kerensky's Provisional Government, which had soon become discredited. "All Power to the Soviets!" was the Bolsheviks' call.

"Either we must abandon our slogan, 'All Power to the Soviets,'" Lenin wrote, "or else we must make an insurrection. There is no middle course....." arguing against others in the Bolshevik leadership who voted against insurrection at an all-night meeting of the party's Central Committee on October 23rd 1917.

The role of Bolshevik women in the years leading up to and during the Revolution was recognised by the party's leader, Vladimir Lenin, when he told German revolutionary Clara Zetkin: "Women workers acted splendidly during the revolution. Without them we would not have been victorious."

After the victory of the Revolution the Bolsheviks immediately removed discriminatory legislation. Children outside wedlock were granted equal rights, divorce was made available on request and both spouses given equal rights to property and earnings.

Women achieved full equal rights to education, which was a turning point in the progress of women towards equality, especially in the backward Central Asian republics of the Soviet Union, which by the early twenties had become part of the USSR.

A Women's Section (*Zhenotdel*) of the RSDLP was set up in 1919, its aims being to inform and educate poor working and peasant women, check enforcement of the new legislation and set up political education and literacy classes for women throughout Russia.

You have only to look at their life stories: Nadezhda Krupskaya, known mainly in the West as Lenin's wife, was a leading Bolshevik who suffered arrest by the tsar's police and exile. She was on the editorial board of RSDLP newspaper *Iskra*, became a leading specialist in education, and in the thirties served as Education Commissar (Minister).

Trotsky wrote of her: "She was at the very centre of all the organization work; she received comrades when they arrived, instructed them when they left, established connections, supplied secret addresses, wrote letters, and coded and decoded correspondence. In her room there was always a smell of burned paper from the secret letters she heated over the fire to read..."

Konkordiya Samoilova, a member of the RSDLP since 1903, spent a year in prison for her views and was the founding editor of *Pravda* and on the editorial staff of *Rabotnitsa* (Woman Worker).

Inessa Armand played a leading role among the Bolsheviks in exile in western Europe and was instrumental in setting up the *Zhenotdel*, chairing the first International Conference of Communist Women in 1920. She was the first woman who, on death, was honoured by being buried in Red Square.

Alexandra Kollontai was a leading feminist who fought for women's equality, not only by means of legal measures enabling that, but by bringing into the open issues of sexual freedom, marriage and the family.

Her book *The Social Basis of the Woman Question* (1909) and her essay *Sexual Relations and the Class Struggle* are still relevant today. Her opposition to the Brest-Litovsk Treaty which ended the war with Germany and to other measures where she found herself in a minority in the Bolshevik leadership do nothing to undermine her weighty contribution to women's equality, but rather show that she was a revolutionary with her own views which she was well capable of defending.

It is salutary, looking today at the Russian Revolution and its legacy throughout the world, among which is the fight for true women's equality, to continue to analyse why women's equality has not been achieved either here in Britain or in Russia. Here we have laws on equal pay – but employers continue to get round them by describing the same or similar jobs done by women as different and thus paying them less than men doing similar work.

In the Soviet Union by the thirties there was not one single woman on the Central Committee of the CPSU; when I worked in Moscow in the eighties there was only one woman in the top leadership.

The *Zhenotdel* was dissolved in 1930. In a Soviet encyclopaedia published in 1987, you can find: "The women's movement reached the Caucasus and central Asia only after the Civil War. As a result of the cultural revolution and in the course of the building of socialism, the women's question in the USSR has been completely solved."

I think Russia's women Bolsheviks who gave their energies, their skills and in some cases their lives to the cause of women's equality under a just, socialist society, would turn in their graves if they could see how much more still remains to be done to achieve true women's emancipation.

APPENDIX VII

Victor's experience at a Pioneer Camp

Every year millions of Soviet schoolchildren go to Pioneer camps for part of their long summer holidays – usually about a month spent in countryside or coastal places, in the company of hundreds of other children of all ages. All sizeable Soviet factories and organisations have their own Pioneer camps for their employees' children; and the trades unions alone run nearly 60,000 Pioneer camps for their members' children. Some are excellent, some are good – and some are not so good, according to reports in the press. There has also been discussion and criticism of old-style methods of work with children at Pioneer camps at the Komsomol Congress in April this year (1987), and in the press as the summer approached. Here are the impressions of a 12 year old – our son Victor - at one Russian Pioneer camp called Pushkino:

Pushkino

This summer I went to Pioneer Camp again. When we got there it was still 11 days till the opening ceremony. At the opening, the entire camp puts on parade pioneer uniforms which consist of a white shirt with gold buttons, and on the left arm a little yellow emblem shaped like a shield with three flames inside. Our Pioneer camp has over 1,000 children it it, and we are all divided up into groups of about 30 children in each.

The opening started with the detachments getting their banners. The pioneer leaders with the banner bearers march up a central alley under a drum roll. The pioneer leaders hold the banners. Then the senior pioneer leaders give the banners of the camp to the banner bearers, chosen from among the children.

Then they hoist the Soviet flag under the drum roll and everybody gives the pioneer salute. Then we all go back to our chalets.

We live in these chalets, with four rooms, two big ones and two little ones. The girls sleep on one side, the boys on the other, and in between them there is a narrow room for the pioneer leaders.

Most pioneer leaders are students from institutes, who work there during their summer holidays. Each detachment or group has two pioneer leaders and a kind of teacher.

We had only one pioneer leader called Lena. Lena was a great friend of everybody's. We all loved her because she was kind, understanding and always telling us stories. She is from Stavropol.

At 8 o'clock every morning we do our exercises at the stadium. We would run there, do the exercises and run back, put on our pioneer scarves and after the bugle call we run to our meeting, as we call it.

There we talk a bit about what is happening in the world. Then we have breakfast, with porridge, bread and butter, coffee or tea with milk, then a piece of ham or sausage with peas. Well, nearly every day we have different meals, but they're always delicious.

We do a lot of sport at the camp. Boys play football, and girls too, but they just wear any clothes, not special football gear. We all play handball, pioneer-ball and hockey, in the older groups.

My group played football for a cup with sweets in, and there were other prizes for other games. We also had a camp Olympics, where we ran 60 metres and 500 metres, threw a tennis ball, pulled ourselves up on to a bar and did the long jump.

My group won 3 records and took first place in the Olympics.

About three or four times during the camp each group has to be on duty. This means doing the washing up for nearly a thousand people. At least there's a giant dish-washing machine. Not only do we do duty in the washing-up room, but at the bike centre, where we can all ride bikes round the camp territory, which is a big area in lovely pine forest.

Every Monday, Thursday and Friday we have films, cartoons or adventure films for children. We have at least two discos, and there is a room called 'igroteka' (playroom) with video-games.

One thing that's really nice - but we don't get enough - is swimming. The camp has its own pool, but we only get about five minutes in the water, because there are so many groups. It's not enough.

Sometimes we go on walks in the forest, and pick wild strawberries and other berries to eat. We learn about nature and the names of the berries.

If it's raining, we can go to the library or to the arts and crafts club where we make woodcuts and models or just draw and paint.

It's great when we have bonfires and singsongs. This year we learnt a lot of new songs like this one which my sisters and I like:

> "There's a kingdom of friendship on this earth,
> the best country there is.
> In this kingdom there is no war.
> Shields and armour are only for playing.
> In this kingdom all the soldiers
> see dreams in colour at night."

APPENDIX VIII

The NUM's official historian Professor Vic Allen[150] made a secret visit to Cuba in 1988 to meet with Fidel Castro. This is his story of their four-hour encounter which showed that already in 1988 Fidel was anticipating the collapse of Soviet socialism.

My secret mission to meet Fidel

By Professor Vic Allen

One day, early in December 1988, during the period of impending crisis in the Socialist world, John Hendy, the NUM's legal advisor, and I, its historian, were asked by Arthur Scargill to accompany Cyril Ramaphosa and James Motlatsi, the general secretary and president of the South African NUM, on a visit to Cuba in order to meet Fidel Castro.

The intention was to discuss with him the impact for southern Africa of Cuba's support for Angola in its struggle for independence against Unita, the rebel force backed by the US and South Africa. Scargill had arranged the meeting through his friendship with Castro but, unfortunately, had had to withdraw from it himself. The arrangements were made in secret because Ramaphosa and Motlatsi had to leave South Africa clandestinely. So, none of us even told our respective families where we were going or that we were likely to be away for Xmas.

We all met up in a café at Heathrow early on 21 December, along with a diplomat from the Cuban Embassy who had brought the visas and rubber franks to stamp our passports in his jacket pockets.

He proceeded to arrange them on the table, as if in his office. It is unlikely that this little ceremony was missed by MI5 that was then co-operating with the London station of the CIA in an intelligence entrapment operation against members of the Cuban embassy. But we faced no visible hitches.

On our arrival in Havana that evening we were met by Angel Dalmau, a representative of the Central Committee of the Cuban Communist Party who was responsible for southern Africa and who was to be our guide. He later became the Cuban Ambassador in South Africa and is now a deputy Foreign Minister. He took us first to be greeted by the leaders of the Energy Workers' Union and then to a spacious marble, colonial-era villa that had been the home of a bourgeois family before the Revolution, where we were to stay as its only guests.

It soon became clear that we were not in Cuba for a couple of meetings. An itinerary had been drawn up that was spread over eight days. During that

---

150 See Footnote 101.

period we were to meet with Fidel Castro but no one knew when or where. Such was the persistence of the threats to his life by the CIA and its cohorts that few people were aware of his daily movements or where he slept each night. We were not informed, therefore, of the day and time of our meeting, only that we should expect to be summoned at very short notice.

Whilst we were waiting we visited the Museum of the Revolution and learned a little about Cuba's incredible transformation – of how the few survivors from the original expedition from Mexico had recruited 150 supporters to attack a garrison town protected by 5,000 troops. And how, in the final push, Castro's motley army of about 2,000 had defeated Batista's 80,000 government troops.

Afterwards, we visited a chrome mine and two factories and talked with trade union and Communist Party officials. We saw the impressive Cuban health service and education systems in action in the countryside. We dined in the bar that had been frequented by Hemingway and developed a taste for Cuban rum. Christmas day passed by with scarcely a mention.

On Boxing Day we had a long meeting with Jorge Risquet, the secretary of the Central Committee with responsibility for foreign affairs. Risquet had been involved in the Angolan operations and had led the Cuban delegation to the United Nations in New York where their outcome had been debated. He briefed us for our meeting with Castro by explaining Cuba's intentions and operations in Angola and its attitude to apartheid in South Africa.

He insisted that there could be no military solution in South Africa so that ultimately there had to be negotiations. It would, he believed, be self-defeating to alarm the white population. The military operations, therefore, needed to be confined to military targets.

The next day, Tuesday, 27 December, we were told to be ready to meet with Fidel Castro. During the evening, just after we had started our dinner, Dalmau came in to say that we had to leave in 10 minutes. The meeting with Castro was to be at 8 pm.

The government's offices were housed in three adjoining buildings, the Central Committee, the Palace of State and the Palace of Ministers. We went into the middle one, the Palace of State, and waited in a large anteroom. The door opened behind us and in walked Castro, Risquet, an interpreter and 2 security guards.

Castro was dressed in his green army fatigues, rather worn boots and was wearing his army cap. He greeted us and we walked along a corridor to his office. John Hendy and I trailed in the rear. It was clear that we were accessories and that we would most probably not be involved in the discussions.

Castro fired a number of questions to Ramaphosa about the mining industry, his union and the ANC. In so far as there was a dialogue it was between those two. Motlatsi, Hendy and myself sat and listened silently.

Then Fidel Castro described in some detail the critical battle of Cuito

Cuanavale in southern Angola, a town vital for guarding the route to South West Africa and the Caprivi Strip, on the border of Botswana. The Cubans, he said, had overwhelmed the South Africans. Their MIG fighters were vastly superior to the South African Mirages; they had more tanks and superior artillery.

They could have rolled the South African forces back over their own borders and into their own territory and, he said, for a brief moment they thought of doing just that. They had intervened, however, only to stop the penetration of the South African forces and once they had succeeded in doing that their job was done. The Cubans, moreover, had no intention of fighting Unita. So, as in any event the Angolans wanted a quick end to the fighting, they held back.

After the Cuban victory, Castro explained, the South African government could only maintain its illegal occupation of South West Africa if it moved two army divisions from the townships and it could not do that without leaving the way open for the ANC to advance.

It had to make a critical strategic choice, therefore, and it chose to leave South West Africa and agree to the formation of Namibia as a newly independent state. Since then, the accolades for Cuba have never ceased in southern Africa. Even now, 14 years after the event, mention Castro, or even simply Cuba, at any gathering of black people there and you will hear roars of approval.

After about an hour, Castro looked clearly tired so we prepared to leave. I had given Risquet a signed copy of my book, *The Russians are Coming*, which the editorial committee of the Communist Party had agreed to translate and publish in Latin America. He asked me if I had a spare copy for Castro but as I did not, he suggested that I should write an inscription in his copy and give that to Castro. This I did, prompting Castro to comment that the book seemed to have been going around a lot.

He flicked the pages and opened the book at a section on Soviet democracy. From that moment the atmosphere in the room changed. He asked if it had been written before the policy of *perestroika* had been introduced. I replied that its publication had coincided with Gorbachev's new policy but that I had since written an article for *Izvestia,* pointing out some of the risks implicit in it. He asked for a copy so that it could be published in Cuba.

After that, Castro began a discussion about Soviet policy and the character of Socialism. He had met Gorbachev earlier in the year and had strong reservations about the course he was pursuing.

We went on to discuss Socialist emulation and the problem of incentives in a Socialist system. He never talked in abstract terms but always through practical illustrations from the experiences of ordinary working people.

He explained how the Cuban government planned to train 10,000 more doctors than it needed so that they could work in Third World countries. A Cuban Medical Brigade was already in the Soviet Republic of Armenia, helping to tend those who had been injured by the earthquake that had devastated the country on 7 December. Cuba's policy turned imperialism on its head because it gave help where it was needed without expecting anything in return.

He was not optimistic, however, about world events in the near future. Indeed, he did not think that the Soviet Union and the socialist countries in central Europe would be able to withstand the destructive pressures for change from western capitalism that were facing them. But he did not have the same view of Cuba.

With great self-assurance, he asserted that Cuba might be the only Socialist star in the sky during the next decade. It turned out that he was right. Cuba was left, almost from that moment, to struggle for its right to self-determination against the corrupting might of the USA, without the backing and material assistance from the Soviet Union, and the GDR in particular.

Cuba had, he said, to make a number of internal adjustments. Because of the growing shortage of petrol it had to make its agriculture less dependent on mechanised methods. Already oxen were replacing tractors.

It had to become more self-sufficient in a whole range of production activities. Moreover, it had followed the rigid Soviet model too closely and needed both to decentralise and draw more women and young people into decision-making operations. He envisaged a difficult decade for Cuba.

Our meeting had been transformed into a vibrant discussion group. As it drew to a close, we walked slowly to the lift but on the way he raised the question of Soviet agriculture and Gorbachev's decision to break up the state and collective farms and distribute their land to small farmers.

I had learned, whilst in Moscow a few weeks before, that the Soviet food problem was primarily caused by the lack of refrigerated transport facilities and not by inadequate levels of production. More than half of Soviet agricultural production perished during the long drives from the farms to the urban centres. Castro agreed. In any case, he said, Cuba had experimented with small, individually run farms and the experiment had failed. They had made virtually no contribution to society but the farmers had succeeded in making themselves rich.

Cuba's task, he said, was to convert the farms into collective ones. He knew that Ramaphosa, Motlatsi and I were going on to Moscow to meet the Soviet Miners' leaders. Such was the consensus of opinion between us that he asked whether we would be meeting any Soviet Politburo members because, he said, "if you do will you press your arguments on them?"

It had taken us half an hour to cover the few yards to the lift. We had been together for four hours. Castro thanked us for talking with him. It had not, he said, been the kind of meeting he had planned. We left Havana two days later.